BELA

Andrew Wilson is professor in Ukrain
don and a senior policy fellow at the Eu
He is the author of *The Ukrainians: U*
What It Means for the West.

Further praise for *Belarus*:

'Andrew Wilson has done all students of European politics a great service by making the history of Belarus comprehensible, and by showing how the future of Belarus might be different than its present.' Timothy Snyder, author of *Bloodlands: Europe Between Hitler and Stalin*

'This book will surely become the starting point for anyone interested in Belarus today . . . with his trademark dry wit, Wilson has done us all an enormous service by bringing together a rich array of western, Belarusian, and Russian material on the challenges of nation building in Belarus.' Lucan Way, *Slavic Review*

'This book is scholarly, lucid, and essential reading for anyone wanting to make sense of Belarus today.' Francis King, *Socialist History*

'An authoritative account . . . One of the most valuable contributions to Belarusian studies and is guaranteed a long shelf life.' Grigory Ioffe, *International Affairs*

'An important and timely reminder of the importance of small states to the security of larger concerns.' Stephen J. Main, *Europe-Asia Studies*

ANDREW WILSON
BELARUS
THE LAST EUROPEAN DICTATORSHIP

New Edition

YALE UNIVERSITY PRESS
NEW HAVEN AND LONDON

For information about this and other Yale University Press publications, please contact:
U.S. Office: sales.press@yale.edu   yalebooks.com
Europe Office: sales@yaleup.co.uk   yalebooks.co.uk

Set in Minion Pro by IDSUK (DataConnection) Ltd
Printed in Great Britain by Clays Ltd, Elcograf S.p.A

Library of Congress Control Number: 2020951288

ISBN 978-0-300-13435-3 (hbk)
ISBN 978-0-300-25921-6 (new edn pbk)

A catalogue record for this book is available from the British Library.

10 9 8 7 6 5 4 3 2 1

To Vitali

CONTENTS

ILLUSTRATIONS AND MAPS

Maps

While the author and publisher have made every attempt to discover the provenance of illustrative material, there are some instances where the photographers remain unidentified.

INTRODUCTION
TO THE NEW EDITION

Condoleezza Rice called Belarus 'the last remaining true dictatorship in the heart of Europe' in 2005.[1] The first edition of this book, subtitled *The Last Dictatorship in Europe*, came out in 2011. In the years following, Belarusian President Aliaksandr Lukashenka liked to play up the idea of being the 'last dictator'; in a 2012 interview he proclaimed 'I am the last and only dictator in Europe. Indeed there are none anywhere else in the world . . . You came here and looked at a living dictator. Where else would you see one? There is something in this. They say that even bad publicity is good publicity.'[2] But after Russia's aggression against Ukraine in 2014, Lukashenka slyly told Bloomberg in a 2015 interview that 'There are dictators a bit worse than me, no? I'm the lesser evil already.'[3] He meant Putin.

Some also saw domestic reasons why the label was outdated after 2014. Belarus's precarious position after the beginning of the war in Ukraine led to some tactical foreign policy diversification, and in turn to some minimal domestic liberalisation, to try and open doors in the West. And if Belarus got a little better, several European countries got a lot worse, some of them, such as Hungary, in the EU. Democratic deterioration elsewhere meant that Belarus was no longer the '*last* dictatorship in Europe'. In 2019 Freedom House and the Economist Intelligence Unit rated Azerbaijan as more autocratic than Belarus; Freedom House had Russia and Belarus at roughly equal pegging, with Russia slightly less bad in the EIU's reckoning.[4] The Belarusian regime started to object to being called 'the regime'.

But the events of 2020 made the label accurate again. Lukashenka had rigged elections before – in 2001, 2006, 2010 and 2015. But the blatant fixing of the 2020 election blew up in his face. Hundreds of thousands of Belarusians took to the streets. Mass imprisonments, beatings and torture failed to disperse the protests, which carried on for months. The mirror-image of a dictatorship is a quiet and submissive population, so whether the protesters would ultimately prove successful in removing Lukashenka or not, their actions served to cast off at least one of Belarus's labels.

Others remain. In the Western imagination there are no proper countries between Poland and Russia. Often presented as the last neo-Soviet state, or seen as Russia-lite, or even as nation-lite, Belarus has been home to disappearing tricks. Its capital city, Minsk, was where President Kennedy's assassin Lee Harvey Oswald stayed as a would-be Soviet 'ordinary worker' in 1960–2. Mythical 'Minsk' is where Phoebe's boyfriend David the Scientist Guy disappears to in the US sitcom *Friends*, which is just a plot device to remove him from the face of the Earth.

Marxists like to talk about 'non-historical peoples' (stateless 'tattered remnants' according to Engels), but every people has a history. The lands that are now Belarus, however, were part of other national 'projects' until the twentieth century. The people contributed to those projects and helped make them unique, but the term 'Belarus' referred to a specific region rather than a nation until late in the nineteenth century. The early proto-Belarusian tribes were originally part of a medieval state with the other eastern Slavs. They then helped form the much misunderstood 'Commonwealth': neither 'Poland' nor 'Lithuania', but a multinational agglomeration of all the lands and peoples (and potential peoples) that lay 'in between', before the Russian Empire won control of most of the region in the late eighteenth century. In the nineteenth century Belarusians still thought of themselves as members of the old Commonwealth, or as 'west-Russians' – loyal to the empire and to the Orthodox Church, despite most Belarusians having been Uniate Catholics only a generation before. A specific national movement appeared relatively late, after the Revolution in 1905, and was still weak in 1917. The unification of Belarusian lands first in the 1920s and then during the Second World War was a project of Soviet power.

Belarus is not a nation without a history. The two main English-language accounts, Nicholas Vakar's *Belorussia: The Making of a Nation* (Cambridge, MA: Harvard University Press, 1956) and Jan Zaprudnik's *Belarus: At a Crossroads in History* (Boulder, CO: Westview, 1993), were written when Belarus was still part of, or just potentially emerging from, the Soviet Union. Both authors wanted to demonstrate that Belarus had a separate history and could one day be independent, strong and free. But Belarus's history has basically been a series of false starts – though each different beginning has left important legacies. The first part of this book looks at all of these pre-histories, before the modern idea of

Belarus began to crystallise around 1900. The second part looks at the rise and possible fall of Aliaksandr Lukashenka, who ironically first won a relatively free election in 1994, before ruling twenty-six years until 2020. Ironically, too, he moulded Belarus in his own image – but Belarus outgrew him. The revolution of 2020 marked another rebirth, and the emergence of a new civic nation. The final irony, however, was that in order to survive Lukashenka looked likely to go in the opposite direction, using Russian support to stay in power. The price could be very high: a hollowing-out of the state and its sovereignty. There are two new chapters and a conclusion for this paperback edition: Chapter 13 takes the story forward from 2010, Chapter 14 looks at the events of 2020, and a new Conclusion discusses whether Lukashenka could survive the protests.

In order to emphasise what is distinct about Belarus's history, I have chosen to use Belarusian names and spellings. So I have written 'Lukashenka' rather than 'Lukashenko'; the former is the Belarusian spelling of his name, the latter is the Russian version. I have spelt the city Vitebsk, famous as the birthplace of the artist Marc Chagall, as 'Vitsebsk', and used words like 'Litvin' that are no doubt unfamiliar to most readers, but which are essential to understanding the story. Sometimes, however, choices have to be arbitrary. 'Vilnius', for example, has many names, because it is at the centre of many national histories. I have chosen to call it 'Vilna' when it was a mainly Slavic city before it became the Lithuanian capital of Vilnius in 1940. It was only really 'Wilno', the Polish spelling, between the wars, and was never really 'Vilnia', which is the Belarusian spelling. I have chosen 'Uladzimir' rather than 'Uladzimer' in the main text, but the endnotes keep the original forms. Finally, I have chosen to transliterate the unique Belarusian letter 'ў' as 'w' rather than 'u', which is how it sounds and is hopefully clearer for the general reader.

I would like to give warm thanks to all those who have helped in the preparation of this book: to Andrei Dynko, Valer Bulhakaw, Mila Bertosh, Dzianis Meliantsow and Vitali Silitski in Belarus; to Father Nadson, who runs the Belarusian Library in London; to Natalia Leshchenko and Elena Korosteleva-Polglase in the UK; to Margarita Balmaceda, John-Paul Himka, Grigory Ioffe, David Marples, Barbara Skinner and Timothy Snyder in North America; to Alexandra Goujon and Anaïs Marin in France; to Rainer Lindner in Germany; to everyone at New Eastern Europe, the Batory Foundation and OSW in Poland; to Miklós Haraszti in Hungary; to Yaroslav Hrytsak in Ukraine; and to all my colleagues at UCL and ECFR, especially Jana Kobzova, Ben Judah, Fredrik Wesslau, Joanna Hosa and Nicu Popescu. At Yale University Press, my thanks go to Heather McCallum, Robert Baldock, Tami Halliday and Joanna Godfrey. Miles Irving and Cath D'Alton at UCL made the maps. This book is dedicated to Vitali Silitski who passed away in June 2011, aged only 38.

PART I

Belarus: A History of Crossroads

CHAPTER 1

POLATSK

Despite its reputation as a country without a history, Belarus has a decent enough potential foundation myth, involving a powerful local kingdom, early status as a centre of Christianity, itinerant Vikings and a sorcerer-prince who could turn himself into a werewolf. It's a story that ought to be easier to sell.

The story is set in Rus, sometimes known as 'Kievan Rus', the proper name given to the sprawling east Slavic polity that dominated Eastern Europe between the ninth and thirteenth centuries AD. Our knowledge of what actually happened in Rus is limited. Local written sources are scarce until local priests began writing chronicles in the twelfth century, and foreign accounts are rare. That does not stop modern historians from filling in the gaps, of course. Most Russian and Western historians depict Rus as a relatively united entity. Many also depict it as an early Russian state. But 'Rus' was not medieval 'Russia'. It was centred on Kiev, and ruled what is now western and north-western Russia, but also covered most of what is now Ukraine and Belarus. The modern term 'Russia' is derived from the Greek-influenced 'Rossiia' which became popular in the seventeenth century. It makes more sense to follow the definition of Serhii Plokhy, who called the Rus a 'multiethnic imperial elite whose identity was quite different from that of the rest of the population.'[1]

Rahvalod and Rahneda

In one of the north-western corners of Rus lay the town of Polatsk, on the western river Dzvina. In those days, rivers made nations. They set trade and population flows; heavily forested hinterlands were much harder to penetrate. The Dzvina is the main river in the east Slavic north. On a modern map, it starts in Russia north of Smolensk, then flows through Belarus past Vitsebsk and Polatsk, then on to Daugavpils in modern Latvia, where the river is called the Daugava, and into the Baltic Sea at Riga. But at the end of the first millennium the other towns downriver weren't there: Polatsk stood alone. Riga, for example, was not founded until 1201, while Polatsk was first mentioned by chroniclers in 862. Those seeking deeper historical roots have cited the scribe Saxo Grammaticus in his *Gesta Danorum* ('Deeds of the Danes'), who suggests that Polatsk fought off the two legendary Viking princes Ragnar Lodbrok and Frode a decade or so earlier.[2] Some local archaeologists claim settlement goes back to the fifth century at least. Whatever the case, Polatsk was undoubtedly the most powerful city in the region for almost two centuries, and Belarusian historians like to claim that, periodically at least, it was 'dependent neither on Kiev nor on Novgorod',[3] the two main centres of power in Rus. Many Belarusian historians also use the anachronism 'Polatska-Rus' to denote the idea that Polatsk was only loosely part of broader Rus, and somehow simultaneously independent.[4]

Polatsk's rise is well documented in the last third of the tenth century,[5] though the Belarusian historian Usevalad Ihnatowski dated both the city's importance and its conflict with Kiev back to the ninth century, claiming that 'already in these ancient times there were some misunderstandings between the [rival] centres of Polatsk and Kiev'.[6] Early links with Kiev seem to have been broken in 945. However, most historians consider that Polatsk's rise to prominence was due to the arrival 'from across the sea' of a Scandinavian overlord, Rahvalod (in Russian Rogvolod, in old Scandinavian Ragnvald), who was ruler of Polatsk to a probable 980. Some argue that Polatsk's Viking links go back as far as 820, though their impact seems to have been intermittent and they failed to establish a clear dynasty. Rahvalod's exact origins are therefore obscure, though there are several theories as to the nature of his Viking links.[7] According to the thirteenth-century *Gutasaga*, adventurers and refugees from the Baltic island of Gotland had been sailing up the river Dzvina for centuries past. Polatsk may have been founded by them, or may have been seized by them. Another version links Rahvalod to the Yngling dynasty of what is now Norway.

However it was established, Polatsk gradually increased in importance because of its strategic position at a local crossroads. It controlled the main route to the Baltic Sea, but also the upper reaches of the river Dnieper down towards Kiev in the south, and the river Lovat towards Novgorod in the north.

Polatsk therefore controlled one of the key trading routes from northern Europe to Byzantium and the riches of the Near East. Rahvalod built up Polatsk as a rival to Kiev and Novgorod to such an extent that Volodymyr the Great (ruled 980–1015), the first real ruler of a united Rus, felt compelled to attack the city in 980 (some historians say 970 or 975–6). In fact, it was the key event in Volodymyr's rise to power. He was then based in Novgorod, and feuding with his rival Yaropolk I in Kiev (ruled 972–80), so he initially wanted Polatsk as an ally. Volodymyr's proposal to Rahvalod's daughter Rahneda (Rogneda, Ragnhild, Ragnheithr) was rebuffed, however. According to the *Primary Chronicle* compiled by Kiev monks in the 1110s, she declared: 'I will not draw off the boots of a slave son, but I want Yaropolk instead.'[8] This hauteur reflected the rumour that Volodymyr was born out of (then pagan) wedlock, and perhaps also the perceived superiority of Scandinavia if not of Polatsk.

Volodymyr was certainly a bit of a bastard. According to the later chronicles, he raped Rahneda in front of her parents, before killing them both and their two sons for good measure, and carrying off Rahneda as booty. This was before Volodymyr's conversion to Christianity in 988. Rahneda became one of Volodymyr's five non-Christian wives, and ultimately bore him four sons and two daughters: but the number of children was no indication of a happy marriage. Legend has it Rahneda was caught trying to kill Volodymyr in his sleep. He only spared her because of the entreaties of her elder son, Iziaslaw. In the operatic version of her life by the Russian composer Aleksandr Serov (1863–5), Rahneda is depicted as scheming against Volodymyr to protect the old pagan gods. In the Ukrainian poet Taras Shevchenko's anti-imperial epic *The Tsars* (1848), Rahneda stands out less, but only because the whole court is depicted as a cesspit of debauchery, violence and incest.

But the key fact exploited by latter-day Belarusian mythmakers is Rahneda's loyalty to her native land. According to the Kiev chronicles, Rahneda took Iziaslaw back to Polatsk after Volodymyr's baptism led to his dynastic marriage in 989 to Anna Porphyrogeneta, daughter of the Byzantine emperor Romanos II. According to Belarusian historiography, the city was 'restored' to Iziaslaw by Volodymyr, though others call him an 'assignee'.[9] One interpretation is that Volodymyr assigned the key principalities to his sons to encourage the spread of the new Christian faith. Historian Simon Franklin's judgement is that Kiev was happy to cut Polatsk so much slack because Volodymyr 'calculated that so strongly rooted a regime would block any future bids for [Polatsk] by outsiders'.[10] Nevertheless, it is significant that after Iziaslaw died in 1001, he was succeeded by the elder of his two sons, Brachyslaw Iziaslavich (ruled

1001–44), who once again broke away from Kiev. Rus was not quite divided by rival dynasties, but there were now two rival branches of the Rus dynasty. One was the 'Rahvalodavichi' or 'Iziaslavichi' in Polatsk; the other was the 'Yaroslavichi' in Kiev. Polatsk had its own cathedral (see below), which housed a powerful local bishop.

Family relations between the two branches were often tense. According to the chronicles, 'since that time [i.e. of Volodymyr] the grandchildren of Rahvalod have raised the sword against the grandchildren of Yaroslav'.[11] Iziaslaw died while his father was still alive and ruling in Kiev, so it appears that Brachyslaw owed the city fealty; but fealty also had to be established militarily. After the civil wars of 1015–19 that followed Volodymyr's death, his nephew's uncle Yaroslav the Wise took power in Kiev and, after his nephew's campaign against Novgorod to win back Vitsebsk in 1021, raised armies which defeated Brachyslaw at the Battle of the River Sudoma in 1021. But Brachyslaw still enjoyed relative autonomy: after 1021, he was able to expand against the Baltic tribes, founding the town of Braslaw, first mentioned in 1065.

Usiaslaw the Sorcerer

Polatsk's next and greatest ruler was Iziaslaw's grandson Usiaslaw Brachyslavich, known as 'the Sorcerer', who ruled in Polatsk for more than half a century from 1044 to 1101. Usiaslaw's name is good enough nowadays for a brand of vodka: his magic powers allowed him to fly, and the vodka is supposed to have a similar effect. He also inspired the closest thing to a Belarusian opera, *Usiaslaw the Enchanter, Prince of Polatsk*, written by Mikola Kulikovich-Shchahlow in difficult circumstances, and without much of an audience, in 1944, the year that Minsk was liberated from the Germans.

The sheer length of Usiaslaw's rule was a triumph in itself. Initially, he deferred to Rahneda's second son, Yaroslav the Wise, who presided from Kiev over Rus at its most united from 1019 to 1054. As the Belarusian historian Henadz Sahanovich admits; 'The first decades of Usiaslaw Brachyslavich's rule . . . passed in peaceful relations with Kiev.'[12]

Yaroslav died in 1054. According to the *Primary Chronicle*, Usiaslaw gathered his strength (slowly) and 'began hostilities' in 1065. 'At the time, there was a portent in the west of an exceedingly large star, with bloody rays . . . this star appeared as if it were made of blood, and therefore portended bloodshed.'[13] And much bloodshed there was. Usiaslaw fought to expand in all directions. He unsuccessfully attacked Pskov in 1065, before sacking Novgorod with more effect in 1066–7. He threatened the Baltic tribes in the west, and expanded beyond Minsk in the south and the upper reaches of the Dnieper just below Smolensk in the east. Crucially, Usiaslaw gained access to the sea by expanding down the river Dzvina towards the Gulf of Riga, which, together with control of the key watershed near Vitsebsk, where boats had briefly to be carried overland from the northern to the southern parts of the route, gave him mastery over the key trade route from 'the Varangians to the Greeks', and threatened to cut Rus in half (Polatsk's strategic importance was due to its position at the junction of the river Palata with the Dzvina). At its height, Polatsk controlled the key towns of Braslaw in the west, Vitsebsk and Orsha in the east, the Jersika principality of the Baltic Latgallian tribe in the north-west and its cousin tribe the Koknese, the main centre of the Selonian tribe further down the river Dzvina (both in what is now Latvia), as well as Minsk in the south (Minsk was then the junior city, first mentioned in 1067). His successor, Uladzimir, campaigned twice down the Dzvina, in 1203 and 1206, but Latvian historians tend to dispute the extent to which Koknese and Jersika were dominated by Polatsk. Moreover the Baltic tribes, they argue, were capable of holding back Polatsk on their own and were not 'saved' by the arrival of the Teutonic Knights.[14] Certainly, by the twelfth century, the Rus were too divided and too preoccupied with the threat from the east, first from the Polovtsians (Pechenegs) and then the Mongols, to carry on attacking the Balts.

Usiaslaw therefore sought to aggrandise his power in his own bailiwick. It is less clear that he had any designs on Kiev; though, for whatever reason, he seems to have upset the normal rules of contestation. The three princes of Kiev, Iziaslav, Sviatoslav and Vsevolod, joined forces with Novgorod and defeated Usiaslaw at the bloody Battle on the Neman near Minsk in 1067. The *Primary Chronicle* describes it thus: 'Though it was the dead of winter, [the Kiev princes] collected a force and set forth against him. They arrived before Minsk, but the citizens barricaded themselves in the city. Then the brethren captured it, put the men to the sword, sold the women and children into slavery', and marched to meet Usiaslaw outside the city, where, 'with heavy snow on the ground, the carnage was severe'.[15] Usiaslaw trusted in the kissing of the cross for safe treatment on surrender, but was betrayed and imprisoned in Kiev.

Usiaslaw's misfortune was short-lived, however. After the unpopular Iziaslav refused to put up a proper fight against the Polovtsians (pagan invaders from the southern steppes), the Kievan crowd turned against him and freed Usiaslaw, who then ruled for seven months as grand prince of Kiev and ruler of all Rus in 1068–9. Iziaslav had to raise a Polish army to oust him.

Usiaslaw then returned to Polatsk, where he ruled from 1071 until his death in 1101. According to the Russian historian Vasilii Tatishchev, this was because Usiaslaw understood that Kiev belonged to a different dynasty.[16] Ironically, this is the period – after its accidental bid for glory had failed – when Polatsk was most independent. Kiev and Polatsk now left each other alone, and the latter was able to continue nibbling away at Baltic territory. Usiaslaw was no longer seen as a contender for the throne. But the very fact that Polatsk was now ruled out of succession politics gave it a distinct status among other principalities like Novgorod or Chernihiv. Historians like Usevalad Ihnatowski have also tried to depict a distinct and more 'European' political culture in Polatsk, with the tradition of noble assemblies (*viche*) balancing the power of kings more common than elsewhere in Rus.[17] According to the British historians Simon Franklin and Jonathan Shepard, however, the conflict between Kiev and Polatsk was 'the most serious threat to dynastic order in the entire pre-Mongol period. . . . Nevertheless, Polatsk was not a foreign country: it shared in the political, economic and cultural developments of the other lands of the clan. . . . Usiaslaw of Polatsk was an outsider from within. . . . Animosity was not automatic.' Usiaslaw campaigned with the other princes in the south in 1060.[18]

Usiaslaw 'the Sorcerer' has had a bad press, largely because most of the Rus chronicles were written in Kiev. According to Omeljan Pritsak, 'the dynasty of [Polatsk] was the only one among the old dynasties that survived the competition with the Rurikids, and in the eyes of the Rurikid chroniclers (and only their accounts have survived) was, as a result, to say the least, suspicious'.[19] The *Primary Chronicle* says that Usiaslaw was 'born by enchantment . . . there was a caul [afterbirth] over his head . . . for this reason he is pitiless in bloodshed'.[20] The twelfth-century saga The *Lay of Ihor's Host* depicts Usiaslaw's use of magic to escape from various predicaments.

> Usiaslaw the prince judged men;
> As prince, he ruled towns,
> But at night he prowled
> In the guise of a wolf.[21]

The Kievan monks who wrote the chronicles even report Usiaslaw's death in 1101 on the Wednesday before Good Friday, as though he had been struck down by the power of the Resurrection. They also report how Polatsk was attacked by ghosts in 1092. In truth, being half-man and half-beast was less of a problem in those days. The Norwegian Yngling dynasty was also reportedly descended from werewolves. Usiaslaw seems to have passed into popular memory as father of Volkh Vseslavich, one of the Bogatyrs – the legendary men-mountain defenders of Rus. 'Vseslavich' is Russian for 'Son of Vseslav' (i.e. Usiaslaw); 'Volkh' can mean 'wolf' or 'pagan priest' – either of which will serve in this case.

Usiaslaw's long reign came to an end in 1101. He left six or seven sons, leading to division and decline. Boris ruled in 1101–6 and 1127–8, interrupted by his brother David from 1106 to 1127. Polatsk's relative independence from Kiev, previously an advantage, now often left it prey to rival principalities, including those supposedly on the same tribal territory, Minsk and Smolensk in particular. The challenge from Polatsk to Kiev wasn't extinguished until the death of Usiaslaw's second son, Hleb, the first 'prince of Minsk' in 1119, after two sieges of Minsk in 1104 and 1115.[22] Fierce fighting between Polatsk and Kiev flared again in 1127–8, after Polatsk refused to help Kiev fight its perennial southern rivals the Polovtsians (also known as the Cumans or Kipchaks). *The Lay of Ihor's Host* makes clear that, while the problem for Kiev was in the south, Polatsk was preoccupied with the Lithuanians: 'Usiaslaw ... rang with his sharp swords on the helmets of the Lithuanians ... and himself beneath the crimsoned shields was laid low on the blood-stained ground by the Lithuanian swords.'[23]

A coalition of other Rus princes attacked Polatsk, and in 1129 Mstislav of Kiev finally took the city, expelling key members of the ruling dynasty to Byzantium. Sviatopolk of Kiev (ruled 1128–32) was, however, the last prince of Kiev to exercise real central control. Dynastic rivalry was now mainly local – particularly between the Borisovichy of Polatsk and the Hlebovichy of Minsk. The exiles returned in 1140, but were forced to fight with Minsk in 1151–67 for control, with the more southerly city temporarily gaining the upper hand in 1167. It is sometimes argued that Uladzimir Valadaravich (Volodar) briefly united the lands of Minsk, Brest and Polatsk to create an 'all-Belarusian' state in 1186;[24] but in truth even the dates of his rule are unknown.

Polatsk's glory days were over by the early thirteenth century, once the Teutonic Knights arrived on the Baltic coast with German traders in their wake, cutting off access to the sea – though also deepening contact with the rest of Europe. According to Henadz Sahanovich: 'In the thirteenth century Polatsk became the main partner for the whole of the Hanseatic League on the Dzvina.'[25] Conflict continued with Vitsebsk and Smolensk, to which Polatsk was briefly a vassal (see below). In the 1240s, Polatsk came under the control of Lithuanian rulers, and formally became part of their state in 1307, after briefly being under the archbishop of Riga. Nevertheless, the city was still showing some signs of independent life, negotiating with the Golden Horde and continuing to expand, reaching a maximum size of 100,000 before the devastating wars of the seventeenth century.

Culture

Usiaslaw's long reign was not quite a cultural 'Golden Age', but there were some stirrings of local culture. Most important was the new Christian faith – though it is a testament to the recentness of its arrival that Usiaslaw should be celebrated both as a church-builder and as a sorcerer. The conventional interpretation is that Christianity came to Polatsk via Kiev, after Volodymyr's baptism of its citizens in 988; but some have claimed that it arrived direct from Scandinavia at an earlier date.[26] However, the founding of the Polatsk eparchy is normally dated to right after 988, in 992 – hence the issue of a special commemorative stamp in 1992. A second eparchy at Turaw was set up in 1005.

Polatsk had its own bishop, and between 1044 and 1066 Usiaslaw built him a new home, the St Safiia cathedral, which was designed to be one of three great churches of Rus, along with the other St Safiias in Kiev and Novgorod, which were themselves based on the great Hagia Safiia in the Byzantine capital at Constantinople. Legend has it that Usiaslaw plundered the bells from the St Safiia in Novgorod and transferred them to his church in Polatsk. Usiaslaw clearly had prestige in mind, though Prince Mstyslav of Chernihiv's equally grand project for building the largest cathedral in Rus after 1030 did not in itself turn Chernihiv into a proto-state.

The new Rus religion was Byzantine Orthodox. Polatsk helped export elements of its culture to its sphere of influence among the still-pagan Baltic tribes; by the end of the twelfth century, there were Orthodox churches in Koknese and Jersika.[27] But influence also flowed the other way. For geographical reasons Polatsk was closer than the rest of Rus to Germanic and Scandinavian Catholic Europe, in addition to the formal schism between the two branches of the Christian faith in 1054. Some see a 'Latin influence' in the Polatsk St Safiia, which is more tower-like than traditional Byzantine, where the church is built with cross domes over a symmetrical rather than elongated cross;[28] though the modern church was substantially rebuilt (it originally had seven domes) after fires in the fifteenth and seventeenth centuries. It was also damaged by Peter the Great, who stored gunpowder in it during the Great Northern War in 1710. The current Baroque appearance of the St Safiia derives from the period of Uniate Catholic control in the eighteenth century.

Also testament to the Christianisation of the region are the nine 'Boris stones' placed by the local princes by the river Dzvina in the twelfth century (two were blown up by the Communists), the largest of which is in Polatsk and is inscribed with a plea to the Lord 'to help God's servant, Boris', thought to celebrate the faith of Boris (or Barys), son of Usiaslaw.

Polatsk's most important cultural figure was St Euphrosyne (Ewfrasinnia) of Polatsk (who lived from around 1110 to 1173). Euphrosyne was probably a granddaughter of Usiaslaw the Sorcerer, a 'virgin saint' who joined a convent at the age of twelve. The myth that she (given name Pradslava) was his daughter is troubled by the fact that Usiaslaw died in 1101. Euphrosyne founded her own convent and monastery at Sialtso, which became the main centres of learning in Polatsk. She commissioned a local architect, Iaan, to build the Church of the Holy Saviour in a local rather than Byzantine style, and in 1161 adorned it with the magnificent 'Euphrosyne Cross', a six-armed (Cross of Lorraine) ensemble lavishly decorated with jewels and enamel made by the local craftsman Lazar Bohsha – Polatsk having developed a supposedly distinctive 'school' of icon and fresco painting in the twelfth century. The cross disappeared in the chaos of the German invasion of the USSR in 1941. One version of events is that the head of the local Communist party, Pantseliaimon Panamarenka, picked it up in person from Mahilew to drive it to Moscow only a day or two in front of the rapidly advancing German armies; another version is that it was plundered by the Nazis.

Euphrosyne died on a pilgrimage to Jerusalem, whence her remains were taken to Kiev after the fall of the city to Saladin in 1187. The remains were symbolically returned with great ceremony to Polatsk in 1910, and she was canonised by the Orthodox Church in 1984 (Belarus has fifteen saints in all). Panegyric *Lives* of Euphrosyne began to appear as early as the fourteenth century and were included in Moscow chronicles of the sixteenth century.

The Kryvichy

Polatsk is now a small town in north-eastern Belarus. One weakness for would-be Belarusian nation-builders has been a peripatetic capital, or would-be capital. Russians always had Moscow, even when St Petersburg was the capital; Ukrainians will always have Kiev. The centre of Belarusian national life was Polatsk, then Navahrudak, briefly Smolensk, and then Vilna (Vilnius). Only in the twentieth century has it been Minsk. One option for Belarusian historians seeking to map the territory of modern Belarus onto the past is to stretch the history of Polatsk backwards from the tenth century by writing it as the history of the local east Slavic tribe, the Kryvichy or Kryvychians, (probably meaning 'relatives by blood'). If Polatsk's territory is defined in this ethnic way, it can be redefined as 'Krywia',[29] and may include the other cities founded by the Kryvichy, particularly Smolensk, but also supposedly Pskov and even Vilna, allegedly once called 'Kryva-town'.[30]

According to Sahanovich, 'the Smolensk Principality was formed on the basis of the union of the Smolensk group of Kryvichy in the eighth to ninth centuries in the upper reaches of the Dnieper and Dzvina'.[31] But although Smolensk may have been ethnically closer to Polatsk, it was politically closer to Kiev. The *Primary Chronicle* says that when Volodymyr of Kiev attacked Polatsk in 980, he 'collected a large army, consisting of Varangians, Slavs, Chuds [a Finno-Ugric tribe], and Kryvichy, and marched against Rahvalod'.[32] The Kryvichy were probably from Smolensk, so they were fighting their own kin. In the late twelfth century Smolensk and Polatsk fought each other frequently, notably in 1186, particularly over control of Vitsebsk (1195). However, Smolensk couldn't challenge the power of Kiev once Prince Volodymyr established control of the trade on the Dnieper in the tenth century. Smolensk became independent in 1120 – just in time to carry the story of the Belarusian nation forward after the end of Polatsk's challenge to Kiev (see next chapter),[33] but by then all of Rus was suffering from a decline in Dnieper trade, with Viking itinerants no longer a force in the region and the Teutonic Knights about to become a power in the Baltic.

Other areas like Briansk in the west of what is now Russia were in and out of Kryvichian 'ethnic territory', although they were still often considered Belarusian in the nineteenth century. Changing political boundaries, in other words, were obviously decisive. The Kryvichy of Smolensk and Pskov eventually became Russians,[34] albeit relatively recently. Polatsk, on the other hand, was not even part of the original Soviet Belarus. It was only added in the major boundary revision of 1924, and was nearly shifted back to Russia again in 1944.[35]

But the more the territory of the Kryvichy is stretched, the harder it is to argue that all the Kryvichy possessed a common identity. Conversely, it can be argued that Polatsk was in fact a multiethnic mini-empire, in so far as it claimed overlordship in the twelfth century of the Latgallian vassal cities of Jersika and Koknese, now in Latvia. Various groups of Livs and Selonians 'also paid occasional tribute to Polatsk'.[36] In the Latvian language – and Latvia is closest to the original territory of the Kryvichy – the term *Krywia* has

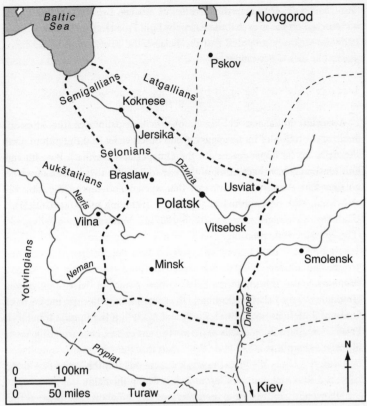

Map 1. Polatsk at the height of its power, twelfth century.

morphed into the modern-day *Krievija*, meaning Russia, and *Baltkrievija*, meaning Belarus.

Polatsk and 'Krywia' were therefore not quite the same. Even more importantly, the Kryvichy did not rule in what is now the south or west of Belarus. The Kryvichy only lived in the northern half, which is just less than half, of modern Belarus.

The Kryvichy theory was popularised by so-called 'west-Russian' historians in the nineteenth century. They were anti-Polish and anti-Catholic, so the rediscovery of specifically east Slavic tribal history was the easiest way to prove that the locals were 'indigenous' and from an older Orthodox culture, as well as matching the west-Russians' power base in the east of Belarus (see Chapter 5). One Belarusian historian, Vatslaw Lastowski (1883–1938), was so keen on the idea that the Kryvichy built Polatsk that for a time in the 1920s he seriously proposed that the Belarusians 'revert' to their old tribal name. The idea never caught on.

Other Building Blocks

The second option for Belarusian historians is to widen the scope of Belarusian prehistory by adding other east Slavic tribes into the picture. One alternative to the Kryvichian theory, the most popular in fact, is to try and knit together the 'ethnogenesis' of three local east Slavic tribes, all of whom are deemed to have been embryonic 'Belarusians'. This 'three-tribe' theory is associated with the historians Yawkhim (Efim) Karski (1860–1931),[37] Uladzimir (Vladimir) Picheta (1878–1947),[38] Mitrafan Downar-Zapolski (1867–1934)[39] and others.[40]

The Kryvichy settled along the river Dzvina, but this is only one river system and modern Belarus has three, the other two being the Neman (Nemunas), also flowing to the Baltic (whose principal Belarusian town is Hrodna), and the Dnieper, flowing to the south (after Smolensk, the towns of Orsha and Mahilew, with Brest, Pinsk and Mazyr on the Prypiat tributary). Polatsk was first among equals in the north-west of Rus, but many Belarusian historians claim that it had two other kin 'states', though the two were linked by a different logic. Whereas Smolensk was founded by the 'same' east Slavic tribe, the Kryvichy, the third 'proto-Belarusian' principality was founded by the Derevliany tribe, whose main settlement was at Turaw. One theory is that the city was named after a wild ram of the same name, now extinct. Another is that Turaw shared Polatsk's links to Scandinavia and was founded by Tur, who was possibly the brother of Rahvalod, the supposed founder of Polatsk.

Turaw city lies to the south-west, at the junction of the rivers Yazda and Strumen, allowing it to dominate the upper reaches of the river Prypiat and the marshy Polessian region. The Derevliany were initially fiercely independent. Their very name means 'free'; they lived in dense forest and inaccessible marshes. They were also somewhat uncultured. According to the no doubt biased account of the Kievan chronicler-monks, they 'existed in bestial fashion, and lived like cattle. They killed one another, ate every impure thing, and there was no marriage among them, but instead they seized upon maidens by capture.'[41] The Derevliany were first conquered by Oleh of Kiev in 884, but rebelled on his death in 912. Prince Ihor of Kiev established a modicum of control in 914 but was murdered when he tried to collect taxes in 945. His wife, Olha, crushed the revolt in 946, executing all the nobility she could find. The remaining Derevliany then surprisingly settled down to a peaceful life of cattle-raising, under satraps sent from Kiev, such as the eight-year-old Sviatopolk, known as 'the Damned' (for killing his half-brothers Boris and Hleb), from 988. Sviatopolk soon picked up local habits, however, and rebelled against Kiev in 1015–19. But Turaw remained under Kiev longer than most cities, even as the unity of Rus was challenged in the twelfth century; despite a rebellion in 1146 and a more successful attempt in 1158–62, when another putative local dynasty briefly flourished but soon conceded power to the rising might of the Galician-Volhynian kingdom to the south. Turaw also gradually lost control over other local towns. Pinsk became an independent power in its own right from the 1180s; Brest (later Brest-Litovsk), under Turaw from 1080 to 1150, drifted into the Galician orbit thereafter.

The third supposedly 'early Belarusian' tribe was the Radzmichy, based to the south-east, around the river Dnieper. Unlike the Kryvichy, who supposedly founded Polatsk, and the Derevliany, who supposedly founded Turaw, the Radzmichy failed to produce their own city-based statelet. There is no reason why they should have, but it breaks the pattern. The Radzmichy seem to be included in the story mainly to prevent Ukraine laying claim to the region, where many Cossacks from the south settled in the sixteenth and seventeenth centuries. The *Primary Chronicle* also mentions a fourth tribe. It says of the Kryvichy that 'from them are the Severiany sprung',[42] but this last tribe seems to have drifted out of the picture (it inhabited the area north-east of Kiev, straddling the modern Russo-Ukrainian border).

The three-tribe theory can't explain why some of the three tribes became Belarusians, while some became Russians or Ukrainians. Others have taken the deconstruction of Rus one step further,[43] arguing that there were in fact two separate ethnic groups on what is now Belarusian territory, until the sixteenth century.[44] The 'White Rus' proper lived in the centre and north, whereas the 'Black Rus' lived in the west around the river Neman at Navahrudak and in Polessia to the south. In the thirteenth century they came under Galicia-Volhynia. Others have agreed that there were effectively 'two states' in this period, based on the Prypiat and Dzvina-Dnieper groups, which were only united by German-Tatar pressure in the thirteenth to sixteenth centuries.[45]

This is a mess, frankly. Once you start saying the 'early Belarusians' were more than one tribe, you start rebuilding the idea of 'One Rus', favoured by most Russian historians. Unless the three had something in common, such as linguistic unity, that also distinguished them from the other tribes of Rus. But any idea of a common proto-Belarusian language is solely retrospective. One suspects that the historians and ethnographers who proposed it were basically working backwards, starting with a territory, normally linguistically defined, and then fitting patterns of tribal settlement to their story. Nor was there any real common early 'all-Belarusian' culture, though historians have often tried to invent one by linking three cultural giants, one per city: Euphrosyne of Polatsk; St. Cyril of Turaw, 1130–81; and Awram (Abraham) of Smolensk, died 1222.

Cyril of Turaw has enjoyed fame and popularity throughout the Orthodox world. He is often considered second in importance only to St John Chrysostom, of Antioch (347–407), patriarch of Constantinople, 398–404, and writer of the Orthodox liturgy. Cyril was dubbed 'Golden Lips' for his eloquence, and played a key role in transmitting Byzantine culture to the whole of the east Slavic world, and in promoting monastic asceticism. Cyril attacked Fedor, the would-be independent bishop briefly promoted by Andrei Bogoliubskii, the independent-minded ruler of Vladimir-Suzdal,[46] which presumably made him a supporter of all-Rus religious unity. Cyril's works, especially his *Sermon on the First Sunday after Easter*, linking the idea of spring to the Resurrection, are still popular today.[47] Abraham of Smolensk was a noted friend of the poor, though not a friend of the local bishops, who twice tried him for heresy. Neither Cyril nor Abraham produced anything that was notably 'Belarusian', however.

Conclusion

The history of Belarus begins with neither a bang nor a whimper. Russia is used to claiming the whole history of Rus as its own. Ukraine can invert that claim by centring its history in Kiev. Belarus can only claim part of the history of Rus, although it can make more of its early history, particularly that of Polatsk, than is sometimes thought. According to Serhii Plokhy: 'The Kryvichy showed surprising tenacity in maintaining their separate identity; unlike many other East Slavic tribes, they never disappeared from the text of the Primary Chronicle. They were also mentioned by the authors of its continuation, the Kyiv Chronicle, where one can still read about the Kryvichian princes in the entry for 1162.'[48] By the thirteenth century, however, although Polatsk is mentioned separately in treaties with Lithuanian princes, and its inhabitants are still referred to as 'Polatskians', it is regarded as part of the broader Rus lands.[49]

But Polatsk's ultimate fate was uncertain at the time. Many medieval principalities became kingdoms and ultimately nations; many did not. Association with some piece of territory in the past is no guarantee of statehood in the present. History is usually written by the victors, but it is always written by the literate, and a literate culture was only just beginning to develop in the eleventh century. Polatsk, in other words, wasn't at this stage writing its own history. The Rus chronicles came later, and were largely written by Kievan monks from a Kievan point of view. Usiaslaw had no team of chronicle writers at his service. He wasn't one of those early medieval rulers who was able to justify his claims to power by embellishing or inventing old stories, like the English earl Richard of Cornwall using Geoffrey of Monmouth's *History of the Kings of Britain* (1136) to reinvent the legend of King Arthur, and relocate Arthur's birthplace to Richard's new castle at Tintagel after 1233, though it is claimed that one local chronicle was destroyed in the St Safiia library during Ivan the Terrible's siege of Polatsk in 1563.[50] Once the Grand Duchy of Lithuania (GDL) won formal control over Polatsk in 1307 (see next chapter), according to the modern commentator Valer Bulhakaw, 'one of the most tragic events in Belarusian history [occurred:] the forcing out from the chronicle writing of the GDL of all memory of the Polatsk Principality as a form of Belarusian statehood'. He argues that this was deliberate. 'For the ruling elite in the GDL the Belarusian lands were potentially dangerously dominant. In order to rule them effectively, it destroyed [all] sprouts of the separate historical, religious or cultural consciousness of Belarusians.'[51]

The reclaiming of Polatsk would have to wait until the nineteenth century, when it was led by the 'west-Russian' historians, who ironically or not were fiercely loyal to the then Russian Empire, but wanted to establish a local Orthodox identity that preceded the later period of Roman Catholic Polish rule.

CHAPTER 2

LITVA

The second act in the history of the lands that eventually became Belarus also has hidden potential – though it has little to do with the first. The decline and fall of Rus was over by 1240, but the 'Grand Duchy' that took its partial place from the fourteenth century onwards became the preeminent power in Eastern Europe – long before the rise of Muscovy. At its peak, the Grand Duchy stretched from sea to shining sea, from the Baltic to the Black Sea – and from Vilna (Vilnius) and Polatsk in the north, to Smolensk and Kiev in the east and the open steppe in the south. Generations of schoolchildren remembered the boast that its rulers could water their horses in either sea – assuming they had a taste for sea water. The Grand Duchy's power matched its size: its armies won great victories against the Teutonic Knights at the Battle of Grunwald (or Tannenberg, 1410), against the Muscovites at Orsha (1514) and the Golden Horde at the Battle of Blue Waters (1362). The power of the Grand Duchy also stretched across five centuries. It was only removed from the map in 1795, and there were many who still sought to revive it in the nineteenth century and even as late as after 1917.

But in the West at least we are used to calling the Grand Duchy simply 'Lithuania'. The grand dukes who metaphorically watered their horses had obviously non-Slavic names like Minduagas and Gediminas. So why is the period so important to Belarus? It hasn't always been: Soviet historians, including native Belarusians like Lawrentsi Abetsedarski[1] and Viachaslaw Chamiarytski in the 1960s and 1970s,[2] preferred to interpret the history of Rus as a single state, as this approach supported the project of building a single 'Soviet People', though a little bit of local pride in Polatsk was permissible.

When President Lukashenka first appeared on the scene in 1994, he was an ardent Russophile, so his 'court historians' also backed the One Rus approach.[3] For example, an official popular history by Yawheni Novik et al. published in 2000 defends the idea of a 'common feudal state of the eastern Slavs' against the 'invention of [nationalist] historians' such as Mikalai Ermalovich who claim that Polatsk stood alone.[4] The history of Polatsk had also been important to the 'west-Russians' in the nineteenth century, if only to prove the Belarusians' cultural affinity with Orthodox Russia rather than Roman Catholic Poland (see page 71). But once a properly independent Belarusian nationalism began to develop in the early twentieth century, it needed a different starting myth which more clearly distinguished Belarusians from Russians. The Grand Duchy fitted the bill. It was independent of Muscovy, and frequently at war with it; and it was periodically one of the most powerful states in Europe. The story could still be backdated to Polatsk, but the Grand Duchy took centre stage in the new national narrative.

White Rus and Black Rus

The traditional interpretation of the end of Rus history tells a story of disunity and decline from the middle of the eleventh century, although this is one reason why Polatsk was able to remain relatively independent and relatively strong. But the story of Rus comes to a traditionally definitive end in 1240, when the invading armies of the Mongol Golden Horde broke up what remained of the political unity of the state. The traditional story about Belarus, however, is that it was not invaded from the east by the Mongols, but from the north-west by the Lithuanians instead.

One common interpretation of the origin of the name 'White Rus' (see pages 134–5) is that it refers to that 'virginal' part of Rus which remained untouched by the armies of the Horde. In the south, in what is now Ukraine, Kiev was ransacked by the Tatars in 1240–1, although the extent of the damage is disputed between Ukrainian and Russian historians (the Russians typically talk of extensive damage, claiming that the only significant civilisation to survive was in the north). On their way west, the Tatars also burnt the towns of Halych and Volodymyr-Volynskyi, the strongholds of Danylo of Halych, beloved by Ukrainian nationalist historians as the would-be Ukrainian reunifier of Rus. The Tatars also wheeled north against Vladimir and other towns in 1238, but spared Novgorod and forced the Muscovites to pay tribute (the 'Mongol yoke') for centuries – although the extent of the tutelage is again disputed between Ukrainian, Belarusian and Russian historians (the

Ukrainians typically argue that Muscovite political culture became 'Mongolised', seeking to show that the only significant civilisation to survive was in the south).

The future Belarusian lands of the north-west, on the other hand, were protected by thick forests and the Polessian marshes in the south, and had fewer problems with the Mongol Tatars, although some historians claim that the *threat* of Tatar attack led Polatsk and others to seek Lithuanian protection. In fact, many friendly Tatars and Karaim (Turkic-speaking Jews from Crimea) would settle in military service to the grand dukes (see page 31). Ironically, the Grand Duchy sent an army under Jogaila (1377–1434), the victor at Grunwald, to the Battle of Kulikovo Field in 1380, which according to Russian historiography marked Moscow's liberation from the 'yoke'. Jogaila's army missed the battle, and would have fought on the other side.

The rising power in the north-west, however, was no longer Polatsk but the town of Navahrudak (founded in 1227), in the area known not as 'White Rus', but as 'Black Rus', near modern-day Hrodna. The growing power of the militant 'missionary' Livonian Order of Teutonic Knights, which built up the city of Riga at the mouth of the river Dzvina (Daugava in Latvian) after 1201, undermined Polatsk's former strategic and commercial advantages upriver. Black Rus, on the other hand, was neatly situated in the territory between the Livonian Knights and the rampaging Golden Horde.

But because it was further to the south-west, in the basin of the river Neman rather than the river Dzvina, Black Rus was more closely connected to the local Baltic tribes than Polatsk. The nearest tribe was the Yatvingians who lived further down the Neman, followed by the Aukštaitians ('Uplanders') from the area around Vilna, which is on the river Neris, a tributary of the Neman. Further north, downriver to the Baltic Sea, were the Samogitians ('Lowlanders'). In Lithuanian, Samogitia is Žemaitija; in Belarusian, the tribe was known as the Zhmudz. Belarusian historians tend to depict Black Rus as a Slavic outpost influencing the Baltic region; Lithuanian historians tend to put things the other way round, claiming that Navahrudak, Hrodna and Volkovosk were 'founded by the Rus [but] on the former territories of the Lithuanians'.[5] Unfortunately, there are no surviving written records, except those written by outsiders. In other words, Black Rus was a transitional zone, and quite a wide one at that. According to Lithuanian scholars, this zone, and the eastern limit of the Lithuanian language, ends just west of Minsk. The Slavs only pushed west in the seventeenth century.[6] According to Belarusians, the western limit for Belarusian influence is north-west of Vilna.[7] Although it was argued at one time that

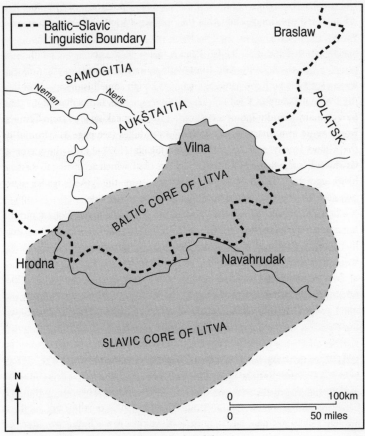

Map 2. The origins of Litva, according to the 'joint' theory.

the Balts eventually fled west as Slavic settlement consolidated, the evidence is actually that they stayed put.[8]

Litva Version I: Lithuania Rising

Navahrudak (or Naugardukas in Lithuanian) played a key role in the rise of the Grand Duchy. The entity referred to as medieval 'Lithuania' in fact had the full name of 'Grand Duchy of Lithuania, Rus and Samogitia'. Its short name was 'Litva'. This is not the same thing as 'Lithuania'. In the modern Lithuanian language, the word for 'Lithuania' is Lietuva. Still the standard Lithuanian version of history takes its founding moment in the thirteenth century. Tacitus and Ptolemy mentioned the Baltic tribes (the Aestians and Galindians) back in the first and second centuries AD, but as they were pagan and illiterate little is known of them until their ruler adopted Christianity in 1251, followed somewhat later by the people as a whole in 1387. The Lithuanians chose to mark Vilna's (to them Vilnius) year as the City of European Culture in 2009 by celebrating 'a thousand years' of the name Lithuania. Certainly the *Magdeburg Chronicle* mentions the visit of a missionary, St Bruno of Querfurt, to the borders of Lithuania and Rus in 1009 – although it also reports that he was brutally murdered.

The Baltic tribes increasingly banded together militarily in the eleventh and twelfth centuries, initially both to fight Polatsk *and* to provide its ancillary armed forces, taking advantage of the increasing feuds between (and within) Polatsk, Minsk and Smolensk to build up their power.[9] But the key catalyst that produced Lithuanian unity out of tribal confusion was the arrival of the 'Crusaders of the North'. After the sack of Constantinople in 1204, the enemies of the Catholic West were just as likely to be the Christian Orthodox as the Muslims, and the popes of the time had also spotted new heathens in the north, with Celestine III declaring a formal crusade in 1193. The Order of the Brothers of the Sword was established in what is now Latvia in 1202. Further south, the Knights of the Cross, who were founded in Acre, Palestine in 1192, came to the Baltic via Hungary at the invitation of Duke Konrad I of Masovia (Poland) to fight against the Pruss in 1230. The two orders did most of their fighting to the west and north of what is now Belarus and Lithuania, defeating and eventually assimilating most of the 'west Baltic' tribes, most notably the Pruss, who left only their name to what became Prussia; and conquering, largely without assimilating, the other 'Saracens of the North' in today's Latvia and southern Estonia. The loose union of the two groups to create the Livonian Order in 1237 was directly aimed at conquering the lands of the Samogitian tribe that lay in between, an expedition the previous year having resulted in defeat at the Battle of Schaulen.

Some Baltic historians accept that the invasion may have been a good thing. The Christianity brought by the Knights may have saved the likes of the Estonians from the assimilation that was the fate of other Finno-Ugric tribes under Russian rule.[10] The Knights brought order. Others argue the Balts did the work by themselves.[11]

But the ancestors of today's Lithuanians lived further inland, as did the Black Rus, and resisted the Knights with much greater force. Other rival Rus principalities fell victim to the Golden Horde at this time, and Moscow would not be a force in the region until the second half of the fourteenth century. Poland was also relatively weak, after the end of the first period of rule by the Piast dynasty in 1138, and its subsequent division among rival principalities until 1295.

But the story of how the Lithuanians and/or Black Rus used the advantages of their geography and relative fighting strength to build a state is less clear. Even modern Lithuanian historians admit that, 'the first historical ruler of Lithuania Mindaugas . . . comes out of the shroud of Lithuanian legends'.[12] He was probably born around 1203, but is first mentioned in the chronicles after a treaty with Volhynia in 1219 and is already being called supreme ruler of the united tribes by 1245.[13] Mindaugas (in Polish, Mendog) converted to Catholicism under Andreas von Stirland, the master of the Riga Knights, and received the blessing of Pope Innocent IV for his rule as king in 1250 or 1251, followed by further licence in 1253 to conquer territory in the east. The first such conquest was supposedly Navahrudak, in the same year, though Mindaugas's son Vaišvilkas had supposedly been overlord of the region since 1239. Lithuanian historians tend to depict Mindaugas's rule in Navahrudak and Black Rus as the consolidation of ethnically mixed but predominantly Lithuanian (i.e. Yatvingian) territory,[14] after Mindaugas expanded out from his original 'patrimonial lands' around Vilna and Trakai 'between the Neris, Nemunas and Verkys rivers'.[15] It was only his successors who ventured further into unambiguously Slavic lands.[16] Only in 1358 did Algirdas (ruled 1345–77) declare his intention to conquer all of Rus.

The circumstances of Mindaugas's apostasy in 1261 and murder in 1263 are not well established, though he had made plenty of enemies on his way up, not least by murdering his brother and nephews. One interpretation is that Mindaugas's conversion was a sign of his westward orientation. But both his tactical Christianity and his eventual apostasy were probably necessitated by internal tensions provoked by the shifting balance of external powers – in the latter case, war with Livonia after the rebellious Samogitians once again defeated the Teutonic Knights at the Battle of Durben in 1260. Mindaugas's rivals restored paganism after him, as they renewed their struggle against the Knights.[17] Mindaugas's project for Litva ultimately failed therefore because it could not unite three different worlds: 'a pagan Lithuania, Catholic Europe, and Orthodox Rus'.[18]

The next version of Litva, so-called 'Geiminid Lithuania', established by Mindaugas's successors Gediminas (in Polish Giedyman, in Belarusian Hedimin, ruled 1316 to 1341), and Algirdas (in Belarusian Alhierd, 1345–77), was more stable, lasting until the sixteenth century.[19] Gediminas added what is now southern Belarus, down to the Prypiat; Algirdas gained Vitsebsk by marriage. But initially the Grand Duchy still looked both east and west. One trend was represented by Jogaila (Jagaila in Belarusian or Jagiełło in Polish, ruled 1377–1434), who, to try and solve the perpetual problem of war on two fronts, signed the Union of Kreva with the Poles in 1385, married the infant Polish queen Jadwiga and became king of Poland in 1386. The other trend was exemplified by Vytautas (in Belarusian Witold, ruled 1392–1430), who is known as 'the Great' because of his ethnically Lithuanian orientation. Christianisation of the Lithuanian lands gradually helped consolidate the new state after the formal introduction of Roman Catholicism there in 1387, and the two trends united to defeat the Teutonic Knights at the Battle of Grunwald in 1410.

Litva Version II: A Slavo-Balto Enterprise

The Slavic side of this history is also obscure. In the north, 'the history of thirteenth century Polatsk is only partially known and the circumstances of the Lithuanian invasions remain obscure'.[20] The city was in decline, but lasting Lithuanian control over Polatsk seems only to have been established in 1307. Arguably, however, it was no big deal for the local Slavs, who had once been ruled by Scandinavians, to swap one set of overlords for another. According to Serhii Plokhy, 'the process of replacing Rurikid princes with Lithuanian ones could last for generations and go back and forth, as was the case in Polatsk'.[21] And for Henadz Sahanovich, 'Polatsk had long experience of close contact with the Baltic tribes. There were never clear ethnic boundaries between the eastern Latgallians [from the south-east of modern Latvia], Lithuanians and Slavs in the Dzvina and Neman basins.'[22] The Slavs moved down the rivers, the Baltic tribes occupied the hinterlands. Inter-ethnic marriage was common among the elite, possibly because the Baltic tribes were less likely to be seen as culturally alien, as they were pagan.

The relationship was therefore far from one-way. At an earlier period the Balts paid tribute to the Rus. The *Primary Chronicle* describes the first attacks in 983. Polatsk defeated the Yatvingians in 1002 (see page 20); this was followed by a more general campaign led by Yaroslav the Wise in 1040. Polatsk at the height of its power ruled many of the peoples on the way to the Baltic Sea as vassals. But, not surprisingly, Lithuanian historians consider that the ebb and flow favoured the proto-Lithuanians at later periods, particularly by the second half of the twelfth century, when they 'took up the offence [sic]' and advanced across the river Dzvina.[23] In 1185, Baltic armies defeated Polatsk, though the defeat was reversed in 1191. But the Balts also increasingly fought for Polatsk – there were common campaigns against Smolensk in 1198 and 1258 – which came to rely on their force of arms. According to the Belarusian historian Yahor Novikaw, 'it was not long before the growing Lithuanianisation of the Polatsk army made Polatsk society think that the energetic Lithuanian dukes and their brave warriors contributed to the defence and security of Polatsk more than Rus royal families, hopelessly stuck in their dynastic disputes. . . . A synthesis of Lithuanian military power and Rus civil tradition was to become the cornerstone of the Grand Duchy of Lithuania.'[24]

Further to the south-west, however, it is also argued on the Belarusian side that Navahrudak was set up precisely in order to project Slavic power over the Lithuanians.[25] Instead of the Teutonic Knights, it could just as easily have been emigrants from Polatsk spreading out downriver who provided the spark for Lithuanian consolidation.[26] According to Ihnatowski, 'the Lithuanian ruler [Mindaugas] well understood that he couldn't rest his construction on the Lithuanians alone. The Lithuanian tribes were not numerous. . . . Polatska Rus gave the new state its orders, habits, powers and culture.'[27] Even some Lithuanian historians admit the Grand Duchy 'lacked an intellectual class' without the Slavs.[28]

Others have argued that a similar political culture was more important.[29] The two overlapping groups faced similar threats. It made just as much sense for the proto-Belarusians as it did for the proto-Lithuanians to unite in a single state. They also benefited from a common opportunity: the Mongol onslaught weakened the power of the more definitively Slavic Galician-Volhynian Principality to the south (in what is now west Ukraine), and Mindaugas successfully fought off the Galicians, or 'Red Rus', when he had to in the war of 1249–54. The local Slavs and Balts had in any case two centuries of previous history living alongside one another along the river Neman. According to Belarusian historians such as Mitrafan Downar-Zapolski, therefore, 'the incorporation of Belarusian lands was not forced. This was an incorporation with the agreement of the population, seeing the obvious political gains from such a union.'[30] Far from being invaded, the Slavs may have petitioned the Lithuanians for help against the Tatars. The new state was therefore 'a union of Lithuanian princes with Belarusian gentry and towns', in which Belarusians did a lot of the fighting.[31] Ihnatowski thus preferred to talk of the building of a 'Lithuanian-Belarusian State' in this period.[32]

As the Lithuanians were pagan, Rus culture was stronger. It is claimed without much evidence that Mindaugas first converted to Orthodox Christianity in 1246. His son Vaišelga (ruled 1264–7) certainly did. Vaišelga even founded an Orthodox monastery at Lawrushava on the Neman, where the *Lawrushava Gospel* was produced in the early fourteenth century.[33] 'The Grand Duchy had separate [Orthodox] metropolitans during 1316–1330, 1354–61, and 1375–1389', which were based at Navahrudak and Vilna, including the eparchies of Polatsk and Turaw, 'but was unable to consistently maintain its own Grand Duchy Orthodox Church separate from the metropolitans of greater Rus.'[34] The new state's rulers only supported the Church for *raison d'état*; a group of 'Vilna martyrs' was put to death in the 1340s for refusing pagan orders to eat meat during an Orthodox fast.

In 1382 Jogaila toyed with the idea of a proper alliance with Muscovy – involving marriage to the daughter of Dmitrii Donskoi and conversion to Orthodoxy. But this would have meant the Lithuanians being overwhelmed by the already numerous Orthodox nobility, and increased the hostility of the Teutonic Knights, to whom Orthodoxy was heresy. An alliance with Roman Catholic Poland made more sense both internally and externally.[35] Significantly, however, when Roman Catholicism began to make inroads into Slavic territory and future Belarusian lands after 1387, this was mainly in Mindaugas's core territory of Black Rus.

The Land of the Snake

One reason for depicting Litva as a Baltic-Belarusian joint enterprise is that mutual influence goes back a long way. The 'Baltic' or 'substratum' theory of Belarusian origin is a rival to the 'Kryvichy' theory mentioned in Chapter 1, and was developed by the Moscow archaeologist Valentin Sedov (b. 1924),[36] and in independent Belarus is associated with Mikola Ermalovich and Anatol Hrytskevich. Unlike Vatslaw Lastowski's 'Kryvichy' theory of the 1920s, the 'Baltic' theory tries to preserve the idea of a common prehistory for all those who are now Belarusians, while stressing their distinction from Russians through the admixture of Baltic 'blood', which would now be called Baltic DNA.

Baltic historians allege that, in addition to the ancestors of today's Estonians, Latvians, Lithuanians and other vanished 'western Balts', the now extinct 'eastern Balts' occupied a huge rectangular territory due east of what is now Lithuania and Latvia, but north of Kiev and south of Moscow. Supposedly *all* the northern neighbours of the Scythians, who occupied the northern Black Sea coast, mentioned by the Greek historian Herodotus were in fact Balts. Controversy continues as to the original 'homeland of the Slavs', but most historians agree that there was hardly any Slavic settlement much north of the river Prypiat, in the far south of what is now Belarus, until around AD 500. Archaeologists therefore argue about whether the Bronze Age 'Bantser culture', relics of which have been found in central Belarus, was a common Baltic culture or a 'local variant'.[37]

Some pockets of 'eastern Balts' survived to be mentioned in the early chronicles. One tribe called the Galindians was still being mopped up in the north in 1147, the year Moscow was founded. Many elements of the thinly spread local ethnic Baltic prehistory, including folklore (dances, songs and ornaments), toponyms and hydronyms in particular, can therefore be found as far away as parts of Kaluga, Tula and Orel, now in western Russia, in the upper Oka, near Moscow, and in Chernihiv, now in northern Ukraine. Baltic 'enclaves', pockets of original settlers rather than more recent migrants, survived in central and eastern Belarus down through the Middle Ages.[38]

The Belarusian argument, however, is that the 'three tribes' mixed with local Balts between AD 700 and 900 to create the basis for Belarusian 'ethnogenesis'. Some Lithuanian historians argue that a fourth east Slavic tribe, the Viatychy, also had Baltic roots.[39] Conversely, the Polessians wouldn't be Belarusians at all on the basis of the 'Baltic' theory, as it is difficult to find anything pre-Slavic in the region after the sixth century. On the other hand, other tribes with Baltic links – the Severiany and even the Paliany – were still being classified as Great Russians in the 1920s.[40] Finally, the mixing was done relatively late. According to Lithuanian archaeologists, 'the entire territory of Belarus was, until the 8th century, occupied by Balts'.[41]

Nevertheless, what is now Belarus was the heart of the 'eastern Baltic' territory. Some key words are only shared by Balts and Belarusians, such as dorzhnik (Belarusian) and daržinīkas (Lithuanian) for 'animal pen', lun and liūnas for 'quagmire', migla for 'fog' and asla for 'dirt floor'. The peculiar position of snakes in folk culture and superstition is unique to both. The pantheon of pre-Christian gods often overlapped, like Piarun and Perkūnas, the god of thunder and lightning.

Litva Version III: Litva Was Belarus

According to the more radical Belarusian version of history,[42] medieval Litva was really medieval Belarus. The modern 'Lietuvians' are really only the 'Baltic Lithuanians', the tribes who lived near the coast, who have stolen the ancient name of the true Slavic locals, like German Prussia taking the name of the Baltic Puss (the Prußen), or the Anglo-Saxons usurping the Celtic name of 'Britain'. The name 'Litva' came from one of the Yatvingian tribes, the

'Yatva'; but the 'Litvins' more generally emerged through a unique synthesis of Baltic Yatvingians and Slavic Kryvichy – the tribe that founded Polatsk. (The Yatvingians have many names: they are also known as the Yotvingians, the Sudovians or the Jotvingiai in modern Lithuanian, the Jaćwingowie in Polish and the Yatsviahi in Belarusian.) Of the then Baltic tribes, the Yatvingians in the west were assimilated by the Black Rus; the Nalshany in the east and Litva in the east and north-east were conquered. The Aukštaitians in the south-east and the Samogitians remained unassimilated, thereby becoming the ancestors of the modern-day Lithuanians.

On this version of events, Mindaugas, the Belarusian version of whose name would be Mindowh, first came to power in Navahrudak in 1239. Black Rus was the original Litva, the territory of the Kryvichy and the related Drehavichy tribe as they moved down the river Neman past what is now Hrodna. Mindaugas may have come from Aukštota but been 'invited' to rule in Navahrudak, possibly as a refugee in search of Slavic money and support. He then proceeded to conquer his homeland in the 1240s, rather than the other way around: that is, Mindaugas attacked Lithuania from Navahrudak, rather than attacking Navahrudak from Lithuania (though it is sometimes argued that Mindaugas was actually from Slavic stock, just as Vilna was really founded by the Kryvichy).

Thus, the original Kryvich-Yatvingian Litvins were supposedly Orthodox. Later, the two pagan Baltic tribes, the Aukštaitians and Samogitians – the 'Baltic' Lithuanians – were forced to join the new state. The location of Mindaugas's capital is placed in convenient obscurity, though some Belarusians say it was first Kreva and then Navahrudak. It is clearer that Navahrudak was indeed the capital immediately before it was shifted to Vilna in or after the latter's first mention in the chronicles in 1323. It is also claimed that the rather stylish coat of arms of the Grand Duchy, the so-called Pahonia (a rearing horseman, in Lithuanian the Vytis), was originally the emblem of Navahrudak, which then gifted it to the Grand Duchy as a whole. For a brief period in 1991–5 Lithuania and newly independent Belarus *both* used it as a state symbol.

As a footnote, the official modern version of Belarusian history under Lukashenka has gradually adopted an intriguing mix of these various versions of events. On the one hand, it suits the president politically to maintain the myth of 'One Rus' and play down the idea of Slavic–Baltic intermingling. On the other hand, he does not want to concede either Slavic purity or preeminence to the Balts. As of 2003, he had settled for the awkward formulation: 'a part of the east Slavic population was forced to unite with the Balts and create

Map 3. Litva, mid-sixteenth century.

their own state. It became a Slavic Forepost, standing against threats from outside.'[43] Instead of conquering Slavic lands in the east, this version of Litva seems to have been pointed firmly west.

Litva, Lietuva and Rus

However it was established, the Grand Duchy had a diverse population, regardless of whether it can be formally viewed as a multiethnic state.[44] At its height, the Lithuanians were a clear minority, outnumbered by Slavs and by large minorities of Jews, Karaim, Roma and Tatars.[45] It is hard to be precise about numbers, however. Some historians argue that the ethnic border gradually shifted down the river Neman, and the new joint state had a Slavic majority.[46] Lithuanian historians tend to argue that 'certain of the Rus'ian lands were sparsely populated due either to unfavourable natural conditions [the Prypiat marshes] or attacks by the Tatars. . . . It was therefore unlikely that, despite the expansion of the area, the Rus'ian population had an advantage over the Lithuanians.'[47]

Modern historians from several of the 'successor nations' of Litva have accepted the idea that the state was led by a multiethnic 'political nation'.[48] This was a 'socio-political community', defined in part by class and partly by rights of political participation. The 'political nation' was therefore only for the upper reaches of society (in Polish the *wspólnota państwowa*). There was no modern idea of 'nation' to encompass the lower orders.

The ethnic Lithuanians were overrepresented in the governing elite, but they were still consolidating the various south Baltic tribes into a single nation and trying to consolidate the new Roman Catholic religion into a united tribal faith. The Battle of Grunwald, for example, was fought to win final control of Samogitia in 1410, so the Samogitians adopted Catholicism late, in 1417. The pagan years left a tradition of secular noble power. The Lithuanian nobility were granted extensive privileges in 1387 and 1434, followed by exemption from taxes and the right to judge their own peasants in 1447. The noble-dominated parliament was increasingly powerful from the late fifteenth century. The Lithuanian nobility soon learned to share power with others, however (see below), which was made easier by its history of fighting increasingly alongside as well as against the nobility of Polatsk and Black Rus.

Both had long fought the Tatars, but the latter weren't all bad. One group, the so-called 'Lipka Tatars', settled in what is now Lithuania and Belarus in the fifteenth century (Lipka was the old Crimean Tatar name for Litva). In 1382 Khan Tokhtamysh sacked Moscow in revenge for the supposedly decisive Muscovite victory in 'throwing off the Tatar yoke' at Kulikovo Field near the river Don in 1380. Tokhtamysh established a great empire, second only to that of Timur the Lame (Tamerlaine), with whom he quarrelled after invading Transoxonia (Central Asia). Tokhtamysh was first defeated by Timur on the Volga in 1391 and again when he joined forces with Vytautas at the Battle of the River Vorksla near the Dnieper in 1399. He died in about 1406, but Vytautas invited his followers to settle in the region around Vilna as a military caste. They remained Muslim and could marry locally. At their peak around 1600, there may have been around 200,000 Tatars living in Litva. The largest numbers were in Lida, Navahrudak and Iwye near Vilna, though Minsk also had a Tatar quarter known as Tatarskaya Slabada ('Free Tatary').

The Lipka Tatars remained in the service of the grand dukes for hundreds of years. Stanislaw Bulak-Balakhovich, who headed the Belarusian People's Republic's limited military forces in 1918, was part Tatar. The Lutskevich brothers, who were prominent national leaders either side of 1917, had some Tatar blood (see pages 78–9) – as did the Hollywood actor Charles Bronson, whose father was from Druskininkai near Vilna. From the sixteenth century, however, the Tatars assimilated linguistically, if not religiously. Remarkably, they produced religious texts (*al-Kittab* or *kitabs*) in the local Slavic language, but using Arabic letters. In fact, because the Tatars cared little for old Church Slavonic traditions, their books were actually closer to dialectical Belarusian than to chancellery Ruthenian (see pages 36–9).[49] Over the centuries, 'Belarusian' has therefore been written in three alphabets: Cyrillic, Latin and Arabic.

The Karaim were Turkic-speakers who used the Hebrew script,[50] and according to one theory were the lost descendants of the Khazars. The Karaim were also often in military service, having also been invited from their Crimean homeland in the fourteenth and fifteenth centuries. Karaim Street still sits at the entrance to the castle at Trakai, the ancient capital of Lithuania.

The Jews arrived in Belarus from the west, migrating from Germany through Chełm – a process accelerated by the Black Death – first under Gediminas (ruled 1316–41), and then Vytautas (ruled 1392–1430), both of whom invited Hanseatic and Jewish traders to strengthen the economic life of the state. The alternative theory that all the local Jews were descended from the Khazars never really gained much traction, as Germany seemed a more civilised place of origin. The Jews were first recognised as a separate group by the charter of 1388. They were temporarily banished in 1495, but returned in 1503, although the Lithuanian Statutes (the Grand Duchy's legal code) confined their economic role to trade and moneylending. Nevertheless, by the end of the eighteenth century, the Jews accounted for one-eighth of the population.[51]

Russian Old Believers began fleeing to the Grand Duchy after the reforms of Patriarch Nikon led to the great 'Schism' in the Russian Church in the 1660s. One group settled near Homel in 1685. Numbers really began to grow, however, after Peter the Great's Spiritual Ordinance of 1721 defined the Old Believers as 'implacable foes'. By mid-century they numbered in the hundreds of thousands, though the figures were hotly disputed as they acted as a *casus belli* for the Partitions (when Russia, Germany and Austria swallowed Poland and Lithuania). Most local Old Believers were Fedoseyans from over the border in north-west Russia, radical ascetics who refused to pray for the tsar and rejected marriage.

The identity of the older local east Slavic population is less clear. Many still had a dynastic identity, calling themselves after their town or principality. The Lithuanians called the Rus the *gudas*, allegedly derived from the local name for the Balts' previous neighbours the Goths. The local Rus eventually solidified a local identity distinct from the Rus of Muscovy over roughly three periods. An early 'Golden Age' of Rus influence in Litva lasted until the illiterate and pagan Lithuanians, under further pressure from the Teutonic Knights, adopted Roman Catholicism in 1387, two years after the Union of Kreva with Catholic Poland in 1385. In this period, the pagan Lithuanians were more likely to assimilate to east Slavic culture than the other way around. The last grand duke to speak Lithuanian was Kazimierz IV (Kazimieras in Lithuanian), who died in 1492.

After the Union of Kreva in 1385, however, the Grand Duchy needed a new narrative to distinguish itself from both Poland and Muscovy, leading to the development of a common identity for the local east Slavs that in English is called 'Ruthenian' (or Rusyn), from the medieval Latin ethnonym 'Rut(h)eni', despite the tensions of the early fifteenth century and the civil war of the 1430s (see next chapter). A third phase in the sixteenth century brought about the partial reconsolidation of Rus identity via the trend towards 'confessionalisation' introduced by the Reformation and Counter-Reformation, at the same time as, and in large part in reaction to, the increasing spread of the Polish language and culture in the region. The 'Ruthenian' language, as it had developed since 1385, now paradoxically 'provided a Slavic platform for the spread of the Polish language and ideas'.[52] But this story will be told in full in the next chapter.

Conclusion

'Litva' has long since disappeared from the map. But as late as the 1920s, when people expressed nostalgia for 'historical Lithuania', they meant multiethnic Litva. According to the modern Belarusian historian Aleh Latyshonak from Białystok, however, its eventual definitive death means that the 'Belarusians are double orphans, because they are Rusyns, deprived of Kiev, and Litvins denied Vilna. We have had to construct a history from the remnants of the history of [both] Rus and Litva.'[53]

CHAPTER 3

RUTHENIA

The new state of Litva divided one set of east Slavic Rus from another. The two would develop separately for over five hundred years, with the western half going through several profound changes of identity between the thirteenth and eighteenth centuries. For most of this time the Rus of the west were known as Rusyns or, in the Latinised form, 'Ruthenians'. The Calvinist writer and folklorist Salamon Rysinski was the first to call himself a Belarusian, in 1586. But most of his contemporaries did not. The historian should therefore guard against 'the inflationary use of the term "Belarusian".'[1] When it was used, 'Belarus' was a variable term, and often meant only the eastern regions of Vitsebsk and Mahilew, which were the borderlands of Litva, plus parts of Smolensk, which was disputed with Muscovy. Most of what is now Belarus was part of 'Litva' proper.

The relative tolerance for east Slavic culture shown by the early Lithuanians meant the Rus initially did not have to develop an identity in adversity. However, after the Union of Kreva in 1385 upgraded the personal union of Polish-Lithuanian kings into a dynastic one, and the Union of Hrodna (Horodło in Polish) in 1413 granted the Lithuanian elite the privileges of the Polish nobility in exchange for the adoption of Roman Catholicism, the Orthodox, i.e. the Orthodox nobility, suddenly found themselves demoted to second-class citizens overnight (had the Orthodox elite been allowed to convert, there may well have been a mass conversion at this time). Moreover, the Lithuanian elite began justifying the move in Vytautas's time (ruled 1392–1430) – as nobilities so often did – by creating a cover story of its 'historical rights'. One document, *Vytautas's Complaint* (an account of his war against his cousins Jogaila and Skirgalia), was supposedly written in 1390 by Vytautas himself, to justify his claim to the throne – though no original survives.

Chronicle Wars

The Orthodox Rus responded with civic strife, an appeal to outsiders, and the beginnings of an identity-building project of their own. Fortunately, they were able to exploit the split in the ruling elite after Vytautas's death in 1430, between the half-Rus Švitrigaila of Polatsk and Vytautas's brother Žygimantas (Sigismund). Švitrigaila attempted to exploit the Rus, backed by Muscovy, to clear his own path to power and was largely supported in the east (Polatsk, Vitsebsk, Smolensk, Kiev, but also Volhynia). But Žygimantas defused the issue by offering the Hrodna privileges to the Rus nobility in 1434, after which the position of the Orthodox Church was temporarily stabilised, and by defeating Švitrigaila at the Battle of Pabaiskas in 1435.

But the Rus scribes were encouraged to put pen to paper in defence of Orthodox privilege. Significantly, *The Chronicle of the Grand Dukes of Lithuania* (1446) and especially *The Eulogy of Vytautas* (*c.* 1428), which propagated the idea of the dual Slavic-Lithuanian origins of the Grand Duchy, were both probably written in Smolensk, where Vilna's power was weakest and the influence of neighbouring Muscovy strongest (Smolensk had only been conquered by Vytautas in 1395). The anonymous author's idea of the Rus land at this time included Muscovy. (The Soviet Belarusian historian Viachaslaw Chamiarytski revived the theory of the Grand Duchy's 'dual origins' in the 1960s.)[2]

These Smolensk chronicles were in part an attempt to build a dualistic historical identity for the new state, as a rival to nascent Lithuanian historiography, particularly the idea that the Lithuanian nobility was descended from the Romans. *The Chronicle of the Grand Duchy of Lithuania and Samogitia* (sponsored by Albertas Goštautas, who ruled in Vilna and Trakai before becoming grand chancellor in 1522 – hence no mention of the Rus) describes how Prince Polemon was said to have left Rome with five hundred nobles from four leading families (the Centaurus, Columna, Ursini and Rose) to escape persecution by Nero, and settled by the river Neman. Some of this flight of fancy may have been inspired by the arrival of Bona Sforza, princess of Bari, as queen of Poland and grand duchess of Lithuania in 1518. However, many nobles took the myth seriously enough to start learning Latin – the 'language of their ancestors'.

This rival fifteenth-century mythmaking was supposedly evidence of what Aleh Latyshonak has called 'the growing enmity between the two ethnic groups.'[3] But the compromise of 1434 led to at least half a century of relative peace before the 'Slavic rebellion' of Mikhal Hlinski in 1507–8. The aristocratic Hlinski, who was part Tatar, dreamed of creating a separate Rus state and occupied Minsk before fleeing to Moscow. Hlinski claimed to be acting in defence of Orthodoxy against attempts to implement the Union of Florence (the abortive reunion of Catholic and Orthodox in 1439), but historians disagree about the extent to which he was supported by the Slavic locals. One argument is that the constant warfare with Muscovy after the threat from the Teutonic Knights was finally ended in 1410, when the combined armies of Poland and the Grand Duchy's rout of the Order at the Battle of Grunwald (Minsk has a 'Grunwald' restaurant which is full of suits of armour and heroic battle paintings) arguably led to the strengthening of a common 'civic' loyalty to the Grand Duchy. There were two wars between the Grand Duchy and Muscovy, in 1445–9 and 1492–4. Then there were five in the sixteenth century, in 1500–3, 1507–8, 1512–22, 1534–7 and 1563–82, and two in the seventeenth century, in 1609–18 and 1654–67. The east Slavic elite was moving towards an identity of *gente rutenus, natione lituanus*; (Ruthenian tribe, Litvin nation)[4] although this was also because 'distinctions were blurred by the process of Polonisation of [both] Lithuanians and Ruthenians.'[5] Maciej Stryjkowski's *Chronicle of Poland, Lithuania, Samogitia, and All of Ruthenia of Kiev, Moscow, Novgorod*, published in 1582, tried to encompass both points of view, as its title suggests.

There was less internal tension after Smolensk went back to Muscovy in 1522 following a ten-year war. Aleh Latyshonak has argued, however, that, after the relative decline of Polatsk and Navahrudak, 'the loss of Smolensk was a terrible blow to the Ruthenian community of the Grand Duchy. Smolensk had [briefly] been its principal intellectual centre. It was here that the conceptions of the Ruthenian nature of the Grand Duchy were formulated. Smolensk had also been the centre of the newly-emerging "White [Rus]". . . . Although Polatsk [also occupied by Muscovy in 1563–78] returned under Polish-Lithuanian rule in 1579 and Smolensk followed suit [temporarily, in 1611, until 1654], the two towns did not regain their former status. Mahilew on the Dnieper became the biggest city' in Lithuanian Rus,[6] but it was a relative backwater. The future Belarusian lands once suffered from having a peripatetic capital. The period of Smolensk's preeminence was relatively short, and it was in any case always in rivalry with Vilna, which now came into its own. (As stated before, the modern capital of Minsk only truly became a rival centre of national life in the second half of the twentieth century.)

The Language Question

Before the Union of Kreva and the coronation of Jogaila as Jagiełło, king of Poland in 1386, Litva had been lightly administered. The Lithuanians were pagan, so the state used a mixture of Church Slavonic and what was known as the *delovoi iazyk*, a 'business' form of Slavic common to the whole of 'East Slavia', i.e. a language used in both Muscovy and among the Orthodox of the Grand Duchy. The two were mixed together in many different versions, often depending on the individual scribe. But after 1385 there was an increasing practical requirement for a new administrative language and a new symbolic need to distinguish Litva from both Muscovy and Poland. Old Church Slavonic was ritualistic and too unintelligible for common use. This led to the development of what was in essence a new language known as the *rus'ka mova* by the Rus clergy who 'manned the state bureaucracy' at the various royal chancelleries,[7] which combined elements of old Church Slavonic with local dialect and some Polonisms.

There were many versions of *rus'ka mova*, however, depending on where the work was being done: at Vilna, at Navahrudak or even briefly at Smolensk.[8] From Mindaugas to Vytautus the chancellery language was based on Volhynian dialects (a region now in north-west Ukraine) and on those of Polatsk-Smolensk. In the second half of the fifteenth century the epicentre shifted to north Volhynia and southern Belarus, then in the first half of the sixteenth century Brest-Navahrudak, and only in the second half of the sixteenth century was it properly but temporarily Belarusianised: that is, dominated by central Belarusian dialects.[9]

But in so far as most of the work was done at the main chancellery in Vilna, the local scribes were using one variant of early 'Belarusian' dialect. Most of the chancelleries were anyway in the north. Lithuanian wasn't much of a competitor: the first Lithuanian book was only printed in 1547. Scribes travelled, of course, and there were many southern 'Ukrainianisms'. But the regional bias was largely accidental. According to the language expert Jan Fellerer, *rus'ka mova*, or 'Ruthenian', was a 'continuum that worked perfectly well in other places as well'.[10] Either by accident or design, the scribes drew on Polessian (northern Volhynia-southern Belarus) dialects because they represented, as they continue to do today, a transitional zone between north and south. And dialect remained: 'there was no assumption that the written and the spoken language had to be the same'.[11]

Rus'ka mova also served to transmit cultural influences from elsewhere. According to Barbara Skinner, around 1500 'European humanism and its emphasis on textual study and vernacular publications influenced educated Ruthenians' like Frantsysk (or Frantsishak) Skaryna (c. 1490–1551).[12] Skaryna is a key cultural icon in Belarusian history: first, because he was a polyglot, born in Polatsk and a major cultural figure in Kraków, Padua, Prague and Vilna; second, because as Henadz Sahanovich asserts, he also embodied the 'cultural synthesis' of 'two traditions – the Greco-Slavic and Western-Latin' (it is not even known for certain whether Skaryna was Orthodox or Catholic),[13] which makes him a useful symbol for latter-day proponents of a distinct Belarusian identity based on cross-cultural borrowing. Skaryna is also argued to have been an embryonic 'confessionaliser'; an accidental or incidental nationaliser of religion through an emphasis on vernacularisation of the Word of God to bring salvation closer to ordinary men and women.

The first Ruthenian book was the *Triod Tsvetnaia* in 1483, a book of services for Easter and Pentecost. With the support of patrons such as the Bürgermeister of Vilna Yakub Babich, Skaryna published a psalter (Book of Psalms) in Prague in 1517 and an entire vernacular Old Testament produced in twenty-three books, with commentaries, in 1517–19, which was before Luther's German Bible (1534). Skaryna also translated the Book of Judith in 1519–21, which is part of the Apocrypha and outside the biblical canon to the Protestants, perhaps undermining the theory of his radical sympathies.[14] Around 1522 he moved back to Vilna, where he set up the east Slavic world's first regular printing press in Babich's home. Skaryna used Cyrillic, but there was no conventional 'vernacular' at the time. He invented his own mixture of Church Slavonic and local dialect, but his work was formal and heavy with the former. His Old Testament was therefore 'not a vernacular work in the strict sense',[15] but a work that used some vernacular. He was also too early to influence nation-building via a modern mass public culture. But this is often the way. Instead of using revealed 'Belarusian', Skaryna helped to reveal a path towards its eventual creation as a modern literary form – a task that would not be completed until the twentieth century.

Besides Skaryna's half-Bible, the Matricula (church records), the state archives, the chronicles and statutes (second 1566, third 1588) of the Grand Duchy were all written in *rus'ka mova*. The most important of these was the Third Statute of the Grand Duchy of Lithuania, produced in 1588 under the guidance of the Ruthenian chancellor of the Grand Duchy from 1589 to 1623, Lew Sapieha. The Statute was the most progressive and comprehensive code of law of its time, and remained in force until it was abolished in eastern Belarus in 1831 and in other Belarusian lands in 1840. Many Belarusian historians therefore refer to the sixteenth century as the 'Golden Age'.[16] The Union of Lublin in 1569 (see below) ushered in further change in the linguistic sphere. Its first effect was greatly to accelerate the penetration of Polish – first in the administration, then in the judiciary, then in belles-lettres.[17] Ruthenian remained the official language of the Grand Duchy until 1697, after which official documents had to be in Polish, but this merely gave formal recognition to a shift that had been under way for some time. The Latin alphabet also spread, assisted by the popularity of the myth of the Latin origin of the Lithuanians and its zealous promotion by the Jesuits whose Academy was converted into Vilna university in 1579.

North and South

The Union of Lublin increased Polish power throughout the region by establishing a political union between Poland and the Grand Duchy on top of the dynastic union established in Kreva in 1385 and Hrodna in 1413. Before 1569 there were few ethnic Poles in what is now Belarus, apart from in Podlasie. But Poland and Polish culture increasingly became the Belarusians' main 'other'. The official name of the new state was the 'Kingdom of Poland and the Grand Duchy of Lithuania', but by the seventeenth century it was also known as 'The Most Serene Commonwealth of Poland' (*Najjaśniejsza Rzeczpospolita Polska*), or just 'the Commonwealth' (*Rzeczpospolita*).

Old Ruthenia was originally a common homeland for both Belarusians and Ukrainians – before either really existed as such. But the Union of Lublin created a border of sorts between the Ruthenian north and the Ruthenian south – a political border between 'Litva' and 'Poland', which was not yet a real ethnic or linguistic boundary (nor an external border). Even in the twentieth century it would not be clear where the difference lay. In particular, it was not clear whether the border region of Polessia was part of Ukraine or of Belarus. Nineteenth-century Belarusian scholars such as Aliaksandr Ryttykh and Efim Karski left it out of their definition of 'Belarus'; the Belarusian People's Republic in 1918 added it in; the Germans gave the region to Ukraine in 1941; the USSR gave it back to Belarus in 1945. But the new border, such as it was, created a virtuous – or vicious – circle. In so far as a good part of the Golden Age came after 1569, the Ruthenians north of the new border identified their language and culture more and more with Litva. The centre of Orthodox culture moved south and merged with the myth of Kiev as the 'New Jerusalem' propagated by southern clerics before 1648.

The common Ruthenian language and culture that had developed by the sixteenth century were north-centred, though only relatively. The Battle of

Orsha in 1514, despite its prominent place in much Belarusian historiography, was in fact won by a 'southerner', Prince Ostrozskyi. A second effect of the Union of Lublin, however, was a gradual shift to the south, for a variety of reasons. First, because Vilna went into relative decline. Second, because of the founding of new centres of learning: the Ostrih Academy in 1576 and the Kiev Mohyla Academy, originally the Kiev Brotherhood School, in 1615. Third was the rise of administrative activity in the south, with the arrival of Polish nobles controlling large estates in the Ukrainian farmlands. Under these pressures, Ruthenian changed from *rus'ka mova* to what became known as *prosta mova*, simple tongue. This new version of Ruthenian contained more southern dialect and more Polonisms. In spite of, or perhaps because of, these two factors, it was used more widely, in biblical books, sermons, practical litera-ture, and even poetry and verse dramas; so the final triumph of Polish was put off until the late seventeenth and eighteenth centuries – though even then it was not complete.

It was therefore not Polonisation as such that created identity problems in the north. The north was cut adrift by the rival identity-building project in the south, and left with an incomplete and inchoate 'Ruthenian-ness' at a time when rising Polonisation in the region left it vulnerable.

Broader Culture

The Ruthenian provinces in the north – Polatsk, Vitsebsk, Minsk, Navahrudak and Brest – enjoyed some limited autonomy. The Orthodox had half the seats on the Vilna city corporation. Unlike in later eras, eastern Slavs dominated the urban population, but not in every city – Vilna had a Ruthenian quarter in the north-east of the city. In fact, it still has a *Rusu gatvė* ('Rus Street') in the old town today, behind the university and a bit bohemian in character. But back in the sixteenth century, the Ruthenians had the grandest churches in town, such as the St Michael built by Prince Ostrozskyi in the Gothic style in 1514, and the St Archangel Michael endowed by Lew Sapieha, the chancellor of the Grand Duchy, in 1594–7 – at least until the Jesuits built the St Casimir, modelled on the *Il Gesù* in Rome, consecrated in 1618. Vilna was the northernmost in Milan Kundera's quintessentially central European 'chain of Baroque cities'. But local architects also developed a 'Gothic-Orthodox' style, as seen in church-castles mainly in the west (near Hrodna) like those at Mozheykovo (1524) and Synkovichi (1518–56), whose present form is also sixteenth-century.

The Kalozhka church of SS Borys and Hleb in Hrodna is one of the last surviving examples of 'Black Rus' architecture. It is recognisably Orthodox, but has colourful stone crosses on the walls.

Wars of Religion

However, the Golden Age was also the time when local Ruthenian society was being torn apart by the religious upheavals of the sixteenth century, particularly after 1569. The creation of a new state came at a bad time for the Ruthenians. Ruthenian identity in the Grand Duchy depended on two factors of which religion remained more important than the de facto dominance of the Rus language.[18] But the Ruthenian Church was isolated and poor after the fall of Constantinople in 1453. The Union of Lublin meant increasing pressure from a Jesuit-dominated state to spread the language, religion and identity of Counter-Reformation Poland. The initial failure of Ruthenian society to compete with either Reformation or Counter-Reformation meant a progressive loss of social elites, though the second half of the sixteenth century produced some tentative attempts at Orthodox reform, sponsored by magnates such as Prince Ostrozskyi. Ruthenian society was open to change, and its pace accelerated by 1600.

According to Barbara Skinner, 'the already multi-confessional Polish-Lithuanian society provided fertile soil for reformed Protestant and Catholic thought'.[19] In the middle of the sixteenth century, under the relative tolerance of King Sigismund (Zygmund) II Augustus (ruled 1548–72), it was Calvinism that made most inroads locally, particularly among noble Ruthenian families like the Radziwiłłs and Sapiehas. Calvinism was therefore strongest in the northern and western parts of the Belarusian palatinates where such families had their estates, as well as in the Ukrainian region of Volhynia. The Radziwiłłs owned property all over, but particularly at Niasvizh, south-west of Minsk; the Sapiehas, who claimed descent from the rulers of Smolensk, at Ruzhany near Brest; the Mirskis and Puciatas near Braslaw. As of 1572, only three secular senators of the GDL were Catholic and three orthodox; the rest, sixteen out of twenty-two, were Protestant.[20]

Antitrinitarianism or 'Arianism', with its social radicalism and argument for individual interpretation of the Gospel, on the other hand, appealed more to the gentry and the lower orders. In Niasvizh, the social radical Symon Budny published daring Antitrinitarian tracts from his own printing shop, including a Lutheran catechism in the Ruthenian vernacular in 1562 (but a Polish New Testament in 1572). One reason why Protestantism spread so quickly was that its more radical strands had a lot in common with the simple ascetic virtues of local Orthodoxy,[21] and with a strong local tradition of Orthodox dissent, including the 'non-Possessors' who opposed the Church's ownership of land, the 'Socinians' and the 'Judaisers' dating back to the late fifteenth century, who questioned the Trinity, rejected icons and criticised indulgent and ill-educated clergy.[22] Budny was even criticised for rabbinical influence.

Protestantism had a potentially broad power base, at least until the rise of the Uniates (see below). Under the threat of the Counter-Reformation, the Calvinists and the Arians briefly united to form a united Church for Litva, the *Jednota Litewska*, in Vilna in 1578. Three out its six districts were in what is now Belarus (Navahrudak, Podlasie and 'Belarus'), but the vast majority of its parishes (98 per cent) were in what is now the west and north. The Protestant influence did not extend to Minsk and the east.[23] The Protestants also attempted to make common cause where possible with the Orthodox, but by mid-century the Counter-Reformation Catholics and reformist Orthodox in Kiev had successfully stolen their agenda. The Jesuits hounded the radical Protestants out in the seventeenth century. In 1647 their schools and printing presses were closed. In 1658 they were expelled from the Commonwealth.

The Union

The northern Ruthenians responded to the Roman Catholic and Protestant challenges in various ways after 1569. Many took up the offer to become Polonised Catholics. The Jesuits founded colleges in Vilna in 1570 and Polatsk in 1581. Ironically, when Pope Clement XIV ordered the suppression of the Jesuits in 1773, the order was ignored in the Russian Empire. The Jesuits continued to operate in Belarus until 1820.

Others sought protection under the umbrella of Orthodox Muscovy. Ultimately, an Orthodox revival would gather pace in the south – much less so in the north. But the main compromise option that emerged was the creation of a new Church, which represented a 'Union' of Catholic and Orthodox traditions. The various parties that supported the new union had different motives. The Orthodox Brotherhoods wanted to encourage a Protestant-style reform from below. The old Orthodox hierarchy was mainly interested in administrative and political matters, i.e. maintaining their administrative control and winning the political and social privileges of the nobles' 'Golden Liberty' (*Złota Wolność*), such as membership in the Sejm (parliament) and the right to set their own taxes. Advocates of union were also split between the idea of a local union, supported by some state realpolitik, hoping that it would help create a more politically united Commonwealth, and more idealistic plans for a broader European ecumenicism to overcome the schism of 1054. The Roman Catholic Church was much stronger after the Counter-Reformation and the Council of Trent, and pushed hard for doctrinal uniformity. The Polish king Zygmunt III therefore failed to deliver full social and political privileges for the new Church. The tensions produced a split, rather than the reinvigorated Church that the reformers had hoped for. Many nobles, the Brotherhoods, most monastic clergy and two southern bishops, those of Peremyshyl and Lviv, refused to back the Union. Barbara Skinner argues that 'generally, the Ukrainian palatinates, where the majority of the anti-Union leaders resided, provided the bulk of the opposition, whereas the Belarusian palatinates became predominantly Uniate, but exceptions occurred within both geographic areas'.[24]

Iosif Rutski, who became Uniate metropolitan in 1614, set up the Basilian Order, which gained official papal approval in 1624. In 1623 the murder of Yasafat Kuntsevich, archbishop of Polatsk, by an angry Orthodox crowd in Vitsebsk, provided the Uniates with a martyr and a foundation myth (among other things, he had refused to allow burial of the Orthodox dead in church-yards controlled by the Uniates). Kuntsevich's beatification by the Vatican was fast-tracked by 1643 – he was canonised in 1867.

In the south, the Orthodox Ruthenians began, but arguably did not complete, the process of 'confessionalisation' (creating a distinct religious identity) under Petro Mohyla, metropolitan of Kiev from 1642 to 1647. According to Skinner, 'the Uniate Church', on the other hand, 'floundered in its quest to create a coherent confessional identity for most of the seven-teenth century'.[25] The Church had no metropolitan between 1655 and 1665. It only established its own printing press, in Vilna, in 1670. 'For the most part, the Uniates continued to rely on the service books issued by Orthodox presses. As a result, Uniate liturgical practices lacked clear delineation or uniformity'.[26]

Kiev's Orthodox revival ultimately led to a strong 'southern' influence on religious practices in Muscovy, contributing to the great schism between New and Old Believers in the 1660s. The 'Belarusian' influence on Muscovy was much weaker, because the local Orthodox Church was weaker, although a specific region in Moscow, Meschanskaia sloboda, was populated with craftsmen from Belarus.[27] By the eighteenth century, little was left of Orthodox culture in the Belarusian lands that remained inside the Commonwealth.

Fewer Cossacks in the North

In southern Ruthenia – the future Ukraine – society was reshaped in the early seventeenth century by an Orthodox revival in clerical circles in Kiev and the increasingly independent Cossack culture in the southern and eastern borderlands. The two did not always sit easily together, but the great Cossack Rebellion led by Bohdan Khmelnytskyi in 1648 created a new independent polity known as the Hetmanate. The northern territories had no equivalent, however. As Plokhy writes: 'the Belarusian national project was based on the Ruthenian identity that had previously developed in the Grand Duchy of Lithuania but failed to produce a distinct identity in early modern times, given the lack of a proto-Belarusian polity comparable to the Cossack Hetmanate in Left-Bank Ukraine.'[28]

But north and south were not yet completely distinct, and there were some Cossacks in what is now Belarus. Several directions were possible for the north in the middle of the seventeenth century.[29] One is that Belarus, or parts of Belarus, could have become part of the Cossack project. Cossack culture spread up the river Dnieper into the south-east and east of what is now Belarus. Several Cossack uprisings spread north up the Dnieper in the late sixteenth century, including those led by Severyn Nalyvaiko in 1594–6 and Hryhorii Loboda in 1596. There were also many echoes in the north of the much larger rebellion that began in 1648. Some historians argue that one local leader, Kanstantsin Paklonski from Mahilew, was a potential 'Belarusian Khmelnytskyi', as he supposedly 'attempted to create a centre of his own political and military power, but he had also to dodge between Muscovites and Zaporozhian Cossacks' in the lands of the upper Dnieper, where he captured several towns, notably Mahilew and Shklow.[30] In fact, although Paklonski called himself the 'Belarusian colonel', he was an instrument of the tsar from the beginning, while Khmelnytskyi only came to a later accommodation with Muscovy in 1654. The real potential Belarusian 'hetman' was Paklonski's rival and Khmelnytskyi's emissary Ivan Zalatarenka, who threatened to kill Paklonski because he wanted to hand Mahilew over to the tsar, not to him.[31]

Khmelnytskyi himself briefly fought in the north alongside Zalatarenka, before the latter was killed in 1655. The two formed a separate Belarusian regiment that functioned until 1657. In 1656 Khmelnytskyi even established a protectorate over the Slutsk principality, formerly the personal property of Prince Radziwiłł. In 1657 Khmelnytskyi added the fortress of Old Bykhaw, and then in July 1657 Pinsk, Mazyr and Turaw. However, Khmelnytskyi's death in the same year largely put an end to these schemes. The 'Belarusian regiment' joined the Polish-Lithuanian side, although Khmelnytskyi's successor, Ivan Vyhovskyi (served as hetman 1657–9), reached an agreement with the Swedes for a more limited protectorate over Brest and Navahrudak.

But these were partial successes. Khmelnytskyi was able to carve out the Hetmanate further south because of the relative weakness of Polish and Muscovite power. There were too many Muscovite troops in the north, where the Cossack war was also mainly with regular troops led by Radziwiłł, who was keen to get his estates back. Unlike Ukraine, few local elites broke ranks and the Cossacks' inroads were resisted by local forces. Many Orthodox sided with Moscow and the Cossacks, but they were now the minority. Most Uniates remained loyal to the Commonwealth when it was under attack, whether from the east or from the south – in fact, arguably more so in the latter case because of the Cossacks' fearsome anti-Catholicism. The era was also one of struggle *between* north and south. Radziwiłł's armies, which defeated the Cossacks at the Battle of Loew in 1649, contained many Ruthenians. Radziwiłł even briefly captured Kiev in 1651. The north was already Catholic – but that meant it missed out on Khmelnytskyi's state-building, which laid the foundations of modern Ukraine.

In the south, the Orthodox were split between supporters of the tsar and supporters of the local Orthodox Church based in Kiev. In the north, the local Orthodox Church was much weaker, so appeals by the Orthodox minority to the tsar were more common. The main apologist for the tsar's policy became an Orthodox writer, Simiaon Polatski (1629–80),[32] who, in his 'Verses for the Arrival in the Native City of Polatsk' for tsar Aleksei Mikhailkovich, launched the idea of a tripartite Rus (Muscovy, Little Rus or Ukraine, and White Rus or Belarus), though Polatski himself bemoaned the Muscovites' destructive path, particularly the taking of the icon of the Holy Mother from Polatsk.

According to the modern historian Aleh Latyshonak, 'for the Orthodox population of the Grand Duchy of Lithuania [the] adoption of the terms "White Russia [Rus]" and "White Russians" was on the one hand a way of making [a] separate identity from Muscovites ("Great Russians") and Ukrainians ("Little Russians"), and on the other hand was an ideological act of divorcing oneself from the state traditions of the Grand Duchy of Lithuania, increasingly Lithuanian and Roman Catholic'.[33] For the tsar it was also a means of keeping Khmelnytskyi out of the Grand Duchy,[34] as Russia regarded the north as its own.

The Ukrainian nationalist Yurii Lypa described the period as 'the war of two Ruses for the third'.[35] That is, the Cossack and all-Rus-ian projects competed for local loyalties in Belarus, which had no real independent identity project of its own.

The Tragic War of 1654–67

The Treaty of Pereiaslav in 1654 between Khmelnytskyi and the Muscovite tsar marked a pause in the war in the south, though conflict between the Cossacks and the Muscovites continued on and off until the Treaty of Andrusovo in 1667. In the north, however, war was just beginning, but it would mainly be a state-to-state conflict between Muscovy and the Commonwealth, with the added complication of Sweden's involvement.[36] In Polish and Lithuanian tradition, the war is known as the 'Second Northern War' (in between the Livonian Wars, 1558–83, and the Great Northern War, 1700–21) or 'The Deluge' – though it hit the Grand Duchy in the north much harder than the Polish lands in the south. The Commonwealth would lose huge swathes of territory in the east and north, become permanently enfeebled until it disappeared from the map a century later, and end its tradition of religious toleration under the strain.

In July 1654 Muscovy invaded from the east, prompting Sweden to invade from the north in response. The lands of the future Belarus saw most of the fighting, which was catastrophic in every imaginable respect – demographic, social and national. According to Latyshonak, 'the process of the growing maturity of the new nation was suddenly arrested by the outbreak of war with Muscovy (1654–1667). Belarus lost half of its inhabitants. Cities were destroyed, the fortunes of burghers, the main adherents of Belarusian national ideas [sic], were dissipated. The nobility converted to Roman Catholicism in droves and adopted both the Lithuanian national myth and . . . Polish culture. Belarus [became] for a whole century a purely geographical notion.'[37]

The physical destruction in the lands of the Grand Duchy was indeed immense. Plague and famine in 1657–8 claimed 40 per cent of the population,[38] were fell from 4.5 million in 1650 to 2.3 million in 1670. Henadz Sahanovich records losses up to 75 per cent in regions such as Polatsk.[39] With the effects of war and population flight, almost three-quarters, 72 per cent, of the population were eventually lost overall.[40] The devastation was even worse in the east. As if this were not enough, there would be further devastation in the region during the Great Northern War, in 1705 and 1708–9. The wars against Sweden, Russia and Ukraine also marked the end of the power of the Protestant and Orthodox elites.[41] The Protestants were seen as a Swedish fifth column, the Orthodox as working for Russia. The Radziwiłłs negotiated the abortive Union of Kėdainiai with Sweden in 1655 which would have broken the union of Poland and the Grand Duchy, turning the latter into a federated state with Sweden instead, though the Radziwiłłs' part would have been basically a private fiefdom. The remaining Orthodox nobility sided with Moscow and the Ukrainian Hetmanate. After the war of 1654–67 the Protestant and Orthodox became real minorities; 'the Counter-Reformation triumphed'.[42] The last Protestant senator, Jan Sosnowski, converted to Roman Catholicism in 1664; the last Orthodox senator, Aliaksandr Ahinski, died in 1667. There would still be an Orthodox lobby in the eighteenth century, but the pro-Russian Confederation of Slutsk in 1767 needed Russian money.[43]

The war was therefore in many ways a more decisive turning point for the region than the Union of Lublin in 1569. In the eighteenth century the old dual monarchy became an increasingly unitary state dominated by Roman Catholic and Polish culture. Both Ruthenian and Lithuanian nobles assimilated. Polish was made the official language in 1697. Ruthenian public culture declined sharply – the last ever Ruthenian book was published in 1722.

The war of 1654–67 also widened the gap between Uniates and Orthodox. The initial offensive against the Uniates in areas occupied by tsarist troops was successful. 'By 1667, the Orthodox Church controlled between two-thirds and three-quarters of all Eastern-rite parishes in the Commonwealth, and many parish churches were either abandoned or destroyed.'[44] All these temporary gains were reversed after the Treaty of Andrusovo. Once the Hetmanate was outside the Commonwealth and linked to Muscovy, the position of the Orthodox still within the Commonwealth became much weaker. The Commonwealth Orthodox also lost the protection of the Cossacks.

In 1676 those remaining Orthodox were prohibited from making contact with the patriarch in Constantinople. The Commonwealth constitution of 1717 banned the formation of new parishes or the construction of new churches for all non-Catholic Christians (though this provision was often waived in Right Bank Ukraine – west of the river Dnieper). There were now no more prominent centres of Orthodox education in the Commonwealth. Once Orthodox communities lost 'access to the basic rites of baptism, marriage and burial',[45] they often turned to Uniate priests instead.

Conclusion

A potential common identity for all the Commonwealth's Orthodox subjects had developed by the sixteenth century. But it was at least partially superseded by rival religious identities after the formation of the new Uniate Church via the Union of Brest in 1596 and a progressively weaker 'multiconfessional' identity after 1596. Moreover, the Orthodox version was increasingly based on Kiev's scholastic culture to the south, and lost substantial ground in the north. That in turn was challenged by various versions of a common identity with emergent Russia, and by a Cossack identity initially based on both sides of the river Dnieper. At first, the latter made some inroads into what are now the Belarusian lands in the north, but eventually morphed into a 'Little Rus-ian (*malo ruskii*) Nation', increasingly distinguished from those left outside the quasi-state called the 'Hetmanate' which the southern Cossacks managed to create in 1648.[46] The lands of modern Belarus were among those left out. They clung to a residual but ever more meaningless Ruthenian identity; as it faded away, the multiethnic idea of a multicultural Litva or general Commonwealth identity made a comeback. Finally, the Uniate Church consolidated its position in the north after the Zamość Synod in 1720.

CHAPTER 4

UNIATE-LAND

The history of what is now Belarus had several false starts in the five centuries between Mindaugas's rule over Black Rus in the 1250s and the final dissolution of the Commonwealth in 1795. 'Litva' was for a time a de facto Lithuanian-Rus state, but succumbed increasingly to Polish influence after 1569. The Ruthenian revival of the sixteenth and seventeenth centuries created a common identity for what are now both Belarusians and Ukrainians. But rather than developing a new identity of their own after 1648, the northern Ruthenians were left with a shrunken version of the old identity after the Cossacks opted out of Ruthenia – at a time when the northern version of that Ruthenian culture was in serious decline, even before the massive economic and social dislocation caused by the war of 1654–67. The consolidation of the Uniate Church in the north after the Zamość Synod in 1720 created a unique local culture, but one that was subordinate to broader Roman Catholic identity and was fated to disappear when the Commonwealth was finally partitioned between the Romanovs, Habsburgs and Prussians seventy years after Zamość. This new Uniate identity, such as it was, was surprisingly viable, but represented a religious community. Even in the north, it did not define itself in national terms. 'Belarus' did not yet exist.

North and South

The one thing that remained after the upheavals of the seventeenth century was religion. Between 1596 and 1648 the rivalry between the Uniates and the Orthodox remained largely an internal Ruthenian affair, but most northern

Ruthenians were increasingly on the Uniate side. After the southern Cossack rebellion in 1648, the Orthodox Hetmanate separated away, but the Uniates grew stronger elsewhere. Between 1720 and 1794 the Uniate faith became more and more coterminous with Ruthenian identity in the Commonwealth – if you were the one, you were the other – while the Orthodox only clung on at the margins. A new identity project came into being. It didn't involve all the Ruthenians, many of whom now lived under the Hetmanate, or the smaller number who were still Orthodox. It was not the same thing as modern-day Belarus or modern-day Ukraine or both. We can call it 'Uniate-land', though the nearest equivalent contemporary term, *uniatsvo*, referred to the people, not to any given territory. The Uniates often called themselves *uniaty* or *Katoliki*, and called the Orthodox schismatics or *nieunity*. That said, alternative concepts, such as the idea of a collective Ruthenia or of Holy Rus, the indeterminate historical community of all the original Rus, Muscovites as well as Ruthenians, were far from dead – helped in part by the fact that the newly dominant Poles made few distinctions among the east Slavic population, whom they viewed as generally or potentially disloyal.[1]

The boundaries of Uniate-land were not fixed, however. The Union was always more popular in the north,[2] which was less affected by the ongoing Cossack disturbances in the south, which left the Uniates' position precarious in the territories of the future Ukraine, particularly in central Ukraine in the Right Bank region – west of the river Dnieper. The majority of signatories to the original Union of Brest in 1596 were from the future Belarus; so were the majority of the metropolitans who headed the Uniate Church: from the very first, Mikhail Rahoza (1596–9, from near Minsk), to Lev Slubich-Zalenksi (1694–1708, from Volhynia), who was the first 'Ukrainian'. The metropolitans resided in Navahrudak; the monasteries at Vilna, Suprasl and Zhyrovitski, which were the other centres of Uniate life, were all in the north.

For political reasons, the Uniate stronghold in the north drifted towards Western culture. The situation was therefore the opposite of that in the twenty-first century, when Belarus has often been perceived as strongly Orthodox and Russophile, and Ukraine – briefly seen as pro-Western after the Orange Revolution – is viewed more realistically as a truculent land of many identities and faiths. Many in seventeenth- and eighteenth-century 'Ukraine' saw the Catholic Poles and the Uniates as the outsiders, whereas in the north, the Uniates or Eastern Rite Catholics saw the Roman Catholics as kin (they were usually treated that way) and the Orthodox as outsiders. According to Barbara Skinner, the two Catholic faiths shared a 'myth of Orthodox backwardness and Russian barbarism and persecution'.[3] The Roman

Catholics could still look down on the ingénue Uniates, but the social distance between the two faiths was smaller than the chasm between the joint Catholic and Orthodox worlds.

Between 1596 and 1648 the Uniates and the Orthodox contested the whole of Ruthenian territory from Vilna down to Kiev. Galicia in the south-west was largely Orthodox, but the Uniate influence extended to Kiev in the east and even beyond. Smolensk briefly had a resident Uniate bishop, Lew Krueza, after 1632 (until 1667). After 1648, the Uniates were wiped out in the Cossack-controlled territory in the south, i.e. in Kiev and further east. Galicia remained mainly Orthodox until the end of the seventeenth century, but then swiftly converted to the Union: first the Premyśl diocese in 1693, followed by Lviv in 1700 (and the Lviv Brotherhood in 1709), and Lutsk in 1702. Pochaïv monastery joined the Uniates in 1713. Before then, the Uniates' only position

Map 4. 'Uniate-Land', early eighteenth century.

in Ukraine was on the Right Bank (central Ukraine west of the river Dnieper), where the Poles were still socially dominant and Cossack influence was still strong. But the Right Bank was never securely in the Union. According to Barbara Skinner, 'Right Bank Ukraine had the most unstable religious history of all Uniate regions in the last half of the eighteenth century, and most parishes did not adopt a firm Uniate identity'.[4] Many locals remained de facto Orthodox, helped by sympathetic priests, despite shifting political boundaries,

But after 1702 the boundaries of the Uniate faith were roughly fixed, and were stabilised by the Synod of Zamość in 1720. Uniate-land then remained a stable entity for another fifty years, until the Orthodox uprisings in the Right Bank in 1768.

The newly consolidated Uniate Church had eight dioceses inherited from the old structure of the Ruthenian Orthodox Church. Three were in what is now Belarus: first among equals was Polatsk, which was home to the Uniate archbishop, followed by Navahrudak and the bishopric of Pinsk and Volodymyr-Brest. The one remaining Orthodox stronghold in the north was Mahilew. Three Uniate dioceses were in what is now Ukraine: the residual Right Bank lands of the old Kiev metropolitan (without Kiev), and the territories of the bishops of Lviv and Lutsk. And two dioceses straddled what is in the twenty-first century the border between south-western Belarus, western Ukraine and Poland – Chełm and Przemyśl. There was a separate eparchy at Mukachevo for the eastern Slavs who lived west of the Carpathian mountains under Hungary, established separately by the Union of Uzhhorod in 1646, rather than the earlier Union of Brest. One school of historical thought maintains that these Carpathian Uniates were also Ruthenians, another that they kept a parochial and distinct identity as a separate east Slavic group until modern times, and paradoxically maintained the name 'Ruthenian' or 'Rusyn', but this time as a badge of identity distinguishing them from modern Ukrainians or Belarusians – though Rusynism also contains a strong pan-Russian element.

On the other hand, the lands of the Union weren't a real country. Political boundaries, i.e. between the Commonwealth on the one side and Russia on the other, were increasingly important. The Uniates more and more defined themselves as loyal citizens of the Commonwealth, while the Orthodox diminished in number and more and more looked to Russian support. The Orthodox in the one remaining diocese of Mahilew and the Right Bank, such as Heorhi Kanisski, the bishop of Mahilew from 1755, increasingly appealed to the Russian empress Catherine for 'protection'. Catherine was happy to oblige, as the issue provided an excuse for the Partitions of the Commonwealth, and sponsored the rewriting of history with the publication in 1800 of the *History of the Union Created in Poland . . . and the Persecution of Orthodox Residents There from the Romans and the Uniates*.[5] According to this view, the inhabitants of Mahilew and the Right Bank spoke for all the Ruthenians, including the former Orthodox, who therefore sought 'reunion' with Russia. This view became the foundation of later Russian and Soviet (and much post-Soviet) historiography and the foundation of 'west Russian' identity (see next chapter). In fact, only Mahilew was run from inside the Commonwealth. The pockets of Orthodox support in Right Bank Ukraine were under the control of the Pereiaslav diocese on the other side of the Dnieper river in the Hetmanate. Its bishops, such as Gervasii Lintsewski (1757–69) and Lew Bazilevich (1770–6) were Ruthenians, but their militant Orthodoxy was working for the Russian state.

Uniate Culture

In the seventeenth century there was an informal shift towards Latin religious culture among the Uniates, but it was neither consistent nor coordinated. Some priests began to speak rather than sing Mass. Uniate churches looked different inside and out. Iconostases, walls of gilded icons that separated the congregation from the priests and some parts of the service, creating the more 'mystical' aspects of Orthodoxy, began to disappear. Open central altars took their place. Confessional booths and even the occasional organ started to appear. Religious art began to escape the formal rules of old Byzantium. Icons became more realistic, and were occasionally oil-on-canvas rather than the traditional Orthodox style of tempera-on-wood. Uniate heroes such as St Yasafat (Kuntsevich) the Martyr were often depicted, in contrast to the narrow range of divine subjects in traditional Byzantine art, as well as Roman Catholic saints such as Francis of Assisi or Casimir of Poland. Marian feasts and (some) Roman Catholic holidays slowly became a shared tradition.

In external architecture, the 'Vilna Baroque' tradition developed. So-called 'Belarusian' Gothic appeared as a result of the merging of Ruthenian-Byzantine cross-dome cathedrals and the compositional characteristics of local castle architecture. The Cathedral of the Saint Virgin Mary, built for the Jesuits in Minsk in 1710, is a fine example of this Eastern Baroque.

On the other hand, Uniate-land retained the Orthodox liturgy. Its cultural sensitivities were not receptive to full-blown Counter-Reformation Baroque, particularly in the visual arts, with its drama and prodigious nudity. Local society was too poor, and the aristocracy too few in number, for the frivolity of the Rococo.

The 'European' political culture of the Uniates (see below) did not go deep. The Ruthenians, as Litvins, had participated to an extent in the aristocratic political culture of the Commonwealth, but only at the elite level. As an identity-forming factor, Catholic, or quasi-Catholic, culture in the future Belarusian lands was never as powerful as the mass Cossack culture of the south – nor the identity myths that the Cossacks left behind.

The Synod of Zamość

The gradual and uncoordinated changes of the seventeenth century were eventually systematised at the synod held in the town of Zamość in 1720, now in south-eastern Poland. One reason for calling the synod was time. The Uniates had not held an equivalent assembly since 1626. Other impulses were political. Russia supported 'its' fellow Orthodox, Poland 'its' Roman Catholics. In 1717 the Polish parliament, the Sejm, passed a law restricting non-Catholics' right of assembly, and in the same year an anonymous 'Project' called for the 'Abolition of the Orthodox and Uniate Faiths in the Ruthenian Provinces of the Kingdom of Poland'.[6] The Uniates had to prove their loyalty.

Some have claimed that, because the synod was supposedly sponsored by Rome, it created a Union that was much more Catholic. According to Plokhy, 'The Zamość Synod drew a clear confessional line between Uniates and Orthodox,' and, 'in the opinion of many scholars, the Zamość Synod also set the Uniate Church on course for Latinisation, introducing numerous Roman Catholic rituals and traditions into its practices. Latinisation implied the cultural Polonisation of the Uniate hierarchy, especially its bishops and monks.'[7] As a consequence, the synod led to a split in the Church, with many in the 'old Union party' now looking to Moscow.[8]

Skinner's view, however, is that

discussing the developments of the Synod of Zamość in terms of the 'Latinization' of the Uniate Church ... misses a critical point. Notably, the Synod of Zamość marks the confessional maturity of the church. It standardized doctrinal, institutional, and educational norms and brought the Uniate Church closer to the rigid standards of confessional identities of post-Reformation Europe. The Synod did institute alterations from the Orthodox doctrine and practice in the direction of Latinization, but this was an attempt to standardize practices already in place in some Uniate regions. At the same time, however, the Synod members promoted Eastern liturgical norms as the essential marker of Uniate confessional identity in distinction from the Latin-rite Catholics. While the actual competence of priests and administrative practices often did not live up to the Synod's decrees, the attempts to carry out the new guidelines significantly altered the character of the Uniate Church .... The Church now had a structure and coherence that had been lacking in the seventeenth century, as well as clear standards of religious practice that distinguished Uniates from both the Orthodox and Roman Catholic faithful .... By the early eighteenth century, with the stress and threat of a competing Eastern-rite church greatly diminished [i.e. the Orthodox], the Uniates could attend more fully to their own confessional development. The Synod of Zamość instituted uniform norms for the performance of the liturgy, the training of priests, the catechizing of the parishioners, and effective adminis-tration – finally giving the Uniate church the kind of confessional guidelines that characterized the reformed Protestant and Catholic Churches.[9]

A *sluzhebnik* (service book) printed at Suprasl monastery in 1727 attempted to standardise the new liturgy. The Church now adopted the *filioque* (the Catholic doctrine that the Holy Spirit proceeds from both Father and Son); the pope was mentioned during Mass. Baptism would be by the pouring or sprinkling of water, rather than total immersion. Children could not receive communion until they knew the catechism. There was greater use of the Latin alphabet, and even the physical appearance of the faith began to change further, with the removal of iconostases from churches and the introduction of organs (although they remained rare) and bells.

Skinner also argues that Uniate 'handbooks embodied West European intellectual traditions that stressed legalistic and rational religious and contractual social foundations. In comparison, Orthodox priests inside the Commonwealth relied primarily on catechisms and instructional materials coming from the Russian Orthodox Church that preserved patristic univer-salism and promoted autocratic political authority.'[10] As in Protestant England, where the process had a massive impact on solidifying English-language culture, 'the Synod required the parish priests to instruct parishioners in the catechism, at least every Sunday and holiday'.[11]

The Basilian Avant-Garde

The Uniates also benefited from the organisational and intellectual leadership of the Basilian Order, which also provided a stronger link to the Roman

Catholic world. The Basilians were first recognised in Vilna in 1624 and then in Galicia, and in 1743 were united in the Ruthenian Order of St Basil the Great by Pope Benedict XIV and governed from Rome. Peter the Great paid the order the compliment of personally strangling one of its priests with his bare hands when he occupied Polatsk cathedral in 1705.

Unlike the autodictat Peter, the Uniate elite was relatively well educated. According to Skinner, 'over three-quarters of Basilian monks – about 77 per cent in 1773 – trained and ordained as priests. Not only does this percentage far exceed that of Orthodox monks (the majority of whom were not ordained), but it places the Basilians highly among the Roman Catholic orders, approaching the Jesuit goal that every novice become a priest.'[12] The main monasteries were in the north, but many of the seminaries eventually set up by the Uniate Church were in the south, in 'Ukraine', which meant that the priests in the north were often poorly trained. A majority of students at Basilian schools were Roman Catholic. Uniate priests came from more diverse social backgrounds. About half of all Basilians were born into the Latin rite, and Latin influences within the order followed naturally from the personal background of so many of its members.[13] But overall the network of Uniate parishes and churches was relatively dense, more so than for the Roman Catholics.[14]

The declining Orthodox community, on the other hand, was poorly served. No Orthodox seminaries existed inside the Commonwealth, and Ruthenian Orthodox priests became by the late eighteenth century largely dependent on the catechisms, instructional materials and liturgical books that came from across the Russian border.

Nevertheless, the situation varied from region to region. Right Bank Ukraine was under the influence of Orthodox rebels or *haidamaki*. The growing consolidation of the Uniates was one factor provoking the 'Koliivshchyna' uprising of 1768. The Orthodox bishops of Pereiaslav constantly sought to expand their influence from over the border, making strong gains after the First Partition in 1772–3, although these were partially reversed as Poland regained precarious control over the region for another twenty years.

The Lost Lands of the Papacy

From 1781, a clear majority of the overall population of the lands that eventually became modern Belarus – some 70 to 75 per cent – were Uniates. Between 430,000 and 440,000 of the same population were Roman Catholic, or 15–20 per cent of the total. The vast majority of these, no less than 84 per cent, were concentrated in the north-west region around Vilna and Hrodna. Only 6 per cent of the overall population were still Orthodox.[15] Even where the Orthodox were strongest, they were in a minority. In the far eastern region of Mahilew, 68 per cent of churches belonged to the Uniates in 1777, and only 22 per cent to the Orthodox.[16]

Catherine was personally hostile to the 'schismatics' of the Union. She was even briefly prepared to promote the Roman Catholics instead. The Uniates were now a long way from Vatican help, and the Empress Catherine wanted to appear tolerant to European Catholic monarchs. In 1772 a Roman Catholic diocese was established in Mahilew, which was elevated to an archdiocese in 1782 and gained jurisdiction over Vilna and Minsk. Uniates began to switch to a safer haven.

As discussed in the previous chapter, the Ruthenian language was also in long-term decline by the eighteenth century. 'By 1795 the Uniate clergy still read the liturgy in Church Slavonic, but they didn't understand it.'[17] The Basilians and the printing press at Pochaïv in Volhynia were able to produce some materials in Ruthenian, but increasingly the Uniates used Polish.[18] Arguably, in fact, the Uniates lost the language of Skaryna to the south, where it became the language of Mohyla. Because of the Uniates, ironically or not, the Polish language became more popular in the north.

Moreover, however popular the Union was, it was known as 'the peasant faith' (*muzhytskaia vera*); as nearly 85 per cent of Uniate parish churches were located in rural areas in 1772.[19] The vast majority of churches were made of wood – many still had dirt floors. High culture meant Polish culture, and in Roman Catholic form. Basilian schooling stemmed but could not stop the ongoing defection of Uniate social elites to the more prestigious Roman Catholic faith.

Skinner has promoted a compromise view. The Uniate Church was certainly a conduit for Western concepts and values. This was indeed Western culture filtered through Polish norms, but it was not full-blown Roman Catholicism. The Uniate confession marked the northern Ruthenians off from all their neighbours, including the Roman Catholics (the Poles, Lithuanians and Latgallians), the Protestant Balts, the Orthodox Russians and the local Jews, and to an extent also the Orthodox of Cossack Ukraine (although the Uniate Church remained a force in Right Bank Ukraine until 1839 and in Galicia until the present day, despite Soviet suppression between 1946 and 1989). The Uniate Church also provided the northern Ruthenians with the halfway house that their identity needed – a way of being between Russia and Poland – although Skinner argues that increasingly their stress on their political loyalty to the Commonwealth meant that 'an emphasis on the Western element dominated'.[20] As for making them 'more European', this would logically only apply with respect to Russia after 1795. Before the dissolution of the Commonwealth, the Uniate faith if anything made the northern Ruthenians *less* European than the Roman Catholic Poles or Lithuanians.

It should be noted that the opposite point of view was popular in Soviet times, and has been recycled by some of the ideologues of the Belarusian regime under President Lukashenka.[21] According to this view, the Uniate Church was simply an instrument of Polish and aristocratic influence. Once it was gone, a divisive internal marker separating Belarusians of different religions disappeared, ultimately allowing the consolidation of a Belarusian national identity on the basis of language rather than faith (rather ignoring the significance of the all-important remaining and now suddenly sharper Roman Catholic–Orthodox divide).

As Ukraine became more Cossack and more Orthodox, Uniate Belarus could have had more in common with increasingly Uniate Galicia, but political as well as geographical barriers after the Habsburgs took over Galicia wouldn't allow it, although there was some traffic between those of the same faith. The Union of Brest wasn't an ethnic project – though it could have had ethnic consequences. In fact, it furthered the division of the Ruthenian people into three confessions.[22] It took a century of state-sponsored recovery after 1772 for the Uniate Church to become a bulwark of Ukrainian national revival in Galicia. Alternatively, a vague common identity for the Orthodox of the future Belarusian north and those of the non-Galician south could have been revived under the tsars.

So the idea often expressed by modern-day Belarusian nationalists that Catherine sought to destroy the Uniate Church to prevent it stoking the fires of a Belarusian nationalism that did not yet exist is fanciful.[23] The Russian Empire didn't really like any type of Catholics. And the Orthodox Church still adhered to the myth that the Union of Brest in 1596 was forcible theft of the faithful. It now saw a chance to win them back. As it thought that the newly acquired 'locals' were 'really Orthodox' at heart, they would not even have to be persuaded to return to the fold.

Despite the promises made after the First Partition in 1772, Catherine introduced a decree on forcible conversion in April 1794, led by Bishop Viktar Sadkowski, archimandrite of Slutsk. The subsequent campaign reduced the number of the Commonwealth's Uniate faithful by a massive 1.6 million out of an estimated 4.6 million Ruthenians (compared to 400,000 Orthodox),[24] although 1.4 million Uniates remained.[25] The decree had its strongest effects in the middle of Belarus, with 80,000 converts in Minsk province. The lands in the east were acquired in 1772, before the 1794 decree – though Mahilëw was Orthodox anyway. The westernmost lands acquired in the third Partition in 1795 were only subjected to the decree for a short time before Catherine's death in November 1796.

The population of the future Belarus in the old Ruthenian lands was then around 3.8 million. This was one of the largest forcible conversions in European history, carried out by the supposedly 'enlightened despot' Catherine the Great. One million of the 'converts' were in the Right Bank region of the future Ukraine, where the Uniates' position had always been precarious, so another 600,000 were in the north.[26]

Some claim that the Church actually enjoyed a measure of institutional stability and even a potential revival of sorts in the first two decades of the nineteenth century, under the relatively liberal tsars Paul I (ruled 1796–1801) and Aleksandr I (ruled 1801–25). The Uniates fell increasingly under Roman Catholic control, but Yasafat Bulhak, who held the post of Uniate metropolitan from 1817, supported an independent line where possible.[27] Crucially, however, the Uniate Church was finally suppressed in 1839, before it could develop any kind of symbiotic relationship with a secular nationalist movement,[28] which in the Belarusian case only really began to develop in the 1900s.

It has been asserted that, before it was suppressed, the Union 'became a catalyst for the growth of ethnic, cultural, confessional and historical self-consciousness'. The argument is that the Church stimulated the education system and intellectual life, and led to Belarus moving 'closer to the West European cultural sphere'. Second, the unique 'synthesis of the Byzantine cultural heritage [and] east Slavic traditions and Western influences in Belarusian Uniatism' created the basis of a pre-modern national identity, especially as proto-Belarusian society was now increasingly differentiated from proto-Ukrainian Orthodox-Cossack society.[29]

The abolition of the Uniate Church on the eve of the modern era certainly was a sort of national disaster, though one best expressed in counterfactual terms, i.e. what might have happened if the Belarusians had entered the modern era with 'their own' Church. The local Orthodox Church was a strong supporter of nationalism, particularly after the Polish Rebellion in 1863–4; but this was the local west-Russian version of all-Russian nationalism.

The Endgame

Russia's religious aims in the Partitions were actually clearer than its political aims. Catherine II's main agent was her favourite, and favourite lover, Prince

Grigory Potemkin; but Potemkin had several possible plans for the old Commonwealth in mind. Its total disappearance was not preordained. Two other possibilities encompassed a series of semi-independent 'Hetmanates', including Moldova, and a Confederation. Potemkin toyed with the idea of leading a Cossack army to create a new Orthodox state. There were many who preferred the Petrine policy of maintaining a weak buffer state.[30] On the other hand, the end of the old Commonwealth was not entirely involuntary. Potemkin courted and sponsored many of its leading citizens, such as Ksawery Branicki, hetman of the Commonwealth, 1774–94, and Stanisław Potocki, *voivode* (governor) of Ruthenian Galicia 1782–91, who set up the pro-Russian Targowica Confederation in 1792. The 'Polish-Russian War' of 1792 was in part a civil war.

Apart from some minor disputed ethnographic territories under Prussian rule or, to be more precise, territories that national linguists and geographers would claim to be Belarusian a hundred years later, Belarus was swallowed almost whole by the Romanov Empire in the three Partitions of 'Poland' (i.e. the Commonwealth), in 1772, 1793 and 1795. Unlike the future Ukrainian lands, the future Belarusian lands were not significantly divided. There was to be no 'fifth column' abroad in the nineteenth century. Białystok initially went to Prussia, but was moved to the Russian Empire by the Treaty of Tilsit in 1807. Ironically, the First Partition in 1772 did create a Belarusian 'Piedmont', but it created it in the east after Russia gained the territory on its side of the Dzvina and Dnieper rivers, including Polatsk, Vitsebsk, Mahilew and Homel. The term 'Belarus' was reserved for these earlier acquisitions, which became the centre of a strong anti-Uniate movement. The territories further west were still known as 'Litva',[31] and were absorbed in the two final Partitions. Russia gained central Belarus (Minsk, Pinsk and Slutsk) in 1793, and the western regions (Vilna, Hrodna, Brest and Navahrudak) in 1795.

Conclusion

Many Russians regarded the Partitions as the completion of the process of 'gathering Rus lands' begun back in the fifteenth century by Ivan III. But they did not restore some kind of mythical status quo ante. The northern Ruthenian territories had been remote from first Muscovite and then Russian influence for over five hundred years. The locals did not become Russians overnight after the Partitions, and the era would also provide a potentially powerful myth for 'revival' nationalists in later years.

CHAPTER 5

BELARUS BEGINS

On the eve of the First Partition of the Commonwealth, in 1771, Jean-Jacques Rousseau urged the Poles: 'if you cannot prevent your enemies [the Russians] from swallowing you, at least you can prevent them from digesting you.' The Belarusians, however, proved eminently digestible, in part because they were not yet Belarusians: they were better, if awkwardly, described as northern Uniate Ruthenians. And northern Uniate Ruthenian society had a tiny local elite: less than 1 per cent of the aristocracy and bureaucracy in Hrodna in 1832 was Uniate,[1] and Hrodna had more Uniates than most other regions.

The study of nineteenth-century Belarusian history is prone to two opposing errors. Either it is argued that the people who eventually became Belarusians some time in the twentieth or even twenty-first century had no real identity or sense of self in the nineteenth century. They were just 'locals' (*tuteishiya*). Or the opposite. The new nation-states of Eastern Europe tend to write their history in what is assumed to be the 'end of empire' era in the nineteenth century as 'national revival' or 'national rebirth', according to the classic schema established by Miroslav Hroch.[2] The story that results is predictable. First, a few lonely academics are identified working at the coalface of defining national identity; then a 'founding father' appears – usually a poet, historian or doomed revolutionary – whose example gives birth to a period of 'mass agitation'. Belarus is no exception. The little-known Romantic intellectuals of the early nineteenth century such as Vintsent Dunin-Martsinkevich (1808–84) are depicted as the precursors of Kastus Kalinowski (1838–64), a Belarusian hero of the

Polish Rebellion of 1863–4, who tried to stir up a peasant revolt and inspired the 'father of Belarusian literature', Frantsishak Bahushevich (1840–1900), who begat a proper national movement grouped around the newspaper *Nasha Niva* ('Our Cornfield') after 1906, which inspired the Belarusian People's Republic that existed for a few weeks in 1918. And nothing much else happened around or in between.

The truth was, of course, much more complex. The Belarusian national movement arrived extremely late, and was but one of a number of options for the local population. Many Belarusians supported class-based socialist parties: the founding conference of Lenin's Social-Democratic Workers' Party was held in Minsk in 1898. But the Belarusians had at least three other 'national' options that are rarely even identified in traditional historiography.[3] The first – residual loyalty to historical Litva based in a Catholic milieu – was the dominant trend until after the Polish Rebellion. Then came 'west-Russism', a movement that supported the tsarist monarchy and the Orthodox Church in the name of 'all-Russian' unity, though with its activists serving at the same time as what Aliaksandr Tsvikevich, who wrote the first and so far only history of west-Russism in the 1920s, called 'Belarusophiles within Russian culture'.[4] As one modern historian has argued: 'in the first half of the nineteenth century a unique Belarusian cultural tradition didn't exist. The process of Belarusian cultural accumulation happened in two directions, which can conditionally be called the "Litvin" (or "Litsvin") and "west-Russian" cultural traditions.'[5]

Third, in the late nineteenth and early twentieth centuries came a revival of the Litva tradition in the form of the multiethnic ideology of the *krajowcy*, who believed that all the local ethnic groups – mainly the Poles, Belarusians, Lithuanians and Jews – should cooperate in the interests of the region or *krai*. The *krajowcy* were mainly Poles, but included many Belarusians, who in the Belarusian language were *krayovtsi*. There were also some local Jews or 'Litvaks' (see pages 80–2), and Lithuanians,[6] whose embryonic national movement was also split between 'old and new Lithuanians' – between empire loyalism, residual *litwini* (the Lithuanian for 'Litvins') and ethnic nationalism, though the Lithuanians had more reason to fear a movement that included both Belarusians and Poles, as they would then be outnumbered by local Slavs. The first stirrings of a properly independent Belarusian 'national idea' came only after the 1905 Revolution, and in a form that still overlapped with the older variants, which remained stronger alternatives.

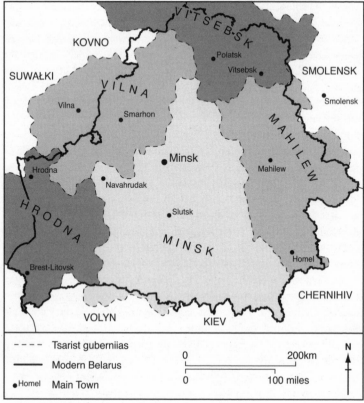

Map 5. Belarusian lands in the nineteenth century.

Religion before Nation

National identities in whatever form came late to Belarus. Religious divides remained more important than national divides right down to 1914, and even arguably thereafter. At the time of the Partitions in the eighteenth century, what is now Belarus was a largely Catholic region, but with a mixed culture of a Roman Catholic elite and a Greek Catholic or Uniate 'peasant faith', alongside an Orthodox minority. In the nineteenth century the same lands became a battleground of intense religious competition, which drove most would-be Belarusians to the extremes of either Russian Orthodoxy or Polish Roman Catholicism. However, Belarus was unable to develop a distinct Orthodox identity of its own, in contrast to developments in the Dnieper Ukraine, where nation-builders like the poet Taras Shevchenko and the historian Mykhailo Hrushevskyi used the Cossack myth to develop a version of identity that was anti-Polish and anti-Catholic, but also Orthodox and specifically Ukrainian. In Belarus, Orthodoxy meant belonging to all-Russian culture, broadly defined. And in Belarus's Orthodox east, unlike the Hetmanate east of Ukraine, there was no Cossack tradition to compete with populist Russophilia.

Nor was Belarus able to develop the kind of Uniate-based nationalism – on the basis of the Uniate culture that undoubtedly did exist in the eighteenth century – comparable to the movement that eventually triumphed in Habsburg-controlled Ukrainian Galicia. The Uniate Church was abolished on nearly all Romanov territory in 1839, with a clean-up operation in the over-looked backwater region of Chełm (Kholm) eparchy in 1875. Moreover, nearly all Belarusian lands were inside the empire, whereas Galicia lay outside. In Ukraine, the long nineteenth century was a story of religious and ultimately ethnic conflicts echoing across imperial boundaries. With Belarus, the conflicts happened within one empire. As a result, it only ever had a weak and embryonic all-national movement, confined to a self-limiting Catholic, but soon enough exclusively Roman Catholic, milieu.

The End of the Union

The last chapter described the campaign against the Uniates that began under Catherine the Great. There was a moment of calm under Catherine's successors. Paul I (ruled 1796–1801) reestablished the Minsk and Lutsk dioceses alongside that of Polatsk in 1798, even if his only motivation was reversing the policy of his hated mother. Aleksandr I (ruled 1801–25) set up a governing board for the Uniates in 1804, and a joint Uniate and Roman Catholic seminary at Vilna in 1805, later moved to Polatsk. In 1809 a new diocese at Vilna was established. However, given the squeeze on the Uniates in the middle, the ranks of both the Orthodox and the Roman Catholics continued to grow. Some 200,000 more souls had left the Uniate Church for Roman Catholicism by 1825, and the number of Roman Catholic parishes had grown from 240 to 325 by 1830.[7]

But from the 1820s onwards the Uniate Church itself was increasingly suffering from its position in the middle ground, and was split between the 'Polish' party and an internal opposition that sought protection from Great Russia, led by Professor Mikhal Babrowski and Iosif Siamashka, a Ukrainian by origin, who lobbied for 'reunion' with the Orthodox as early as 1827 – even before the 1830–1 Uprising led the authorities to clamp down on all forms of 'disloyal' Catholicism. The new tsar, Nicholas I, was against the Uniates from the moment he came to the throne in 1825. In 1826 he published a decree banning the sale of Uniate literature outside of Uniate churches. In 1827 the Basilians were banned from training Roman Catholics to be Uniate priests, their primary source of recruitment in the past.

Discussions on abolition of the Uniate Church began in 1828,[8] but after the Polish Uprising, when many Uniates sided with the rebels, the tsar gave Siamashka the task of abolishing the Church for good. Siamashka first forced it to use Russian, and then closed the Basilian Order in 1832. But the ambitious Siamashka still had to defer to the veteran leader of the Church, Yasafat Bulhak, metropolitan since 1817, who did not die until February 1838. Siamashka was then duly appointed to take his place, and promptly convened a 'synod' without papal authority in Polatsk in 1839 (in Usiaslaw the Sorcerer's Cathedral of St Safiia), which denounced the 1596 Union of Brest and proclaimed a 'reunion' with the Orthodox Church. An estimated 1.6 million converted to Orthodoxy, along with 1,300 priests.[9] Siamashka duly got his thirty pieces of silver as the new Orthodox archbishop of Vilna eparchy.

The historiography of the end of the Union is dominated by Orthodox triumphalism and Catholic 'victim literature' (some priests went underground and others fled to Austrian Galicia),[10] but some have argued that the process was largely peaceful and involved many concessions to the Uniates which allowed them to keep certain practices in place,[11] in part because the Orthodox clergy at this time were largely little educated and socially inferior to the Poles.

But the Orthodox Church in the Belarusian lands moved into an infrastructure that already existed. Many churches in Belarus still look Catholic, some new churches were built after 1839, followed by a massive building programme after 1863, such as the Holy Virgin church in Hrodna in the Russian Revival style (1904) and the Aleksandr Nevskii church in Vilna (1898), and the conversion of the Baroque St Casimir into the neo-Byzantine Orthodox St Nicholas. Most notable was the Church of SS Michael and Konstantine in Vilna (1913), financed by a descendant of the great Ostrozskyi family, though this time as a monument to Russian imperial (and, of course, family) glory.[12]

On the other hand, the 'Red Kostel' in Minsk (the Church of SS Simon and Helena, built in 1905–10, which was restored to Roman Catholic control in

1990) arguably exported a more Central European style to what was now Orthodox territory.

Catholic-Orthodox antagonism became much sharper after 1839, and society split more clearly along religious lines, although arguably these dividing lines were not really sharp until after 1863.[13] But the religious split was also geographically polarised. The Roman Catholic areas were in the far west. In addition to the 'old' Orthodox in Mahilew and the eastern lands of the First Partition, the large majority of the population in central Belarus who had been Uniate were now overwhelmingly Orthodox. The religious 'border' now advanced to the west (and north) of Minsk.

The authorities obviously favoured the Orthodox. By 1897 the balance of the population was about 4.6 million Orthodox to one million Roman Catholic, with the latter representing around 15 per cent of the total population.[14] The authorities' assumption that making the peasantry Orthodox would render them more loyal was proved right: first in 1863, when few local peasants sided with the rebellion of the Polish *pany*; second, in 1905, when the tsar published his decree on religious freedom and only 50,000 immediately left the Orthodox church.[15] There was no mass 'return to the faith', i.e. Uniatism. An estimated 230,000 switched to Roman Catholicism by 1909, but nearly all of these were in the far western, half-Polish districts of Chełm and Podlasie.[16]

But the end of the Uniate Church led to a certain regression in identity terms. A local peasant in the middle of the century would have called him- or herself *chelovek russkoi very* ('a person of Russian/Rus faith'), but without any implications of Russian ethnicity. As the Ukrainian historian Yaroslav Hrytsak has argued, the eastern Slavic peasantry shared a common culture of Holy Rus, but by the nineteenth century this was a concept only vaguely rooted in any specific sense of territory.[17] Most would-be Belarusians identified with locality, a phenomenon known as *tuteishyia* (in Belarusian, coming from 'here', *tut*, *tuteshni* in Ukrainian), but that was not unusual in the nineteenth century. Many Estonians still thought of themselves as *maarahvas* ('people of the land').[18] Even many 'Poles' had primarily parochial identities until 1905 or the First World War.[19]

The White *Kresy*

In the western and central regions nothing much changed between 1795 and 1830. Polish culture still dominated. In fact, with the expansion of the

University of Vilna in 1803,[20] then the largest seat of learning in the empire, the surrounding area became one of the key centres of the Polish nation-(re) building project in the borderlands (*kresy*). As Bulhakaw puts it, as far as St Petersburg was concerned 'in the first third of the nineteenth century Belarus remained foreign territory . . . and its history and geography were excluded from the integrated narratives of the empire'.[21]

But intellectual climate was changing under the influence of the Enlightenment and Romanticism. If, in the late eighteenth century, the 'science and literature of the time were not interested in the linguistic and cultural uniqueness of the Belarusians',[22] by the early nineteenth century an interest in 'the people' was stirring – the people as defined by Poland, that is. Polish Romantics in the early nineteenth century viewed Belarus romantically, as *terra incognita* or *terra exotica*.[23] The locals were deemed to be Poles who spoke *slaviano-krivich* or *slaviano-litovskim*, the *język krewicki*, *język ruski* or the *język polsko-ruski*, *ruteńskim* or *rusińskim*.[24] The last version of Old Ruthenian – *prosta mova* – was in decline, but this was arrested to an extent by Belarusian Polish-speaking writers such as Jan Czeczot (1796–1847). Aleksander Rypiński produced a local geography in 1840.[25] Much of Hroch's phase A – that is, the initial academic work of defining a potential nation by studying its language and culture – was therefore completed in the Polish language. Many so-called 'founders' of the as yet nonexistent Belarusian national movement were in fact Polonophiles, at least in so far as the likes of Dunin-Martsinkevich supported the expansion of Polish schools.[26] Nevertheless, a sprinkling of academics such as the linguist Mikhal Babrowski (1784–1848) represented what has been dubbed 'university regionalism'.[27] Aliaksandr Tsvikevich argues that Babrowski hoped that Tsar Nicholas I would support a Uniate renaissance that would allow it to become independent of Roman Catholicism and preserve 'old-Belarusian [i.e. Litvin] culture'.[28] Not enough was done by the 1830s, however, before the failure of the Polish Uprising in 1830–1 led to the suppression of much Polish academic activity in the region. Thereafter there was a long hiatus until work was resumed by others after the failure of another Polish Rebellion in 1863–4. In many respects, this was a great missed opportunity.

The most famous graduate of the University of Vilna was Adam Mickiewicz, Poland's national poet, who studied there in 1815–19. Mickiewicz was born in Zaosie near Navahrudak in 1798. Belarusians, Ukrainians, Poles and Lithuanians have tried to claim him as their own, but he was really a 'Litvin' in the geographical sense, whose primary loyalty to Polish high culture was perfectly natural at the time.[29] His great epic poem *Pan Tadeusz* famously begins thus:

Litva! My country! like art thou to health,
  For how to prize thee alone can tell
 Who has lost thee. I behold thy beauty now
  In full adornment, and I sing of it
    Because I long for thee.

Litva was one thing, but according to Bulhakaw, 'Mickiewicz conceived of [actual] Belarusians as something incomplete, existing not in real but in mythological time, as hangovers or enchantments'.[30]

In the end, the impact of these largely Polish-culture intellectuals was limited. They couldn't bridge the enormous gap between the nobility and the peasantry, which would still be there at the time of the next rebellion, in 1863-4. 'Society on the eastern periphery of the former Commonwealth was split between elites, attached to early national identities, based on a noble culture, a knightly ethic, a Catholic and Latin cultural code; and Belarusian, Ukrainian and Lithuanian common folk (*prostonarode*).'[31] The local Poles eventually chose a different way forward, and by adopting 'modern Polish [ethnic] nationalism, the Polish nobility on Belarusian lands committed political suicide'.[32] If Poland was to be only for the Poles, it would end up smaller.

Only in the second half of the nineteenth century did the Belarusians finally define their way out of Ruthenianism – later than the Ukrainians – and much of this work was done by west-Russian intellectuals rather than Poles.

The Last Ruthenians

The Litvin tradition was still dominant in the early nineteenth century, and still capable of developing as a joint national idea for those who eventually chose a different path as Belarusians and Lithuanians.[33] Moreover, for the would-be Belarusians at least, the disappearance of the Uniate Church in 1839 meant the loss of a religious identity option: so a certain revival, or revisiting, of the political 'Litvin' identity was natural.

The authorities' reaction to the 1830-1 Uprising showed a fairly good, if brutally pragmatic, understanding of where things, from their perspective, were going wrong. Vilna University was closed down in 1832 (and stayed shut until 1919), thus depriving any potential national movement (of whatever type) of a focal point. The Ukrainians had the universities of Kharkiv and Kiev, the Estonians had Tartu: the Belarusians now had nothing. In 1836 teaching in Polish was banned in Vitsebsk and Mahilew. In 1820 the Jesuits were expelled from Polatsk. The Lithuanian Statutes were abandoned in 1840. Mikhail Muraviev, who was governor of Mahilew in 1828–31, nevertheless managed to complain about the lack of positive Russification measures.

One complication was that the use of the Roman alphabet was relatively widespread in Belarus, more so than in Ukraine.[34] Roman script originally meant Polonisation. In Austrian Galicia in 1859 the Polish viceroy, Agenor Gołuchowski, tried to impose its use on the Ukrainians. Nicholas I discussed the opposite possibility, of shifting Polish into Cyrillic. In 1835 the Vilna Roman Catholic eparchy produced a Belarusian-language catechism. Some of Jan Czeczot's folk songs were in Roman script. But the 1859 version of *Pan Tadeusz* in Roman script produced a ban on its use for both the Belarusian and Ukrainian languages, followed by a ban on its use for Lithuanian in 1865. (Latvian was mainly written in Gothic script until 1908; in eastern Latvia it was written in Cyrillic.) 'The goal was not to turn Lithuanians into Russians, but to put maximum distance between them and the rebellious Poles', especially with the peasant emancipation in 1861. Polish insurgents in 1863 appealed to Ukrainians in Cyrillic, but to 'our' Roman Catholic Belarusian peasants in Latin script; the Russian authorities' own appeals were, of course, in Cyrillic.[35] In 1901–17 nine out of twenty-five new Belarusian periodicals were in Latin. The two main papers, *Nasha Dolia* (Our Fate) and *Nasha Niva*, appeared in both alphabets. The use of the Latin script of course reduced the Belarusian national movement's appeal in the eastern guberniias, where peasants couldn't read it. But in the last analysis 'the Latin alphabet was a component of its sacral world'.[36] In Belarus the Roman alphabet deepened the religious divide rather than serving as an instrument of nation-building.

A False Start: The Kalinowski Myth

Poland was still culturally attractive, but the reality was that the Polish nobility still owned half of the local land, which was mainly toiled by Belarusian peasants. Not surprisingly the great Emancipation of 1861 upset the balance. However, it was largely for social reasons that the local Belarusians participated in the 'Polish' Rebellion of 1863–4. They didn't yet have a national movement.

However, Belarusian historiography makes much of local hero Kastus Kalinowski, a great Romantic figure, who fought for the peasants and died a martyr's death. It has often been claimed that Kalinowski was an early representative of 'the modern Belarusian idea'.[37] But there is almost no real evidence for this. Kalinowski's propaganda broadsheet *Muzhytskaia prawda* ('Peasant's Truth') may have been written in Belarusian, such as it then was, using the

Roman alphabet;[38] but, as Bulhakaw argues, 'in his texts, apart from the language, you won't find the other necessary elements of nationalist thinking, including the spatial localisation of Belarus .... Not once in the texts of Muzhytskaia prawda does he mention the exact term "Belarusians".[39] In fact, he usually addressed his audiences as *Dzetsiuki*, which just means 'men' or 'lads'.[40]

The one respect in which Kalinowski's message was more than social was in his appeal for the restoration of the Uniate Church: it was, after all, the old 'peasants' faith. 'Since the time of our ancestors we have had the Uniate faith,' he argued, 'which means that we, being of the Greek faith, acknowledged the Saint Fathers of Rome as the governors.' Orthodoxy was imposed artificially, as the faith of the distant tsars. 'Thus we were separated from the true God .... We lost our spiritual merit, our Uniate faith.'[41] Kalinowski viewed the Orthodox as 'schismatics',[42] but the majority of his would-be fellow countrymen were Orthodox.

Kalinowski's execution in Łukiszski Square in the centre of Vilna in March 1864 made him a national hero to later generations, but in reality his impact was limited at the time. He had no movement to lead. But he did provide inspiration for those who came later.

West-Russism

Kalinowski had a large potential audience of disgruntled peasants. He couldn't yet speak to a 'nation', however. As Bulhakaw states, 'Belarusian identity didn't exist in the middle of the nineteenth century.'[43] The building blocks simply weren't there. Belarus needed to be imagined as a region first. Paradoxically, much of the initial work would be done in the 1860s and 1870s by a very different group of people, the so-called 'west-Russian' movement (*Zapadno-russizm*). Paradoxically or not, this strongly Orthodox movement was the main successor to the Uniates. By the end of the century its centre of gravity lay more in the east, but early on many of the leaders of the movement, like the archaeologist and historian Ksenafont Havorski (1821–71) and the historian Mikhail Kaialovich (1828–91),[44] were from former Uniate families. The west-Russian movement was initially strongest in Hrodna in the west, as well as Mahilew in the east.[45] In fact, Kaialovich was born far to the west, near Białystok, in 1828, where ethnic and religious markers were sharper.[46] His Uniate father ended up an unwilling citizen of Prussia after the final divisions of the Commonwealth and fled east. Kaialovich was initially unsure about his identity and called himself a 'Litvin',[47] but he ended up, at least in terms of his

Polonophobia, *plus royaliste que le roi*. He switched to Orthodoxy as an adult, and his most famous work was in celebration of the 'Reunification of the West-Russian Uniates' with the Orthodox in 1839.[48]

In the first half of the century, former Uniates like Siamashka were better described as Russifiers *tout court*. After the 1863–4 Rebellion, however, the embryonic west-Russian movement acquired a self-consciously political motivation. In Bulhakaw's words: 'West-Russism as an ideology was . . . set up to block Polish nation-building on Belarusian lands, above all by means of weakening the old elite.'[49] According to Tsvikevich, ' "Fear of Poland" was the most characteristic mark of west-Russian circles.' Poland was seen as a 'Jesuitical', 'non-Slavic civilisation' (sic), and Polish landlords were universally depicted as cruel usurpers. Havorski was determined to show that 'the Russians are masters in this land, and the Poles either renegades or immigrants'. When Kaialovich quoted Cato in the pages of the Russian nationalist paper *Den'*, declaring *Delenda est Carthago!* ('Carthage must be destroyed!'), he clearly had Russia in mind as Rome and Poland as Carthage.[50]

Havorski and Kaialovich also railed against what modern analysts would call an 'ethnic division of labour', i.e. the fact that the Poles were landowners and the west-Russians were mainly serfs. But unlike Kalinowski, they were able to exploit popular hostility to Catholicism, which became increasingly narrowly associated with the nobles' religion. Kaialovich and Kalinowski both defined nascent Belarusian identity by exclusivist reference to religion; but for Kaialovich, any Catholic, whether Roman Catholic or (former) Greek Catholic, 'was already not a proper Belarusian, not a proper west-Russian, but kind of half-Polish. For Kaialovich, faith defined everything – both nationality and ethnicity, and the "Russian spirit" itself. And for Havorski, "outside of Orthodoxy" Russia could not exist.'[51] Hence 'the historical popular striving of West Russia to the East'.[52]

The alternative approach of using language to define identity, although advocated by the likes of Pavel Babrowski (1832–1905), a military historian of Hrodna and Białystok,[53] didn't suit this approach or the needs of the imperial bureaucracy,[54] even though, without it, it was logically difficult to tell an Orthodox west-Russian from an Orthodox Ukrainian, or, indeed, in the eastern guberniias an Orthodox west-Russian from an Orthodox Russian. Overall, Kaialovich looked not to language, 'not to material Russian force, or even to Russian reason, but to the Russian spirit . . . the hope of all the Slavic peoples'.[55] In practical terms, Kaialovich was keen on the use of the Cyrillic alphabet throughout the region.

After the Polish Rebellion in 1863–4 the movement could count on some limited state sympathy. The leading Slavophile Ivan Aksakov wrote in 1863 that 'the peasant must understand and carry out the orders and suggestions of Russian power ... he must feel himself completely Russian, and for this he must feel himself above all Belarusian'. In other words, Bulhakow writes, 'in order to assimilate Belarusians, it was first necessary to perceive them as a separate nationality'.[56] Aksakov wrote to Kaialovich in 1861, 'the most important question for us at the moment is the Polish question and the question about Polish borders ... the relation of Lithuania and Belarus to Poland can be properly determined only with the help of historical, statistical and ethnographic data'.[57]

After the 1863–4 Rebellion, the tsarist authorities were therefore keen to establish the 'ancient' Russian identity of what they now called the *Severozapadnyi krai* (the 'North-western territory'). As it hadn't ever really been contemporary 'Russia', this meant going back to the old 'Rus', 'Ruthenian' or parochial east Slavic traditions of the region. For example, one study of Vilna in 1904 described how 'from the earliest times, the Lithuanian tribe lived in close proximity to the neighbouring Russian tribes, and since the time of its foundation, Vilna has always been a half-Russian town ... a *Civitas Ruthenica*'.[58] It was west-Russian historians who revived (or created) interest in Polatsk: first, because they wanted to demonstrate that the region didn't belong to the Poles; second, because Polatsk was Orthodox almost four centuries before the creation of a Roman Catholic Lithuania in 1387. Writers like Ihnat Kulakowski (1800–70), the rumoured author of the popular primer *Tales in the Belorussian Dialect*, published in 1863,[59] were unaware that their work would one day be used to help underpin a more specifically local 'national idea'. When Vosip Turchynovich wrote the first real history of Belarus in 1857, he concentrated on the Kryvichy and Polatsk, safe in his assumption that the history of Belarus as an independent subject had ended in the seventeenth century and Belarus was now part of Russia.[60] The west-Russians wanted to suppress the idea of a country called Litva and a people called the Litvins in fundamental existential conflict with Moscow for the control of Eastern Europe. The west-Russians, rather than the Belarusian nationalists who came later, were therefore responsible for popularising the terms 'Belarus' and 'Belarusian' as a safer alternative.

Men like Havorski and Kaialovich hoped that the early signs of state sympathy for the embryonic west-Russian cause would be backed up by positive discrimination in their favour. But the state's response to the Polish Rebellion ultimately proved to be remarkably pragmatic.[61] Just *before* the rebellion, in February 1862, Vladimir Nazimov, who was governor-general of

Vilna from 1855 to 1863, had proposed setting up networks of 'people's schools' for the local Orthodox.[62] In January 1863, the tsar himself allocated six thousand roubles annually for a potential local hearts-and-minds project, and a 'Friend of the People' journal was planned.[63] Dmitrii Bludov, the chair of the Council of State, proposed to the tsar the establishment of a loyalist 'West-Russia Association' in April 1863, although this ultimately came to naught.[64] The ban on the use of the Belarusian 'language' in Roman script in 1859, although that language was still uncodified, was primarily a measure to combat Polish and Catholic influence, rather than a measure against Belarusian speech as such. Havorski was able to set up a paper *Vestnik zapadnoi Rossii* ('West-Russia News'), first in Kiev in 1862, and then in Vilna from autumn 1864 (it folded in 1871). Other institutions – the Vilna Archaeological Commission, the Vitsebsk Archive of Ancient Acts, and the North-Western Department of the Imperial Russian Geographical Society, established in 1867 and revived in 1910 – were also natural homes for west-Russism.[65]

But the Polish Rebellion ironically scuppered these plans. When none other than Mikhail Muraviev returned to the region as governor-general of the North-western territory in May 1863, it was obvious he only had 'pacification' in mind rather than campaigning to win hearts and minds. Indeed, he quickly earned himself the nickname 'the hangman' by overseeing more than a hundred public executions, while hundreds more were exiled and whole villages were razed. Moreover, Muraviev increasingly only trusted 'pure Russians'. According to Tsvikevich, 'to Muraviev's point of view all local people tended towards Polonism, regardless of whether they were Catholic or Orthodox; the difference between Poles and west-Russians, and those more Belarusian, wasn't crucial'.[66] Loyalty to tsar and Church was what mattered. Muraviev recruited Orthodox priests from Bessarabia to serve locally. All Catholics were repressed, with a ban on new Catholic churches, on Catholic crosses (hence their importance in Lithuanian culture), and even for a time a ban on funereal black. The idea was even privately floated to corral all the locals into a new 'Catholic-Slavic Church'.[67] Ironically, this might have re-created the Uniate Church in a different form, which is no doubt one main reason why the idea was stillborn.

Aleksandr Potapov, the governor-general in 1868–74, applied a softer touch, reaching out over the heads of Belarusian peasants to build bridges again with the Polish landlords – not unlike in the other post-rebellion Reconstruction at this time, thousands of miles across the Atlantic in the former Confederacy. The west-Russians represented the middling social orders at best, those downtrodden by Polish landlords. And in the last analysis, Tsvikevich points out, 'clerks, schoolteachers and mere bureaucrats of "local origin" to high-ranking aristocratic Petersburg were too small a class of unfamiliar people'.[68] More generally, by the 1870s 'Russian politics wasn't interested in Belarus: it almost forgot about its existence . . . just like after the 1831 Rebellion, St Petersburg was happy with the simple fact of Belarus belonging to the empire'.[69] A proposal by the minister of education Dmitrii Tolstoi to set up a university in Polatsk in 1873 was quietly forgotten.[70] Significantly, therefore, according to Theodore Weeks, 'while the government never repudiated russification as a long-term goal, it did not devote significant resources to this goal'.[71]

A new generation of west-Russians came along in the 1880s and 1890s, but the situation did not change radically until 1905. Until then, the west-Russian movement was largely academic, concentrating on 'philology, cartography and ethnography'.[72] After a false start with Havorski, individuals such as the linguist Ivan Nasovich (1788–1877)[73] and the ethnographer Efim Karski (1861–1931) took up the slack. Piatr Bessonov collected songs. 'For the construction of Belarusians as an ethnic nation' they 'used the standard nationalist instruments: maps, censuses and ethnographic data'.[74] But 'the pulse of west-Russian intellectual life and work was now not in Vilna. It moved to the east, to provincial towns – Vitsebsk, Polatsk, Mahilew', and even Smolensk.[75] Vitsebsk was home to the historian Aliaksei Sapunow (1852–1924), Mahilew and Homel to the local historian and ethnographer Ewdakim Ramanaw (1855–1922), Smolensk to the linguist Uladzimir Dabravolski (1856–1920), who produced a *Smolensk Regional Dictionary* in 1914 recording the mixed Belarusian-Russian language of the borderland. Though their output was limited in scope. Sapunow 'was not a leading figure'. Even Kaialovich 'can hardly be considered a father of the nation'.[76] The closure of Vilna University after the 1830–1 Uprising limited the entire region's potential as an intellectual centre. There wasn't even an equivalent of Kiev University, set up under Nicholas I in 1834, to provide an imperial loyalist message in competition with that of the Poles.

However, west-Russism wasn't just a preliminary transitional phase; it wasn't simply superseded by a more 'mature' Belarusian nationalism. By the early twentieth century the two were in competition, and west-Russism often had the upper hand, after the 1905 Revolution, and the authorities' reaction to it, helped it to a revival of sorts. Unlike in the aftermath of the rebellions of 1830–1 and 1863–4, the regime now had other options than the Polish aristocracy. The new prime minister, Piotr Stolypin, hoped to build the regime's social basis of support by developing a new class of small- and medium-size property holders in the countryside, like the conservative yeomanry he thought was the hidden secret of England's status quo. He was well acquainted with Belarus thanks to his time as governor of Hrodna in 1902–3 and hoped 'that the west-Russians [now] stood at the head of the new class – the peasant kulak bourgeoisie'.[77] West-Russism began to make new allies among the Russian nationalist movement and, equally importantly, in statist bureaucratic circles. The movement's newer leaders were now welcomed, Tsvikevich records, 'in St Petersburg salons, in ministerial offices, at the tsar's own receptions'.[78]

The 1905 Revolution also resulted in the creation of an all-Russian parliament, the State Duma, where public opinion in Belarus could be put to the test, although the changes in election rules that Stolypin engineered for the Third Duma in October 1907 worked in the west-Russians' favour. Whereas the Poles and the *krayovtsi* (see below) had dominated the first two Duma elections in 1905–6, local representation was now dominated by the west-Russians. In Hrodna guberniia, one priest and three peasants sympathetic to Russian monarchist parties were elected; in Minsk, two priests and four rightist peasants (out of nine); in Vitsebsk (again out of nine) two rightist peasants, one priest and one member of the intelligentsia (Aliaksei Sapunow); in Mahilew, one priest and one peasant. Polish candidates did well 'only in Vilna guberniia where they received five mandates'.[79] Of the twelve Belarusians elected to the Third Duma, 'one was a member of the Octobrists' faction, two were progressives, and the rest belonged to the Russian national faction and right group'.[80] In total, Russian nationalist parties and west-Russians won a clear majority of thirty-six mandates in the Belarusian guberniias (80.5 per cent). No radical socialists were elected.[81] Explicitly Belarusian national parties had minimal support. Only six Belarusians were elected to the Fourth Duma in 1912. Of these, four belonged to Russian nationalist groups and two to the moderate right.[82]

The west-Russians also began to establish political organisations at this time. Tsvikevich records that the idea of a local loyalist party had been around since 1893, or even earlier,[83] though Havorski and Kaialovich's musings about a 'People's Party' in the 1860s and 1870s came to nothing. In 1905 a 'Peasant Society' was founded in Vilna. In 1907 the 'Krai Society' (*Okrainnoe obshchestvo*) was established in St Petersburg; several of its leaders sat in the Duma. In 1908 the West-Russian Orthodox Brotherhood was set up, followed by the West-Russian Society in 1911, again in St Petersburg. Finally, the Union of Belarusian Democracy, which included Efim Karski as a member, appeared in 1917.

Somewhat to the left was the 'Belorussian Society' (spelt in the Russian fashion) founded by Luka Salanevich in Vilna in 1908 (first meetings were held in 1905). Salanevich's group is often dismissed as a Russian nationalist organisation but, according to one modern history, its 'ideology of Russian provincialism coexisted with elements of separatism. Distancing itself from the Black Hundreds, who were not prepared to recognise the selfhood of the Belarusians, and saw in them only ethnographic differences from the great Russians and developed the idea of west-Russism, Luka Salanevich and his followers grew closer to the national movement.'[84] Salanevich considered the natural language of Belarusians to be Russian, but he called on the tsarist authorities to do their duty to their own by backing a populist agrarian programme to squeeze out the Polish landlords. Prime Minister Stolypin might have supported this policy, but it seemed too radical. Salanevich's supposedly loyal opposition had its paper, 'Belorussian Life', suspended between 1909 and 1911. It may be too simple to seek a parallel between Salanevich and Lukashenka, president of Belarus since 1994, but Lukashenka didn't come from nowhere. Belarusians have a long tradition of voting for populist Russophiles.

As one of their number Aliaksandr Tsvikevich argued in the one and only book on the subject, first published in 1929, 'the kulak-Orthodox basis of west-Russism in Belarus was its Achilles heel'.[85] Although the authorities considered the movement potentially useful after 1905, they still normally thought of class and religion before nation. Another fatal weakness identified by Tsvikevich was the west-Russians' passive 'ethnographism'. Despite 'loving ethnographic Belarus', he wrote, and 'studying Belarusian folklore, they could not create a Belarusian literature'.[86] Many west-Russians were in fact quite disparaging about the 'weak' or underdeveloped Belarusian language.

The closest analogy to west-Russism was 'Little-Russianism' (*malorosiistvo*) in Ukraine, but the differences are also instructive.[87] Little-Russianism also drew on various forms of overlapping identity, most commonly the idea that there were separate Ukrainian and Russian folk cultures and a third over-arching 'all-Russian' 'high' culture, which, because it was genuinely synthetic, was something both groups could share. The problem for the west-Russians was that their idea of Belarusian identity and folk culture was little more than ethnographic. Whereas many Ukrainian 'Little-Russians' combined regional patriotism with imperial loyalism, and advocated the use of Ukrainian for folk culture, the west-Russians saw little need for the Belarusian language at all. They argued that Belarusians should use the 'one and the same Russian literary language' as the Russians.[88] Some hoped that a 'Belarusian Gogol'[89] might come along – someone who could bring the two cultures together or move both onto a higher level – but he never did. Crucially, the west-Russians ceded the key theatre of education to Russian, where the identity of future generations would be developed. The most they might advocate was some primary schooling in Belarusian. Tsvikevich's ultimate damning judgement is that too many 'saw in Belarus only a transition phase from Poland to Russia'.[90]

A second big difference is that Little Russianism was in competition with a relatively vigorous Ukrainian 'national idea'. The two also developed in tandem, often leapfrogging one another in popularity. In Belarus, however, west-Russism came first, inchoate as it was, two generations before the creation of a rival national movement.

Traditionally, west-Russism was treated dismissively in the national school of history, if it was mentioned at all, while Soviet historians focused on the development of left-wing precursors of 1917. However, a younger generation of Belarusian historians has looked again at west-Russism since 1991. Pavel Tserashkovich argues:

> west-Russism included not only truly odious figures like Havorski, but also personalities like Nasovich, Ramanaw and Karski, without whom the formation of the Belarusian national idea would scarcely have been possible. In any case it must be noted that a general line between 'west-Russism' and proper Belarusian national positions in the 1870s to 1890s would be difficult enough to draw. Polarisation happened considerably later – in the second half of the 1900s, when a Belarusian national movement [first] became a noticeable political and cultural force .... On the whole in the second half of the nineteenth century 'west-Russism' played the role of the first stage in the 'ethnographic' phase, characteristic for the majority of peoples in Central-Eastern Europe [in the scheme of Miroslav Hroch]. It was a stage of the accumulation of empirical material, but without it the national-political projects of the start of the twentieth century would scarcely have been possible.[91]

The nation first had to be defined and described before activists could argue over what to do with it.

Bulhakaw even argues that Kaialovich, in other words, despite his natural inclinations, was 'the first Belarusian nationalist, that is a man who used a modern understanding of Belarus as a nation', despite being a 'monarchist, imperial historian and Orthodox reactionary'.[92] West-Russism condemned 'separatism' and sought integration, but emphasised elements of Belarusian identity (*samabytnasts*).[93] One of Kaialovich's famous statements embodied the dilemma: 'between the Russians and us there is not [yet] full unity. How can we make it whole?'[94] He wanted to close the gap, but he admitted the gap was there.

Four Nations, One *Krai*

Another identity option ignored in most traditional histories was the *krayova* idea (*krajowość* in Polish) – the persisting loyalty to a civic Litva or more general Commonwealth.[95] The *krayovtsi* (*krajowcy* in Polish, *krajovcai* in Lithuanian) believed in the idea that the interests of the region as a whole (the *krai*) should come before those of any one ethnic group, and adhered to a political idea of Grand Duchy patriotism and a common Polish high culture, distinct from, and even superior to, ethnic Poland,[96] representing a unique synthesis of cultures, albeit on the basis of Catholicism and the Polish language.

The five guberniias corresponding to what is now Belarus certainly had a diverse population: ethnically, linguistically and religiously. Only in Minsk and Mahilew were the Belarusians truly numerically dominant. (Though the 1897 census was based on language not ethnicity, and the local tellers who collected the information often treated it as a 'social project.')[97]

Composition of the Five Guberniias Corresponding to Modern Belarus by Linguistic Group, 1897 Russian Census (by Percentage)

Guberniia	Belarusians	Jews	Poles	Russians	Other
Vilna	56	12.7	8.2	4.9	17.6 Lithuanian
Hrodna	44	17.4	10.1	4.6	22.6 Ukrainian
Minsk	76	16	3	3.9	
Vitsebsk	52.9	11.7	3.4	13.3	17.7 Latvians (Latyshskie)
Mahilew	82.4	12.1	1	3.5	

Belarusians also made up 6.6 per cent of the population of Smolensk guberniia, and 6.6 per cent in Chernihiv. In Avgustovskii uezd (district), Suwałki guberniia, on the border of East Prussia, 36.4 per cent of the population were Belarusian.[98]

Source: http://demoscope.ru/weekly/ssp/rus_lan_97.php?reg=0

The *krayovtsi* had both a democratic strand represented by Mikhal Romer (1880–1945), and a conservative-liberal strand led by Raman Skirmunt (1868–1939). Romer set up the 'Lithuania' society in Paris in 1904; Skirmunt made tentative attempts to set up a Krai Party of Litva and Belarus in 1906–8, with three separate national sections for Belarusians, Poles and Lithuanians and a paper, *Glos Polski* ('Polish voice');[99] which made it seem too pro-Polish to many. The real meeting place for *krayovtsi* like Romer and the Lutskevich brothers was in the Masonic lodges of Vilna, such as 'Unity' set up in 1910, 'Litva' in 1911 and 'Belarus' in 1914. The city's Society of Art, founded in 1908, also aimed to be multinational.[100] The Vilna *krayovtsi* published one newspaper in Russian, the daily *Vecherniaia gazeta* (1912–15), one in Polish, the weekly *Kurier Krajowy* ('Regional courier') (1912–14), and two in Belarusian, *Nasha Niva* and *Sakha* ('The Plough'). The Lutskevich brothers saw no contradiction in backing the relatively 'nationalist' *Nasha Niva*; its pages were still full of *krayovtsi* appeals for building a multiethnic political nation.

According to Zakhar Shybeka, 'the *krai* movement was of exclusively local origin. It was the response of the Belarusian and Lithuanian intelligentsia of Polish culture to Russian chauvinism on the one hand and Polish nationalism [of the exclusivist type backed by Roman Dmowski] on the other, and based itself on the preservation of common Polish-Belarusian-Lithuanian cultural traditions in the Vilna region.'[101] It was therefore more common in the west, where there was still a mix of such cultures, as compared to eastern Belarus. The *krayovtsi* looked to the equality of the three peoples in some form of revived Grand Duchy, without Poland if necessary, as argued by the Polonised Lithuanian Mikhal Romer;[102] or in some kind of decentralised cantonal arrangement – like an eastern Switzerland of three or four cultures. Vitald Zhukowski in his 1907 book *Poles and Belarusians* simultaneously argued against the tsars and against the advocates of 'all-Polish union' and foresaw a tripartite union 'in mutual defence against Germany and Russia.'[103]

Normally, the *krayovtsi* argued that the 'interests of the *krai* as a whole' were higher than 'the interests of any one national group'.[104] But, suggests Ales Smalianchuk,

> there was no unity in how the *krai* idea was understood. The *krayovets* Romer foresaw the merging together of all the indigenous ethnoses of the *krai* and the formation of a new political nation [which others took to mean joining Poland]. Raman and Kanstantsa Skirmunt understood *krai*-ism as Belarusian-Lithuanian patriotism [and] the domination of general *krai* interests over the needs of particular ethnoses and social groups. For Liudvik Abramovich the *krai* ideology would lead to the good-neighbourly coexistence of all the ethnoses of the *krai*.[105]

In a 1913 article entitled 'About our Land', Romer talked of 'creating one political (civic) nation' out of three 'national-cultural zones' (three zones, rather than three peoples).[106] The first zone was Lithuania proper, namely Kovno guberniia and most of Suwałki to the south-west. The second zone was 'Litowska Rus' or Catholic Belarus, comprising the middle zone of Vilna guberniia and west and north-west Hrodna, which Romer described as a 'classical region of localism' (*klasichny krai tuteishastsi*), which was 'not Poland, not Lithuania [and] not Belarus'.[107] All three cultures in the region were incomplete and subject to mutual influence, including Lithuanian, which was subject to some linguistic Slavicisation. The third zone was orthodox Belarus, further to the east and including Minsk, where the overlap with Russian culture was strong. Romer's personal journey was incidentally similarly complex: he originally seemed Polonophile, establishing the newspaper *Gazeta Wileńska* ('Vilna Newspaper') in 1906, but sided with Lithuania after the war. Preserving multiethnicity was therefore key: as Smalianchuk again points out, Romer argued that 'the loss of the Catholic regions could lead to the complete Russification of Belarusian lands'.[108] Romer had some success in working with the Lithuanian Democratic Party and the Constitutional-Catholic Party of Litva and Belarus headed by the bishop of Vilna, Edward von Ropp, who were sympathetic to *krayovism* and dominated Duma representation in what is now Lithuania, including the 'ethnic' parts of Vilna guberniia.[109]

The main Jewish party, the Bund, technically had no regional focus. The Polish *krayovtsi* (*krajowcy*) (the Polish Socialist Party, the 'Liberation' Peasant Party – the early Piłsudski-ites) had proposed a voluntary federation of Poland 'proper' with the *kresy* back in the 1890s, though there were too few Poles in the east, where they feared being swamped if they cooperated in circles that were too wide. Local Poles became more radical after the coup against the Second Duma, but Belarusians 'of Polish origin' like Romer and the Lutskevich brothers continued to cooperate with figures in the Belarusian, Lithuanian and Jewish movements.

In the elections to the First Duma, all versions of the Belarusian movement remained weak, but the *krayovtsi* dominated until the election was fixed in 1907 (see page 74). In 1906 'nearly all of those elected from all five Belarusian guberniias were Poles'.[110] (The radical socialists boycotted the first Duma elections.) Not all local Poles were *krayovtsi* by any means. The narrowly ethnic nationalist Polish National-Democrats (*Endecja*) were growing in popularity, but they were more popular in the Polish heartlands. Nevertheless, out of fourteen Poles elected in the region, nine were conservative liberals sympathetic to the *krayovtsi*, as were another four members of the all-Russian liberal 'Kadet' party. Only one was a National-Democrat. In the Second Duma, elected in January 1907, eight out of ten Poles were *krayovtsi*, two were National-Democrats.[111] Overall, therefore, in the words of Smalianchuk, most followed 'the conservative-liberal direction of the *krai* ideology'.[112]

Many modern historians argue that the *krayova* ideology remained dominant among the Belarusians until 1916–17.[113] As it allowed more room for an assertion of Belarusian identity than west-Russism, it overlapped to a considerable degree with the 'national' movement. Indeed, the national movement was but a later offshoot of the *krayovtsi*. Many of its leaders, such as Skirmunt, started out as *krayovtsi*. According to Smalianchuk, 'the idea of the statehood of historical Litva dominated in the Belarusian movement west of the front line [in the First World War] through to 1917. Only at the start of 1918 were the Belarusians finally forced to reject it'[114] – although some continued to pursue the option into the 1920s.[115]

The Litvaks

Significantly, the local Jews also often thought of themselves, if not exactly as members of the *krai*, then as members of a specific 'Litvak' subgroup of Russian Empire Jews.[116] East European Jewish identity as a whole was closely bound up with the old Commonwealth, sometimes satirised as 'Yiddishland', in part because it was relatively tolerant of the Jews.[117] Self-governing *kahals* (councils for Jewish officers) existed until 1844, and the central Jewish *Va'ad Medinath Lita* (Rabbinical Council) gave the Jews of the Grand Duchy considerable autonomy from 1623 to 1764. The short-lived 1791 Commonwealth constitution would have given the Jews civic freedoms; Russian rule did not. But Catherine II's attempt to confine the Jews to the 'Pale of Settlement' in 1791, a more or less porous version of the old Commonwealth, slightly adjusted in the nineteenth century, only confirmed this residual loyalty.

There were many important differences between the former Commonwealth Jews of the north and the south – though it has also been argued that the empire's separate Jewish communities were increasingly united from the 1860s, and increasingly dominated by an elite that had slipped beyond the Pale to settle in St Petersburg.[118] Traditionally, however, the Jews of the north called themselves Lithuanian Jews or Litvaks, which in Yiddish made them 'Litvish', from 'Litah' or 'Lita' – as opposed to the 'Galitzianers', or Jews from Ukrainian Galicia, or the 'Lettish' Jews from Latvia. Jewish Vilna (Vilne in

Yiddish) served the whole hinterland of shtetl life in the northern half of the Pale of Settlement, 'the heartland of Ashkenazi Jewry, where important developments in modern Jewish history – Zionism and Yiddish culture – came into maturity'.[119] The more mystical and anti-formalist Hassidic movement was born in modern Ukraine, while Litva was home to the more self-consciously scholarly Lubavitchers, named after the Liubavich shtetl, east of Vilna in Mahliew guberniia. According to Benjamin Harshav, therefore, 'Jewish Litah is marked by a distinct Yiddish dialect, a particular Jewish cuisine, a "Litvak" mentality, and admiration for learning'.[120] Litvish in the north was one of three major Yiddish dialects in the Pale: the others were known as 'Poylish' (Polish-influenced, in the west), and Ukrainish, divided into 'Galitzianer' (from Ukrainian Galicia in the south-west), 'Volinyer' (from Volhynia), 'Podolyer' (Podil) and 'Besaraber' (Bessarabia, now Moldova) in the south.

The Litvaks thought of themselves as more educated than the more emotional Galitzianers. There was even an alleged culinary boundary, known as the 'Gefilte Fish Line', between more savoury Litvak food and its richer Galitzianer equivalent. Famous Litvak Jews include Menachem Begin, Shimon Peres, Irving Berlin, Louis B. Meyer, Michael Marks, the founder of the UK retail giant Marks & Spencer, Sholom Aleikhem, the painter Isaac Levitan, Eliezer Ben-Yehuda, initiator of the Hebrew revival, and Ludwik Lazar Zamenhof, the inventor of Esperanto. It was therefore often the Vilne version of 'Yiddishland' that survived and prospered in New York or Paris.[121] Not for nothing was Vilne known as the 'Jerusalem of the north' or *Yerushalaim d'Lita*, or the great Talmud scholar Eilyahu ben Shlomo Zalman (1720–97) as the 'Gaon ['Genius'] of Vilne' – a direct ancestor of Benjamin Netanyahu. The Gaon and the northern Misnagdim ('opponents') fought against Hassidism as a charismatic deviation, and defended traditional Torah-based learning.

The most famous local Jew was the painter Marc Chagall. Benjamin Harshav writes that 'Chagall always identified himself as a Litvak, even though he came from eastern Byelorussia' and Russified his name – he was born Moyshe Shagal and also tried out Moses Chagaloff.[122] His paintings show how the Litvak Jews both adapted to local culture and led separate lives alongside and in the shadow of Orthodox Christian culture. The then venerable Russian painter Ilia Repin, who was born in what is now Ukraine but bought an estate nearby, called Chagall's home town of Vitsebsk the 'Russian Toledo', where the domes of Christian churches shared the skyline not with minarets but with Jewish synagogues.[123] Chagall painted a series of paintings such as *The Blue House* (1917), with its Jewish *izbas* (log cabin) foregrounded but still overshadowed by the local Orthodox church. In another series, *Over Vitsebsk* (1915–20), he shows the Jew as a dream-like outsider, floating above the domes. Chagall took these and other leitmotifs from local Kabbalist stories and imagery.

Vitsebsk has a long artistic history. Repin helped found the Russian Empire's first private school of art there, which also produced the abstract painter El Lissitzky. A People's Art School under Chagall as commissioner of artistic affairs for Vitsebsk briefly flourished in the city from 1918, until Chagall, no natural friend of the Bolsheviks, fled to Paris in 1923. But Vitsebsk is now home to Belarus's premier annual cultural festival, the 'Slavianski bazar'.

All this, of course, made the local Jews Litvak Jews, Lithuanian Jews or Grand Duchy Jews rather than 'Belarusian Jews'.[124] But Belarusian culture is still marked by the centuries of intermingling with the Litvaks. Because of the Pale of Settlement, there were fewer Jews in 'Russia proper' – hence the ease with which they were so often depicted as outsiders. Many Belarusians, however, spoke or understood some Yiddish. Unwittingly or not, the Litva and *krayova* ideas overlapped and reinforced one another. And in the present day, the Belarusian-Jewish writer Paval Kastsiukevich has maintained the tradition of crossover, with his tales of nostalgia for the 'rare perfume' of the Minsk of the 1970s and Yiddish-influenced dialect (Trasianka).[125]

The Belated National Movement

The founding father of Belarusian nationalism is the writer Frantsishak Bahushevich (1840–1900). He wrote in and simultaneously helped to invent modern literary Belarusian. Given the decline of both the medieval *rus'ka mova* and later *prosta mova* (see page 39), Bahushevich had to base his project on local dialect. His most notable work, *Dudka belaruskaia* ('Belarusian Fiddle'), was, moreover, based on Polish literary models. It even had to be smuggled across the border from Kraków, then part of the Habsburg Empire. Bahushevich's son ended up a Polish nationalist. But, like Kalinowski, Bahushevich was ahead of his time. The Belarusian national 'movement' only belatedly struggled into life after the empire's near-collapse in the Revolution of 1905.

But there were still many versions of the 'Belarusian idea' – in the early twentieth century at least four.[126] The first was represented by the Belarusian Socialist Hramada, which emerged in 1903–4, initially as an informal club, before becoming a proper party after the 1905 Revolution.[127] As throughout the Russian Empire at this time, Hramada activists debated the relative importance of the national and social questions, but emphasised the latter, appealing to the 'working poor people of the Belarusian land without differentiating any nationalities'. According to Smalianchuk, 'the national component of the idea was considered as a means of mobilizing Belarusian peasants for the political struggle'.[128] Their paper was *Nasha Dolia* ('Our Fate'), which appeared briefly in 1906, but after six issues was banned by the authorities in December of the same year.

The polar opposite of Hramada was represented by Anton Bychkowski (1889–1937) and Baliaslaw Pachopka (1884–1940), who founded the weekly *Belarusian* paper in Vilna in 1913 to 'defend Christian and Belarusian values'.[129] Instead of class before nation, it put religion first, and Catholicism at that, thereby limiting its maximum appeal to a fifth of the population. Pachopka was the author of a Belarusian grammar in the Roman alphabet. His patron was Countess Maria Magdalena Radziwiłłowa, from one of the oldest families in the region. Interestingly, therefore, moderate versions of Belarusian nationalism did not lack elite support. Countess Radziwiłłowa also backed the *krayovtsi*,[130] which was no real contradiction.

The alternative option, of putting nation and mother tongue before class, was represented by the newspaper *Nasha Niva* ('Our Cornfield'), which began publication in 1906. Whereas the west-Russians had stressed Orthodox history to distinguish themselves from the Polish-leaning 'Litvins' in the first half of the nineteenth century, the 'Nashanivtsy' were now reacting against the west-Russians in turn, who had neglected the Belarusian language. Language 'revival' was therefore the Nasha Niva leitmotif, producing a new definition of the nation which they hoped would unite Orthodox and Catholics, based on the language maps ironically made by the west-Russians Aliaksandr Ryttykh (1875)[131] and Efim Karski (1903–4).[132] Their maps were sketchy however: their vision of would-be Belarus in areas like Smolensk often amounted to little more than a few of the building blocks of Belarusian dialects, like a palatalised 'dz' and 'ts'.

The Nashanivtsy also sought to write a new version of national history that was broader than the history of Polatsk or one or more particular east Slavic tribes. In this, they were helped by Lithuanian historians of this period such as Simanas Daukantas (1793–1864) and Jonas Basanavičius (1851–1927), who sought to reclaim their national history from Poland by concentrating on the period before the 1385 Union of Kreva and the coming of Christianity in 1387.[133] Daukantas in particular eulogised the pagan period. Arguably this helped the Belarusians muscle in on the later history of the Grand Duchy. The three founding fathers of this new Belarusian historical school were Vatslaw Lastowski, Usevalad Ihnatowski and Mitrafan Downar-Zapolski, whose work bridged the *Nasha Niva* and early Soviet eras (see page 104).

Many classics of Belarusian history and literature would be produced between roughly 1906 and 1930, but this was extraordinarily late compared with other national movements in Eastern Europe. The first Belarusian dictionary – in Roman script and based on the Czech alphabet – was only published in 1906. Yanka Kupala (the pen name of Ivan Lutsevich, 1882– 1942) published his first poem *Muzhyk* in 1905. Yakub Kolas (another pen name, this time for Kanstantsin Mitskevich, 1882–1956) published *Songs of Captivity* in 1908. Branislaw Tarashkevich's first Belarusian grammar, half in Roman and half in Cyrillic script, was only published in Vilna in 1918.

Without such basic materials, there could be no real Belarusian school movement. Much Belarusian literature therefore developed under Soviet auspices, allowing Soviet patriots to depict 1917 or even 1945 as a cultural year zero in Belarus.

Nasha Niva liked to think of itself as a 'literary academy',[134] but it had a circulation of only 4,500. Initially it published in both the Cyrillic and Roman alphabets.[135] In 1912 it switched to Cyrillic only in an effort to win a bigger market in the east, then home to only 12 per cent of its readers. Unlike the previous generation, which had largely sidestepped the religious question, *Nasha Niva* was marginalised by its plans for a revival of the Uniate Church, which by the 1900s was a radical and probably utopian position to adopt. The Lutskevich brothers made tentative contact with Andrei Sheptytskyi, the Uniate (now Greek Catholic) metropolitan in the Galician centre of Lviv, who made an incognito visit in 1908; but without much result. According to one retrospective account: 'It was planned that the reborn Uniate faith would play a dual role. On the one hand, it should become the social "cement" which would unite religiously diverse people into one spiritual monolith. On the other hand, it was intended as a spiritual shield, which could protect the national organism in the process of consolidation against the destructive influence and aggression, which came from both "spiritual empires" – Russian Orthodoxy and Polish Catholicism.'[136] Despite their best intentions, however, the Nashanivtsy largely remained in a Roman Catholic milieu. According to Smalianchuk, 'most easterners . . . regarded the programme of Nasha Niva as too radical'.[137] Unfortunately, not many from the western guberniias heeded the call either. The purpose of *Nasha Niva* was 'to make all Belarusians who do not know who they are, realise they are all Belarusians'; but many remained blissfully ignorant.[138]

Aleh Latyshonak argues that the Nashanivtsy only really made an impact in the ethnically mixed middle region: 'the Belarusian national movement was practically nonexistent in the relatively homogeneous sites of either Catholics living in the Belarusian-speaking neighbourhood of Vilna – or Orthodox living in eastern Belarus.'[139] By 1911 there were two Belarusian-language periodicals in Vilna, but its polyglot citizens could also choose from thirty-five publications in Polish, twenty in Lithuanian, seven in Russian and five that were in Yiddish (Jewish).[140] Belarusian parties like Hramada were also a sideshow compared to all-Russian parties like the Jewish Bund, founded in Vilna in 1897, and the Communists. Lenin's Russian Social Democratic Workers' Party (RSDWP) held its first congress in Minsk in 1898 – before the split into 'Bolsheviks' and 'Mensheviks' in 1903. The Minsk building is a more popular tourist destination than the revamped National Museum of Culture and History.

Why Was the National Movement So Weak?

This is really two questions: Why was the Belarusian national movement so weak? And why would any movement have been weak?[141] Barbara Törnquist-Plewa argues that 'the roots of modern Belarusian nationalism can be found in the identity crisis which the Ruthenian gentry experienced after the fall of the Polish-Lithuanian state.'[142] Many assimilated. Most early activists were Roman Catholic. 'Later a small group of Orthodox Belarusians joined the movement, having rejected Russian state-nationalism as undemocratic and turning to Belarusian nationalism, which appeared emancipating by contrast.'[143] But there was no real spark to set the movement alight. The local population was relatively stable. There were no population interchanges of the kind that helped create, for example, Young Turk nationalism in Anatolia;[144] or dramatic status reversals like the changed perception of the Baltic Germans after German unification in 1871. The Poles were viewed as traitorous after 1863, but then they had always been distrusted. There was less pressure or repression from the authorities than in Ukraine or Lithuania;[145] in fact, the authorities helped the west-Russians at least to get off the ground.

Academic analyses of national identity and nationalism talk about 'social communication' – the importance of education and mass media in spreading notions of identity.[146] Belarus was severely handicapped in this sphere by any measure, both in terms of message delivery and potential audience. Belarus had middling peasant strata, but hardly any middle class. There was no local equivalent of the 'free peasants' to be found in the Baltic or in New Russia (the northern Black Sea coast recently conquered from the Ottomans), or of the still partly free Cossacks in Left Bank Ukraine. In 1858, on the eve of the Emancipation of 1861, a massive 64.7 per cent of the population of Mahilew guberniia were serfs, and 60.7 per cent were so in Minsk.[147] Belarus had relatively few big towns, and the railways arrived late, from the 1870s. The region was an economic backwater. According to the economic survey undertaken in parallel with the 1897 census, 'commercial and industrial turnover per capita' was 205 roubles in Latvia, 85.5 in Estonia and 70.3 in Ukraine, but only 25.8 in Belarus, making it one of the most impoverished parts of the empire, on a par with Arkhangel in the far north.[148]

Schooling was extremely patchy. In 1856, thirty-three per thousand children were in school in Estonia, but in Mahilew the figure was just five.[149] The lack of a university anywhere in the north-west was a notable handicap, especially in an era when nearly all revolutionaries were students or former students. Many activists were based in St Petersburg. The new organs of local self-government, the zemstva, were established late in Belarus, in 1911.

Literacy was not widespread. It was higher for Catholics, at 29.9 per cent, than among the Orthodox, at only 11.2 per cent.[150] Overall, only 13.5 per cent of Belarusians were literate compared to 80 per cent of Estonians and 71 per cent of Latvians, although the high number of Roman Catholics meant that the Belarusian figure was just above the Ukrainian figure of 12.9 per cent.[151]

There were very few conscious Belarusians among the elite, though there were notable exceptional patrons such as Magdalena Radziwiłłowa (see page 83). Many writers emphasise the loss of the Greek Catholic Church, which is true enough, but other national movements made do without clerical leadership, like the Dnieper Ukrainians. In any case, the Uniate Church in Galicia took a century under the Habsburgs to become a real national institution.[152]

Existing towns were either Jewish or Polish, and minorities were relatively large. Belarus was 17.9 per cent Catholic and 10.4 per cent Jewish, compared to 4.2 per cent and 6.2 per cent in Ukraine.[153] This was a similar pattern to Right Bank Ukraine, but other parts of Ukraine, the Donbas in particular, already had large Russian populations. However, towns like Poltava had ethnic Ukrainian majorities, and there was no real equivalent in Belarus. Belarusian peasants were not made mobile by the market; instead of taking their goods to urban markets, Jewish middlemen often came to them.

The old problems of a peripatetic capital and lack of a primate city were still acute. Vilna was now the centre of the embryonic national movement, but was also the centre of the much stronger Lithuanian movement, and the centre of its new version of an imagined Lithuania.

There was no foreign territory that could serve as an incubator of the national movement, perhaps helped by hostile foreign powers, like Galicia for the Ukrainians or East Prussia for the Lithuanians (though the Lithuanians in 'Lithuania Minor', after several hundred years under the Teutonic Knights before falling under Prussia, were subject to often severe pressures of Germanisation). Vice versa, there was no ideological 'backyard' like the Hetmanate for Ukraine, though the Ukrainian example was a spur to many.

But as Bulhakaw argues, 'the main reason for the lateness of Belarusian nationalism is not material, but ideological (*ideinaia*)'.[154] The main weakness of the Nashanivtsy was that they didn't have that strong a story to tell. The national movement had the wrong myths. The west-Russians developed the historiography of Polatsk, but it wasn't an ecumenical myth. Vilna intellectuals didn't embrace it, as Polatsk was in the east. The Grand Duchy myth, on the other hand, fuelled the *krayovtsi* movement instead. This lack of a usable joint historical memory was notable, compared to the Hetmanate in Ukraine where many former Cossacks had only recently lost their freedom, though Belarus wasn't a complete tabula rasa – legends of Rahvalod and Rahneda still circulated among the peasantry.[155] Other nationalists in other countries have filled in the gaps, as with Latvia's epic poem *Lāčplēsis* ('The Bearslayer'), which required a considerable amount of poetic licence on the part of its author, Andrejs Pumpurs; but the Belarusians were too honest.

The Nashanivtsy also had threadbare material for their language-building project. Church Slavonic was already archaic back in the Middle Ages. The functions of administrative language once enjoyed by *rus'ka mova* had passed to first Polish and then Russian. Even the *prosta mova* tradition had disappeared by the early nineteenth century. All that was left was dialect.

The quality of culture is also key. Russia's Pushkin was a good writer. Ukraine's Shevchenko was a good poet. Nineteenth-century Ukraine enjoyed the first stirrings of national opera and symphonic music, but mostly the new Ukrainian literate public got middlebrow fare like the comedy of manners *Chasing Two Hares*. The Belarusians didn't even get that. There was no Belarusian Shevchenko, not even Bahushevich as much of his popularity was retrospective. Even the most enduring writers of this period like Yanka Kupala and Yakub Kolas only gained a mass readership in the Soviet era.

Conclusion

In 1914 the two most significant national movements in Belarus were the Roman Catholic *krayovtsi* and the Orthodox west-Russians. In the struggle between Holy Rus and civic Commonwealth the *krayovtsi* were strongest in the two western guberniias – Vilna, where 58.5 per cent of Belarusian-speakers were recorded as Roman Catholic in 1897, and Hrodna, where the figure was 30.3 per cent.[156] The west-Russian movement predominated in the other three eastern guberniias – Minsk, Vitsebsk and Mahilew – where Orthodoxy was the norm. The Belarusian national movement, on the other hand, barely figured at all, and least of all east of Vilna. As Bulhakaw writes, 'the Orthodox hierarchy was far more consolidated and right up to the events of 1917 did not allow the smallest manifestation of Belarusian nationalism in its surroundings'. Consequently, 'until the revolution of 1917 the idea of Belarusian nationalism had barely penetrated to the east of Belarus'.[157]

The Belarusian national idea emanated outwards from Vilna, but not in the manner of the traditional nation-building model of a primate beacon city and eager hinterland. The Belarusian message coming out from Vilna was relatively weak, and weaker than the rival Polish, Lithuanian or Jewish messages. The Belarusian message was mainly passed on by a small number of literate peasants and small-town intelligentsia. The writer Frantsishak Bahushevich was born in tiny Smarhon, east of Vilna (current population: 36,000). The national movement therefore remained parochial and less than national. Bulhakaw argues that the area around Vilna was also peculiar: 'historically these lands were never either Rus-ian or purely Orthodox: they were either never a part of so-called Kievan Rus or were the extreme periphery of so-called Kievan Rus. Already at the start of the second millennium they were settled by Baltic tribes, Christianised into Roman Catholicism in 1387. At the moment of the ruin of the [old Commonwealth these] Roman Catholics made up 14–15 per cent of the confessional structure of the Belarusian population',[158] and were assimilated to the Belarusian language. The Belarusians of the 'core', in other words, were unlike the other Belarusians they sought to convert to their cause.

There were some possibilities for accelerated nation-building during the First World War (see next chapter), but Vilna was seized by the new Polish state between the wars, though the remaining Belarusians had some success in strengthening a regional version of Belarusian identity. But once Vilna was decisively lost to the Belarusian cause after the Second World War, it was like a dead star. Its signal was still being received in the neighbouring region, but the source was gone. Vilna was never an equivalent of Ukrainian Galicia.

Russia, on the other hand, missed many nation-building opportunities in the north-west. The national state's bureaucratic presence remained weak. St Petersburg bet the house on religious loyalties, which made sense so long as local society remained premodern, but it never invested in a school system to develop a more modern network of cultural loyalties. Tension with the Poles helped to win the loyalties of most eastern peasants, but a large part of the local elite was in the Roman Catholic camp. The war in 1914 further divided loyalties. The Germans made early advances into Belarusian territory: national feelings were intensified on the front line, but many Belarusians were behind it. 'Russia' or 'Holy Rus' remained an abstract idea for most.

CHAPTER 6

BELARUS BEGINS AGAIN: THE TRAUMATIC TWENTIETH CENTURY

If there had been many versions of the Belarusian 'national idea' in the nineteenth century, there would be again in the twentieth century too. The period of civil war, which raged throughout the tsars' old empire from 1917 to 1921, was particularly fluid. Soviet and Belarusian nationalist historiographies emphasise their preferred single stream: Soviet power or national destiny. In reality there were many rival projects, and many different possible outcomes, though some rival projects were more plausible than others. The First World War was a time of accelerated nation-building, but the German occupying forces never backed the Belarusian cause as they did the Ukrainian cause in 1918. 'White', i.e. monarchist, forces were less important in Belarus than further south. Unlike in Estonia, where the British Navy helped secure independence, the Entente's impact was mainly indirect, through the advocacy of the 'Curzon Line' dividing historical Poland on ethnic lines. And as well as the Poles, the Belarusians faced an extra rival in the Lithuanian national movement, which targeted Vilna (to them, Vilnius), though not quite all of historical Litva.

A specifically Belarusian National Republic was in many ways the least likely outcome of all. Most Belarusians, if they were political at all, backed transnational class parties. According to Aliaksandr Smalianchuk: 'In Belarus [1917] was a social revolution with [only] some signs of national revival.'[1] The real contest was between the Polish project for the region, in whatever form it might take, and the Bolshevik project for the region, in whatever form it might take – and there were several versions of both. Even after a Belarusian Soviet Socialist Republic was established, no other Soviet republic changed its shape and size as frequently and fundamentally as did the Belarusian Republic between 1918 and 1945. Belarus also lost more of its putative territory in the Civil War than Ukraine, its nearest equivalent, and also lost the more important parts. Not only was the city of Vilna lost to Poland, but almost the whole of the old tsarist guberniia surrounding it was divided between Poland and Lithuania. Most of the ethnically mixed territories that had previously served as something of an incubator of national consciousness were therefore now under Poland. The new capital of Minsk was only a partial substitute.

Ober Ost

Russia's imperial armies began the First World War well, but after their initial advance through East Prussia in 1914, the subsequent German push-back went farthest at the northern end of the front: German occupation therefore began much earlier in Belarus than in Ukraine. Coincidentally, as it was fixed entirely by the military ebb and flow, the front line that was settled by late 1915 passed more or less between historical Litva and 'Belarus' proper in the east, running from Braslaw in the north to Pinsk in the south, east of Navahrudak but west of Minsk. Vilna was occupied in September 1915. In the far north the German advance stopped at the river Dzvina, short of Riga. The front line therefore coincided with the limits of prewar Belarusian activism. The Belarusian national 'movement', such as it was, was therefore under the Germans for two years before 1917. By contrast, the Germans didn't arrive in Ukraine until February 1918.

But, unlike Ukraine, the Germans had no plans for puppet Belarusian statehood, or even for annexation. Instead, they set up a broader administrative region, *Ober Ost* ('Upper East', the mirror image of Imperial Russia's equally anodyne *Severo-zapadnyi krai*, or 'North-western territory'), stretching from Brest to Braslaw. Eastern Belarus was for military operations only, where occupied territory might be a useful bargaining chip – but was assumed to be naturally 'Russian'.[2] The Belarusians in general were not a factor in German calculations. In the words of one German account: 'the German districts, especially the Balts, had welcomed our troops. The Letts [Latvians] were opportunists. The Lithuanians believed the hour of deliverance was at hand. . . . The White Ruthenians [i.e. Belarusians] were of no account, as the Poles had robbed them of their nationality and given them nothing in return.'[3]

However, it is often argued that the German occupation gave an unintended and allegedly 'artificial' stimulus to the Belarusian movement: first, because it encouraged the mass migration of the Orthodox to the east, while most Catholics stayed put; second, for practical military reasons, Marshal Hindenburg, the Supreme Commander East in the occupied territories (and eventual German president), promoted the 'languages of the local population (Polish, Lithuanian, Belarusian) and banned the use of Russian in education, printing and administration'.[4] He conducted educational reform in Vilna, Hrodna and Białystok in 1915–16 that led to the opening of the first ever Belarusian elementary schools – though most schools in the occupied area were still Polish. The first such school opened in Vilna within two months of the city's occupation in November 1915. Arguably, however, the Belarusian intelligentsia's 'collaboration' in the occupiers' schemes further alienated them from the masses.

Limited political activity was allowed in *Ober Ost*, but significantly it was the *krayova* idea that was the first to be revived. The lawyer and literary critic Anton Lutskevich set up a 'Belarusian People's Committee'; and in December 1915 a 'Council of the Confederation of the Grand Duchy of Lithuania' was organised after a German-sponsored conference on the issue, which in February 1916 called for 'historical Litva' to be revived, uniting 'Belarus, Lithuania and Courland' with its capital in Vilna. Via coastal Courland, this version of the Grand Duchy would even have had access to the sea. But the project was soon beset by arguments between the four main nationalities (Belarusians, Poles, Lithuanians and Jews). The fact that the Belarusians were the idea's main supporters, when others had moved on, showed a certain lack of political development. Since the 1905 Revolution, most Lithuanians preferred the idea of 'ethnographic Litva', or 'Lithuania for the Lithuanians';[5] though, of course, they defined it in expansive terms to include the Vilna region, Suwałki to the south-east and even Hrodna (the abortive Soviet-Lithuanian peace treaty of July 1919 offered them all three). Many peasants in the Vilna region had been Slavicised in the nineteenth century and Lithuanian nationalists now feared that this process might continue in a joint Belarusian-Lithuanian state. The Lithuanians also felt, probably justifiably, that Russia would never be reconciled to the loss of Slavic territory and given half a chance would seek to detach it from a new 'Litva'.[6] A Vilna Belarusian Council was formed in January 1918, but after Germany announced its preference for the Lithuanian cause in February, it was forced to look east. Nevertheless, it was 'only at the start of 1918 that the Belarusians finally gave up on the *krai* conception of statehood'.[7]

A newspaper, *Homan* ('Hubbub'), began to appear in February 1916, edited by the historian Vatslaw Lastowski, which attempted to continue in the tradition of *Nasha Niva*. However, its circulation was tiny and its impact minimal. In the summer of 1917 Lastowski founded the underground society Independence and Unity of Belarus.

The BNR

East of the front line, on the side of Romanov Russia, the only really active Belarusian organisation was the apolitical *Khatka*, or Society for Helping Refugees, headed from late 1916 by the *krayovets* and one-time Polonophile Raman Skirmunt. After the February Revolution in 1917, Belarusians in the east were suddenly able to play catch-up with their brethren under the Germans in the west, but their natural inclinations were more on the left. According to Smalianchuk, 'while Belarusian politicians [under German occupation] in Vilna paid more attention to the problem of state self-determination, their Minsk colleagues kept to social priorities'.[8] The newspaper *Hramada* was primarily socialist. The Belarusian Socialist Hramada was revived in March 1917, but it only had a maximum of 5,000 members and split over how to respond to the October Revolution.[9] Unlike Ukraine, the Belarusians had no real populist socialist party capable of combining national and social messages.

After the February Revolution in Petrograd, Raman Skirmunt emerged as the head of a new Belarusian National Committee in March 1917. But many locals saw the committee as a '*pans*' [nobles'] intrigue',[10] and helped form the alternative Cultural Soviet of Belarusian Organisations to bypass Skirmunt's conservative circle of landowners. Skirmunt helped establish a Belarusian Central Council in late 1917, but it still 'acted mainly as a national-cultural organisation'.[11] Most Minsk Belarusians were *ablasniki*, i.e. parochial, thinking only of their own region (*voblasts'*). Unlike their more radical counterparts in Vilna, they did not yet think in terms of national independence. In Ukraine eastern leaders based in Kiev were also more moderate than those in the former Habsburg west, but unlike those in Belarus they were able to organise before those west of the frontier. The east Belarusians had almost no base of support. The often-quoted figure for the east Belarusian parties' lack of support is taken from the all-Russian Constituent Assembly elections held in November 1917 – 0.6 per cent – but refers only to the three eastern guberniias of Minsk, Mahilew and Vitsebsk, where the national movement was traditionally weakest.[12] No voting was possible in the areas controlled by the Germans in the west. The Bolsheviks' local vote, on the other hand, was highest among soldiers and in the frontline guberniias. Back east in Mahilew they won only 23 per cent, where the peasant-based Socialist Revolutionaries (SRs) triumphed instead.[13]

In the immediate aftermath of the Bolsheviks' seizure of power in Petrograd in October 1917, Belarusian activists tried to convene an All-Belarusian Congress in December, but it was disrupted straight away by local Bolsheviks. A minority of Belarusian activists went underground, led by the poet and journalist Yazep Varonka, which might have been the end of their story, had if not been for the German advance in February 1918 immediately after the signing of the Treaty of Brest-Litovsk, when Lenin and Trotsky gave away huge slices of old imperial territory in the west. The German occupation now extended across almost all of Belarus, all the way up to the river Dnieper.

But Belarus had not been mentioned at the negotiations in Brest-Litovsk. Germany now recognised new states in the Baltic and in Ukraine, some with various degrees of puppet government – but not in Belarus. Nevertheless, the German advance had one advantage, as it meant that the Vilna Belarusians and the Minsk Belarusians could finally join forces. The arrival of the Lutskevich brothers and Vatslav Lastowski in Minsk in 1918 greatly strengthened the supporters of independence. But the combined forces of the intelligentsia soon began to outstep their local support. The Belarusian Central Council split. The representatives of the towns, *zemstvas* and the Bund opposed a declaration of independence, so when a decision was finally made on 9 March 1918 to establish a 'Belarusian National Republic' (BNR), relations with Russia were left undefined.

The third Charter (*Hramata*) of the republic, issued on 25 March 1918, was a final formal declaration of independence. But it didn't lead to a Belarusian state, though it did help consolidate the idea of a Belarusian political nation.[14] The BNR may have transcended *krai*-politics, but it still thought in terms of some kind of confederation with Poland, an alliance with Ukraine or the Baltic States, or German protection. But Skirmunt's telegram to the Kaiser on 25 April asking for his protection led to a split among the leaders of Hramada.[15] According to Shybeka, 'the German occupiers saw the government of the BNR as a reserve option', but no more.[16] Nevertheless, it had some achievements to its name, particularly setting up a network of between 150 and 350 Belarusian schools and beginning preparations to create a university in Minsk. Although an embryonic foreign mission in Berlin had two thousand diplomatic passports printed, the BNR was only ever internationally recognised by other new East European states. Only in 1919, after the war was over in the west and the Germans faced chaos in the east, did Berlin have a belated change of heart, providing four million marks in subsidies to the BNR in March.[17]

But by December 1918 the leaders of the BNR had been forced to leave the country. Yet another split in its ranks occurred in December 1919. Fifty members supported the anti-Polish line of Piotr Krachewski and Vatslaw Lastowski, and thirty-seven the pro-Polish Lutskevich line.[18] The Krachewski/ Lastowski wing eventually moved to the new Lithuanian capital of Kaunas in November 1920. The Lutskevich group secured Polish sponsorship in autumn 1919 for two national battalions. But ordinary Belarusians failed to show much willingness to fight for the cause. Two-thirds of the money were embezzled. Only five hundred troops could be raised.[19]

The dying BNR had two notable afterlife episodes. The first involved a brief military fight-back under the magnificently named General Stanislaw Bulak-Balakhovich, one of many itinerant soldiers in this period, who had switched sides from the Imperial Russian to first the Red and then the White Army, before joining the Poles in 1919. But some Belarusian historians have still seen Bulak-Balakhovich as Belarus's potential major Major, a military saviour like Napoleon, Piłsudski or Symon Petliura in Ukraine. For a brief period in 1920 he commanded seventeen thousand men, and in November of that year declared yet another 'Belarusian Republic' in Mazyr, on the river Prypiat in the south-east. He even briefly captured the much larger town of Homel. In reality, however, Bulak-Balakhovich was not an independent actor; his advance came in the wake of the then current high-water mark of Polish success. In any case, his amorphous forces were east Slavic rather than strictly Belarusian and were originally named the 'Russian People's Volunteer Army'. Piłsudski said of him disparagingly that 'today he is Russian; tomorrow, Polish; the day after, Belarusian; and the next day, a Negro' (he was in fact part Tatar).[20] In the event, Bulak-Balakhovich's unconvincing transformation into a temporary Belarusian Napoleon made little difference, as Soviet forces drove him out in little more than a fortnight.

A second coda was provided by the 'Slutsk uprising'. After Polish forces left the region south of Minsk in November 1920, a regional congress was organised by veterans of the BNR and Belarusian SRs, though initially its aims were vague. The 'Slutsk congress' rejected overtures from Bulak-Balakhovich to join forces and appealed to both 'sister Poland' and 'the brotherhood of all the Slavic peoples'.[21] Though it claimed to act in the name of the local authority of the BNR, nobody else in Belarus came to its support. Nevertheless, its ragtag army of four thousand briefly engaged the advancing Red Army on 27 November 1920 – 'Heroes' Day' to some Belarusian nationalists – but was soon defeated.

After the body had stopped twitching, the BNR government-in-exile moved first to Berlin and then to Prague in 1923. The Soviet secret services (then called OGPU) considered it worthwhile to mount a 'special operation' to split the émigrés at the second All-Belarusian Conference in Berlin in 1925. Thereafter the BNR de facto ceased all hostile activity and many key figures were persuaded to return to the new Belarusian Soviet Republic. The BNR carried on a symbolic existence, with its scattered representatives dispersing into remoter exile in North America and the UK. Its current president is Ivonka Survila, who lives in Ottawa.[22]

Interestingly, after years of taking the Soviet line that the BNR was either irrelevant or a foreign-inspired bourgeois plot, President Lukashenka's regime adopted a softer line in 2008. Paradoxically, the BNR could not have been so insignificant if the Soviet secret services sought to destroy it in exile. More seriously, the official historians now argued, the BNR may have been only a 'political centre with pretensions to state status', which not even the inhabitants of Minsk had necessarily heard of; but it laid the basis for later, more successful attempts at building Belarusian statehood.[23] Even Soviet Belarus owed something to the BNR.

Soviet Belarus: Version One

The BNR lacked the strength to sustain itself for even the briefest of periods once the Germans were gone. The vacuum was filled quickly enough when Soviet troops first arrived in Minsk on 11 December 1918. But the Bolsheviks' plans for Belarus were extremely vague – when they were about Belarus at all. When Lenin's RSDLP had held its first congress in Minsk in 1898, the delegates unthinkingly assumed they were assembling in Mother Russia, although they would not have spoken of it in such affectionate terms. In 1918, the Bolsheviks therefore initially assumed that the local territories would just be another part of the new Russia.

In November 1918 Anton Lutskevich had proposed to Lenin a federal union of the BNR with Bolshevik Russia on the basis of the latter's constitution,[24] but his hand was weak. Lenin's sudden shift to backing the idea of a technically separate Bolshevik Belarus was entirely pragmatic. There was a noticeable shortage of Belarusian Bolsheviks; war with Poland was still raging; and Lenin wanted Poland to be 'in conflict with buffers' rather than with Russia itself.[25] And as the war wasn't going well, Lenin sought to claim the maximum possible territory for his would-be satellite. So, paradoxically or not, the borders of the first Belarusian Soviet Socialist Republic (BSSR), established on 1 January 1919, were a nationalist's dream. Based on the ethno-graphical maximalism of coopted intellectuals like Efim Karski (see below), the Bolsheviks' definition of their new Belarus included Minsk, Mahilew, Hrodna, Vitsebsk (though not Latgallia), a good part of Smolensk, and parts of Kaunas, Vilna and Suwałki; and even the mixed Belarusian-Ukrainian lands of Chernihiv.

But the government headed by Zmitser Zhylunovich – a Belarusian writer, but based in Moscow – only lasted two weeks, and never really controlled any of its would-be territory. Smolensk was soon reassigned to Russia. The first Belarusian Soviet Socialist Republic was a will-o'-the-wisp.

White Poland

The next possibility was that more or all of Belarus might have ended up under Poland, assuming more extensive Polish gains during the Polish-Bolshevik war of 1919–21. Since 1863 Polish 'National Democrats' like Roman Dmowski had abandoned the idea of a multinational commonwealth for a more 'modern' Polish ethnonationalism. A stress on 'Poland for the Poles' ought to have narrowed their focus and their territorial ambitions, but in practice they often claimed territory as far away as Minsk – the 'borders of 1772' or the Dzvina–Berezina–Dnieper line. The National Democrats didn't think that ethnic Poles had to be in a majority in every region of the restored Poland, just present in sufficient numbers in areas that belonged to 'Polish-Western culture'. The new Poland should swallow as many minorities as 'it could assimilate in one generation'.[26] In practice, this meant that the National Democrats targeted all of the Catholic lands – including all of Białystok, Hrodna and Vilna. The predominantly Orthodox Belarusian territories could be left to Russia. However, as all of Ukrainian Uniate Galicia to the south was also assumed to be naturally Polish, the National Democrats also targeted the largely Orthodox lands in between, namely Ukrainian Volhynia and Belarusian Polessia, so as to form a more 'natural' border against the Bolshevik east.[27] Eastern Belarus, on the other hand, was seen as a card to trade in return for the Bolsheviks' cession of western Belarus.

The Polish leader Józef Piłsudski, however, was in Polish terms a 'confeder-alist'. Like Adam Mickiewicz, Piłsudski was an archetypal Litvin, born in 1867 on his family estate in Zalavas (Zułów) in Vilna guberniia (now in Lithuania, north-east of Vilnius). His followers were later dubbed the 'Prometheans', supporters of Poland's *mission civilisatrice* in the east. But like other Poles he still thought in terms of a Catholic west and Orthodox east. According to the

Polish historian Jerzy Borzęcki, at best 'Piłsudski expected the Belarusians to give up their claims to the regions of Wilno [Vilna] and Grodno [Hrodna] in exchange for a Belarusian national entity in the region of Minsk and possibly further to the east'.[28] Some Polish federalists discussed the possibility of adding this Minsk as some kind of Belarusian autonomous region under Poland, but were concerned that such an Orthodox area might prove a fifth column that could eventually reverse its loyalties and back Russia.[29] In the early 1920s Piłsudski also toyed with the old *Krai* idea of rebuilding the Grand Duchy in three parts: a Litva based on Kaunas which would be Lithuanian-speaking, a Central Litva speaking Polish, and a Minsk Litva where the Belarusian language would be adopted. But at other times, Piłsudski mocked 'the fiction of Belarus'.[30] He never backed the idea of real Belarusian state-hood. The best he could offer was the creation of some kind of 'Belarusian Piedmont' aimed at the east, but *within* Poland.

Piłsudski's ally the future prime minister Kazimierz Świtalski admitted that the region was 'not Poland', but fretted at the idea of a new Polish Catholic frontier stretching precariously all the way to Daugavpils, in what is now Latvia.[31] Ironically, Piłsudski was eventually driven back by a Soviet counter-offensive launched from east Belarus in 1920. In January 1920 Piłsudski abandoned plans to hold a referendum on the issue. The Polish government washed its hands of the idea of a Belarusian state or even of Belarusian autonomy in March 1920. Modern historians are rightly sceptical of the idea that Poland rejected a Bolshevik offer of some form of Polish Belarusian protectorate in late 1920: Lenin's priority was to bury Piłsudski's federalist programme.[32]

In the end, neither Poland nor Lithuania (see below) was a sufficiently interested patron for the Belarusians. Ultimately, everything depended on whose army ended up on top. It was military campaigns that shifted the border backwards and forwards, rather than politicians or ethnographers. In August 1919 the Poles were in Minsk and in June 1920 they were in Kiev; two months later, in August 1920, they were fighting with their backs to Warsaw. The border ended up somewhere in the middle.

Lit-Bel

The second Soviet attempt at winning power in Belarus was the remarkable 'Lit-Bel': remarkable because, literally understood, it aimed to re-create the medieval Grand Duchy in simplified Bolshevik form, as a joint Lithuanian-Belarusian republic. Unfortunately, neither set of local Communists was keen – particularly the Belarusians. For good reason: 'Lit-Bel' was hardly intended as a marriage of equals. With its eastern territories assigned to Russia, including Polatsk, Vitsebsk and Mahilew, only a rump of western Belarus – basically the old Litva territories of Minsk and Hrodna – was left attached to Lithuania when the 'Lithuanian-Belarusian Soviet Socialist Republic' was declared in Vilna on 28 February 1919. There were no significant Belarusians in the government.[33]

In theory Lit-Bel existed until 25 August 1919, but its forces were on the run from the Polish invasion that began in April 1919 and reached Belarusian territory in July. Lit-Bel forces fled gradually east. Their first capital was in Vilna, the second Minsk, the third Smolensk – a movement born out of necessity rather than historical symbolism. The Bolsheviks soon gave up on the idea.

Nevertheless, Lithuanian–Belarusian cooperation continued in attenuated forms. Priority number one for the new truncated Lithuanian state was regaining Vilna, taken by the Poles in the war of 1919–20, and it would accept any ally in the process. In fact, to its neighbours like Latvia, 'the foreign policy of Kaunas – "the enemy of my enemy is my friend" – was dangerous to the [other] Baltic states.'[34] The temporary compromise of a second quasi-independent quasi-state of 'Central Lithuania' (*Litwa Środkowa*) of October 1920 lasted only until disputed elections created a local Sejm dominated by local Poles which voted to join Poland in February 1922 (Mikhal Romer turned down the chance to be its president).

After a Lithuanian–Belarusian agreement was made in 1920, Lithuania therefore briefly gave tactical support to moderate versions of the Belarusian cause which might help them regain Vilna, or make them stronger against the Polish common enemy. The exile government of the BNR was based in the new capital, Kaunas, receiving two million marks in Lithuanian government support between 1920 and 1922.[35] These former 'Vilna Belarusians', who set up another 'Belarusian National Committee' in 1920, still clung to Romer's prewar idea of a confederation of three cantons: a mainly Lithuanian West Litva based on Kaunas, a mixed Polish-Belarusian Middle Litva based on Vilna, and a mainly Belarusian East Litva based on Minsk.[36] Lithuania set up a Ministry of Belarusian Affairs, and in 1922 there were even joint Belarusian-Lithuanian partisan actions against Poland, which were strongest in the Hrodna and Białystok regions, including the forest of Belovezhkaia pushcha, near the spot where a different kind of joint action would bring down the USSR sixty-nine years later. Some ten thousand were at one stage involved in the fighting.[37] In May 1922 Lastowski and Tsvikevich signed away to Lithuania the theoretical right to Vilna, if it were ever to be won back from Poland, to try and keep the project going.[38] However, Lithuania changed tack at the end of 1923, as the postwar settlement solidified and the largely conservative government in Kaunas grew impatient with the left-leaning Belarusians, and closed down most local Belarusian operations. Lithuania therefore never became a real launch pad for the Belarusian idea, the equivalent of Habsburg Galicia for Ukraine or Prussia for Lithuania itself before 1914.

But some elements of Lit-Bel lived on. Its language policy was revived by the Bolsheviks in 1924, when four state languages were confirmed for the Belarusian Soviet Socialist Republic (BSSR) (minus the Russian, a policy first laid down by the occupying Germans). The principle was still present in the 1927 constitution. Most important was the intellectual legacy. In the nineteenth century the main line of dispute between historians had been the tsarist-sponsored west-Russians' attempts to prove that 'Belarus', initially meaning the more easterly territories, was not Polish because of the legacy of Polatsk. Given the way that territories were divided in 1917–21, a three-way struggle, between the Poles based in Vilna, the Lithuanians in Kaunas and the Belarusians in Minsk, now began to claim the legacy of the historical Grand Duchy of 'Litva'. Elements of the mythology of the Belarusian Middle Ages had already emerged before 1914, but now they were systematised by the new Soviet Belarusian intelligentsia, many of whom were veterans of the national movement. This was no real irony, as it suited the Bolsheviks' political goals as they sought to expand farther west. Many of the classics of Belarusian history, by Usevalad Ihnatowski, Mitrafan Downar-Zapolski and Uladzimir Picheta, were first published or written in the mid-1920s.[39] At the same time, Vatslaw Lastowski was refining his theory that the Belarusians were really the 'Kryvichy', at first in exile in Kaunas and then in Minsk, inspired in some degree by the need to reclaim Polatsk, which was part of the Russian Soviet Republic until 1924.

Western Belarus under Poland

By the mid-1920s, therefore, the main antagonists in the region were Poland and the USSR. Poland had not won all the territory it had once sought, but somewhere between one and three million Belarusians became citizens of interwar Poland.[40] Efforts to revive the Uniate Church, now also called the Greek Catholic Church, had little success. Some thirty parishes and two monasteries were organised, but the authorities in Warsaw obviously favoured the Roman Catholics. (Soviet Belarus meanwhile declared all of its Catholics to be Poles. Many, perhaps half, were deported to Siberia in the early 1940s, followed by 'voluntary' movement to Poland in the late 1940s and 1950s.)[41] The local Orthodox were granted autocephaly under Poland by the patriarch of Constantinople in 1924. Attempts to force them to unite with Rome failed, resulting in an anti-Orthodox campaign in the late 1930s. Protestants, particularly Baptists and Methodists, made some progress in the south-west, and dominated the Belarusian Peasants-Workers Society (BSRH) until measures were taken against it in 1927 and the 'trial of the 56' in 1928.

Warsaw saw the Belarusians as relatively loyal, at least compared to the Ukrainians, though this was in part because they were relatively poorly organised and in the early 1920s Soviet-sponsored radicals organised multiple attacks on local Polish organs of state. In the early 1920s it was still possible to believe that elements of the old multiethnic 'Commonwealth' Poland could be reborn. The Polish Belarusians did not boycott the 1922 elections, in which the Belarusian Central Committee under Anton Lutskevich managed to elect eleven representatives to the Sejm, though the autonomy project they presented to parliament in 1923 was ignored. The Belarusians had a Polonophile paper, *Hramadszki holas* ('Civic Voice'); and leading lights like Lutskevich, Radaslaw Astrowski, former minister of education for the BNR, and Branislaw Tarashkevich, the compiler of the first Belarusian grammar in 1918, founded a Belarusian Polish Society in Vilna in 1924, followed by the Polonophile Central Union in 1930. While Piłsudski was Polish leader (1918–22 and 1926–35), the 'Prometheans' urged support for all the non-Russians in the USSR and, less consistently, some support for multiethnic rights in the new Poland as Shybeka states, 'In 1926 there were several state projects to end the assimilation of Belarusians and turn them into Polish partners by means of widening their cultural rights.'[42]

But Poland had already begun reducing minority rights. The number of Belarusian schools fell from four hundred to twenty in the early 1920s.[43] Political trials against Belarusian leaders began as early as 1923; over 1,300 people were imprisoned.[44] Piłsudski returned to power at the wrong moment for the Belarusians in 1926, with the BNR finally discredited and more and more Belarusians choosing what even Piłsudski saw as the disloyal pro-Soviet option. 'Prometheanism' had gone into reverse; Belarus was more likely to be a channel for Soviet influence further west than the other way around. As Belarusian national identity was weaker than Ukrainian, the Belarusians were more open to Soviet propaganda from the east. Former SRs set up the pro-Soviet Belarusian Revolutionary Organisation in 1922. In 1923 it became the basis of the Communist Party of Western Belarus (CPWB), which enjoyed a brief early 'independent' period in 1924–5; thereafter Minsk and Moscow were in control.[45] Stalin ordered the party's dissolution in 1938. The Belarusian parties were unable to win any seats in the 1935 elections, which were followed by yet another round of arrests and the closure of remaining organisations in 1936–7. There were fewer Belarusians who regretted the end of Polish rule in 1939 then welcomed its start in 1921.

Soviet Belarus

The first really stable Soviet project, after the Bolsheviks' phantom initial attempt and Lit-Bel, was actually the third: the second version of the original BSSR that existed from 1920 to 1924. But, like the first Soviet Republic, the second BSSR initially only existed on paper. Its revival was officially declared on 31 July 1920, when the outcome of the Bolsheviks' military struggle with Poland was still highly uncertain. The Bolsheviks wanted to put pressure on Poland and Lithuania by claiming territories in the west like Hrodna and, perhaps, Vilna. Significantly, therefore, the BSSR's putative western borders were set along 'ethnographic' lines (i.e. using the idea of a Belarusian identity to push as far west as possible), whereas its borders with the Russian and Ukrainian republics were left initially undefined. The government structures of the BSSR were then hastily upgraded in September 1920 to try and sneak an extra Soviet delegation into the Treaty of Riga negotiations.[46]

But the Bolsheviks' more ambitious plans were rebuffed by the Treaty of Riga. Given the combined losses of 1919 (Smolensk and the eastern regions to Russia) and March 1921 in the Treaty of Riga (the Vilna region, Hrodna and Brest to Poland), the new BSSR was clearly too small. In contrast to the first BSSR, as it had briefly existed on paper in 1918, the second coming was tiny, at least in the geographical sense, amounting to a strip of land around Minsk, but not even the whole of the tsarist guberniia of the same name, the western parts of which were now lost to Poland. Even some Bolsheviks like Adolf Ioffe were thinking aloud as early as December 1920 that at least Homel and Mahilew should be shifted back to Belarus 'so that one would get something a little more like a state'.[47]

Ultimately however, the justification for an expanded BSSR, as with its foundation in the first place, was realpolitik. The Bolsheviks still needed a buffer against Poland. They also needed a counterbalance to the new Ukrainian Soviet Republic, some of whose leaders were seen as potentially anti-Russian. As Bolshevik power stabilised, the Piedmont principle in reverse meant that all of the western Soviet republics (Belarus, Ukraine, Moldova and even

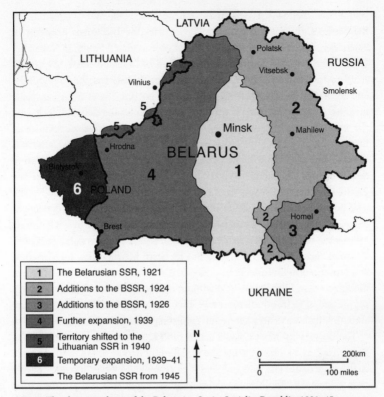

Map 6. The changing shape of the Belarusian Soviet Socialist Republic, 1921–45.

Karelia in the north to target Finland) were used to appeal to ethnic kin in the new central European states – in this case, the Belarusian minority in Poland. So the BSSR existed, but mainly for instrumental reasons. Homel, on the other hand, was originally made part of Russia so as to facilitate control of the rail link to Ukraine. Moreover, only 11 per cent of the Communist leadership were ethnic Belarusians, and the party itself was tiny. It had a mere 1,500 members in 1921, rising to only 6,600 in 1926.[48] Nor was its authority yet secure: in early 1921 there were still 3,500 'bandits' active in the BSSR, including the semi-mythical 'Green Oak'.[49]

Once the decision to expand again was made in the mid-1920s, the Bolsheviks looked to intellectuals to define the new Belarus, though the main centre for the Soviet Belarusian intelligentsia, 'Inbelkult' (Institute of Belarusian Culture), was set up relatively late (the Ukrainian Academy of Sciences was founded before the Bolsheviks consolidated power, in November 1918). Inbelkult was provisionally established in 1922 and converted into an Academy of Sciences in 1929. Most of the Vilna Belarusians, the Polonophiles and former BNR activists were now abroad, but the Soviet Belarusian elite included a significant part of the 'intellectual core of the nation',[50] including the writers Yanka Kupala and Yakub Kolas and a paradoxical mixture of former west-Russians and Nashanivtsy. The most prominent of the latter was the amateur historian Usevalad Ihnatowski, who became 'the theoretician of Soviet Belarusianisation'.[51] In 1927 he was joined by his colleague Vatslaw Lastowski. The most venerable of the veteran west-Russians was Efim Karski. The Bolsheviks even briefly tolerated an attempt to set up an independent Belarusian Orthodox Church. A Belarusian Autocephalous Orthodox Metropolia was set up at a sobor (council) in Minsk in July 1922, a year after a similar move in Soviet Ukraine. But its head, Metropolitan Melkhisedek, was sentenced to three years in prison in 1925 and died in 1931 in Moscow, though a second sobor was held without him in 1927. The tiny Church was suppressed in 1938, but there are still some 'Autocephalous' Belarusians living abroad. Minsk was also a centre for Yiddish-speaking intellectuals.

The Bolsheviks' most notable act in the 1920s was allowing the BSSR to grow. And, as so often during the USSR's foundation phase, borders were changed by diktat and national identities assembled by bureaucrats – in this case, principally Efim Karski, whose language arguments and preference for the 1897 census over that of 1920 trumped the self-declaration of individuals.[52] Therefore, according to Francine Hirsch, 'from the start, the creation of the Belarusian republic was an example of nation-making "from above" – based on ethnographic data, but with limited public support'.[53] There was ambiguity on both sides. In many regions, it proved impossible to distinguish between a 'Belarusian' and a 'Russian' village. (Similar ambiguities existed in western Belarus under Poland.)[54] Zakhar Shybeka claims that 'Pskov gubkom [regional party committee] was not against joining the BSSR'.[55] But mostly the boot was on the other foot: many peasants, particularly in the eastern regions of Vitsebsk and Homel, let alone further afield in Smolensk, were reportedly not keen on becoming Belarusians, especially given the supposed threat of the forcible imposition of the Belarusian language.[56]

Moreover, the lands that were added in two enlargements in 1924 (Polatsk, Mahilew, Vitsebsk) and 1926 (Homel) had been the prewar centres of west-Russism (see pages 69–77). Paradoxically, enlargement to the east eventually 'severely weakened the position of the representatives of Belarusianisation'.[57] The local Bolsheviks in the new districts were reluctant to make such a move in 1924; in 1926 it was the central Moscow leadership that had its doubts.[58] Belarusianisation – the promotion of the Belarusian language and of ethnic Belarusians to senior posts – was decided over the heads of the local party in Minsk as part of the all-Soviet 'nativisation' or *korenizatsiia* campaign decreed in Moscow in June 1924 – i.e. before the eastern territories were added to the BSSR.

But this was later than the equivalent policy launched in Ukraine (1923): Belarusianisation therefore had a more truncated effect, both in time and in regional scope. It did not apply in the western territories then under Poland, which, unlike Galicia, had never been under the Habsburgs, and only took hold in the east at the point when the programme was winding down anyway. The new Soviet Belarusian intellectuals, moreover, were soon purged. According to Per Anders Rudling, the threat from Piłsudski's Poland was also creating something 'close to a popular uprising' in the western borderlands of the BSSR. As a result, 'The purges of the BSSR elites were more thorough than in any other republic, leading to the demise of 90 per cent of the Belarusian intelligentsia. The national mobilization was interrupted. For the next six decades the Soviet Belarusian nation building was carried out from above.'[59] After a show trial was organised against the 'Union for the Liberation of Belarus' in 1930, 108 people were arrested, including Lastowski, the geographer Arkadz Smolich and the chronicler of the west-Russians Aliaksandr Tsvikevich. Ihnatowski committed suicide in 1931.[60] Only twenty out of a cultural elite of 238 survived. During the Great Purges in 1937–41 between 100,000 and 250,000 were murdered and buried in the woods outside Minsk at Kurapaty.[61]

Unlike Soviet Ukraine, there was only limited industrialisation in Belarus in the interwar period. The Soviet leadership regarded the region as too exposed to the threat, first from Poland and then from Germany – quite rightly as it turned out.[62]

Vilna Becomes Belarusian for a Fortnight

Soviet Belarus grew even bigger in 1939 as a result of the Nazi–Soviet Pact. To be precise, the Soviet Union actually made two very different agreements with Germany, the first on 23 August 1939 and the second a month later, on 28 September. In between, the Soviet authorities gave every impression that Vilna would be added to the Belarusian SSR. Vilna 'went Belarusian' for all of two weeks after the arrival of the Red Army in the region on 17 September. The leadership of the Communist Party of Belarus was in town, organising a local Belarusian paper and setting up the organs of power of the BSSR. In fact, the Nazi–Soviet Pact divided Poland by extending the BSSR as far west as Białystok.[63] This brief version of Soviet Belarus was much more multiethnic, with a massive Polish majority, but there were plenty of similar experiments all along the western border of the USSR (Moldova, the Budzhak on the lower Danube, Transcarpathia in 1945), when Stalin grabbed multiethnic territory for geopolitical reasons, but with elements of an ethnic cover story. The eventual borders set for the BSSR after the war were only slightly less artificial than those that were briefly contemplated in September 1939.

This policy was reversed after 28 September, however, and the city and region of Vilna were transferred to Lithuania to sweeten the pill of its forthcoming annexation by the USSR. Vilna (the Slavic spelling), which had been Wilno (the Polish spelling) for eighteen years, which never quite became Vilnia (the Belarusian spelling), now became Vilnius (the Lithuanian spelling). Three further pieces of border territory between Vilna and Minsk – Druskininkai, Dieveniškės and Švenčionys – were shifted from the Belarusian to the Lithuanian republic when the latter 'joined' the USSR in November 1940. The region around Białystok (the Polish spelling; the Belarusian version is Belastok) would also be abandoned after 1941, even though it had hosted the carefully stage-managed congress to 'reunite' Belarusian lands in 1939. In fact, when the Red Army returned, Białystok's fate was still uncertain: the region was not formally relinquished to Poland until 1945. The absence of the Białystok bulge (see map at page 103), along with some lost mixed Polish-Ukrainian districts in Chełm, was in fact the major difference between the western border of the USSR in 1939 and the border settled in 1945.

Imagine, nevertheless, a Belarusian SSR developing after the war with its capital in what had become Vilnia. What would it have been like? There would have been an alternative Soviet Belarusian Academy of Sciences churning out the same kind of capital-centric ethnogenesis myths as in other Soviet Republics. Soviet Belarusian historiography would have given pride of place to the new Litva. Logically, the Polatsk myth would have faded somewhat, while that of the Grand Duchy assumed greater importance. The internal weight of the Belarusian west would also have grown – within the actual postwar Belarus, towns like Hrodna were relatively small and lacked the historical and cultural capital to take the place of Vilnia.

A second possible route to the creation of an even larger Belarusian Soviet Socialist Republic was that East Prussia could have been divided differently after the war, with parts going to the BSSR. The Allies were happy to see Germany punished by the loss of its eastern territories, but the spoils could have been divided in many different ways. This would have profoundly changed the regional dynamics. Quite a lot of territory – the intervening zone could have been given some historical legitimacy as the 'Samogitia' of the Middle Ages – might have gone to Belarus, whose new western territories would have been much more industrialised, which could well have encouraged Soviet planners to continue shifting the balance towards a more developed Belarusian west versus a neglected agricultural east, as was the case in postwar Poland. This counterfactual BSSR would also have had access to the sea and a major port.[64] As it was, the northernmost part of East Prussia, including the city of Memel, now Klaipėda in Lithuania, but not the region of 'Lithuania Minor', home to the Prussian Lithuanians or *Lietuwininkai*, eventually went to Lithuania. The great 'King's city' of Königsberg, home to the philosopher Immanuel Kant, became 'Kaliningrad', a dour and highly militarised postwar rebuild named after a Bolshevik president; and Moscow settled for the anomaly that it would be a noncontiguous part of the Russian Soviet Federative Socialist Republic. As a consequence it has been an even bigger anomaly since 1991, a part of Russia stranded between Poland and Lithuania, and since 2004 surrounded by the European Union. A 'Greater BSSR' that included part of the region instead would have been no more illogical.

On the other hand, realpolitik gifted the Brest region to Belarus. The famous treaty signed by Leon Trotsky in March 1918 is known as the Treaty of Brest-Litovsk, i.e. 'Brest-the-town-in-Litva', but most tsarist ethnographers defined the region as 'Ukrainian', without asking the inhabitants, on the basis of 'objective' language or dialect information. In fact, most locals had only a parochial identity, and many voted for the Ukrainian slate in Polish Sejm elections in the 1920s. In 1939 Nikita Khrushchev, then the head of the Communist Party in Ukraine, wanted to add the region to Ukraine, but the Belarusian Communist leader Pantseliaimon Panamarenka trumped him with the argument that the Moscow–Warsaw–Berlin railway passed through Brest and the whole region should be part of a single 'western front', separate from the 'south-western front' south of the Prypiat marshes in 'Ukraine proper'.[65] 'Stalin didn't want the main east-west railway via Brest being under the control of Ukraine.' As a result, comments Andrei Dynko, 'Panamarenka got Brest, Khrushchev got the marshes' to the south and east,[66] which was a pretty good deal. Brest was also some compensation for Belarus not getting Vilna in 1939. The Nazis, on the other hand, agreed with Khrushchev in 1941, and

included the region in Reichskommissariat Ukraine. In 1945 the Soviet authorities returned it to the Belarusian SSR.

The War

In their desperate situation between the wars, many Belarusians in Poland,
Lithuania or in exile further afield in Warsaw, Berlin or Prague looked to the
new Germany. The Nazis' Department of Foreign Politics (APA) established
contact with at least one would-be Belarusian Führer, Fabiian Akinchyts, in
1933.[67] Akinchyts set up a Belarusian National Socialist Party in 1936, but by
1937 it was 'practically banned' in Poland.[68] In November 1939 the German
Ministry of Internal Affairs helped set up the 'Belarusian Representation'
under Akinchyts. The newspaper *Novy shlakh* ('New Path') was published in
Vilna; an Alliance of Belarusian Students was set up in Germany.

But the right-wing nationalists were not the only Belarusian voice in the
west. There was the Communist Party of Western Belarus until 1938, the
centrist Belarusian National Union, and the conservative Catholic nationalists
led by Father Vintsent Hadlewski. And there were at least three groups of
exiles: Akinchyts tended to operate in Berlin, while other groupuscles,
including Vasil Zakharka, the head of the exile BNR,[69] the Ivan Ermachenka
group in Prague and the faction led by Mikola Shchors in Warsaw all
looked to Nazi Germany. But the Party of Belarusian Nationalists, including
Vatslaw Ivanowski and the writer Yan Stankevich, based in Warsaw, looked
to the Allied Powers,[70] as did the small Belarusian Independence Party set up
in Minsk in July 1942, led by Hadlewski, Usevalad Rodzka and Mikhail
Vitushka.[71]

Belarus was route number one for the Nazi invasion of the USSR in 1941,
but at first it seemed to play little part in the Nazi war plans – other than
negatively, as a home to *Untermenschen* – Slavs and Jews marked for extermi-
nation, slave labour or starvation. Initially, there was no separate Belarusian
administration, only the larger Reichskommissariat Ostland. Belarus was run
from Riga and was only a *Generalbezirk* ('General District'). It was also small,
like the republic of 1921–4. Its eastern border was only just east of Minsk. As
the Nazis carved up Eastern Europe, Vilna went to Lithuania and Brest to
Reichskommissariat Ukraine; Hrodna was made part of a separate Białystok
Bezirk, administered out of East Prussia.

However, the local Nazi chief, Wilhelm Kube, claimed to like the
Belarusians.[72] In fact, he liked one of them, his mistress Alena Mazanik, so
much that she was able to murder him by putting a bomb in his hot-water

bottle in September 1943. His successor, Kurt von Gottberg, more actively sought Belarusian props for his regime, but in truth his policy was dictated by desperation after the German military disasters at Stalingrad in the winter of 1942–3 and in the great tank battle at Kursk in the summer of 1943. Many Nazi leaders believed that terror and propaganda were merely different sides of the same coin (though the one, of course, usually undermined the other), and they set up a considerable propaganda apparatus in Belarus.[73] A local militia of sorts, 'People's Self-Help', had existed since October 1941. The SS helped set up a 'Belarusian Autocephalous Orthodox Church', independent of Moscow, in September 1942. (It reformalised itself at a sobor in Germany in 1948 and was then built up in exile, mainly in the US and Canada. The current head, since 1984, is Metropolitan Iziaslaw.) In June 1943 Kube had set up a Council of Elders under Vatslaw Ivanowski. Also in June 1943 Kube offered to decollectivise agriculture, which might have won hearts and minds in 1941, but was now a meaningless gesture as so much of the countryside was controlled by the Soviet partisans, who would have shot any defectors from the collective farms.

The most important collaborationist structure was the Belarusian Central Council set up in December 1943, with Radaslaw Astrowski (1887–1976) as 'president' (Astrowski had by this time been arrested both by the Poles and the Soviets). This in turn organised a twenty thousand-strong Home Defence Force (BKA) in February 1944 under Ermachenka. But the BKA was mainly used against partisans, on the very eve of their victory. A symbolic All-Belarusian Congress was held in June 1944, but its leaders had to flee west by train before the Red Army arrived six days later. A coda involved nation-alist partisans being parachuted in in late 1944, in an operation known as 'Black Cat', but they did not last long.

The fleeting political structures set up in wartime had a lasting effect, however. In the 1990s moderate Christian Democratic Belarusian politicians were outraged to be stigmatised by new president Aliaksandr Lukashenka as 'Nazis'. The idea that anybody carrying the white-red-white national flag was a Hitler sympathiser was patently absurd, though collaboration had been widespread.[74] In fact, Lukashenka was just overplaying his strongest card. By setting up a quasi-state under the Nazis in 1943–4, Belarusian nationalists discredited themselves more thoroughly than their Ukrainian counterparts. There were plenty of individual Ukrainian police officers and militia members in German service. There were Ukrainian divisions that fought in varying degrees of closeness to the Germans. There were Nazi-backed administrations in cities like Dnipropetrovsk, but there was no Ukrainian Nazi-backed state, only Reichskommisariat Ukraine (Dnipropetrovsk was just outside). The Ukrainians could also place wartime events in a broader historical context. But as the Belarusian People's Republic made only a limited impact in 1918, the Belarusian Central Council of 1944 has received more historical attention. Its 'national' symbols, the Pahonia and the white-red-white flag, were the symbols of local administration and more prominent in 1943–4 than in 1918. A formally organised Belarusian militia operated alongside the Germans. And the state was set up relatively late, not in 1941 (the Organisation of Ukrainian Nationalists made a symbolic declaration of independence in Lviv in June 1941), when naïve illusions about German intentions may have been more common, but in 1943–4, after Stalingrad, with the Red Army about to launch the massive Operation Bagration and the forests full of partisans. One small consolation was that Astrowski's Belarusian Central Council had few followers, so there was less controversy over large-scale collaboration than in the Baltic States.

The positive power of the myth of Soviet victory, on the other hand, runs deep in Belarus.[75] After the war, it was normally estimated that 2.2 million local inhabitants had died. Some 810,000 of these were combatants – not all of whom were originally from Belarus. The first figure represented a staggering quarter of the prewar population.[76] In the 1990s some raised the estimate even higher, to 2.7 million.[77] According to Timothy Snyder, 'by the end of the war, half the population of Belarus had been either killed or moved. This cannot be said of any other European country'.[78] Even on the original lower estimate, no single European country suffered so much. An additional 380,000 Belarusians were forced to serve as *Ostarbeiten* ('East workers', slave labour in Germany). Two hundred and nine out of 270 towns and cities were more or less destroyed, and a total of 1.2 million buildings.[79] One hundred and eighty-five villages that were burnt or destroyed were never rebuilt – though the Soviet decision to evacuate as much industry as possible to the east also contributed to the general decline. Minsk in particular was razed to the ground. It was even thought for a time that it would be easier to rebuild it elsewhere. Modern Minsk is therefore one of the most Soviet of former Soviet cities. Minsk was named a 'hero-city'. Its reconstruction was seen as a genuine achievement, just as the painstaking reconstruction of Warsaw Old Town in the 1950s was genuinely popular. Brest was named a 'hero-fortress' in 1965 for its defence at the sharp end of the German invasion in 1941.

Belarus was also home to the largest Soviet partisan movement in the war (only Titoist Yugoslavia had a similar proportion of inhabitants under informal arms). The partisan movement began as early as late 1941, with twelve thousand already active at the end of the year according to Soviet sources,[80] helped by the local terrain of marshes and forests and by the large number of Red Army soldiers who had been left behind or bypassed by the sheer speed of the initial German advance. But the Belarusian partisan movement was really kickstarted by the opening of the 'Surazh Gates', a 40 km hole in the front between the German Army Group North and Army Group Centre east of Belarus near Vitsebsk, which allowed supplies to flow back into Belarus between February and September 1942. In May 1942 a Central Staff of the Partisan Movement was established in Moscow, and Communist Party structures were reestablished on the ground, underground. At this time, however, the Soviet partisans did not really operate in the former Polish lands west of the 1939 border, owing to Stalin's cynical temporary courtship of the Polish exile government under Władysław Sikorski after the German invasion.[81]

Still, Zakhar Shybeka has argued that 'only at the start of 1943 did the partisan movement receive an organised and mass character', although numbers had grown to fifty thousand by the end of 1942, with the partisans controlling 30 per cent of Belarusian territory.[82] The German rout at Stalingrad gave the movement its biggest fillip – in February 1943 twelve thousand policemen defected almost overnight.[83] Victory at Kursk gave yet another boost, as did the Nazi campaign to seize locals as *Ostarbeitern* that began in October 1942. So 1943 was the peak year of the partisans' success. A total of 153,500 were under arms by the end of the year, and 370,000 by mid-1944, controlling 60 per cent of Belarusian territory.[84] There were even partisan collective farms to feed the forest men, as well as mini-factories for arms repair and up to fifty secret air strips. The partisans conducted a 'railway war' in 1943 that severely disrupted German supply lines: up to ten divisions had to be diverted from the front line to Belarus to keep the situation from getting even worse. One hundred and forty seven thousand joined the Red Army after the Germans were pushed out of Belarus in 1944.[85]

But the sheer number of partisans meant that Belarus suffered uniquely heavily from German reprisals. According to Timothy Snyder, a staggering 350,000 'the vast majority of whom were unarmed civilians', including thirty thousand Jews, were shot in reprisals, which further polarised the situation.[86] Belarus was a playground for notoriously brutal sadists like Kurt von Gottberg, whose unit killed an average of two hundred a day in the winter of 1942–3, and Oskar Dirlewanger, whose 'Poachers' Brigade' specialised in burning barns with the entire village population huddled inside.[87] The partisans themselves had executed 17,431 people who had been formally dubbed 'traitors' by the beginning of 1944, and many more without such labels.[88]

Only in the early 1990s could the 'partisan myth' be challenged.[89] A new generation of historians, and some politicians who wished to rehabilitate the Belarusian Central Council, criticised the partisans for bringing on reprisals and for the Moscow leadership's lack of concern for human losses. The Soviet myth of an 'all-people's struggle' against a collaborationist minority was partially deconstructed. Shybeka has argued, for example, that at earlier periods, and in western Belarus, because the partisans were fewer in number, there were often equal or comparable numbers of Belarusians in the partisan units and serving under the Germans as police.[90]

In 1944 Belarus was also the site of one of the great dramas of the Second World War. 'Operation Bagration' was named after the tsarist general, fatally wounded at the Battle of Borodino, who had harassed Napoleon's troops as they crossed Belarus from west to east in 1812. This time the blow would be dealt in the other direction. The offensive against Army Group Centre did the German Army as much proportionate damage as Stalingrad or Kursk. From June to August 1944 the Germans suffered 670,000 casualties, including 300,000 dead, and the entire eastern front was rent asunder, never to recover. But, as Mark Mazower has bemoaned, it is D-Day that gets all the headlines in the West: 'how many people have even heard of Operation Bagration, the simultaneous Soviet offensive through Belarus, that engaged almost 10 times the number of German divisions, and destroyed three Wehrmacht armies? . . . Yet Bagration, the biggest and most successful surprise attack in history, dwarfed what was happening in Normandy.'[91] As Snyder has commented: 'West Europeans would generally be surprised to learn that Belarus was both the epicentre of European mass killing and base of anti-Nazi partisans who actually contributed to the victory of the Allies . . . .While Lukashenka prefers to ignore the Soviet killing fields in his country, wishing to build a highway over the death pits at Kurapaty, in some respects Lukashenka remembers European history better than his critics.'[92]

The Holocaust

Belarus was also one of the epicentres of the Holocaust.[93] According to the 1897 census in the Russian Empire, there were then 725,000 Jews in the Belarusian guberniias, making up 13.6 per cent of the local population. The number of Jews when the Germans invaded the USSR in 1941 was estimated to be around 900,000 (Belarusian territories were divided between the wars, and Stalin repressed the results of Soviet censuses after 1926, so it is impossible to be precise). Hrodna had 40,000 Jews, Brest had 34,000, Vitsebsk and

Mahilew had 20,000 each, and there were scores of smaller shtetl towns throughout the region. The Minsk ghetto was one of the biggest in Eastern Europe, with an estimated 100,000 Jews crowded in by 1941. Vilna, now Vilnius, the new capital of Lithuania, had 60,000 Jews (54,600 in the 1931 census), using 105 synagogues and prayer houses.

Hardly any survived to the end of the war. Snyder estimates 500,000 Jews were killed on Belarusian territory during the war, including 30,000 in the indiscriminate 'anti-partisan' operations.[94] Yitzhak Arad counts between 556,000 and 582,000, not including Vilnius.[95] The normal estimate by Belarusian historians is that 810,000 Jews were murdered on Belarusian territory during the Holocaust, including 53,000 who were moved there from Western Europe.[96] Part of the problem is what to count as Belarusian territory: the borders of 1991 or some kind of ethnographical Belarus? Should Vilna be included or not? But the sheer numbers killed were not due to Belarusian anti-Semitism or collaboration with the Nazis – although, as noted above, there were plenty of Belarusians in the service of the Nazi police and their own auxiliary formations like the BKA were often put to questionable use. One recent study of the Minsk ghetto by Barbara Epstein argues that Jewish–Belarusian relations were still relatively good.[97] The figures were largely due to the sheer comprehensive ambition of the Nazi killing machine in the east.

And this was despite the illogicality of the Nazis' initial approach, identifying the Jews with the Bolsheviks or the partisans. Synder describes how on the Nazis' first Revolution Day in occupied Minsk on 7 November 1941, they organised a 'carnivalesque death march', dressing up 6,624 local Jews with Soviet flags and making them sing Soviet songs.[98] All were then removed to an old NKVD warehouse at Tuchinka just outside the city and murdered. But the killing fields of Belarus were literally that. As Snyder writes, 'most Jews in the East were killed where they lived'.[99] Ironically, the Nazis used many such NKVD facilities: there was a camp built outside Minsk at Maly Trastsianets, where forty thousand were killed. The Nazis planned to build an incinerator for their own style of death in Mahilew,[100] but on the whole the Jews of Belarus were killed by single bullets or burnt to death in their shtetls. Ironically, this was made easier because, in Snyder's words again, Belarus 'was home to one of Europe's densest populations of Jews, doomed to destruction, but also unusually capable of resistance'.[101] Even the Minsk *Judenrat* that had to answer to the Nazis was subverted by the underground in the winter of 1941–2; thereafter thousands escaped to the forests. 'Yet partisans did not necessarily welcome Jews. Partisan units were meant to defeat the German occupation, not help civilians endure it.'[102]

The partisans saved some thirty thousand Jews.[103] But they also tied down German forces behind the front lines, who often switched to the easy target of mopping up remaining Jews. Increasingly, therefore, the Jews set up their own partisan units. The most famous, thanks first to a book[104] and then a Hollywood screen version of their lives – the 2009 film *Defiance*, starring Daniel Craig – were the Bielski brothers in western Belarus, who took to the forests and saved 1,200 Jews. Some critics, particularly in Poland, accused the film of whitewashing the partisans' role in an attack on the village of Naliboki in 1943 in which 128 were killed,[105] and in collaborating with Soviet units against the Polish underground. But the Bielskis were a symbol of the important fact that the Jews did not go passively to their deaths. There were in any case many other groups: Sholem Zoryn's force even raided the Minsk ghetto to free Jews.

Year Zero: The Partisan Myth

The Belarusians were certainly guilty of downplaying, or even ignoring, their local Jewish tragedy, like the postwar USSR as a whole. After the war, uniquely among Soviet republics, the local Belarusian Communists monopolised the myth of resistance to cement their power as the partisan generation. Michael Urban argues that they grew used to the relative autonomy they enjoyed behind enemy lines, and after 1945 exploited the prestige of their leadership and sacrifice to succeed in 'constructing a particular national myth which situated the ideals of a heroic *national* resistance movement within the larger framework of the heroic sacrifices of the *Soviet* people'.[106] To them, history started almost *ex nihilo* in 1941, whereas party leaders like Petro Shelest in Ukraine sought to bolster their position by reinventing the Cossack myth. 'The new ruling class formed its ideology on the basis of its own Victory, not thinking too deeply about historical events which came "before them".'[107] The partisans possessed a valuable self-confidence in the Soviet context, skilfully spinning the myth that 'our' Communists were good Communists. There were plenty of purges in Belarus, but no single symbolic Purge or other event, like the Holodomor in Ukraine (the Famine of 1932–3), the deportation of the Crimean Tatars or Chechens, or the forcible sedentarisation and consequent starvation of the nomad Kazakhs.

The partisan myth was *the* central trope of postwar Belarusian culture. BelarusFilm, which churned out war epics, was nicknamed 'PartizanFilm'. Even the favourite film of the twenty-first-century opposition intelligentsia, *Mysterium Occupation* (Andrei Kudinenka, 2004), is about the partisans, although most are anti-heroes in this retelling. The great writer Vasyl Bykaw wrote about little else, but wrote about it with élan. Hence the shock of the eventual discovery of the Kurapaty graves in the Gorbachev era – and Lukashenka's subsequent denial, or near-denial, that the massacre ever happened.

The partisans walked tall in postwar Soviet politics. Leaders like Kiryla Mazuraw, first secretary of the Communist Party in Belarus from 1956 to 1965, could use their prestige to exert leverage to win resources. Mazuraw's group even built a career for itself in all-Soviet politics, playing a key role in the removal of Khrushchev in 1964, and benefiting from Brezhnev's subsequent patronage. Mazuraw moved to the Politburo in 1965 as first deputy chairman of the Council of Ministers (i.e. the all-Soviet government) until 1976. Other Belarusians rode on his coattails, like Mikhail Zimianin, who became editor of the Soviet newspaper *Pravda*. Mazuraw was no liberal: he delivered the Soviet ultimatum to Czechoslovakia in 1968. Hundreds and thousands of ordinary Belarusians made solid all-Soviet careers, like Pawel Sukhi of the aircraft designers Sukhoi, or the truck designer Barys Shaposhnik.

But Mazuraw also delivered the bacon. Postwar economic development was extraordinarily rapid, in part because Belarus was an ironic beneficiary of the new Soviet Empire in Eastern Europe. With Soviet satellite states in Poland and East Germany, Soviet planners could now belatedly industrialise the region (the Polish-German threat having been a strong disincentive to local industrialisation in the 1930s). In fact, Belarus was one of the key hubs of the new Comecon system linking the interdependent economies of the Warsaw Pact. Output increased ninefold. In 1955 the population was still overwhelmingly rural, with 80 per cent living in villages or small towns. In 1970 the urban population was still only a third, but by 1985 that figure had surged to 62 per cent. The local Communist Party expanded from a relatively elite group of 119,787 in 1945 to a mass party of 520,283 in 1978, 57 per cent of whose members were recruited from the new 'working class'.[108]

The partisans were all technocrats; most were also only a generation removed from the village. Lukashenka did not come out of nowhere – the entire Soviet Belarusian elite was provincial: Viacheslaw Kebich, the first leader of independent Belarus, was a similarly rough diamond, just higher up the nomenklatura ladder. The lack of local universities had been a key factor handicapping the national movement before 1917. Now they expanded rapidly, but the local intelligentsia was a technical and scientific intelligentsia. The humanitarian sector was weak and had shallow roots.

Ironically the postwar boom ultimately undermined the partisans too. To some in Moscow, they had always been a bit too big for their boots. The rival Brezhnev and Andropov clans began making inroads into Belarus in the 1970s and 1980s. As the economy grew, local power was increasingly concentrated in the hands of the Minsk City Industrial Group, with strong links to Moscow and powerful enough to be given its own acronym, the 'MCIG'.[109]

The Masheraw Myth

Belarus's second great 'partisan' leader was Piotr Masheraw, who headed the local party from 1965 to 1980. Many myths grew up around him, especially after his sudden death in October 1980. Masheraw drove a small car. Masheraw was incorruptible. Masheraw was a war hero, who had led the partisans in his native region of Vitsebsk. Brezhnev wasn't any of these things, despite the best efforts of his biographers to make his service in the Caucasus sound a bit more heroic or at least more military. So there were many reasons why Brezhnev and Masheraw didn't get on. Some of the supposed tensions are invented, however. Some historians and politicians have retrospectively depicted Masheraw as a closet Belarusian nationalist. He wasn't. Under both Mazuraw and Masheraw, Belarusian language schools were closed and 'Russification' proceeded apace, though Masheraw did put up statues to the writers Kupala and Kolas in Minsk (see page 84).

The strongest myth about Masheraw is that he was murdered to get rid of a key rival to the ailing Brezhnev, who died in November 1982. Masheraw was killed in a car accident in October 1980, after a potato truck pulled out in front of him on a local highway, a common way for enemies of the KGB to meet their deaths. Whether this is a mere conspiracy theory or not, the myth of Masheraw as the 'good Communist' and people's servant has been a powerful resource in Belarusian politics. Lukashenka has both depicted himself as Masheraw's natural successor and resented his continuing popularity. There is a website dedicated to Masheraw at http://masherov.na.by (Masherov is the Russian spelling).

After Masheraw's death in 1980, local power was increasingly in the hands of the Minsk City Industrial Group. The latter was noticeably less 'national' than the partisans had been. Its network didn't cover the republic in the same way, and its economic power was 'structured on a Minsk–Moscow axis'.[110] The ties between Moscow and the local Communists remained strong in both the Gorbachev era and even after independence in 1991.

Conclusion

There was little sign that Belarusians were unduly unhappy with their lot when Gorbachev came to power in Moscow in 1985. The economy was doing well enough. Late twentieth-century Belarus had became a much more homogeneous society, though the religious cleavage between what was now the Orthodox majority and the Roman Catholic minority was still there below the surface. The war was a key social turning point. The Holocaust, population exchanges and huge social changes cleared the towns of Jews and Poles, and meant Belarusians dominated urban life for the first time.

But Belarus was also one of the most loyal Soviet republics, not so much because Belarusians were naturally passive, but because they did so well out of postwar reconstruction, which most felt was only just compensation for the horrors of the war.

PART II

Independent Belarus

CHAPTER 7

THE BUILDING BLOCKS OF NATIONAL IDENTITY

The next chapter will deal with the events that took Belarus to unexpected independence when the Soviet Union collapsed in 1991. But what type of society was the Belarus that emerged? A small band of committed nationalists assumed Belarus was a nation-in-hibernation already formed, or that an incomplete nation-building project dating to roughly 1905–30 could now be completed. A larger number were left disoriented by the end of the USSR. Belarus had one advantage: its internal divisions were not as profound as those in states like Georgia or Moldova, which were plunged into civil wars at this time. But any sense of positive identity and external boundaries remained inchoate.

Belarusians

In ethnic terms at least, the new Belarus was more homogeneous than at any time in its history. The 1989 Soviet census recorded a healthy ethnic Belarusian majority of 77.9 per cent. The two traditional minorities were much reduced: the Poles numbered 4.1 per cent and the remnants of the once proud Jewish population stood at 1.1 per cent. Ethnic Russians had increased their numbers steadily in the twentieth century to reach 13.2 per cent. The Ukrainians who lived mainly in the south were still at 2.9 per cent; but the Lithuanian minority represented only 0.1 per cent, as did the Lipka Tatars and Roma. In the next census, in 1999, the number of Belarusians actually went up, to 81.2 per cent. The rise seems to have had nothing to do with either differential migration or death rates, but with a common east Slavic tendency to identify with their local state, ironically in part because east Slavic identities are vague and overlapping. The number of Ukrainians in Ukraine also went up, and minorities everywhere (Belarusians in Russia, Russians in Ukraine) showed a trend towards assimilation, though the number of Russians in Russia was complicated by larger migration levels.

The number of Russians recorded in Belarus in 1999 correspondingly fell to 11.4 per cent, and of Ukrainians to 2.4 per cent. The Polish minority was only slightly smaller, at 3.9 per cent. Jewish out-migration had reduced their numbers to 0.3 per cent.[1] The trend continued through the 2009 census, with the Belarusian population at 83.7 per cent, the Russians at 8.3 per cent and the Poles at 3.1 per cent.[2]

Multiethnicity was not long in the past, however. An ethnographic tourist could visit the Lipka Tatars who live in Iwe, south of Vilnius but just inside the Belarusian border; the Lithuanian villages in the Astravets and Ashmiany regions which were patrolled by German-backed Lithuanian police in the Second World War; the Braslaw region near Vitsebsk which was part of the Swedish kingdom for several decades; and the Old Believer Orthodox communities in the east.[3]

The once thriving Jewish population almost completely disappeared in the Holocaust. The 1989 census recorded only 111,977 remaining Jews, falling to 27,810 in 1999, though this did not stop President Lukashenka from reviving old stereotypes, describing Babruisk near Mahilew as a Jewish 'pigsty' on a visit in 2007. 'You know how Jews treat the place where they're living. Look at Israel,' he bizarrely proclaimed.[4] According to the 1999 census, Babruisk's population of 250,000 included only 4,000 Jews.

The Poles were no longer the ruling class, but had not really disappeared either. They remained heavily concentrated in the western areas of Hrodna and Brest, with scattered numbers in the Vitsebsk and Minsk regions (see pages 38 and 97). The Second World War had sharply reduced their numbers, but population flight and deportation were not as brutal as in neighbouring Ukraine in 1944–6. Many locals still had overlapping religious, ethnic, linguistic and regional identities, and their ultimate loyalty was up for grabs. The Belarusian Communists were happy to see the back of the Polish intelligentsia, but thought the less definitively Polish local peasants would end up on their side. On the other hand, many non-Poles sought to register as Poles, just to get away from the USSR. A total of 232,200 eventually went west, although 520,500 had wanted to go. Smaller numbers, some 36,000 in all, nearly all ethnic Belarusians, travelled east from Białystok to the BSSR, although this was only 30 per cent of the total originally planned.[5]

The Belarusian Language

The Belarusians may be a majority, but Russian is the language you would normally hear in Belarus. On the other hand, Belarus is not split more or less in two by the language question like Ukraine: almost everybody speaks Russian. Knowledge of Belarusian is reasonably high, but its everyday use is restricted.

In 1989, 80.2 per cent of ethnic Belarusians, or 66 per cent of the whole population, said that Belarusian was their 'native tongue'. In 1999 the figures were actually higher: 85.6 per cent of Belarusians claimed their titular language was their native tongue, which meant 74.5 per cent for the population as a whole.[6] But in 2009 the first figure dropped sharply to 60.8 per cent, meaning only 53.2 per cent for the population as a whole.[7] The concept of 'native tongue' is well known to overlap with that of ethnicity, defining the language that is 'native' or ancestral to the group in question, regardless of whether people actually speak it. In Belarus the 'native tongue' is still often referred to by the premodern label of *prosta mova* – the 'simple tongue', which is indeed 'ours' but is from the village, and is associated with low, not high, culture.

The 1999 census added a second question: 'What language do you normally speak at home?' This time a majority of Belarusians cited Russian, 58.6 per cent, but 41.3 per cent still claimed it was Belarusian. The 'home language' figure for the population as a whole was 62.8 per cent Russian and 36.7 per cent Belarusian. The situation deteriorated further by 2009, when only 21.8 per cent of Belarusians said they normally spoke Belarusian at home, and only 30 per cent of the population as a whole.[8] Overall, therefore, there is a clear paradox: more people identify as 'Belarusian' than speak the language.

One reason is that, apart from a brief rise in the early 1990s, the number of Belarusian schools has been declining since the end of the Soviet 'Belarusianisation' drive of the 1920s and early 1930s. Belarusian was used in 83 per cent of four-year primary schools in 1927 and 60 per cent of seven-year schools.[9] But in the late Soviet era the figure was less than a quarter. In 1989 only 22 per cent of year-one schoolchildren studied in Belarusian-language classes. After briefly rising to 76 per cent under Kebich in 1993, the figure was back down to 23.3 per cent in 2006.[10] Looked at in this way, the decline of Belarusian in the Lukashenka era only restored the status quo of the late Soviet era, but of course dashed the hopes of nationalists that the clock could be turned back to the 1920s. Less than 15 per cent of the total number of books printed in Belarus today are in Belarusian.[11]

The 'home language' question may still have a subtext of ethnic loyalty. Other surveys show that less than a quarter of the population know Belarusian well, which, given the data on schooling, seems logical, if depressing for Belarusian nationalists.[12] A poll from 2009 shows that the number of regular Belarusian-speakers is less than 8 per cent, even in domestic situations.[13] Another survey in 2004 showed that only 13.7 per cent use Belarusian as the primary means of communication at home, compared to 73.6 per cent for Russian, 6.8 per cent for both and 4.7 per cent for other languages.[14]

A further complication is the split between what are effectively *three* versions of the Belarusian language: 'Tarashkevitsa', 'Narkamawka' and 'Trasianka'. The first version of literary Belarusian is named after the linguist Branislaw Tarashkevich (1892–1938). The dialectical line in Belarus runs from north-east to south-west. Tarashkevich was born in a village near Vilna and politically was a 'Polonophile' (see page 101), but his dream was a united ethnographic territory based on Karski's maps. When Tarashkevich produced his pioneering grammar in Vilna in 1918 he therefore based his language project on the dialects of the south-west. But by the mid-1920s these territories were in Poland, and cut off from the east. Not that the Polish authorities approved of Tarashkevich – they twice arrested him as a spy, in 1927 and 1931.

The Soviet Belarusian authorities and the intellectuals gathered at Inbelkult had their own views on the language issue, but the purge of 'nationalist' sympathisers from the local Communist Party leadership in 1930 meant that the new authorities wanted Belarusian to be closer to Russian. In 1933 they formalised Narkamawka (a nickname based on the abbreviation for 'People's Commissariat'), this time based on the dialects of the north-west and south-east. Critics called the changes 'Russification', most notably the Polonophile West Belarusian linguist Yan Stankevich (1891–1976),[15] who began pressing unsuccessfully for his approved version of Belarusian to be called the 'Great Litowska' language instead – and for a revived use of the Roman alphabet. Further changes facilitating the transfer to Russian were made by the Soviet authorities in 1959.

The 1989 law on languages made Belarusian the state language and Russian the 'language of inter-ethnic communication', but did not define which version was to be used. There was some limited success in pushing Tarashkevitsa in the early 1990s, but it was rapidly reversed once Lukashenka became president in 1994. Following a referendum in 1995, Russian was made a second state language. In 1998 amendments to the language law stipulated that state documents should be in Belarusian or Russian – which normally meant Russian, although there was some sign of revival in Lukashenka's third term (see page 226). Changes to orthography were enforced in 2006.

'Trasianka' (literally: low-quality hay, diluted with straw), on the other hand, is a mixture of Belarusian and Russian involving an extensive use of Russian words and forms on an imperfectly Belarusian grammatical base. It is also known as 'Meshanka' (mixture). It tends to be seen in pejorative terms as a lower-class pidgin or creole language form used mainly in the countryside or by those who have recently left the countryside who wish to upgrade from *prosta mova* to a language of 'culture'. In the past, this meant Polish or Russian; nowadays it suggests Russian in Belarus itself, though it would still mean Polish in Białystok. There are some regional variations in Trasianka, but because of the overwhelming influence of Russian not as many as with its equivalent, Surzhyk, in Ukraine. Its use is widespread enough for some optimists to consider it could be a means for consolidating a more synthetic but at least formally non-Russian version of Belarusian identity (see page 205).[16]

Belarus: Regions

Belarus is not as sharply divided into east and west as Ukraine,[17] where the river Dnieper, the historical limit of the Commonwealth in the south-east, has often seemed to mark a cultural or even civilisational divide. In Ukraine there is also a strong regional divide between Galicia and the rest of Ukraine, creating different political cultures in the former Habsburg and Romanov lands.

Since Lukashenka came to power in 1994, his 'policy has been very effective in homogenising the country'.[18] Moreover, without much privatisation to date, Belarus does not yet have the same regionally based economic 'clans' as Ukraine. There are notable regional economic differences, however. Mazyr in the south and Navapolatsk in the north are home to Belarus's two giant oil refineries, which are vital contributors to the state budget and their managers' pockets. Rechytsa in the south-east has a small oilfield. Salihorsk, south of Minsk, produces 30 per cent of global potash. Zhlobin, near Homel, is home to Belarus's biggest metallurgy plant. In the west at Hrodna is the giant Azot fertiliser plant. It makes exotic fertilisers from gas, so is dependent on Russian supplies. Azot is the only major industrial employer in western Belarus. Out of necessity, therefore, and because of its geographical closeness to the newly expanded EU in Poland and Lithuania, there has been more development of small enterprises, a trading and service sector, in western Belarus.

But historical differences are still strong and subnational identities are still important. The 1999 census allowed Belarusians to describe themselves as Belarusians, Breschuks (from Brest), Litvins (various spellings), Litvaks, Pinchuks, Poleshuks (from Polessia) and Tuteishiya (locals). The east–west axis is still the main line of difference. One possible dividing line is sometimes argued to be a split between two nations: the 'Black Rus' of the north-west and parts of the west, and the 'White Rus' of the east and centre – a reinvented version of the historical divide between 'Litva' and 'Belarus'. There is even a Litvin revival movement. In May 2000 it solemnly passed an 'Act of Proclamation of the Revival of the Litvin Nation' (see www.litvania.org), which it argues was formed from the union of the Kryvichy and the Baltic Yatvingian tribe with the 'Liutichi', who were Polabian Slavs, driven east from their original homeland on the river Elbe by German tribes between the eleventh and thirteenth centuries AD (with, apparently, some splitting off to move south to what is now Bohemia).

Another theory is that the locals are not Slavs converted by the Union of Brest in 1596, but the remnants of the local Baltic population who gradually assimilated linguistically but kept the Catholicism they adopted in 1387. (This theory, it should be noted, is different from the earlier theory of Slavic-Baltic 'ethnogenesis' in the first millennium AD – see pages 24–7.) The area also experienced a much stronger Germanic influence from the Teutonic strongholds of Königsberg, Klaipėda (Memel) and Riga, though the it became more solidly Catholic in the seventeenth century, when the greater Catholic region included the four districts of Vilna, Troki, Minsk and Novahrudak.

Vilna's Dead Star: The North-West

Regardless of these theories, more recent historical effects are stronger. The core region for the would-be Nashanivtsy version of Belarusian identity is neither 'Black Rus' as a whole nor the strict geographic west, as with Galicia in Ukraine, but the north-west. According to one modern scholar, 'Contrary to the received view of Western Belarus as the center of opposition at the level of small towns and rural areas, we have grounds to assert that this centre is located more northward, along the Lithuanian border, not the Polish one', and comprises roughly the 'triangle whose corners are Minsk, Lida and Braslaw. Formerly, this area was almost entirely part of the historic Vilna province.'[19] As argued here in Chapter 5, if Lviv is the historical epicentre of Ukrainian nationalism, then in Belarus it was supposed to be Vilna. It was in the historical Vilna province that modern Belarusian nationalism was born around the turn of the twentieth century. But Vilna became Vilnius and was lost to Lithuania, though Chapter 6 speculated on what a Belarus with its capital in Vilna (in Belarusian, Vilnia) might have been like. Without it, the nearest equivalent would be Smarhon, the birthplace of Bahushevich. But Smarhon is a tiny provincial town. It was only joined to Russia in 1793, but for most of the nineteenth century was the private property of the Radziwiłł family. Three-quarters of the population of no more than ten thousand were Jewish in 1897.

The historical effect of nationalist agitation emanating from Vilna was therefore weak. It was also truncated and relatively small. Ironically, the signal is still being received in the minority part of the old Vilna guberniia that became part of independent Belerus after 1945, but the source of the signal is gone.

The West: 'Church Poles'

Hrodna (Grodno in Russian and Polish) is one of the most evocative remnants of the old Commonwealth, whose parliaments often sat in the city where the last king, Stanisław August Poniatowski, abdicated in the New Castle in 1795. It has some of the best surviving examples of Baroque architecture in Belarus, but its traditionally multiethnic population (even some Lithuanians have claimed the city which they call Gardinas as their own at various times) has been reduced to Belarusians and Poles. Hrodna also has a good claim to be considered the religious capital of Belarus (see below).

Some Belarusian activists assert that many or most of the local ethnic Poles are really *Kastselnyja paliaki*, so-called 'Church Poles' (the Polish for 'church' is *kostol*, the eastern Slavic is *tserkva*). That is, they are Roman Catholics who speak Polish in church, but they are 'really' Belarusian. There is some supporting evidence for this stereotype from census data, according to which only 16.5 per cent of the 396,000 Poles in Belarus (3.9 per cent of the total population in 1999) gave their home language as Polish, while 57.6 per cent cited Belarusian. In fact, this was a higher figure than for ethnic Belarusians, only 41.3 per cent of whom gave Belarusian as their home language.[20]

The Far West

There were 48,700 Belarusians still living in Poland in 2002, according to the Polish census of that year. The vast majority of these, 46,400, lived in the border regions of Białystok and Podlasie (Padliashsha in Belarusian).

Belarusian activists, as activists usually do, claim the real figure is much higher, more like 150,000 or 200,000. Białystok was part of Soviet Belarus in 1939–41. In fact, it was the location for the Communist-organised 'People's Congress of Belarus' which proclaimed all-Belarusian unity in 1939. Many locals call themselves *padlashy* or *litsviny* and speak a Polish-Belarusian version of Trasianka, which one activist, Jan Maksimiuk, proposes could be a new language called *Svoja* (the possessive 'ours' or 'yours', depending on who's talking).[21] Just to make things even more complicated, there is a rival movement asserting the Ukrainian identity of the population and region.

Historical Belarus never really had a 'Piedmont' – a safe haven for developing the 'national idea' while the rest of Belarus was controlled by unfriendly forces. But Białystok may be becoming one. Under a much more liberal Poland which still has an interest in the historical *kresy* and in the remaining diaspora in the east, Białystok has become a leading centre of Belarusian studies. It has also provided shelter for activists fleeing Lukashenka's Belarus. But, to state the obvious once more, the Belarusian population of Białystok is relatively small, probably too small a tail to wag the dog of Lukashenka's Belarus.

The South-West: After Ruthenia

The south-west region around Brest is variously known as Polessia, Polissia or Podelesia. It is not clear, however, whether the southern border of the region is defined by the limits of the Prypiat river basin and the surrounding marsh and forest, or by language, or by the political border created between Poland and Litva in 1569. The remoteness of the area makes it an ethnographic museum. It is one of the candidates in the long-running dispute among historians, archaeologists and linguists about the birthplace of all the original Slavs: though, paradoxically or not, it still retains a highly local identity. Activists like Mikola Sheliahovich have argued that the locals are a separate West Polessian 'nation', called the Poleshuks, Poleszuks (Polish), Polishchuks, or Pinchuks.[22]

Polessia was partly settled by the Derevliany tribe and then part of the principality of Pinsk-Turaw. Then, in the later Middle Ages, it was influenced by Volhynia and its Orthodox Brotherhoods to the south, whereas the Orthodox tradition in eastern Belarus was always linked to Russia. The local dialect is strongly influenced by Ukrainian, that is, by Ukrainian dialect rather than standard literary Ukrainian. Ukrainians, Belarusians and Poles disputed the region after 1917. The Poles won, but during the interwar period the Baptist and Methodist Churches gained in popularity. The previously relatively numerous local Polish population (14 per cent) was almost all expelled or fled west in 1944–6, leading to the decline of the Roman Catholic Church (and its churches). The relative closeness of the Orthodox Church to the Soviet regime (its periodically militant atheism not here being a contradiction) in the postwar period has led to the renewed growth of evangelical Protestantism since 1991, particularly the Pentecostal Baptists centred around the town of Stolin.

The Brest region has been traded back and forth between Belarus and Ukraine, most recently in 1939–45 (see pages 107–8). Soviet rule also meant a wild scheme to drain the marshes in 1952. The 'amelioration' of the wetlands from the 1960s onwards created some new farmland in the short run, but also turned much of the region into salt fields. 'Further west' does not necessarily mean 'more liberal' in Belarusian politics. The Brest region has backed Lukashenka heavily in all elections, giving him his second highest score in 1994. One possible reason is the region's historical anti-Catholicism (Shushkevich and Pazniak were both Catholic candidates in 1994), although another is its relative backwardness.

Homel and Mazyr in the south-east, on the other hand, were the key areas where medieval Cossack culture extended up the river Dnieper into what is now Belarus. The Cossack leader Bohdan Khmelnytskyi attempted to add them to his 'Hetmanate' state in the 1650s (see pages 43–4). Slutsk and Mahilew were also occupied during the earlier Nalyvaiko rebellion in 1594–6. Since these unsuccessful attempts, all but residual linguistic influences have faded away. The characteristically Russian form of communal land ownership, the *obshchina*, was more common in Homel and the upper Dnieper region. Unfortunate geography meant the region was the worst hit by the fallout from the Chernobyl plant in northern Ukraine in 1986.

The Eastern 'Borderlands'

The influence of Belarus's other east Slavic neighbour is of course most marked in the east. One academic study produced by R.A. Grigor'eva and M. Yu. Martynova in 2005 argued that the 'Belarusian-Russian Borderland' – defined as the three oblasts of Vitsebsk, Mahilew and Homel on the Belarusian side, and the corresponding trio of Pskov, Smolensk and Briansk on the Russian side – was a transitional zone, 'a specific regional culture with its local variants' that transcended vague ethnic boundaries.[23] Many locals have traditionally identified themselves as 'locals' (*tuteishiya*), or claimed 'Orthodox' as a religious rather than a national identity, or had no clear idea of their identity.

Statisticians in Novozybsk uezd (district) in 1917 counted 11 per cent who were Belarusians and 55 per cent of 'unknown nationality'. 'Almost all' the inhabitants of Starodub (to the south-east) and Klintsy (now in Briansk) were unable to specify a nationality.[24] 'Inter-marriage' is frequent, and often enough not even recognised as such. According to the 1999 census, 1.36 million lived in mixed Belarusian-Russian families.[25]

A first reason for this ethnic blurring is the uncertain history of the Kryvichy culture in the region – uncertain both in its territorial extent and in its cultural legacy. Second, the border between the Grand Duchy and Muscovy cut through the region from the fourteenth century and was constantly changing. Unlike other additions to the Russian Empire that occurred as single events, Russia/Muscovy and the Grand Duchy/Commonwealth swapped control over different regions at different times. Polatsk was under Muscovy from 1563 to 1578. Smolensk was under the Grand Duchy from 1404, and under Muscovy from 1522, until it was ceded by the Truce of Deulino in 1618. It was the unobtained object sought by Moscow in the 'Smolensk War' in 1632–4, before finally ending up in Russia again in 1654. Only with the Treaty of Andrusovo in 1667 did the Commonwealth finally renounce its claim. In 1862 the Russian ethnographer Mikhail Tsebrikov still considered half the local inhabitants to be Belarusian.[26] The folklorist Sergei Maksimov 'referred to Smolensk as the capital of Belorussia'.[27] The first congress of the Communist Party (Bolshevik) of Belarus in December 1918 briefly and ineffectively awarded Smolensk to Belarus. On the other hand, others have proposed shifting the ethnic border westwards, to the Russians' advantage. In 1864 the notorious Mikhail Muraviev, governor-general of the North-western Territory (see page 72), proposed shifting several districts (uezdy) from Mahilew and Vitsebsk to the more properly 'Great Russian' guberniias.[28]

Third, there was frequent population interchange in both directions, particularly, for example, during the war of 1654–67.[29] After the Partitions of Poland, the 'borderlands' were all under the Romanov state, but remained a backwater until 1917, and often enough beyond. In the 1920s Soviet nationality policy planners made several attempts to settle a border between the Belarusian and Russian republics on the basis of ethnicity (see pages 104–5), but in effect things worked the other way round. The boundary-makers' decisions created or firmed up identities that had previously been only vague, although surveys done in the region in the 1950s and 1960s still found it hard to locate clear boundary markers.[30] According to Grigor'eva and Martynova, 'on the territory of Belarus the majority of inhabitants *became* Belarusian, and in Russia [became] Russian. However this was not always based on the ethno-cultural differences of Russians and Belarusians.' Rather, 'one of the most important factors exercising an influence on the ethnocultural map of the borderland territories was changes in administrative-territorial borders'.[31]

In theory this cut both ways. The eastern half of Belarus is clearly marked by its longer and more intimate Russian influence. Some Belarusian national-ists, on the other hand, claim that large areas of Smolensk, Briansk and Pskov are 'really' Belarusian. They also like to point out that in the early fifteenth century the border between the Grand Duchy and Muscovy was so far to the east of Smolensk that it was 650 km from Vilna and only 120 km from Moscow.[32] According to the 1897 census, there were almost 100,000 Belarusians in the Smolensk guberniia, mainly living in the Krasnin district, and in Surazh in Chernihiv (now Ukraine). In the three districts that went to Pskov in Russia in 1924 (Nevelsk, Velizh and Sebezh) there were some 220,000 Belarusians, or 80 per cent of the population. According to the 1926 census, there were suddenly only 30,600, though the Pskov statistical bureau had calculated 135,500 only months before the census, indicating 'the compli-cated ethnocultural and linguistic situation [that still prevailed] in the border-land'.[33] On this type of reasoning, the composer Glinka, who was born near Smolensk, was really a Belarusian.

Eastern Belarus still has some scattered Old Believer communities, dating from the times of Tsar Aleksei Mikhailovich (1645–76), when the persecuted adherents of the old faith could find sanctuary by fleeing across the then border of the Commonwealth. Most are now assimilated, but there are notable communities in Vitsebsk and at Vetka, near Homel.

Faith

Despite Lukashenka projecting the image of Belarus as monolithically Orthodox, the country has in fact always been multiconfessional. No one Church has ever dominated. In fact, on one interpretation, the divide between Catholic and Orthodox has been a problem for every state on Belarusian terri-tory since the time of the Grand Duchy.[34] At the time of Polatsk, the main religious difference was between the Orthodox Rus and the pagan Balts, before the Lithuanians adopted Roman Catholic Christianity in 1386. In the fifteenth century there were hopes that Roman Catholicism might spread on the basis of the Florentine Union. After 1596 the Uniate Church gradually overcame Orthodoxy in what is now Belarus. The suppression of the Uniates in 1839 did not prevent the struggle between residual Roman Catholicism and

Orthodoxy defining Belarusian identity until well into the twentieth century, and arguably still today. Protestantism has already flared twice, in the sixteenth century and in interwar Poland, with yet another revival in the present day.

According to official statistics, as of 2009 there were 1,498 registered Orthodox parishes in Belarus, with 32 groups of Old Believers, 18 of which were in the Vitsebsk region. Roman Catholic communities numbered 470, no fewer than 170 of which were in Hrodna, but Uniates or Greek Catholic communities numbered only 13. Protestant communities were the fastest-growing, with 996, including 501 Evangelical and 271 Baptist. Only 46 Jewish communities were recorded, and 24 Muslim.[35] More general estimates are that around 80 per cent of 'believers' are Orthodox and 15 per cent Catholic (only 3.9 per cent of the population are Polish), with only 2 per cent Protestant, despite the fact that the latter are growing controversially quickly. In fact, Aleh Latyshonak's somewhat alarmist view is that 'in Belarus *la revanche de Dieu* is of a Protestant rather than an Orthodox character'.[36] Even that in the not-too-distant future the number of adherents of Western Churches (Catholic and Protestant) might outnumber those of the East (Orthodox) – or even that the Protestant Churches might make it on their own.[37]

One rarely noticed fact is that *all* the main Churches are strongest in western Belarus, including the Orthodox, owing to the Soviet imposition of atheism in eastern and central Belarus in the 1930s, when the western territories were part of Poland. In 1939 there were fewer than 10 active churches in the BSSR, but there were 700 Orthodox churches in Polish western Belarus, and more than 200 Catholic and almost 100 Protestant communities.[38] (Though, of course, religious repression by the Soviet Belarusian authorities in the west was strong after the war.) Even the apparently dominant modern-day Orthodox Church suffers from both a weak and corrupt hierarchy and weak *klir* (parish clergy). Until recently, there was only one Orthodox monastery, at Zhyrovitski, near Hrodna, where a seminary was added in 1989. The Catholic Church meanwhile is reliant on foreign-born, usually Polish, priests – there was no Catholic monastery in Belarus after 1820 until one was opened in Hrodna in 1989. In 2007 the authorities began a campaign against 'foreign priests'.

The Roman Catholic Church divides Belarus into three. The main episcopate is based at Hrodna; Brest serves the south-west; and a Minsk-Mahilew episcopate covers the east. Hrodna is dominated by 'traditional Polish' religion, but the Belarusian language has begun to be used in recent years. Communities in Brest are relatively small. Only in Minsk, where the

Church is relatively weak, does it come under the influence of Belarusian national-democrats.

The Orthodox Church also has regional differences. In 1995 Archbishop Maksim of Mahilew, the only region not to succumb to the Uniates in the eighteenth century, tried to found a militantly pro-Russian Orthodox party, but without success as President Lukashenka doesn't like political parties in general. In western Belarus, however, the Orthodox Church must still compete for souls. The Orthodox Church has grown since the late 1980s, but not at the same rate as the various branches of the Orthodox Church (one loyal to Kiev, one to Moscow and one 'autocephalous', i.e. independent) in Ukraine. Many Orthodox feel 'surrounded' by the Roman Catholic revival in north-western Belarus, in Poland, in Galicia in western Ukraine, in Lithuania and in Latgallian Latvia. And the Protestants are strong in the south-west.

None of three main Churches is therefore a traditional carrier of the 'Belarusian idea'. The Orthodox have a strong pan-Russian wing, the Roman Catholics a Polish core, and the Protestants are less interested in such secular affairs. Many Protestant activists backed the main opposition candidate Aliaksandr Milinkevich in 2006, but because they thought his was a 'values-based campaign'. Belarus has two émigré Churches, which use the vernacular and support the 'national idea', but neither has found it easy to return since 1991. With both the modern Greek Catholic Church and the Belarusian Autocephalous Orthodox Church (BAOC), one often gets the impression of the cart being put before the horse. They were founded by small circles of nationalists to promote their version of the national idea, and have remained small. Metropolitan Iziaslaw was elected head of the BAOC in Manchester, England in 1984.

Lukashenka claims to be that interesting combination of things, an 'Orthodox atheist'. His regime has exploited both Soviet nostalgia and its connections to the Orthodox Church. According to the 2002 law on religion, the Orthodox Church plays 'the defining role in the state traditions of the Belarusian people',[39] something that government officials are obliged to take into account in their dealings with other religious organisations. In its 2003 concordat-style cooperation agreement, the Belarusian state also guaranteed the Orthodox Church 'the right of ecclesiastical jurisdiction on its canonical territory' and endorsed its collaboration with a broad range of government ministries.[40] Church and state are not truly separate, as evidenced by the existence of the Committee of Religious and Nationalities Affairs of the Council of Ministers. This has, for example, largely prevented the official return from exile of the BAOC. In 1989 Belarus became an exarchate of the Russian Orthodox Church and gained some formal autonomy in 2000, but is essentially still part of the Russian Church.

Metropolitan Filaret, the head of the local church stood in the 2009 election for the sixteenth 'Patriarch of Moscow and all Rus'. He won sixteen votes in the first round and backed the eventual winner, Kirill of Smolensk, in the run-off.

Lukashenka briefly embraced the myth of Belarus as the most Orthodox of lands, the opposite of Uniate-land (see Chapter 4), and even the idea that Minsk was the 'fourth Rome' (see pages 203–4). But the chameleonic president swung to the idea of Belarus as a religious crossroads in 2009 when he thought he could suddenly gain an advantage by posing as an intermediary between the new pope and the new Russian patriarch, now declaring that 'Belarus is a sacred place because there are no disagreements here between Catholics and Orthodox'.[41] But this conversion is only skin-deep, since picking on the Polish minority still makes political sense for Lukashenka.

Name

What is Belarus? Where does it begin? And where does it end? The proper name should be some help in answering these questions.[42] Previous versions of would-be Belarusians, the Kryvichy and the Litvins, didn't really know. The former was a relatively narrow tribal label, the latter a relatively broad civic-political identity. The first attempts at a proper definition were made in the late nineteenth and early twentieth centuries by linguists and ethnographers like Aliaksandr Ryttykh and Efim Karski. But theirs was always an incomplete and to most seemingly uncompletable project, allowing strange mutations like Vatslav Lastowski's 'Kryvichism' in the 1920s.

The Belarusian idea has undergone further mutations in more recent years. Soviet Belarusianism (or Belo-Russianism) survived long after 1991 and is still the fundament of identity for many. A revived version of the Nashanivtsy project supported by the 'Belarusian Popular Front' (see next chapter) flourished briefly in the early 1990s, but since the election of Aliaksandr Lukashenka as president in 1994 it has lacked a secure anchor – though one strain grew more extreme in noisy exile. A younger generation began reconciling themselves to the reality of Lukashenka's Belarus, especially after his rule extended into a third term (2006–10). Lukashenka himself was initially more of an anti-ideological populist than a nation-builder. He flirted with all-Russian nationalism in the late Yeltsin era, and with the idea of Belarus as the superior embodiment of that idea in the early Putin era; but with Putin consolidating his own version of Russian messianism, Lukashenka switched to concentrate on cultivating his own backyard. Several commentators have called the resulting ideological grab-bag 'creolic nationalism'.

To many Belarusians, 'Bela' (white) means freedom, in the original historical sense of independence from both Tatars and Lithuanians (see page 19). The nineteenth-century writer Frantsishak Bahusevich argued it had a more specific related meaning, which was that the Belarusians themselves had never oppressed anyone else. But these myths of national character don't really sit with the reality that the term has been applied variably over the years and to many different territories.

The historian Vatslaw Lastowski argued in the 1920s that the national place name was derived from the locally popular pagan god Bielboh ('White God'), the father of all the other local gods. Others have said more or less the opposite. 'White Rus' represented the first Christian lands in the region, while 'Black Rus' stayed pagan longer, under the influence of the pagan Yatvingians. One slightly boring possibility is that 'Belarus' is derived from the Turkic for 'west' – which makes some sense from the Turks' geographical point of view.

In the fourteenth and fifteenth centuries, 'White Rus' often meant the triangle of Polatsk, Pskov and Novgorod – another alternative Belarus further to the north of present-day borders, before the fall of Novgorod to Moscow in 1471–8. The name 'Belarus' was first used with its modern meaning by Poles in the sixteenth century, and by 'the second half of the seventeenth century "White Rus" in many sources already had a more exact geographical localisation'.[43] Salomon Rysinski, the 'first Belarusian' (see page 33), followed their lead. Many foreigners referred to Lithuanian Rus as 'Rutheni Albi' or 'Alba Ruscia'. But this was still a geographical term. In the 1588 Lithuanian Statute the border between 'Litva' and 'Rus' ran east of Minsk, and this distinction between White and Black Rus (the western part of Lithuanian Rus) held until the eighteenth century, even the nineteenth.

One explanation is that

having conquered Belarus, the Muscovites realized that it was not in their favour to call Belarusians the 'Litsviny' (i.e. their second original name, along with the 'Kryvichy' one) as it would always remind our people about the times when our ancestors happened to constantly fight against Moscow. Therefore, the Muscovites applied the term of 'Belarusians' to our people while the name of 'Litsviny' was attributed to the Lithuanians; at the same time the propaganda publications tried to propagate the idea that the Grand Duchy of Litwa was [a] Lithuanian state, i.e. it was a foreign country that did not have any close ties with Moscow.[44]

Myths of Identity

Whatever their origin, national names are never neutral. They encode certain ways of thinking about geography, history and identity. Belarus is no exception, though there is a broad range of myths associated with its national geography.

Nowhere land. One of the 'Nashanivtsy' was also a geographer, Arkadz Smolich (1891–1938).[45] In his view, Belarus had no natural or naturally notable borders. It is also generally flat, with no great mountain ranges. A third of the country is still uniform forest. The only territory of special note, he thought, was Polessia – the marshes in the south-west – which has its own distinct history. Belarus is also landlocked. Despite sitting atop three great rivers – the Dzvina, Neman and Dnieper – it never managed to reach the sea, though Polatsk once thought it could; its city symbol is a ship on the open sea. It may be several hundred kilometres from the Baltic, but Polatsk's one-time power came from its position in the Baltic hinterland before the rise of Riga, when it did actually control vassal city-states downstream on the Dzvina. Had Polatsk consolidated this position, it is possible to imagine the three east Slavic nations developing separately around 'their' river systems: Belarus closer to the Baltic Sea and Scandinavia; Ukraine on the Dnieper flowing south; and Russia on the Volga, via the rivers Moskva and Oka. There might then have been a more even contest for control of Novgorod and its links to the Gulf of Finland. Expansion to the river Neman, which also flows into the Baltic Sea via the towns of Navahrudak and Hrodna, failed to give Belarus another out-route. In any case, 'ethnographic' Belarus is now spread too far and too wide to concentrate just on the Baltic.

The quiet land. According to the Russophile politician Valer Fralow, upland Belarus also has its own 'rough history', with Swedes, Germans, Poles and Russians crisscrossing its territory. The Belarusians "hid in potato plants" and tried to survive during these periods.'[46] Belarus is therefore the quiet nation: 'We Belarusians are peaceful people' is the first line of the national anthem (the words were finally fixed in 2002). Unlike the Russians, who have constantly spread across Eurasia, the Belarusians have largely stayed put.[47] Unlike the Ukrainians, they have not been overly colonised. In the Middle Ages, the Poles moved east to Ukraine's fertile farmland and steppe, but few ventured to the north-east until after 1569. Under the Russian Empire, there were few Russians, at least until after the Rebellion of 1863–4. The Jews were the great exception, dominant in many cities until the Holocaust.

The downside of this passive status is that often 'Belarus is [like] a chess piece that fell off the chessboard'.[48] Or that, as the motorway or doormat of Europe, it has known more than its fair share of war, which has not only decimated the population, but also prevented continuity of elite development. So often in Belarusian history one embryonic culture has been replaced by another. The Livonian Wars of 1558–83 were followed by the catastrophic war of 1654–67, the Great Northern War of 1700–21, Napoleon's 1812 campaign, and the First and especially Second World Wars, particularly Operation Bagration in 1944. In this sense, the current Belarusian elite, both the Soviet partisan generation and the Lukashenka coterie, with its limited interest in anything before the Second World War, is not that unusual in Belarusian history.

Everywhere land. The real key to Belarusian history is that it lies at the crossroads of many cultures as well as sitting upstream on so many rivers. According to a more synthetic view, Belarus is therefore an in-between, cross-cultural kind of place.[49] Belarusians have a long tradition of bandwagoning – of seeking out and joining the stronger side.[50] Lukashenka's on-off courtship of Russia in the modern era is strongly reminiscent of the local knights backing the Grand Duchy of Lithuania in the Middle Ages. Belarusians also have a long tradition of joining other people's Churches: Catholic, Protestant and Orthodox. To some commentators like Sviatlana Kalinkina, this means a tendency towards national dilettantism: 'one moment we were going to join Russia, at another we were not. And this zigzagging appears to have prevented the Belarusians' self-identification.'[51] But it is also another reason why profoundly opposing myths can flourish simultaneously.

Nationalists would argue that Belarus is an inherent part of Europe, with a European political culture.[52] For some, Belarus is also the *edge of Europe*, particularly if they want to depict Russia as beyond Europe. According to Zianon Pazniak, Belarus is a frontier of European civilisation against the barbarian East, the *antemurale christianitatis*:

> During the whole Belarusian history until the end of the 18th century Belarus was the shield of Europe in the East. The Belarusian Slavic principalities have united into the powerful state – the Great Lithuanian Principality (the GLP) or Litva (according to the name of the central Slavic tribe whose princes had initiated the unification of the Belarusian territories). The Great Principality has stopped the Mongol aggression against Europe and established the border of the empire of Chingiz-Khan. The Great Principality resisted and fought against the East during the centuries (against the Golden Horde and then against Moscow). The border between the Great Lithuanian Principality and Russian Principality of Moscow represented at the same

time the border between two different political systems, different civilizations and different worlds – the democratic, cultural European world and
the Eastern despotic tyrannical world.[53]

Belarusian nationalists tend to get frustrated by historical counterfactuals.
They therefore look for compensation in absolutes: 'total victory' against
Muscovy at the Battle of Orsha in 1514 (and against the Tatars at Kletsk in
1506); and 'eternal struggle' against the evil empire. But the idea of a pseudo-
imperial Belarus founding Litva, driving back Muscovy, reaching the seas and
stretching out between them has little contemporary resonance. The idea of a
militantly Catholic Pazniak (see page 154) trying to implement such a vision as
president after 1994 is pretty scary. He would have split the country to a greater
extent than Lukashenka has ever done. The idea that *all of* Belarus is an outpost
of European civilisation in confrontation with Orthodox and authoritarian
Russia is also absurdly ahistorical. Andrey Dynko writes: 'The Belarusians
harboured suspicions about the flourishing Europe for a long time. Until
recently, an ordinary Belarusian above all associated Europe's *mission civilisatrice* with "Hitler the Liberator" posters. It was hard for a person who had gone
through experiments in amputation without anesthesia in the Nazi death camp
of Auschwitz to agree that Europeanness means civilization.'[54]

Alternatively, Belarus is depicted as *the Centre of Europe* – which is only
geographically possible if Europe includes Russia at least as far as the Ural
mountains. Dynko continues,

All people in Belarus know that their country is located at the centre of
Europe. If we take it from Belarusian geographers that it is so, the centre of the
continent lies in the waters of a small lake bearing the lapidary name of Sho.
Everyone in Lithuania also knows that the centre of Europe is somewhere
near the town of Alytus. Meanwhile, Ukrainians would confidently locate this
centre in the incredibly beautiful landscapes near the town of Rakhiv in the
Carpathians.[55]

Lukashenka has talked of Belarus in neatly opposite terms to Pazniak as a
'Slavic forepost';[56] the East Slavic *antemurale* against the West rather than the
other way around. This myth can be traced back to the long wars between
Muscovy and Poland–Lithuania, but it derives its most resonant power from
Belarus playing this role in 1941–4.[57] But Belarus is still a central part of
Europe in a roundabout way. According to Lukashenka: 'we were, are and will
be an inalienable part of pan-European civilisation, which is a mosaic of

different cultures.' But not part of the Catholic and Protestant bits, which are 'alien to Belarusians who are predominantly Orthodox and for centuries coexisted in the same political setting with Russia and Russians'.[58]

Lukashenka has also played up Belarus's role as a Russian redoubt, especially after the expansion of NATO to Poland in 1999 and the Baltic States in 2004. In 2005 Lukashenka presided over celebrations of the 'Stalin Line' that bravely resisted the German advance in 1941. Except it didn't. The line was built just west of Minsk in 1931–2, and was never fully finished, to protect the then border of the interwar Belarusian SSR. It was therefore nowhere near the new border when the Germans attacked in 1941, and in a state of considerable disrepair. There was no real engagement as the Germans advanced past it.

A related myth is the short-lived idea of Minsk as the fourth Rome (see pages 203–4).[59] The idea that Belarus is 'the spiritual leader of east Slavic civilisation' has slightly more staying power.[60] But there are few surviving Orthodox churches that were originally built for the Orthodox, particularly before the Grand Duchy. Belarus has few local myths and symbols that are exportable to the rest of the east Slavic world – except perhaps Euphrosyne of Polatsk and Cyril of Turaw (see page 16).

Conclusion

Belarus's identity is still malleable. It is still being remade. But most of the remaking was and still is governed by political circumstances. The Soviet version of Belarusian identity seemed stable for forty years after the war. A new anti-Soviet opposition tried to revive the Nashanivtsy tradition in the late 1980s and early 1990s but failed to become hegemonic. For better and for worse, modern Belarus has developed its identity under Lukashenka, both because of his longevity in office since 1994 and because of his construction of an eclectic identity closer to the median Belarusian than the purist project of the opposition. Once Lukashenka had consolidated his power, the Nashanivtsy culture became a minority counter-culture. Only very recently have there been any signs of cross-fertilisation. The next chapter therefore looks at the events leading up to independence from the Soviet Union in 1991 and the three years of turbulent political life before Aliaksandr Lukashenka emerged as president in 1994.

CHAPTER 8

POLITICS EITHER SIDE OF INDEPENDENCE, 1989–1994

The basic question about Belarusian history is: 'Does it have one?' The basic answer is a qualified 'yes', although Belarus's history is really a series of false starts. The basic question about Belarus since it unexpectedly gained independence when the Soviet Union collapsed in 1991 is: 'How did it get stuck with an authoritarian populist leader like Lukashenka?' Was he, in the words of one Russian book, an 'Accidental President'?[1] Or was he in truth a reflection of Belarusian society after 1991, and more broadly of its stop-start, jump-start history?

Weimar Belarus?

Part of the answer to the second question can be found in the period before Lukashenka came to power, between the Gorbachev reforms that brought real politics to the USSR in 1989–91 and Belarus's first presidential election in the summer of 1994. Lukashenka would later enjoy contrasting his presidency with the chaos that supposedly went before him. Many of the tropes that Kremlin ideologues would use under the Putin presidency were coined in Belarus, including the humiliation of a former great power by a triumphalist and hypocritical West, democracy as anarchy, and post-Soviet 'freedom' as freedom only for gangsters and the super-rich. Lukashenka was hunting down domestic 'oligarchs' long before Putin. He took office declaring the 'end of anarchy has arrived',[2] and has consistently returned to this theme ever since. In a 2003 speech, for example, he lambasted 'parliamentary anarchy, where everyone just talks, though nobody answers for anything or builds an effective vertical of state power with personal accountability'.[3]

As in Weimar Germany, the self-interested manoeuvrings of petty politicians supposedly allowed a dictator to come to power on their blind side,
claiming the necessary imposition of 'order' after 'chaos'. Of course, Belarus
before Lukashenka wasn't literally like Weimar Germany in the 1920s or even
Russia in the 1990s.[4] It did have hyperinflation, but it wasn't a former imperial
heartland, agonising over the territory that it had lost. Though many
Belarusians were Soviet enough in their mind-set to feel the loss of the Great
Power status in which they had shared as part of the USSR as a personal loss,
Belarus was more analogous to Austria after 1918, the rump state that didn't
want to be born. Or, more exactly, just like Austria, it was profoundly divided
over the issue. Austria was initially the 'Republic of German-Austria' in
1918–19, before seemingly stabilising as an independent state in the 1920s,
until the *Heimwehr* ('Home Army') began agitating again for union with
Germany in the 1930s, before the *Anschluss* in 1938. Belarus in the early 1990s
was similarly divided over whether it should even exist. The main opposition
force, the 'Belarusian People's Front' (BNF), revived the cultural nationalism
of the 'Nashanivtsy', but never actually came to power. At the opposite
extreme was the Russophile 'White Rus' movement, which argued for Soviet
reunion. In the middle sat the former Communist elite, hedging its bets,
happy enough to be in power in its own state after 1991, but not really
knowing what to do with it.

But Lukashenka's caricature of Belarusian politics shouldn't be taken
entirely at face value, as he has used it to justify the aggrandisement of his own
power. One point of view, expressed by the American political scientist Lucan
Way, is that the early 1990s were indeed a mess, and prime minister Viacheslav
Kebich was simply an 'inefficient authoritarian'.[5] Another perspective is that
these were years of incipient pluralism and missed opportunities. Belarus's
nascent parliamentary democracy was noisy and anarchic, but maybe there
was some good fortune in being late to introduce a presidency (in 1994). If
Lukashenka hadn't come along and spoiled things, Belarus might have
muddled through the rest of the 1990s like Ukraine or Moldova – not exactly
a success story, but not exactly a disaster zone either, though under Kebich's
continued rule it would probably have developed a Ukraine-like version of
local oligarchy: most likely an alliance between the Minsk City Industrial
Group (see page 116), energy transit interests, particularly in the oil-refining
sector, and associated Russian oligarchs. Either way, Belarus's first and so far
only truly competitive presidential election in 1994 was a pivotal event.

The period 1989–94 was in any case divided in two. First, in the short time
between the emergence of real pluralism after the all-Soviet elections in

March 1989 and the failed Moscow coup in August 1991, real politics came late to still-Soviet Belarus, which largely played catch-up with events elsewhere. Then, from 1991 to 1994, Belarus struggled to make its mark as a new and unexpectedly independent state.

The Vendée of Perestroika

In the context of the turbulent politics of the late Soviet era, Belarus was relatively quiet, competing with other conservative republics or regions like Crimea or the über-Soviet 'Dniester Republic' in Moldova for the title of 'the Vendée of perestroika'. (The Soviet Communists always liked to draw analogies between their own revolution and its French predecessor; the Vendée region at the Atlantic end of the Loire was the stronghold of Royalist forces in 1793–6.) In a poll taken across the USSR in 1991, the Belarusians were the most likely to identify themselves as 'citizens of the USSR' (69 per cent) rather than 'citizens of their republic' (24 per cent), even more than the Russians (63 per cent to 25 per cent), and more than Russians resident in other Soviet republics (66 per cent to 22 per cent). Ukrainians narrowly identified with Ukraine (46 per cent over 42 per cent), Kazakhs with Kazakhstan (52 per cent over 48 per cent) – to say nothing of Estonians, only 3 per cent of whom identified with the USSR, or Armenians (only 8 per cent).[6]

According to the memoirs of Piotra Krawchanka, the Communist boss of Minsk and the first foreign minister of independent Belarus, 'the system in which we worked was absolutely unprepared for challenging times – because of its sluggishness, lack of agility and, yes, because of the banal stupidity of many Party bosses. At the end of the 1980s there weren't any National-Communists in Belarus. . . . And for the new generation of party intelligentsia, to which I belonged, it was very difficult to keep the national component in everyday life.'[7] Belarus had no Gorbachev and no Shevardnadze. Nor did it have any equivalent of the local leaders who made a career for themselves by hijacking national causes elsewhere in the USSR, like Algirdas Brazauskas in Lithuania or Leonid Kravchuk in Ukraine.[8] The Communist Party of Belarus (CPB) never really split in the Gorbachev years, and never really disappeared thereafter (it was banned for a few months, but revived as early as December 1991).

Unlike Ukraine, Belarus had no strong regional 'clans'. In part this was because both national and regional identities were weak. There were some vague geographic identifications: Masheraw, for example, preferred people from his home region of Vitsebsk. But, according to Krawchanka again, 'these mini-groups had only a rather conditional character. They weren't cemented by some or other interest, like family relations or finances.'[9] This had advantages and disadvantages. The CPB changed its mind en masse, but changed it slowly. On the other hand, it would prove hard to establish governments with a strong sense of united purpose after 1991.

According to Aliaksandr Feduta, former head of the Belarusian Komsomol who ended up working for Lukashenka, 'there was no [local Belarusian] nationalism in Belarus' under the Communists. 'Masheraw was the "boss" in "his" republic. But he wasn't a nationalist.'[10] Belarus was the most Soviet of republics. Masheraw and Mazuraw managed to exploit the partisan myth to screw the maximum out of the central Soviet budget. But Belarusian schools disappeared from most large towns under their watch. Power in the republic was increasingly held by the 'Minsk City Industrial Group'.[11] The CPB was a tight-knit group without any real inferiority or guilt complex.

Masheraw's successors were mainly colourless time-servers, though at least they kept some central investment rolling in. Tsikhan Kisialiow (1980–3) kept alive the last remnants of the old partisan group, but Mikalai Sliunkow (1983–7) was sent back home from Moscow by Andropov to try and stamp them out. Under Yafrem Sakalow (1987–90), the Minsk City Industrial Group therefore confirmed its ascendancy.[12] Anatol Malafeew took over in November 1990 without realising he would be the last leader of the Belarusian Communists. Malafeew was made of sterner stuff, but would also have a short career at the top.

The Popular Front

The other side of the fence was not exactly crowded. Belarus is often described as having no real dissident movement. Indeed, the number of active opponents of the Soviet system in the 1960s and 1970s, like Aliaksei Kawka or Mikhas Kukabaka, who was sentenced to seventeen years in prison in 1979, could be counted on one hand. One recent account claims that semi-public dissent was a much broader phenomenon, profiling around seventy figures;[13] but Belarus had nothing on the scale of the Movement in Defence of the Catholic Church in Lithuania or the Ukrainian Helsinki Group. Belarusian dissent had no organised structure. Nor, going back further, did Belarus have any anti-Soviet 'forest brethren', like the Armed Fighting Alliance in Estonia, whose last active member died in 1980, or the Ukrainian Insurgent Army, whose last commander was captured in 1954. The Belarusian forests had been full of Soviet partisans, and the nationalists who set up the Belarusian Central Council in 1943–4 nearly all escaped to the West.

Nevertheless, the Gorbachev era unleashed intelligentsia-based dissent throughout the Soviet Union, In fact, its *raison d'être* was to encourage the 'working intelligentsia' to revivify through constructive criticism a party-state to which ultimately they were still beholden. The first sign of the thaw in Belarus was the 'Letter to Gorbachev' that emerged in 1987 signed by twenty-eight leading Belarusian writers, which forecast 'spiritual death' if nothing was done to raise the status of the Belarusian language in Belarus.[14] Small 'informal' clubs appeared in 1988: mainly youth and cultural organisations like the history society Talaka (society) and the club of young writers with the ironic name Tuteishyia (local). However, as Alexandra Goujon points out, 'most of the informals were made up of students',[15] rather than the veterans of the 1960s or the venerable writers who gave similar movements much more clout elsewhere in the USSR. Moreover, despite these early stirrings, the Belarusian opposition under Gorbachev needed two key stimuli to really take off. The first, the Chernobyl disaster in 1986, led to generalised protest, if not initially to any real protest movement – 1986 was just too early for mass protest in Belarus. But Chernobyl was corrosive: as a public-health disaster unfolded in the south of the country (Chernobyl is just over the Ukrainian border, but the winds blew north), the local regime was undermined by its own incompetence. Chernobyl also became a powerful retrospective rallying cry, not least at the annual rallies marking the disaster's anniversary every 26 April which grew progressively bigger through the late 1980s.

The second key event was the Kurapaty finds in June 1988. The archaeologists Zianon Pazniak and Yawhan Shmyhalow found five hundred mass graves in the forests outside Minsk, where the local victims of the Great Purges had been murdered in 1937–41.[16] Later the two would claim that 300,000 bodies were buried there. The numbers were hotly disputed, but, unlike the Polish dead at nearby Katyń, the regime couldn't even try, however implausibly, to blame Kurapaty's thousands of prewar victims on the Nazis. This was a severe blow to the local Communist myth that there were no 'blank pages' in the BSSR's past. In the 'partisan' view of Belarusian history, writes Aliaksandr Feduta, purges and their like were far-off events, for which, in so far as they were belatedly admitted to, 'the NKVD, which was always Muscovite', was to blame.[17]

The consequent Kurapaty demonstrations led to the formation in October 1988 of a society named Martyrology of Belarus and, most importantly, to the creation of an organising committee of the Belarusian People's Front (BNF) in the same month, actually earlier than the equivalent movement in Ukraine. At the same time as denying their brutal past, however, the local Communists were still using the local police, armed with clubs and tear gas, to disperse demonstrators. The founding conference of the BNF in June 1989 had to be held in Vilnius, which made it feel 'foreign' to many.

No less than 70 per cent of the original members of the BNF were from the intelligentsia. The BNF's members were also younger than those of its Ukrainian counterpart, Rukh: no less than 30 per cent of the Belarusian Frondeurs were under thirty, compared to only 16 per cent in Ukraine,[18] where the 'generation of the 1960s' had resumed control. This lack of an older protest generation proved a double-edged sword: many of the Ukrainian leaders of Rukh had been corrupted or compromised by the KGB back in the 1960s or 1970s, but at least they provided a steadying hand. The BNF was also comparatively small. It had only 10,000 members in April 1989 and 50,000 by the end of the year,[19] compared to 280,000 for Rukh in 1989. Even this modest strength was illusory: at various times the BNF's ranks were swelled by opportunistic bureaucrats, who came and went.

The BNF was led by Zianon Pazniak, who, Goujon fairly points out, 'before 1988 was unknown to the broader public and little known in intellectual circles'.[20] Kurapaty catapulted him forwards. But Pazniak was symptomatic of a leadership that always overvaulted public opinion in its relative radicalism. The BNF saw itself as both a 'general-democratic' and a 'national revival' movement. Its founding statements indicate a certain inner conflict,[21] but it soon come to be dominated by the second of these ideas, denouncing Soviet 'genocide' against the Belarusian people.[22]

The BNF also found it relatively difficult to penetrate the corridors of power, compared to Yelstin in Russia or even Rukh in Ukraine, and its voice grew shriller as it struggled to be heard. This also made the BNF concentrate more on street protests. Aliaksandr Martynaw makes the shrewd point that the 'top tiers of the ruling party and the opposition were from non-intersecting social environments'.[23] The ideal BNF member was a writer or an academic from the humanities; the nomenklatura were mainly factory bosses from the Minsk City Industrial Group, collective farm bosses, technical intelligentsia and military men. In other republics there was a more intimate or overlapping relationship – sometimes too intimate, as so many former dissidents had been corrupted or compromised by their Party controllers. But in Belarus the BNF and the Party had almost no common ground, either ideological or social.

The broader 'opposition' was also split from the start. The BNF was made up of Belarusian-speakers, but many members of the Belarusian intelligentsia, particularly outside the humanities, were Russian-speaking and even Russophile. In 1987 they set up a discussion club, *Sovremennik* ('Contemporary'). Then, together with Belarusian members of the Democratic Platform, which split from the all-Soviet Communist Party in 1990, they set up the United Democratic Party of Belarus, which became the first officially registered party in Belarus, beating even the Communists to the gun. Similar organisations were the Movement for Democratic Reforms, set up in February 1992, and the United Civic Party, established in 1995.[24] But the Russian-speaking opposition never really provided an effective third force between the nomenklatura and the BNF, apart from a brief missed opportunity in 1995–6 (see pages 176–7).

The BNF was based in the old Nashanivtsy strongholds of the north-west. But Minsk was also a relative centre of protest at this time. Demonstrations typically pulled in tens, even hundreds of thousands of people, albeit usually because of all-Soviet concerns (price rises) or specific local events such as Kurapaty and Chernobyl. The concentration of industry in the capital also allowed the BNF to dream of mobilising working-class support, though this never materialised on a scale comparable to Solidarity in Poland.

All-Soviet elections were organised by Gorbachev in March 1989. They were only partly free: the rules were skewed, there was competition between individual candidates in most seats, but the Communists were still the only legal party. Only a handful of BNF sympathisers were elected to the Moscow assembly from the eighty-three constituencies in Belarus, including the academic Stanislaw Shushkevich, the writers Ales Adamovich and Vasyl Bykaw, and the economist Aleksei Yurauliaw. A strong local protest vote also claimed the notable scalp of Minsk Party secretary Nikolai Galko. But the CPB remained firmly in control.

The 1990 Elections

The initial enthusiasm for the new quasi-parliament in Moscow did not last long. The open debate that was at first seductive soon come to sound more like empty talk rather than preparation for practical action, and was in any case constantly manipulated by Gorbachev as chairman. The next round of elections, held in the Soviet Union's fifteen constituent republics a year later, in the spring of 1990, was actually more democratic, and power began to haemorrhage away from the Moscow centre to the periphery, including Minsk. Across the USSR this meant two new trends: 'popular fronts', based in local civic movements and representing local nationalisms, were empow-ered by the elections in their republics; and local Communists increasingly built their own power bases, where necessary in alliance with the popular fronts – though they largely went their own way in Belarus. The BNF was relatively weak, and the local Communists seemed reluctant to play the same role as their equivalents in Lithuania or Ukraine, and were more likely to be involved in Moscow intrigues than Communists in neighbouring republics. The BNF rode the wave that was building up throughout the USSR, but it would never be strong enough to take power, although it could put 100,000 people on the streets of Minsk at events such as its preelection rally in February 1990.[25]

The 1990 elections therefore had a similar dynamic to those in the other republics, but only superficially. There were 360 seats in all for the elections to the Belarusian Supreme Soviet, but forty-five were preselected from 'social organisations' like invalids and army veterans, who normally backed the ultra-conservatives, so only 315 seats were potentially competitive. Thirteen seats were never filled because of low turnout. The BNF won between 25 and 37 seats (not all of those elected had formal membership; the higher number was 12 per cent of the total), which in the light of subsequent elections wasn't actually that bad. Most of these were in Minsk, where the opposition won 20 seats out of 22. The rest were scattered in the north-west in the old Vilna region and in the west around Hrodna; but the BNF had no true regional stronghold of the kind that Rukh enjoyed in Galicia, western Ukraine, even in the north-west. Up to a hundred deputies were members of a broader 'Democratic Club'.[26] Sixty belonged to the Belarusian Language Society.[27] But these broader numbers gave the BNF only an illusory strength: it looked powerful, but its core was small.

Once again, there were some high-profile casualties among the top Communist leadership. On the other hand, between 120 and 150 deputies represented the 'second rung' of the party nomenklatura, albeit not enough to secure control on a simple vote. By January 1991, when factions had settled down, this meant the Communists still controlled the largest group, with 170 MPs (49 per cent), plus two satellite nomenklatura factions of the 'Industrialists' (35 MPs, or 10 per cent) and 'Agrarians' (40 MPs, or 12 per cent), with 30 MPs in the hardline 'Union' faction (9 per cent) at one extreme opposing the BNF faction of 27 MPs (8 per cent) at the other.[28] Following the model set by Aleksandr Rutskoi's centrist Democratic Party of Communists of Russia in Moscow, a Belarusian version dubbed 'Communists for Democracy' appeared in June 1991, with 33 MPs,[29] though it failed to make the same impact as Rutskoi's group, confining itself to a few declarations in the press.[30]

Enter the Pig Farmer

The leader of the Communists for Democracy group was none other than Aliaksandr Lukashenka, who at this time was a political gadfly, hanging around with any party that would have him – as long as they would have him as leader. His first try had been with the liberal Party of Popular Accord (PNS). According to PNS leader Aliaksandr Sosnow, 'Lukashenka came to us. In truth, he had no ideas at all, except how to put forward his own candidacy for the leadership.'[31] The Communists for Democracy group was also vaguely centrist, but at this time Lukashenka was also writing articles with titles like 'Dictatorship: A Belarusian Variant?'[32]

Lukashenka was, quite literally, a bastard. He was a youthful thirty-six in 1991, the only child of an abandoned mother from the eastern wasteland of Shklow. He had grown up an archetypal Soviet Man. According to Feduta, when young, Lukashenka 'was completely Soviet, and intended to lead a typical Soviet career',[33] which had so far included stints as a border guard, as an ideology lecturer and as head of the Horodets collective pig farm in 1987–90. By the late 1980s Lukashenka fancied a career in politics: 'it was clear that [he] thirsted for power,' Feduta writes somewhat floridly, 'like a sixteen-year-old youth wants intimacy with a woman, so Lukashenka with every fibre of his spirit, every cell of his organism, desired power as such.'[34]

In his first contest he lost to none other than the future prime minister Viacheslaw Kebich in the 1989 all-Soviet elections in Mahilew, though only by the narrowest of margins, 51 per cent to 49 per cent.[35] Kebich's abuse of 'administrative resources' to win the election provided an interesting lesson for the future dictator. Moreover, already 'he knew what people wanted to hear and what to say'.[36]

Lukashenka showed his ambition by standing and winning with 68.2 per cent in the second round against his immediate party superior at Horodets in the 1990 elections, once again near Mahilew.[37] Interestingly, the constitutional immunity granted by his status as an MP was already proving useful: he was able to quash an investigation into claims that he had assaulted not just one but more or less all of his former employees at Horodets.

Belarus Practises Politics

The mainstream Communists' apparent dominance at the 1990 elections was confirmed in the opening vote to determine who would chair parliament, and therefore control both its machinery and the 'Presidium', which served as a kind of quasi-presidency. It took two rounds to impose the Politburo member Mikalai Dzemiantsei, but the scientist and moderate opposition figure Stanislaw Shushkevich was appointed as his deputy. Three opposition members made it onto the collective Presidium. The old guard would have preferred Dzemiantsei to head the government as well, but the position went to Viacheslaw Kebich, a leading member of the Minsk City Industrial Group, after the initial favourite, Mikhail Kovalev, fell ill.[38] The Communists therefore had a collective leadership troika: Dzemiantsei, Malafeew, the CPB boss, and Kebich – but Kebich was clearly the dominant figure. However, he had become leader without really working for it, and 'was one of the few executives in the region who had not gained power because of his ability to deal with challenges from below'.[39]

The Communists' instinct was to manipulate the opposition. On 21 March 1990 the CPB Central Committee took secret 'decision number 86' to combat the Democratic Platform, a move that was leaked to the press.[40] In the summer of 1991 Malafeew planned to make himself president and introduce a state of emergency.[41] But the conservatives' plans were disturbed in April 1991 when Belarus was convulsed by a month-long strike wave, albeit one caused by all-union issues, namely Soviet prime minister Valentin Pavlov's ham-fisted imposition of sharp price increases for basic products. Hence Belarus was rocked by socioeconomic, not nationalist, protests, with an estimated 200,000 out on strike.[42] The local Communist authorities were caught off-guard. Kebich and Dzemiantsei favoured compromise; Malafeew and, surprisingly, Shushkevich wanted to use force.[43] On 20 April Malafeew called for a state of emergency at the CPSU Central Committee plenum in Moscow. Shushkevich called a session of the presidium of the Belarusian Soviet in parallel, and invited the local *siloviki* (the security services) to restore order. He was opposed by Georgii Tarnavskii, the prosecutor general. In private Eduard Shyrkowski, head of the local KGB since October 1990, was not surprisingly also a hawk, saying to Kebich: 'Viacheslav Frantsevich, you only have to say the word, and all those on the square or going to the square [main city], I'll smear them against the wall! We have the strength for it.'[44] In private Shyrkowski even thought of asking the hardline Soviet interior minister Boris Pugo for a brigade of special forces that had cut their teeth in Nagorno-Karabakh. In the event the strikers were bought off with wage increases instead.

The BNF was unable to make common cause with the strikers. In fact, it was able to achieve little in 1991 after its first partial successes in 1990 (Shushkevich's election and a Declaration of Sovereignty passed in July 1990 – the law on languages which made Belarusian the official language of the BSSR, was actually passed by the old Supreme Soviet in January 1990). In March 1991, 83 per cent of Belarusian voters opted to preserve the USSR in the referendum called by Gorbachev, higher than the average across the USSR of 76.4 per cent. Unlike in Russia (on introducing a Russian presidency) and Ukraine (on a looser 'Union of Sovereign States' based on Ukrainian sovereignty), there was no second question in the vote in Belarus.

The August Putsch

When hardliners in the Soviet leadership attempted a coup in August 1991, Malafeew backed them to the hilt and was in Moscow to support them.[45] On 20 August the Communist group in the Minsk Supreme Council tried to force through its plan to select Malafeew as president and declare a state of emergency in Belarus.[46] Had it had more than two days to achieve its goal, it would undoubtedly have prevailed. Unlike Ukraine, where a presidency was planned as early as June 1991 as a means of defending Ukrainian sovereignty, the idea of a presidency for Belarus was therefore discredited as a Communist plot until 1994. The BNF now assumed, probably correctly, that an ex-Communist would win the presidency, and got cold feet. But when it became independent, the new state was therefore deprived of a key institution for resisting Russian pressure.

Shyrkowski, despite being the first ethnic Belarusian to head the local KGB, kept his likely support for the plotters private. Parliamentary chairman Dzemiantsei made the mistake of backing the coup in public and was forced out on 25 August (his Ukrainian counterpart, Leonid Kravchuk, equivocated, but carefully so, and survived and prospered). The CPB was therefore left leaderless. Generals Anatol Kastenka and Pawel Kazlowski of the Belarusian Military District backed the coup.[47] On the other hand, many local bureaucrats kept a low profile until the victors emerged. Krawchanka describes his own decision to take 'leave as a form of sabotage'. He phoned Kebich on the morning of 19 August, the first day of the coup.[48]

– Viacheslaw Frantsevich, what's to be done? What to do?
– Petr Kuz'mich! Are you on leave?
– Yes.
– Well, stay on leave!
– Understood, Viacheslaw Frantsevich.

Kebich also stayed at his dacha,[49] but not because of his liberal conscience. In his memoirs he claims the coup was a put-up job by Gorbachev, and that the Soviet Union should have been preserved by force, just as the 'minimal victims' at Tiananmen Square in 1989 had 'saved the lives of hundreds of thousands, maybe millions of people'.[50] In other words, Kebich was not exactly Lukashenka's liberal predecessor. But Krawchanka considers that Kebich would not have survived if the coup had been successful.[51] As it happened, it was spectacularly unsuccessful. Its collapse after only two days on 21 August led to another wave, this time of copycat independence declarations among the Union republics. But, however tempting it might be to see Belarus's declaration of independence as an import,[52] the key actors behaved differently from those in Russia, Ukraine or Moldova. There was no equivalent of the anti-Communist mood that flared all too briefly in Russia. The Belarusian Communists did not defect en masse to the old opposition, as in Right Bank Moldova, which raised the real threat of a drive to rejoin Romania and prompted the rebellion on the Left Bank (the self-styled 'Dniester Republic'). In Belarus, independence was actually proposed by the Communists, rather than reluctantly supported by them, as happened in Ukraine.

Moreover, Ukraine declared independence outright, as quickly as possible, on 24 August, before the all-Soviet parliament had a chance to reconvene on 26 August. Belarus was more cautious. On 25 August the Supreme Soviet gave the 1990 Declaration of Sovereignty the status of constitutional law – which wasn't quite the same as an unequivocal declaration of independence. Kebich thought it didn't change much.[53] On 19 September the Supreme Soviet voted to change the name of the old Belarusian Soviet Socialist Republic to the 'Republic of Belarus'. Most importantly, unlike in Ukraine, the declaration of independence, such as it was, was never backed up by a referendum. Ukraine held a popular vote on 1 December 1991, when 90.3 per cent backed parliament's decision. Whenever independence has seemed under threat since, Ukrainian nationalists have always been able to point to this. The BNF would not have the same asset.

The BNF-led opposition was still too weak to take power on its own, or even to threaten to take power. It couldn't even force the former Communist elite to the negotiating table. Essentially, the old guard did a deal with itself, unlike in Ukraine, where the 'National Communists' did a deal with Rukh. With the hardliners in retreat, the relatively orthodox Kebich agreed to share power with the relatively BNF-friendly but still traditionalist Shushkevich. Both men were from the old Communist nomenklatura. The former Communist majority made Shushkevich the nominal head of state simply to stop Pazniak.

Still the two men fought like rats in a sack. Initially, neither could prevail over the other to replace Dzemiantsei; finally, Kebich withdrew, allowing Shushkevich to be elected by 214 votes to 98 on 18 September. Independent Belarus would be plagued from the beginning by the dysfunctional leadership tandem at the top. Shushkevich was unable to build a power base of his own. He had no force or party behind him. He was a physics professor, who tended towards 'the idealisation of social reality'.[54] Bizarrely, Shushkevich had taught Lee Harvey Oswald some Russian when he was in Minsk in 1960–2. Shushkevich naïvely thought he could outwit the cruder apparatchiks around him. The apparat meanwhile dominated the government under Kebich, and the administrative machine, such as it was, was still controlled by the old guard. They tied Shushkevich's hands in parliament by manoeuvring the leading conservative, Viacheslav Kuznetsow, into position as deputy chair parliamentary in April 1992.

A final difference with Ukraine is that Ukraine held its first ever presidential elections in December 1991. Kravchuk won the vote with 61.7 per cent, which gave him an impressive mandate – not that he made the most of it. Shushkevich by contrast lacked the power of popular election.

The former Communist elite didn't take the meaning of 'independence' too literally. Even Shushkevich favoured Gorbachev's proposal for a new Union Treaty until the Ukrainian referendum killed the idea on 1 December, though Krawchanka at least tried to fend off some of the pressure from Moscow to sign the treaty.[55]

The 'Other Coup', This Time in Belarus

The Ukrainian referendum changed everything. On 7–8 December 1991 the leaders of Russia, Ukraine and Belarus arranged a crucial meeting at a state dacha in the Belarusian forest of Belovezhkaia pushcha near Brest, where Leonid Brezhnev had once hunted drugged animals tied to trees. By most accounts, including that of the Ukrainian president, Leonid Kravchuk,[56] the initiative was taken by Shushkevich.[57] Despite the myth that the famous meeting was held near the Polish border to facilitate a quick getaway if necessary, the plush complex built for Khrushchev in 1957 was simply the most logical place for nomenklatura guests to gather. The participants also had no idea they were risking evoking the symbolism of the 1918 Treaty of Brest-Litovsk.

The meeting wasn't an auspicious start for the new Belarus. The initiative was largely taken by Yeltsin and Kravchuk. Krawchanka paints an unflattering picture of Shushkevich, who, he says, was 'always scared of political independence, contriving to find himself an influential patron at every step of his career. At first that was . . . Malafeew. After the ruin of the Communist Party Shushkevich for some time found his protector in the person of Mikhail Gorbachev.[58] After the dacha meeting, Shushkevich was therefore still happy to go and see Gorbachev in Moscow, though Kravchuk, his Ukrainian equivalent, refused, and Gorbachev didn't want to see the Belarusian leader on his own.[59] Shushkevich was by now shifting his attention to Yeltsin. In later years, he would proudly show off a watch Yeltsin had given him, supposedly for saving his life. What had actually happened was less heroic than this boast makes it sound: Yeltsin had tottered halfway up the stairs at the dacha and almost fallen over backwards, before Shushkevich caught him.[60]

Despite acting as host, the Belarusian leadership was deeply split by the resulting accord, which effectively marked Belarus's birth as an independent state. Shushkevich and Foreign Minister Krawchanka were happy to see the end of the USSR. Prime Minister Kebich claims not to have been kept informed of the Belovezhkaia 'plot': attendance was only widened from heads of states to include prime ministers at the last minute. At the meeting he claims to have been resolutely opposed, and assumed that, after this 'formal act', 'a new state formation' would replace the USSR, 'like a phoenix from the flames'.[61] Retrospectively, he says he thinks he should have done everything in his power to stop the meeting happening.[62] KGB head Shyrkowski, on the other hand, was very well informed of proceedings, and called it a 'most brazen state coup'; having secretly contacted the Central Committee in Moscow, he 'waited for Gorbachev's team' to come and arrest the participants.[63] In an interview given just before his death in 2002, Shyrkowski expressed regret that he hadn't arrested everybody himself.[64] Kebich, on the other hand, made sure that all the Belarusian *siloviki* were present, not so much to protect the participants, but so that he could keep an eye on them.[65]

But the Russians and Ukrainians prevailed – but once again, there was no referendum. The accord was ratified in the Belarusian parliament on 10 December, with a massive 263 votes in favour, two abstentions and one against. Lukashenka later liked to claim that he cast the solitary negative vote, but it isn't true. Voting was secret, so names were not recorded; but Lukashenka wasn't even in the hall at the time. The vote against was in fact cast by Valer Tikhinia,[66] one-time minister of justice, who argued it was absurd to override the March referendum on preserving the USSR.

For a brief moment, it seemed like Belarus was the centre of at least some of the world's attention. Yeltsin arrived at the Belovezhkaia conclave via Minsk, addressing the Belarusian parliament first, making a cack-handed gift of a document showing Belarusian losses in the war of the 1660s. On 18

December US secretary of state James Baker came to Minsk. The new headquarters of the Commonwealth of Independent States (CIS) were to be
there. But Belarus would be marked by its failure to establish a '1991 myth'.
Rather, for conservatives across the USSR, events in Belarus in December
1991, the 'Belovezhkaia myth', became their equivalent of Hitler's 'stab in the
back' – the empire that died without a fight.

The Self-Limiting Ideology of the BNF

The new ship of state was in choppy waters from the start, and its direction
unclear. There was no basking in the warm glow of independence long sought
and suddenly achieved. Politics in the new state was totally polarised. The
BNF was more radical than its equivalents elsewhere. It pursued abstract goals
and didn't really engage with the state, while the nomenklatura monopolised
almost every position of power. There was no middle ground. Forces sympathetic to the anti-Yeltsin Russian opposition were already active in Belarus.
Shushkevich's hands were already tied. The old guard was closing in.

Meanwhile, the ideology of the BNF was based on a very narrow social
stratum. Pazniak was too radical for Belarusian society as a whole.[67] There
was no 1960s' generation to lead the opposition. Pazniak was an obscure
figure until 1988, and has lapsed into obscurity again since his exile in 1996.

For the BNF, language and historical consciousness were the main and
sometimes only badges of identity. But, despite the BNF's superficial success
in getting the new state to adopt its preferred national symbols in 1992, especially the white-red-white flag and the Pahonia, (a knight on horseback) as the
state emblem, the number of people who spoke the BNF's preferred version of
national purity – Tarashkevitsa rather than Narkamawka (see page 124) –
represented under 10 per cent of the population. In general, the BNF over-
emphasised the language issue. Pazniak, for example, obsessively attacked
Trasianka as a 'pseudo-language'.[68]

A second factor, although it was rarely noticed abroad, was just how many
of the leading BNF or BNF-friendly politicians in 1990–4 were Roman
Catholics: Pazniak was one, of course, but so too, nominally, was Kebich, as
well as Shushkevich and his successor, Mechyslaw Hryb, and Stanislaw
Bahdankevich, head of the National Bank.

Kebich-land

Kebich, on the other hand, set about building an early type of 'managed
democracy'. There were plenty of new independent parties, but parliament

was dominated by the conservative 'Belarus' faction established in March 1992, which had 120 members by 1994 – nearly all former nomenklatura. Its bland name offered a good indication that it had no real purpose other than retaining power. Kebich's circle also helped set up two corporatist 'regime parties' the Agrarian-Democratic Party (from 1994, the Agrarian Party) and the Scientific-Industrial Congress.[69] And the Communists weren't gone for long. A 'new' Party of Communists of Belarus (PCB), little different from the old-style Communist Party of Belarus (CPB), held its founding congress on the very same day the CIS accords were ratified in December 1991.[70] By 1992, fifty-eight MPs had rejoined the Communist faction, although only twelve were direct members of the PCB.[71] Waiting in the wings was the even more radical Movement of Workers of the Republic of Belarus for Democracy, Social Progress and Justice, led by Viktar Chykin.

But the Kebich regime didn't much care about ideology. It sought to neutralise the Communists' support by enveloping it in the pro-regime 'People's Movement of Belarus', set up in October 1992 – a clone version of the BNF to support, not opose, the regime. The operation was run by the KGB and other *siloviki* and inspired by Kebich's link-man to the security services Henadz Danilaw, who found a tame Soviet ultra-patriot to front it in the form of former Red Army colonel Siarhei Haidukevich,[72] a sort of Belarusian version of Russia's scarecrow nationalist Vladimir Zhirinovskii. Haidukevich would have a long career playing similar roles.

Politics was therefore both increasingly polarised and simultaneously static. Kebich criticised the BNF for creating 'dual power' and blocking reforms that he didn't really want to introduce anyway.[73] The lack of progress compared to the Baltic States or even Ukraine at least produced an early reaction. An 'Anti-Crisis Committee' was set up under BNF auspices in March 1992 and the BNF began a campaign to collect signatures for a referendum on early elections in the autumn. By April an impressive 442,000[74] signatures had been collected; and in May the Central Election Commission (CEC) validated 383,000, 33,000 more than the legal minimum to force a referendum, which was 5 per cent of the electorate or 350,000 people (though 60 per cent of these were from the opposition strongholds of Minsk and Hrodna). The plan was to hold new elections using a mixed, half-proportional/half-majoritarian system, like that used in Russia after 1993 and Ukraine after 1998, which would have led to stronger parties. But the nomenklatura were afraid of any proportional element. Others 'had long since lost contact with their constituencies, lost all influence and support in the regions they represented and had no chance of reelection'. Kebich considered the BNF was creating an artificial campaign, backed by the West, as a means of usurping power.[75] But even the nominal 'democrats' weren't keen: the resistance to early elections was headed by none other than the speaker of parliament, Stanislaw Shushkevich.[76]

So the BNF was on its own. In October 1992 the regime felt confident enough to go for broke. Parliament simply voted to reject the referendum campaign by 202 to 35, and without a new constitution there was no other body to which the campaigners could now appeal. The one concession was that the next parliamentary elections were supposed to be held a year early, in March 1994.[77] But even this promise was not kept. Protests were loud but ineffective.

The BNF thinks it would have benefited from early elections. Most of Kebich's camp were happy to sit in unelected power, but a minority, including the then foreign minister, Piotr Krawchanka, consider this was a great missed chance to strengthen the political centre before someone like Lukashenka came along. It was actually Kebich, claims Krawchanka, who was at the 'peak of his popularity' in 1992.[78]

The defeat of the BNF campaign allowed Kebich to move on to his next target: Shushkevich. Throughout 1993, he was constantly trying to clip his wings. In April 1993 parliament ordered Shushkevich to sign the CIS security pact, which Kebich supported (Kebich was also pitching to rejoin the rouble zone). In June a No Confidence motion against Shushkevich was backed by 168 of the 204 deputies registered to vote. Technically, this was six short of the necessary constitutional majority required to remove him (which was 174 votes, or half of the total number of MPs, which was 347), but Shushkevich was effectively a dead man walking.

Sasha against the System

The killer blow would be dealt from an unexpected source – Aliaksandr Lukashenka. Since his near-debut in Belarusian politics in 1991, Lukashenka had lapsed back into obscurity. But Kebich needed someone to pull the trigger on Shushkevich. An earlier report into corruption in September 1992 by KGB chief Shyrkowski had proved a damp squib. Now Kebich planned to do the job properly. Or rather, he planned to do a proper job on his opponents. He had no intention of actually doing anything about corruption. He therefore set up a parliamentary committee to investigate the issue in June 1993, which all of Belarus's unprincipled parties thought they could exploit. Shushkevich now claims that Kebich 'buttered up Lukashenka and began to give him all [sorts of] materials that would place me in a difficult position'.[79] In fact, Shushkevich and the BNF had originally pushed for the commission themselves, which several of Kebich's allies had turned down the right to head.[80] Anatol Liabedzka proposed Lukashenka as head of the committee. Shushkevich played along, hoping that the handful of Belarusian liberals that provided Lukashenka with his current home of convenience, the informal group of so-called 'Young Wolves' would join him against Kebich.[81]

Lukashenka was well aware that the corruption committee had been set up by others for their purposes, but thought he could exploit it for his own, following the example of Telman Gdlian and Nikolai Ivanov, who had risen to fame in the Gorbachev era by investigating corruption in Uzbekistan, albeit without producing many concrete results.[82] In his speech to parliament on 15 December 1993, Lukashenka dramatically declared, 'I have the most terrible facts here [shows his batch of papers] and about many sitting in this hall.'[83] But his actual 'evidence' didn't amount to much, beyond a garage that had been built for a private dacha at the state's expense.

Shushkevich was briefly hospitalised the very next day, conveniently absenting himself from the political fray, but leaving no one to put up a fight against Kebich. In January 1994 US president Bill Clinton visited Minsk to try and bolster the new state, since Belarus had taken the enormous step of relinquishing any claim of control over the Soviet nuclear weapons left on its territory in 1991, and ratified the Non-Proliferation Treaty (NPT) and Strategic Arms Reduction Treaty (START 1) in 1993. But the symbolism did little to stop the conservatives' advance, largely because Kebich had never had any real control over the nuclear weapons anyway and used the issue as a smokescreen for his pro-Russia policy. As soon as Clinton was gone, Shushkevich's supporters were picked off one by one, as parliament began a 'war of censure' against the Shushkevich camp, particularly those, like Uladzimir Yahoraw, the minister of the interior, whom Kebich considered to be secret allies of the BNF.[84] Over the winter Yahoraw and Eduard Shyrkowski, head of the KGB, had circulated a private letter among MPs accusing Kebich of planning to transfer the new state lock, stock and barrel to Russia (now that he was posing as a patriot; Shyrkowski was clearly a contradictory character). In January 1994 Kebich used the arrest by Lithuanian special forces on Belarusian territory of two former Communist leaders accused of involvement in the killings of January 1991 (Mykolas Burokevičius and Juozos Jermalavičius) to get rid of both Yahoraw and Shyrkowski. Shushkevich naïvely failed to protect them. Others to go were Piotr Krawchanka at the Foreign Ministry and Pavel Kazlowski at Defence.

On 26 January the preliminary skirmishes gave way to a straight fight. A cynical deal between the former Communist majority and the reformist Young Wolves brought down Shushkevich by 209 votes to thirty-six,[85] while the BNF largely sat on its hands. Kebich easily survived Shushkevich's attempt to turn the tables, winning his vote by 175 votes to 105. The votes were secret, but Shushkevich was convinced that 'the majority of the BNF' had stabbed him in the back and cynically voted against him.[86] The alliance of convenience did not last long. Nine were originally in the race to succeed Shushkevich, three of whom made it to the first vote: the conservative Mechyslaw Hryb and two of the Young Wolves, Mikhail Marynich and Viktar Hanchar. Hanchar came bottom of the first ballot and dropped out, allowing Hryb to be elected over Marynich by 183 votes to fifty-five. The 'first Belarusian bison has fallen', Feduta wrote but Kebich had miscalculated: 'the people demanded more and more victims. It was just like a television serial.'[87] Lukashenka would be the ultimate beneficiary by promising more sacrifices. The BNF meanwhile had acquiesced in creating a bandwagon they could not control. Some thirty thousand protested in support of Shushkevich on 15 February, but to no avail.

After Shushkevich

With Shushkevich gone, Kebich could press on with consolidating his rule. Spring 1994 brought two potential turning points. The old parliament's singular achievement was the passing of a new constitution in March 1994. This was certainly an improvement on the amended 1978 Soviet constitution that Belarus had been lumbered with since 1991, not to mention the authoritarian constitution that Lukashenka subsequently replaced it with in 1996, but it was designed by Kebich, so it was hardly perfectly democratic. Nevertheless, if someone other than Lukashenka had won the first presidential election, then Belarus would most likely have become a reasonably well-functioning semi-presidential system, with at least a partially effective balance of powers between president, parliament and judiciary. As with the new Russian constitution passed in December 1993 and the Ukrainian version of June 1996, the parliamentary non-experts who drafted the Belarusian constitution went for an amalgam of the only two systems they knew, which were those of the USA and Fifth Republic France. But, compared to the Russian constitution, which quickly became 'super-presidential', and the Ukrainian constitution, which has been constantly argued over and amended since 1996,[88] the 1994 Belarusian version might have established a more stable political system if it had been given time to work. As well as a presidency, a new Constitutional Court also began to operate in 1994.

The other key potential turning point was the abortive currency union with Russia. Kebich had declared that Belarus would accept the Russian rouble as legal tender as early as March 1993. In April 1994 he thought he had negotiated an agreement that pointed towards complete monetary union; customs restrictions would be removed; and large amounts of credit would allow Belarus to cover any initial balance-of-payments deficit with Russia, with 200 billion roubles being provided to strengthen the financial system in Belarus. Moreover, the agreement offered to exchange basic holdings of Russian and Belarusian roubles one to one, like Helmut Kohl's gambit with the old East Germany in 1990, whereas the real rate was more like one to four. Shushkevich and Pazniak attacked each other on the right; meanwhile Kebich considers he would have seen off Lukashenka had he been able to implement the currency agreement before the election.[89] But the Russians felt lukewarm about Kebich at best, so they dragged things out. The monetary 'union' was only a ploy in Russian domestic politics to restore Yeltsin's nationalist credentials between the Duma elections in 1993 and 1995, and didn't address basic questions such as what would happen to the National Bank of Belarus. Lukashenka felt obliged to oppose the union when it still looked as though it might happen – then simply stole Kebich's programme.[90]

The 1994 Election: The 'Accidental President'?

With Shushkevich removed from office, Kebich was overconfident. He ran the machine. What could go wrong? In January 1994, the leaders of the regions assured him in private: 'Viacheslaw Frantsevich! Don't be afraid of elections. We completely control the situation in the regions. As we say, so the people will vote.'[91] Having ended the temporary diarchy with Shushkevich, Krawchanka argues, 'all power (silovye) structures were returned under Kebich's control: he had promoted the loyal Mechyslaw Hryb to control parliament; he controlled practically all the state apparatus, the majority of mass media and, particularly importantly, television and radio. Boris Yeltsin won the 1996 Russian election from a much worse starting position.'[92]

Kebich had indeed assembled 'administrative resources' in the same way as Yeltsin, but he didn't employ them with the same ruthless cynicism. He later regretted he hadn't used them more.[93] Yeltsin asserted with characteristic bluntness when he met Lukashenka after the election: 'You didn't take power. Kebich lost it. You either keep power or you lose it.'[94] Kebich also shared a particular problem with Yeltsin, which was common enough locally, but far from ideal in a new country's new prime minister – he drank too much. This may have helped him bond with Yeltsin, but he was often incapacitated for days.

Nor did Kebich get his campaign message right. He had no 'greater evil' to fight like Yeltsin's nemesis, the Communist leader Gennadii Ziuganov, in Russia. With the BNF in decline after its failed campaign for early parliamentary elections in 1992, the bogeys for most ordinary Belarusians were the nomenklatura and establishment corruption. Kebich's greatest problem was that he had been in power since before the fall of the USSR – since 1990, in fact – which was all the more obvious now that Shushkevich was gone. Kebich persuaded 203 out of 260 deputies to back his candidacy in an attempt to demonstrate force majeure, but this only served to remind the people that he was the public face of the apparat. To ordinary voters, Shushkevich and Kebich represented twin sides of the ruling elite, and the two were mocked as 'ShushKebich'.

Lukashenka came up on many people's blind side, though there was a natural space to exploit between the unelectable BNF and the increasingly unpopular Kebich. As Alexander Martynaw points out, Lukashenka was certainly not 'accidental' in so far as he found just the right way to sidestep the tired four-year-old psychodrama between the nomenklatura and the BNF.[95] Lucan Way argues that the authorities, on the other hand, were trapped in the old Soviet mentality that only the nomenklatura and the intelligentsia, and certainly not former pig farmers or border guards, could be part of the political elite.[96] Kebich concentrated on attacking his mirror image, Pazniak, assuming that Shushkevich had been dealt with. As well as distracting his attention, this had the dangerous side effect of setting up an anti-BNF dynamic that Lukashenka was later able to exploit. Pazniak and Lukashenka were both after the protest vote, but Pazniak's advisers made a disastrous decision to present him more soberly as a conservative authority figure. Ordinary people wanted the Soviet version.

The right were also naïve about Lukashenka, having already underestimated the impact of his anti-corruption 'report'. Pazniak and Shushkevich played into Lukashenka's hands by obsessively pursuing Kebich as their main opponent. Even the BNF was still uncertain as late as March whether to back Pazniak or support Shushkevich as a common 'democratic' candidate.[97] As a result, the right remained divided.

Dirty Tricks

Kebich had used Lukashenka to smear Shushkevich and now thought he could dispose of him. In April 1994 he ensured that Lukashenka's 'corruption committee' was disbanded. Krawchanka, who now headed the publicity side of the Kebich campaign, later said, 'I know that in Kebich's circle there were constant conversations about how to neutralise Lukashenka' by sabotaging his signature campaign.[98] According to Feduta's inside account of the campaign, Henadz Danilaw, who was 'Kebich's right hand and ran the security ministries from the Cabinet of Ministers',[99] was 'proposing different variants for the use of force to Kebich all the time'.[100] One idea was only to allow candidates over the age of forty – Lukashenka's fortieth birthday being due after the election. Kebich's press secretary, Uladzimir Zamiatalin, manipulated the media. In June the leading official paper, *Sovetskaia Belarus* (Soviet Belarus), reprinted an article about Shushkevich supposedly taken from a Dutch paper that depicted him as a militant Catholic and extreme nationalist. No Dutch original has ever been found. Two weeks before the vote Zamiatalin inspired another story accusing Lukashenka of harassing an air stewardess on a government flight.

Kebich's team also attempted to pressure the leaders of the White Rus movement to persuade their members that Lukashenka wasn't pro-Russian enough.[101] Some did withdraw their support – a 'special operation' that perhaps left Kebich overconfident that he had dealt with the man he certainly did not then regard as his most dangerous opponent. On the whole, however, Kebich was too disorganised to steal a win.

The power of the KGB was a factor in the election, but not necessarily one that worked in Kebich's favour. In 1993 the then KGB head, Shyrkowski, sauntered into Krawchanka's office and calmly played him a tape of Kebich talking with the US ambassador, David Schwartz, in a car, with Kebich promising to get rid of Krawchanka by the end of November (a date that wasn't too far off).[102] Even the guy who served Kebich's drinks in the government dining room was one of Shyrkowski's men.[103] But Shyrkowski was aggrieved at his loss of office in January 1994 and, with Shushkevich looking weak, he needed someone else to unseat Kebich. He therefore reportedly 'fed Lukashenka with material aimed at undermining Kebich's reputation'.[104] Former interior minister Uladzimir Yahoraw backed Shushkevich in the election, but managed to survive as Lukashenka's first head of the KGB.

Lukashenka also pulled his own stunts. In June his car had to speed off when it was supposedly shot at near Liozna, a former shtetl near Vitsebsk – though it was later claimed the car was stationary and the shot had come from inside. Viktar Sheiman, a veteran of the Afghan War who served as Lukashenka's shadowy 'security chief', organised the set-up. Sheiman, Lukashenka and his business backer Ivan Tsitsiankow (see page 164) were the only three people in the car,[105] though Tsitsiankow later claimed he had been alone with Lukashenka.[106] Sheiman's reward was to serve as Lukashenka's head of security after 1994, then as Procurator in 2000, and as head of the Presidential Administration from December 2004. Lukashenka's staff reported the Liozna incident eight hours after it supposedly happened. The pistol was never found. One insider later claimed Sheiman had asked him to supply a 'neutral' weapon for a few days.[107] Lukashenka may also have been helped by Henadz Lavitski, Shyrkowski's successor as head of the KGB, who enjoyed a cosy ten-year stint as ambassador to Israel once Lukashenka was president.[108] The drama doubled up with a bizarre attempt (whether real or not) by the local police to bar Lukashenka from his own office, obstructing the 'people's friend' from doing his work.

Too many candidates were fighting dirty. There were also too many candidates. Henadz Karpenka was a potentially strong opponent, feared by all sides for his appeal to both the intelligentsia and nomenklatura. Like everybody else, he needed either 100,000 signatures to stand or the support of seventy MPs. Initially he attracted seventy-eight MPs, but dirty tricks left him with only sixty-four. He didn't bother to appeal. 'Perhaps he was just lazy,'[109] Feduta suggests. His supporters stood down, fearing he would take votes from Shushkevich.[110] Aliaksandr Sanchukowski, the director of the Horizont TV company in Minsk, was initially put forward by his fellow 'Red directors' (nomenklatura factory bosses) in the 'Belarus' faction, only then to be appointed Kebich's campaign manager instead.

Other minor candidates were actually secret 'clones', intended by one side or another to take votes away from their opponents. Vasil Novikaw for the Communists (who eventually won 4.3 per cent of the vote) and Aliaksandr Dubko for the Agrarians (5.9 per cent) were designed by Kebich's team to siphon off votes that would otherwise go to Lukashenka.[111] The 'new' Communists had for a long time obediently followed in Kebich's slipstream.

But once again Kebich wasn't as fully in control as he thought he was. The clone candidates may even have taken votes off him. Indeed, Krawchanka says of them: 'I am certain that their appearance was initiated by the same forces that stood behind Aliaksandr Lukashenka . . . . The idyll [between Kebich and the Communists] continued to the start of 1994, when the party bosses suddenly . . . went into opposition.'[112] Krawchanka hints the Kremlin might have been involved. The leader of the Agrarian Party, Siamion Sharetski, was another traitor who had deserted Kebich after failing to win a significant place under him in 1992–3,[113] and was deaf to all attempts at compromise.

The accusations from opposite camps can't be right – unless, of course, the clones had sold themselves to both sides, which is entirely possible. But the important point is the general one. Everyone was plotting against everyone else and thought everyone was plotting against them. There wasn't much strategic thinking going on.

Supporting Sasha

Lukashenka was more than just a one-man campaign. After his 1993 corruption speech, he attracted all sorts of fellow travellers and even some true believers, including liberals, albeit 'liberals' in the Russian mould, i.e. Russian-speakers whose idea of 'reform' had little in common with the BNF, but who wanted to take Belarus along Yeltsin's path. These Young Wolves, such as Viktar Hanchar and Dzmitry Bulakhaw, who chaired the parliamentary legislation committee, saw Lukashenka as a battering ram 'to destroy the old machine of executive power and take power in their own hands'.[114] They had been seeking a candidate for a long time, also considering but discarding Henadz Karpenka as too much of a dilettante. Lukashenka, on the other hand, was 'more ambitious, much more hard-working, and, most importantly, knew clearly that he wouldn't get a second chance'.[115]

But, according to Aliaksandr Feduta, who played a key role in the campaign as Lukashenka's media adviser and PR man, many of those who joined his team were 'cynical people, of a kind we weren't used to at that time'. In one discussion over coffee about forming a group of 'trusted persons' to back Lukashenka, Hanchar suggested: '"a pensioner, a doctor, a teacher." Then Bulakhaw asked [jokingly]: "Vitia, what about prostitutes? Who among us will work with prostitutes?"' To which Hanchar replied: "Dima, why does he need prostitutes? He's already got us."'[116] Others waited in the wings, confident they could manipulate Lukashenka in their own interests, or steer their own craft in his wake. Politics was divided between those who were traumatised by the rise of the pig farmer and those who failed to take him seriously.

Businessmen

Feduta refers to Lukashenka's outfit as having 'the cheapest election campaign and the cheapest headquarters of all',[117] though he also says, 'you can't carry out any election campaign without money'.[118] Lukashenka was backed by certain business circles, whose money perhaps seemed modest, certainly compared to Yeltsin's campaign in 1996, or even Kuchma's in Ukraine in 1994;

but it nonetheless helped the neophyte populist make his mark. Would-be Belarusian 'oligarchs' were still relative small fry. Lukashenka wore the same jacket with pride throughout the campaign. On his first visit to the Kremlin, he and his aides looked like 'some Makhno band' (Nestor Makhno was an anarchist leader in Ukraine during the Civil War).[119]

But Lukashenka wasn't the ingénu he seemed. He was running as a populist against nomenklatura privilege and corruption, so his business supporters stayed in the shadows. But they were still there. First among these was Ivan Tsitsiankow, who like Lukashenka came from the Mahilew region, and worked for the less than perfectly transparent Legacy of Chernobyl Fund. Tsitsiankow's reward from 1994–6 was to be the 'de facto administrator of the "second budget of Belarus", the "zavkhoz of the republic" (steward)'.[120] Tsitsiankow was personally somewhat rough.[121] When the Young Wolves complained he was in their offices too much, Lukashenka reassured them: 'Ivan is a businessman. He needs patrons (*babki*). We'll be running the country'.[122]

Other sponsors included Leanid Sinitsyn, whom Feduta called 'the Belarusian Frankenstein',[123] Aliaksandr Samankow, of the First Republican Investment Fund or PRIF (later jailed for bribery), Mikhail Chyhir (later Lukashenka's first prime minister) and Arkadii Borodich, who brought resources from Belahroprombank, which channelled state-subsidised loans to the agricultural sector. These loans could be creamed off, but their distribution was also a potent weapon. Staff would get free petrol from Belahroprombank.[124] Chyhir donated $5,000 of his own money, which at the time was a substantial amount in Belarus – though not in Russia, where it would have been seen as a joke.

On the other hand, Aliaksandr Pupeika, then the biggest Belarusian oligarch,[125] founder of the business empire PuShe, was not in the Lukashenka camp, although Hanchar and Bulakhaw went to the Minsk 'Directors Club' in March 1994 to pitch for his support. Pupeika preferred Shushkevich.[126] In the early 1990s PuShe became Belarus's biggest company with the help of soft credits from Belahroprombank, selling Skodas and Phillips and Whirlpool products, and was also involved in food-processing and the Olimp bank. By 1996 it had an annual turnover of $200 million.[127] Pupeika's empire did not survive Lukashenka's victory for long. He ended up in asylum in Poland in 1998, after an attempt to have him seized on an Interpol warrant at Warsaw airport. Pupeika claims he was targeted because he started to give money to Yury Khadyka of the BNF and the paper *Svaboda* ('Freedom'). Pupeika's summary fate, like that of Mikhail Khodorkovskii under Putin, was designed to show the embryonic business elite there was a new power and new rules. As

Feduta aptly summarised it, 'the absolute majority of those businessmen who sided with Lukashenka in 1994 are silent today, although in truth they repent their choice'.[128]

Rats

As his bandwagon began to roll, Lukashenka was joined by a motley crew of turncoats and careerists, including many who were nominally in the Kebich camp. Mikhail Miasnikovich, who was deputy prime minister and favourite to become prime minister after a Kebich victory, was supposedly Belarus's most 'honourable bureaucrat', but was in secret negotiations with the Lukashenka camp.[129] (His reward would be to be deputy prime minister again after 1994, then head of the Presidential Administration and head of the Academy of Sciences after 2001 – the latter a notable coup for a non-academic.) It was obvious in 1994 that Miasnikovich 'was already playing on two fronts'.[130] He was even giving out instructions in private to regional bosses to go slow on harvesting the vote for Kebich.[131] According to Feduta, he told the Lukashenka team in private, 'You have a good chance. I will be on your side, as it were'.[132] Others who jumped Kebich's ship included Siarhei Linh (later prime minister in 1996–2000), Ivan Tsitsiankow and Leanid Sinitsyn. Uladzimir Harkun whom Lukashenka would make deputy prime minister in charge of agriculture after the election, allegedly helped siphon off money from the agricultural budget.[133]

Russia

Moscow's role is less clear. But Kebich was lumped in with the motley crew from across the former USSR who had supported the Russian White House during the confrontations in Moscow in late 1993, so were hardly flavour of the month with the recently confident Yeltsin in early 1994. Lukashenka's trip to address the Duma in May 1994 at Zhirinovskii's invitation gave him an official seal of approval. Yevgenii Primakov, the Russian Head of Counter-Intelligence, allegedly supplied Lukashenka with information about the Kebich government's arms sales to Croatia.

Lukashenka's Landslide

In the event Lukashenka won comfortably, as he has done in every subsequent election – but his first win was for real. Populism proved to be popular in

Belarus. And Lukashenka was a skilled campaigner, as well as 'his own image-maker and director'.[134] His slogan was: 'Neither with the left nor with the right, but with the people.' Lukashenka has occasionally claimed that he actually won on the first round.[135]

Results of the 1994 Election (by Percentage)

	First Round	Second Round
Aliaksandr Lukashenka	44.8	80.1
Viacheslaw Kebich	17.3	19.9
Zianon Pazniak (BNF)	12.8	–
Stanislaw Shushkevich	9.9	–
Aliaksandr Dubko (Agrarians)	5.9	–
Vasil Novikaw (Communists)	4.3	–

Turnout: 69.9.

In terms of the regional breakdown of votes, Lukashenka was much further ahead in the east and south-west, with a highest score of 63 per cent in Mahilew. Kebich's 'administrative' vote was more evenly spread across the country. Pazniak and Shushkevich did best in the capital, but it was Pazniak who did best in the former 'Litva', in the historically ethnically and religiously mixed 'hotspot' districts of the north-west, winning 21.2 per cent in Hrodna and 21 per cent in Minsk city.

First-Round Vote by Region (by Percentage)[136]

	Lukashenka	Kebich	Shushkevich	Pazniak
Hrodna	36.3	14.6	10.4	21.2
Brest	53.5	13.9	8.7	11.7
Minsk	44.5	14.9	8.7	15.3
Minsk City	26.5	18.2	21.2	21
Vitsebsk	46	19.3	7.1	9.4
Mahilew	63	17	3.8	4.7
Homel	45.6	23.1	8.6	6.3
National	44.8	17.3	9.9	12.8

The combined 'democratic' vote of Pazniak and Shushkevich (22.7 per cent), on the other hand, ought to have put one or the other in the second round instead of Kebich, had they pooled their forces in the campaign. It was a great irony that, despite all the turmoil of the years from 1991 to 1994, the 'democratic' vote was actually higher than in 1990, but counted for less.

According to Krawchanka, 'in the first days after voting many people, including opposition deputies said to him [Kebich] not to allow Lukashenka power at any price. They suggested the most diverse scenarios: from introducing changes to the constitution to abolishing the post of president or disrupting voting in the second round to introducing a state of emergency. But Kebich stayed silent'.[137] Mechyslaw Hryb floated the idea of cancelling the second round of voting, as constitutionally Kebich would then be in charge. According to Feduta, 'we were very scared of this [scenario] in our campaign HQ'.[138] But Kebich stayed his unsteady hand. He knew the jig was up. He tried secret power-sharing negotiations with Viktar Hanchar and Dzmitry Bulakhaw from the Lukashenka team, but sent Henadz Kozlaw and the unreliable Miasnikovich from his side. Not surprisingly, the talks broke down over the obvious first question of who would serve as prime minister and who would be president.[139] Lukashenka romped the second round.

Conclusion

The Kebich elite might well have achieved more if Lukashenka hadn't come to power. His supporters might claim he was an 'inefficient reformer' rather than an 'inefficient authoritarian'. Among his limited achievements, Belarus adopted a new constitution and abandoned nuclear weapons, and the post-Soviet economic collapse was not as severe as elsewhere. But the Kebich elite were certainly guilty of cynicism and short-sightedness. Kebich was no new-model democrat, but a creature of the old Soviet elite. And Shushkevich wasn't much better. The two men constantly fought each other and ignored the real threat from someone they both thought they could manipulate.

Lukashenka, on the other hand, had no intention of being an 'inefficient authoritarian'. He intended to stay in power *vser'ez i nadolgo* ('serious and long term').[140] Feduta records that ' "Sasha" (short for Aleksandr) suddenly insisted on being addressed as "Aleksandr Grigorevich" ' (his more formal Russian patronymic).[141] As Way argues, the 'key authoritarian institutions were already in place when Lukashenka came to power'.[142] He would make better use of them than Kebich.

CHAPTER 9

BUILDING AUTHORITARIANISM: LUKASHENKA'S FIRST TERM

Political leaders often arrive in office claiming to be all things to all men (and women). Lukashenka was no exception, having managed to convince different audiences that he was simultaneously a populist, a liberal reformer and an ardent Russophile. Two years later, he engineered a coup d'état to overthrow the established constitutional order. Could he have been stopped if he had been more forcibly opposed? Could he have been pressed into a different mould in 1994–6? Countervailing domestic forces were weak after the war of all-against-all of the Kebich years, though they were stronger than they would be in subsequent years. Russia was highly factionalised, but Yeltsin needed Lukashenka just as much as the other way around, as an alliance with Belarus helped draw the sting of his nationalist and Communist opponents after their triumph in the Russian Duma elections in 1993 and 1995. The West was engaged early on in Lukashenka's term, though not at the crucial moment in late 1996: some US goodwill carried over from Belarus's earlier adherence to the NPT and START 1 in 1993, the EU initiated – but never formally ratified – a Partnership and Cooperation Agreement in 1995, and the IMF issued Belarus a loan in 1995. But the ailing President Yeltsin badly needed Lukashenka's help to secure his reelection in the summer of 1996, and was willing to invest generously to secure his support. Arguably, however, the West's mistake was then to withdraw too quickly after 1996, and have so little influence on Lukashenka subsequently.

A Liberal, Briefly

Initially, Lukashenka wanted to be a 'reformer', whatever that was, especially as this was then the Russian fashion. He made serious overtures to none other than Russian liberal supremo and later conservative bête noire Georgii Yavlinskii to run the Belarusian economy.[1] Michel Camdessus, the then managing director of the IMF, made a successful visit to Minsk in August 1994, and in January 1995 the IMF approved a loan of $103 million to support economic reforms (after an earlier loan in 1993). The IMF was still praising Belarusian policy in August 1995,[2] just before it suspended its loan programme in November. Belarus hoped for a larger loan, of the order of $700 million. Interestingly, in the light of subsequent events, the IMF was also considering at this time helping Belarus underpin its sovereignty with a more diversified energy supply.

Ukraine also had a new president at this point, Leonid Kuchma, similarly elected on a platform of restoring links with Russia; but Kuchma had launched an apparently serious economic reform plan in October 1994 (although this soon ran out of steam after a good start). For several months, Lukashenka appeared to be treading a similar path, looking for a compromise economic programme to marry the proposals of deputy prime minister Siarhei Linh, an old-style Gosplan 'economist', with the reform plans of Stanislaw Bahdankevich, head of the National Bank.

Lukashenka posed as a man of the people. Feduta quotes his reluctance to raise prices, as 'the president sure can't mess his people around'.[3] On the other hand, he had no apparent fear of the social consequences of reform. In private he dismissed prime minister Mikhail Chyhir's predictions of unemployment and social protest: 'Nobody will be going to the square here. Here there'll be tanks and machine guns, and not one will [dare] step out here. The square will be free! You can do whatever you like.'[4]

But in practice Belarus under Lukashenka was never likely to follow even the semi-reformist path of Ukraine, let alone the radical steps taken by the Baltic States and Poland. Lukashenka and his entourage may have stolen Kebich's campaign, but they were instinctively pro-Russian and bet their hopes for economic revival on Russian assistance. They also wanted to build up their own personal power and bash the BNF – Russia would not object, but the West might. And Lukashenka, the former collective farm boss, understood the planning system, but not the market. Despite his campaign sponsors, in 1994 he had relatively few links with Belarus's 'Red directors' who were tempted by the idea of enriching themselves in a wave of Russian-style 'privatisation'. Lukashenka understood that he had a social base among pensioners and factory workers and wanted to preserve it.

In November 1994 he made up his mind. According to Feduta, 'the country completely changed, and in a single day'.[5] After popular protests at an increase in dairy prices, Lukashenka rushed home from a meeting with Boris Yeltsin in Sochi, and demonstrated his future governing style by lambasting his entire government on live TV, adding in the National Bank and parliament for good measure – though they were only following the course he had set in the first place. Lukashenka's theatrically rhetorical question 'Do you know what a market economy is, can you work in market conditions?' received a firm 'no' by way of answer, meaning that the answer to the next question, 'And do you know what a planned economy is?', had to be a 'yes'. 'Right,' said the president, 'we will build what we know.'[6] In private the Young Wolves, Chyhir, Bahdankevich, the then deputy prime minister Viktar Hanchar, and Uladzimir Yarmoshyn, the mayor of Minsk, all wanted to continue with the reforms. But only Hanchar and Bahdankevich (in September 1995) ultimately resigned. Despite Lukashenka's claim that 'I don't give up my own',[7] his campaign team from 1994 were already almost all gone. The change was symbolised by the appointment in April 1995 of Uladzimir Zamiatalin as deputy chief of the administration in charge of ideology. Zamiatalin had previously done a similar job for Kebich, but his cynical definition of 'ideology' had been no obstacle to dumping him for Lukashenka during the campaign and now serving as the latter's 'enforcer'. Instead of the Young Wolves, the regime now increasingly relied on the old nomenklatura. In 1997 Lukashenka engineered a seemingly ridiculous row with the foreign embassies based in the plush Minsk suburb of Drazdy. He managed to break international law by forcing them out (cutting off their water and electricity) – showing his mettle, but only deepening his international isolation. His purpose became clear when Drazdy was then turned into a haven for the new elite.

Lukashenka's initial 'reform' period is perhaps best taken as evidence for the hypothesis that he was a total opportunist. He wasn't even originally a Russophile. Russia itself had good relations with the IMF at this time, but Lukashenka was looking for a model of relations that suited his own domestic purposes. Crucially, though, the reform period bore some fruit: Feduta considers that 'two and a half years [from 1992] turned out to be enough for the economy to start slowly reviving'.[8] Lukashenka's rapprochement with Russia reinvigorated export markets, but the reforms helped the economy actually produce goods to sell.

Time to Rewrite All the Books Again

The biggest problem with the idea of Lukashenka-the-liberal was that he wasn't one. He had won power by exploiting two big negatives, against both the nomenklatura and the BNF. In Ukraine in 1994 new president Leonid Kuchma famously expressed his indifference to the 'national idea' and the state, which were 'not an icon to which one should pray'. But he was indifferent rather than hostile, and would end up plundering what he needed from the nationalist agenda once he was in office. Lukashenka's animosity towards the BNF was of a different order.

In so far as Lukashenka had a clear ideological position in his early years, it combined elements of Soviet restorationism with what could be called 'Panrussism'.[9] Lukashenka's otherwise nonsensical description of himself as an 'Orthodox atheist' fits this combination perfectly. Regime ideologues played up the idea of Belarus as part of the same 'civilisation' as Russia and the inevitable 'clash of civilisations' with the West – Samuel Huntington's thesis being a boon to so many half-penny ideologues justifying authoritarian regimes. Local hacks like Lew Kryshtapovich talked of 'the large East-West megacycle in world history'; the 'non-objective' end of the USSR was just one phase in this struggle rather than the supposed 'end of world history', and had in any case already been succeeded by a new cycle marked by the revanchism of the East against the materialistic and decadent West, aided by the backlash caused by 'the expansion of Western principles in the non-Western world' – the true cause of terrorism and fundamentalism, a mirror image of the West's own 'consumer-hedonist utopia'.[10] Belarus's unique position was to have been the 'first to realise the destructiveness of the division of the fraternal peoples and mighty state [that was the USSR] and set out on the road of [re]developing a union.'[11]

Lukashenka and his followers were part 'west-Russian', in the sense of being Russian nationalist-lite; but they could also outflank Yeltsin on the right. Domestic critics could be hyperbolic. Piotr Rukowski called Lukashenkaism 'a sort or replica of Russian national-Bolshevism',[12] first seen under Stalin in the late 1930s,[13] and currently represented in Russia by the likes of Aleksandr Dugin.[14] But Lukashenka was still an opportunist. He and Yeltsin were populist mirror images of one another, with each stealing the other's tricks. The aims of the rapprochement with Russia were practical.

Smashing his domestic enemies was the top priority, so the propaganda drive by Lukashenka's acolytes concentrated on dealing the BNF some heavy blows. A black PR campaign on TV fronted by Yury Azaronak crudely caricatured all 'nationalists' as Nazis. The state symbols introduced in 1992, the Pahonia emblem and the white-red-white flag of the Grand Duchy, were now depicted as artificial inventions of Radaslaw Astrowski's Belarusian Central Council in 1943–4. The new schoolbooks that had been tentatively introduced in the early 1990s were rewritten again in 1995–6, to stress the Belarusians' joint development with the Russians in 'the common feudal state of the east Slavs', and restoring the official Soviet Belarusian version of Second World War history to its key place in the pantheon of national glory.[15]

The BNF also destroyed itself. Its zero-sum radicalism and single-minded concentration on cultural and historical issues at a time of extreme economic hardship were already losing it support. Its egotistical leaders fought like rats in a sack, and Pazniak's messiah complex didn't help.

Ya khochu spasti tebia, Rossiia ('I want to save you, Russia')[16]

Lukashenka's strategic choice of economic policy and geopolitical direction in 1994 made him a serious player in Russian politics. The president comes from Shklow, just north of Mahilew, which is an old settlement, with records dating back to 1535, but nowadays a hick town with a population of only sixteen thousand. But Shklow, like Lukashenka himself, has had a colourful history moving back and forth between Russia and Belarus, most notably when it was depopulated in the 1654–67 war, with 195 families being resettled in Muscovy at the time.[17] Shklow is also from where the 'False Dmitrii' – the Polish-backed imposter who claimed to be the son of Ivan the Terrible during Russia's ruler-less 'Time of Troubles' – set out to seize power in Moscow in 1604.

In private Lukashenka was mocked as the new False Dmitrii, the *Shklovskii samozvanets* – the 'self-proclaimed' saviour of no less than two nations.[18] He moved quickly after his election to link his animus against the BNF to leveraging resources out of Russia. Luckily for him, he was pushing at an open door. Yeltsin's Houdini reelection strategy in 1996 depended in large part on stealing the clothes of his opponents by expunging his Belovezhkaia guilt, and showing that the process of Soviet dissolution announced in December 1991 could begin to be reversed. The first practical step was a Friendship and Cooperation Treaty signed in February 1995, which allowed Russia to maintain its military in Belarus until at least 2010 and keep control of Soviet forward air defence systems free of charge. Just as importantly, the treaty established open borders, so that Russia could use Belarus as a giant transit corridor for huge volumes of exports and imports – not all of them legal – and Belarus could rebuild its truck and tractor markets in Russia (the iconic MTZ series of tractors beloved of Socialist Realist painters was produced at the Minsk Tractor Works, founded in 1946). Russia also began channelling arms exports to controversial regimes through Belarus (see pages 186–9). The March 1996 agreement establishing the 'Community of Russia and Belarus' promised the latter important concrete benefits: the write-off of $1 billion of debt, and the opportunity to purchase oil and gas at the heavily subsidised price charged in the Russian market. The latter deal alone would be worth billions.

For once, however, Lukashenka was outmanoeuvred, albeit only briefly, once the 1996 Russian election was out of the way. Yeltsin hollowed out or vetoed the creation of 'Union' institutions that Lukashenka hoped would have been his future playground. An even grander 'Reunion' project, which envisaged a bicameral parliament with equal voting rights for Russia and Belarus and a rotating presidency being put to a referendum in both states within three months, was vetoed on the Russian side by Anatolii Chubais.[19] Yeltsin came to his senses and sacked the overreaching Dmitrii Riurikov, his chief foreign policy assistant, to make sure the project didn't happen.[20] Riurikov was made ambassador to Uzbekistan.

Lukashenka quickly recovered to become the dominant force in the relationship again by 1998–9, when the Yeltsin regime was in terminal decline. Many Russian nationalists seriously thought that Lukashenka could be their saviour; Vladimir Zhirinovskii claimed, 'If everyone in the CIS had followed the same path as Belarus, as Lukashenka, it would have been better for us.'[21] One key reason why Yeltsin chose Putin rather than another liberal as his successor was to forestall this possibility.

1995: The First Referendum

In December 1994 the trade-union leader Siarhei Antonchik of the BNF made a bold anti-corruption speech. It had much more substance, detail and serious import than Lukashenka's more famous earlier speech in 1993, and this time targeted those around the new president. But Lukashenka completely outmanoeuvred him, theatrically ordering and then withdrawing the resignations of all the accused, while preventing the press from publishing the contents of the speech – during typesetting, leading to large blank spaces in the papers the next day. Although Antonchik's speech was made on his own initiative and Pazniak had tried to dissuade him from making it, Lukashenka considered it a casus belli, and it prompted him to begin a campaign to destroy the BNF as a political rival.[22] Antonchik himself, thanks to Lukashenka's long memory, would serve several prison sentences.

Lukashenka's chosen tactic was a referendum which cynically but skilfully linked all his priorities together. The first question, concerning giving 'the Russian language equal status to Belarusian', was likely to be supported by almost all the population, as nearly everyone spoke it. This was designed to bolster support for the second question, which concerned using modified versions of the Soviet Belarusian flag and national emblem, instead of the white-red-white flag and Pahonia of the Grand Duchy supported by the BNF. But, as Feduta noted, the affair was about politics: it wasn't about heraldry at all.[23] Lukashenka cobbled the new design together in his private office. The third question contained the suppressed premise that reintegration with Russia would save the Belarusian economy. The fourth was designed to undermine the credibility of parliament. But Lukashenka's shrewdest move was his timing. The deal with Russia and various trade scams (see pages 185–6) gave him sufficient funds to begin building a 'social contract' after 1995, allowing him to link the use of neo-Soviet symbols with the restoration of a neo-Soviet welfare state.

In April 1995 BNF deputies began a hunger strike in parliament, led by Pazniak, claiming that Lukashenka's state-symbol reform would lead the country back into the arms of Russia. Lukashenka simply sent the security forces into the building to 'look for a bomb', and cleared it by force. The thuggish Zamiatalin did what he was hired to do, and disposed of a video that had been made of the event.[24] Zamiatalin was also in charge of the practical preparations for the 'right result' in the referendum. Lukashenka duly got four 'yeses'.

Results of the May 1995 Referendum (by Percentage)

	Yes	No
1. Do you agree to give the Russian language equal status to the Belarusian?	83.3	12.7
2. Do you support the suggestion to introduce a new state flag and state emblem of the Republic of Belarus?	75.1	20.5
3. Do you support the actions of the president, aimed at economic integration with the Russian Federation?	83.3	12.5
4. Do you accept the necessity of changes to the constitution of the Republic of Belarus, which provide for the early termination of the plenary powers of the Supreme Soviet by the president of the Republic of Belarus in the event of systematic or gross violations of the constitution?	77.7	17.8

Turnout: 64.8. The Constitutional Court insisted that the fourth question was only 'consultative'.[25]

The 1995 Parliamentary Elections

The referendum in May 1995 was also designed to spike the guns of Lukashenka's main institutional rival, the parliament elected in 1990, as it was due for reelection at the same time. Belarus had put off parliamentary elections for as long as possible. Russia had held elections in December 1993, Ukraine in March 1994. In all three countries reformers regretted that elections had not been held sooner, assuming they would have done much better in the immediate aftermath of the Soviet dissolution, before the economic collapse of the early 1990s had turned public opinion against reform and while local Communist parties were still banned. Poland had already had three parliamentary elections and one presidential election since 1989. The missed opportunity to hold elections in Belarus in 1992 was mentioned in Chapter 8. The 1995 parliamentary elections were, however, reasonably free and fair, at least compared to later elections. There was genuine party competition.

Lukashenka encouraged a boycott of the vote, but was only semi-successful. In the first round of voting in May 1995, less than half the seats, only 119 out of 260, were filled (50 per cent of the vote was necessary to get elected), which was well short of the necessary two-thirds quorum of 174 seats. Repeat elections in the empty seats were scheduled for November and December, but the 1994 constitution also said that parliament had to start working within thirty days. The old parliament therefore changed the rules, lowering the turnout requirement from 50 to 25 per cent. It also recalled itself after the first round – a move of questionable legality. Lukashenka therefore had a case when he tried to stop the second round of voting taking place: any act of the outgoing parliament artificially prolonging its life or trying to influence the composition of its successor was legally dubious. But in October 1995 the Constitutional Court sided with parliament, or rather with the two potentially overlapping parliaments; but then it would – its eleven members were all originally elected by parliament, as per the 1994 constitution.

When the repeat elections were held in November and December 1995, a further seventy-nine seats were filled, making 198 in total. There were still sixty-two empty seats, but parliament was now technically quorate.

Individual candidates, particularly those from the BNF, complained about dirty tricks in individual campaigns, but the overall result was not fixed. One opinion poll recorded that 10.4 per cent had voted for the Communists, 6.6% for the Agrarians, and only 5.6 per cent for the BNF and 2.1 per cent for Popular Accord,[26] which was roughly in line with the official result. The BNF

Elections to the Belarusian Parliament, 1995 (Number of Seats Achieved)

Party of Communists of Belarus (Kaliakin)	42
Agrarians (Sharetski)	33
United Civic Party (OGP)	9
Party of Popular Accord (PNS)	8
All-Belarusian Party of People's Unity and Accord	2
Belarusian Social-Democratic Assembly (Hramada)	2
Other	7
Independents	95
Total elected	198
Empty seats	62
Total	260

Source: http://binghamton.edu/crc/elections/blr95par.html.

had lost at least half of its base vote from 1990, which, given the electoral system, meant it was overtaken by the new left and centre parties and won no seats at all. Pazniak left the country in 1996. Lukashenka's antipathy to the BNF was such that in 2005 he signed a decree prohibiting the use of the words 'Belarus', 'Belarusian' or 'national' in the names of public organisations.

The various Belarusian liberals, however, the United Civic Party and the Party of Popular Accord, did well. Lukashenka had gambled on a boycott and didn't have his own party, so part of his electorate voted for the revived Communist Party and the Agrarians. The BNF was vanquished, but there was now a 'new opposition'. Lukashenka had miscalculated.

Once the dust had settled, there were four main groups in parliament. The Communists gained a few independents to take around fifty seats, while the less political Agrarians gained more, mainly collective farm 'independents', also to take around fifty seats. The liberal group Civic Action had twenty-one. Lukashenka's administration managed to cobble together a loyalist group dubbed *Soglasie* (Accord) with sixty seats; leaving thirty to forty deputies in vaguely defined opposition.[27] The BNF press talked of a 'melon' parliament – green (Agrarian) on the outside, but red (Communist) inside. Lukashenka hadn't wanted the new parliament at all and had loftily refused to endorse any particular party, so the Accord group was relatively small. At best, Lukashenka could command barely a quarter of the new MPs. In private, he offered money and cars ('Let deputies have the salaries of ministers', 'Just don't disturb me from working'), if parliament agreed to downgrade its role to a couple of ceremonial meetings a year, as had been the Soviet practice.[28]

However, when parliament finally assembled, the Communists, Agrarians and Civic Action combined against Accord to elect the Agrarian leader, Siamion Sharetski, as chair in January 1996. Sharetski made conciliatory noises, but parliament and president were almost instantly at odds. In February 1996 parliament refused to confirm Lukashenka's appointee, Tamara Vinnikava, as head of the National Bank. Lukashenka considered her appointed anyway. He unilaterally took over the parliamentary paper *Narodna hazeta* ('Peoples Newspaper') as his own propaganda sheet.

Faking the Opposition

Faced with a new opposition in parliament, Lukashenka set about creating an opposition of his own. He never went as far as Russia under Putin, where a whole virtual universe of loyal satellite parties was created by the Kremlin; but Lukashenka went further than Kebich in using 'clone' parties to displace the real opposition. But as soon as the job was done, their role also diminished. Lukashenka didn't want to rule through any collective organs. Divide-and-rule and the use of masses of government informers and agents became his favourite methods of control.

There were three 'cloning' operations in and after 1996. The strongest parties to emerge from the 1995 elections were no longer the BNF, but the Communists, Agrarians and centrists. Lukashenka had no intention of being outflanked on the left, where the Communists had renamed themselves the Party of Communists of Belarus (PCB), and their leader, Siarhei Kaliakin, although strongly in favour of Lukashenka's then Russophile foreign policy, opposed his increasing authoritarianism, if only because it threatened the party's traditional power base in the local soviets and among Belarus's 'Red directors'.[29] In late 1996, therefore, Lukashenka decided to restore the old Communist Party of Belarus as a rival. A PCB defector, Viktar Chykin (later first deputy mayor of Minsk and head of the state TV and radio company from 2000), was gifted 'administrative resources', including money to pay for the new party's founding conference. The PCB, on the other hand, had its business support cut off. The party's leading financier, Anatol Lashkevich, ambitiously nicknamed the 'Belarusian Engels', left for Russia in 1997, where he took up the post of head of Rubin TV. It was easy not to notice there were now two Communist Parties. The opposition Communists lingered on until 2009, when its Veterans' Faction, supported by the KGB, backed a merger with Lukashenka's Communists. Kaliakin's party renamed itself the 'United Left – Just World'.

The Agrarian Party was easier to deal with, as it had always been close to the powers-that-be. Siamion Sharetski was forced into exile in 1999, and a new version of the party, led by Mikhail Shymanski, editor of the now pro-government paper *Narodna hazeta*, was declared the official one.

The new liberals were hardest to deal with. The newly united United Civic Party had won most seats in Minsk in 1995 and formed the powerful Civic Accord faction in parliament. The centre parties rather than the BNF were also the natural home for any defectors from Lukashenka's regime, and along with the revived left were a natural channel for potential Russian support, so their 'safe haven' had to be destroyed. Lukashenka's administration therefore helped build a rival centre party from the splinters of two others.[30] Henadz Karpenka, the original leader of the Party of Popular Accord and deputy chair of parliament, was forced out and replaced by Leanid Sechka, who 'was rewarded with a high post in the Committee of State Control'.[31] The centre-left Hramada, one of modern Belarus's first ever parties, both in its original incarnation in 1903 and in its revived form in March 1991, also split during the crisis in autumn 1996. Thereafter a constant series of splits left everyone totally confused and the old 'centre' totally ineffective.

The final element in the political crackdown took the form of two decrees closing many local NGOs in 1997 and 1999. The first targeted a selective number of organisations that Lukashenka deemed to be dangerous, ranging from George Soros's Renaissance Foundation to the Children of Chernobyl charity. The second ordered all NGOs to reregister, resulting in their numbers falling from 2,500 to 1,300.[32]

The 1996 Crisis

Lukashenka didn't like the new parties and he wasn't about to share power with the new parliament. One of the questions in the 1995 referendum had been designed to be used against the latter. But a new referendum would make doubly sure. However, in order to win it, he would have to take on all the institutions set up by the 1994 constitution. He therefore drew up a new constitution that would replace them, but had to get it legitimised first. In August, after seventy-three MPs petitioned the Constitutional Court for Lukashenka's impeachment, he announced a referendum to be held on 7 November 1996, the old Soviet Revolutionary holiday, although Lukashenka's side had been planning the referendum since at least June.[33] In September, parliament made the mistake of switching from outright opposition to Lukashenka's plans to negotiating a joint referendum, in which Lukashenka would ask his questions and it would put its own alongside. Parliament also negotiated for a different date, 24 November, which was when yet another round of elections was scheduled to take place to fill the sixty-two seats still vacant in parliament; it hoped in this way to boost its own position with a bigger vote.

Parliament, however, overplayed its hand by amending the 1994 constitution and proposing to abolish the presidency in its new draft, meaning it could no longer pose as the conservative defender of the constitutional status quo. It was also outmanoeuvred, as Lukashenka again constructed a multipart exercise to bandwagon support for his key referendum questions. This time, the principal 'enticer' question concerned shifting 'Independence Day' from celebrating the Belarusian People's Republic's declaration of independence in 1918 to liberation from the Nazis in July 1944. Lukashenka then bridged to parliament's questions via two questions that implied parliamentary support for the sale of private land and the abolition of the death penalty, neither of which were popular causes in Belarus (public opinion in many Western European countries still supported the death penalty in 1996). Parliament was soon backtracking to argue that the whole exercise should be purely 'consultative', which looked both weak and duplicitous.

Another weakness was that parliament, or more exactly the new liberal opposition, couldn't really put people on the streets. The BNF could, but it was now an extra-parliamentary force. It organised a 'hot spring', with mass demonstrations in Minsk on 25 March 1996, the anniversary of the founding of the Belarusian People's Republic in 1918, and 26 April, the anniversary of Chernobyl, with the latter drawing some fifty thousand people. However, Pazniak ruined much of the effect by leading a minute's silence in memory of the recently murdered Chechen leader Dzhokar Dudaev. Pazniak still concentrated his fire on Lukashenka's threat to Belarusian national identity rather than on his drive to undermine the constitution. The parliamentary and extra-parliamentary oppositions therefore had no common agenda.

Lukashenka's main advantages were that he had moved quickly to control the state media and purse strings (including his own shadow funds). And after abandoning the Young Wolves in 1995, he had rebuilt his power base among the state conservatives and security services (the so-called *siloviki*) – if anything, the BNF campaign only drove him further into their arms. Lukashenka would try not to play dirty too early, as he still needed foreign, particularly Russian, support; but he was prepared to play much dirtier than the opposition realised.

The War against Institutions

As with the opposition parties, so with the main institutions of state: but rather than outright confrontation, as when Yeltsin sent in the tanks to shell the Moscow White House in October 1993, Lukashenka chose more subtle 'cloning' tactics. Instead of having to deal with the troublesome parliament, for example, he would set up his own. Fortunately for Lukashenka, Sharetski, the new parliamentary chair, didn't want confrontation. Parliament was afraid to appeal to the people. Lukashenka had won the 'war of symbols' in 1995, and the economy was starting to recover, allowing Lukashenka to rush through some populist measures by decree in September 1996, raising pensions and ordering state enterprises to pay all unpaid back wages.

In fact, parliament was cloned twice. First, Mikhail Miasnikovich, the head of the presidential administration, devised the idea of setting up an 'All-Belarusian People's Assembly' in October 1996. The Assembly was a giant Soviet-style corporatist pseudo-consultative body, with enough old party 'patrons', such as Anatol Malafeew and Metropolitan Filaret for the Orthodox Church, attending to give it some clout,[34] though prime minister Chyhir chose a veiled form of protest, giving a long and boring speech about economic technicalities.[35] The Assembly, of course, backed Lukashenka's referendum plans and proposals for a new constitution by an impressive vote of 4,942 to eleven.[36]

The second long-term clone was a bicameral 'parliament', consisting of a 'House of Representatives' and a 'Council of the Republic', that Lukashenka planned to introduce to replace the parliament elected, painfully, in 1995. This shadow parliament would be shadowed in turn by the All-Belarusian People's Assembly, which Lukashenka would call again on the eve of each subsequent parliamentary 'election'.

The 1994 constitution, which had set up the presidency, also set up a powerful Constitutional Court. Its rulings were not subject to appeal, and its eleven members were all elected by parliament (to serve for eleven years). For the two years from 1994 to 1996 it served as the main constraint on Lukashenka's power, striking down no fewer than seventeen presidential decrees in 1995–6.[37] In 1995 Lukashenka was not yet powerful enough to do away with the court and was temporarily forced to compromise with it, as with the ruling in February that the fourth question in his first referendum (on confidence in parliament) should be only 'consultative'. In October 1995 the court sided with parliament and ruled that it could sit, despite its problems actually getting itself elected.

1 The St Safiia cathedral of the Holy Wisdom, Polatsk, above the river Dzvina. Built in the eleventh century, but with Baroque (Unaite) additions in the seventeenth and eighteenth centuries.

2 Synkovichi fortress-church, in the unique local 'Gothic-Orthodox' style, built 1518–56.

3 Euphrosyne's Cross, twelfth century. Also the symbol of the Youth Front.

4 The great Orthodox scholar Cyril of Turaw.

5 The Resurrection cathedral in Barysaw, north of Minsk, 1874, in the 'Russian Revival' style.

6 Icon of Our Lady of Minsk, mid–late sixteenth century, showing a more naturalistic post-Renaissance style.

7 Cathedral of St Virgin Mary, finished 1710; Central European Baroque in the middle of Minsk.

8 The Red Church, Minsk – the Church of SS Simon and Helena, 1905–10. Scene of the demonstrations in December 2010.

9 Valiantsin Volkaw, *Minsk: 3rd July 1944*, (1955). A Socialist Realist classic showing Soviet troops returning to the ruined city in 1944. A massive painting, it took Volkaw nine years to complete.

10 Marc Chagall, *The Blue House* (1917).

11 Marc Chagall, *Over Vitsebsk* (1915–20). The local Jews and Orthodox lead parallel but separate lives.

12 Lukashenka's neo-Soviet national emblem, replacing the Pahonia after the referendum in 1995. The green outline in the middle is actually Belarus.

13 'The Belarus' MTZ – the iconic Soviet Belarusian product. To some, Belarus is still better known as a tractor.

14 The white-red-white flag, the state flag in 1918, 1943–4 and 1992–5, now a symbol of opposition to Lukashenka; at protests after another election fix in 2006.

15 For Belarus! Slightly more orchestrated demonstrations in support of the government.

16 The new National Library, Minsk. Symbol of Lukashenka's social contract and kitsch architectural taste.

17 Lukashenka (far right) plays ice hockey against a Russian team. The president's men lost diplomatically to a Gazprom side, 5–9, in 2008.

18 When first introduced in 1992, the new Belarusian money showed animals in ascending sizes, starting with the 'hare' on the one rouble note (above). By 1998 inflation had forced Belarus to move on to buildings instead (below). The reverse of the 1992 'hare' note shows the Pahonia ('The Chase'), the state symbol of Belarus from 1992 to 1995.

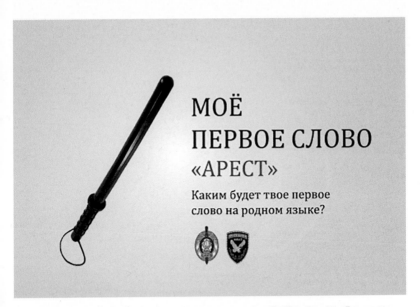

19 The Ministry of Culture produced an advertising campaign called 'My First Word', promoting the use of the Belarusian language. These posters were swiftly adapted by protesters who produced alternative versions mocking the campaign – this poster reads 'My First Word: "Arrest"'.

20 A government propaganda poster, featuring the first line of the national anthem: 'We Belarusians are peaceful people'.

21 The return of the white-red-white flag at anti-Lukashenka protests in Minsk, August 2020.

22 Belatedly organised pro-Lukashenka rallies were poorly attended.

23 Police violence following the protests.

24 The feminisation of the protests. On the wall you can see a graffito of '3%' – Lukashenka's supposed poll rating.

25 Lukashenka's notorious helicopter flight.

26 The opposition leader, Sviatlana Tsikhanowskaya.

But by 1996 Lukashenka was in open confrontation with the Constitutional Court. Valer Tsikhinia, the head of the court, instead of remaining aloof and independent, was drawn into the negotiations with parliament and allegedly made private compromises.[38] Lukashenka also set up a rival Legal Constitutional Council, to indicate he would also replace the Constitutional Court if need be. The court lost its desire for confrontation at the height of the crisis. Three of its judges resigned on 3 December 1996, by which time it was too late to have any effect.

The Procuracy was also potentially dangerous. According to Feduta, it had 'lots of material on Tsitsiankow', the steward of Lukashenka's unofficial budget.[39] But the Procuracy depended on Interior Minister Yury Zakharanka, who was feeding it (the Procurary) some of that information,[40] and he was forced out of office in October when parliament idiotically failed to support him.

Lukashenka's biggest other potential problem was with the Central Election Commission and its ambitious chair, Viktar Hanchar, who could declare the result of the referendum invalid – as seemed likely since Hanchar had already called it a 'piece of legal idiocy'. Hanchar also accused Lukashenka of secretly setting up illegal district election commissions to fix the referendum, and of forcing businesses to pay into a semi-secret 'referendum fund' that had been covertly established on 1 January 1996. On 14 November 1996 Hanchar was forced out after a presidential guard was sent to his office. He was replaced by Lidziia Yarmoshyna, whose subsequent conduct of elections was so bad and so biased as to earn her a visa ban from the EU and the US alongside the members of Lukashenka's supposed 'death squad' (see pages 190–2).

Finally, unreliable ministers were forced out: there were always others prepared to do the dirty work. Lukashenka's private blandishments and skilful combination of sticks and carrots worked against mass defections during the crisis. The interior minister Zakharanka went in October 1996, only to be replaced by the much more hardline Viktar Sheiman. The prime minister Mykhail Chyhir resigned on 18 November. Both would pose a problem at a later date.

The Referendum

The dénouement came in November 1996. The Constitutional Court declared on 4 November that the referendum as a whole should be only 'consultative'. It failed, however, to take the much bolder but more logical step of ruling that, as Lukashenka's proposals clearly replaced rather than amended the existing constitution, the vote was in violation of that original constitution. It also backed away from a decision on impeachment, as between ten and twelve MPs had supposedly withdrawn their signatures.[41] On 6 November Lukashenka issued a decree – of no legal authority at all – saying the referendum would be legally binding after all, though he offered a fig-leaf compromise by accepting parliament's date for the vote. On 12 November Lukashenka addressed the Russian Duma and persuaded Russia to send a fake 'mediation' team, which arrived on 21–22 November, made up of prime minister Viktor Chernomyrdin, Gennadii Seleznev, head of the Duma, and Yegor Stroiev, head of the Russian upper house, the Federation Council. Yeltsin himself was in poor health at this time. Sharetski, the head of the Agrarian Party, thought he had good links with Stroiev, who was in charge of agriculture at the Moscow CPSU Central Committee before 1991; but Seleznev was at the centre of the Moscow network of 'left' parties and oligarchs that Lukashenka had been courting for several years.

The Russians backed out of the 'zero variant' option – no impeachment of Lukashenka in return for no referendum – that the opposition thought they had secured. According to the Russian-backed compromise, the referendum would not be binding, so parliament all too hastily dropped its impeachment plans. As soon as the ink was dry, Lukashenka once again declared the referendum would be 'official'. The compromise also mentioned a 'Constitutional Assembly' of a hundred venerable talking heads, half appointed by parliament and half by the president, which would be tasked with thrashing out an agreed version of a new constitution. It never met.

The Russians had no grand geopolitical concessions in mind. They wanted a factory as their 'reward' – the Belarus Metallurgical Factory (BMZ) to be precise.[42] BMZ seems to have passed under Boris Berezovskii's informal control in the late 1990s via a shadowy company, EL Petroleum, whose head, Yurii Foektistov, was arrested in 1999. Yegor Gaidar also considers that the Russian elite's acceptance of Lukashenka's consolidation of power, with its mission beginning on 21 November, was not coincident with the final removal of nuclear weapons from Belarus, on 27 November.[43]

Lukashenka campaigned for a 'Yes-Yes-No-No-No-No-No'. The key result was the 70.5 per cent support Lukashenka claimed for his new constitution, compared to a mere 7.9 per cen t for parliament's amended version of the 1994 constitution. The opposition claimed up to half the vote was falsified.[44] Local leaders were pressed to maximise early voting, which began as early as 9 November. The opinion polls had showed rising support for most of

The November 1996 Referendum (by Percentage)

	Yes	No
The President's Questions		
1. Shifting Independence Day to 3 July – the day of Belarus's liberation from Hitlerite aggressors in the Great Fatherland War	88.2	10.5
2. Adoption of the 1994 constitution with the changes and additions proposed by the president of Belarus	70.5	9.9
3. Do you support the free buying and selling of land, without restrictions?	15.4	82.9
4. Do you support the abolition of the death penalty in the Republic of Belarus?	17.9	80.4
Parliament's Questions		
1. Adoption of the 1994 constitution with the changes and additions proposed by the Communist and Agrarian factions	7.9	71.2
2. All local councils to be elected	28.1	69.9
3. Do you agree that the financing of all organs of state power must be public and only from the state budget?	32.2	65.8

Turnout: 84.1.

Source: www.rec.gov.by/refer/ref1996resdoc.html.

Lukashenka's options, but not to the levels eventually claimed. The difference was most obvious on the last two of parliament's questions, its 'bandwagon' questions that the public might have been expected to support. Lukashenka didn't want parliament to have even a partial victory.

Four new deputies were elected to the vacant parliamentary seats on the same day, but this no longer made much difference. Another thirty-odd might have been elected in a second round, but this never took place. Parliament's days were numbered anyway, and MPs were no longer showing a united front.

Opinion Poll Predictions for the 1996 Referendum (Yes Vote, by Percentage)

	Two Months Before	On Eve	Claimed Actual
1. Independence Day	35.8	54.1	88.2
2. President's constitution	40.7	62.1	70.5
3. Sale of land	28.0	19.2	15.4
4. Death penalty	20.6	17.4	17.9
5. Parliament's constitution	9.4	8.7	7.9
6. Local councils	86.2	73.7	28.1
7. State budget	79.2	72.5	32.2

Source: *Sovetskaia Belorussiia*, 3 December 1996.[45]

More than half (110 out of the original 198) turned up to meet Lukashenka on 19 November. The same number accepted unelected posts in the new 'parliament'.[46] About forty die-hards tried to continue meeting, but the administration had shut the parliament building 'for remodelling', and Lukashenka formally closed it down on 29 November, though it was still recognised as the real parliament by many in the West. Unlike Russia in 1993, the opposition quietly left the building. The EU broke off relations with Belarus in 1997.

The three new pro-regime parties were the only ones allowed representation in the remodelled puppet parliament. Chykin's new Communist Party had twenty-two seats, Shymanski's Agrarians fourteen and the Party of Popular Accord five. Formal political parties quickly lost their importance, however. In his second term, Lukashenka began setting up pseudo-civic front organisations, so-called 'Lukamol' (like the 'Komsomol' but under Lukashenka) parties like the 'Sporting' Party, aimed at youth, and the Party of Labour and Justice, a pseudo-leftist party aimed at pensioners. The local Liberal Democratic Party, like Zhirinovskii's Russian equivalent, maintained its covert links with the regime (see page 197). But rumours of a new 'official' Lukashenka party never bore fruit. He didn't need one.

Lukashenka's Constitution

The power grab was unmistakable. Lukashenka's first presidential term would be extended from five to seven years, on the pretext that it was beginning again from scratch in 1996, to 2001 rather than 1999. The new constitution paid lip service to, but did not enforce, the separation of powers: the powerful unicameral parliament would be replaced by a much weaker two-chamber system, made up of a Palace of Representatives and a Council of the Republic. This time the 110 members of the first House of Representatives were hand-picked by the president; meaningless elections were then held every four years from 2000. The Council of the Republic, the 'senior' chamber, was not even elected. Eight deputies were appointed from each of Belarus's six oblasts and the city of Minsk, and another eight were appointed directly by the president. Presidential decrees would now have the force of law, higher than parliament's laws. Parliament could not adopt any law to increase or decrease government spending without the consent of the president or the government. Parliament had only minimal control of government. If the Palace of Representatives, the lower house, twice fails to approve the president's choice of prime minister, it faces dissolution. The president appoints six out of the twelve members of the Constitutional Court and the Central Election Commission, with the other six appointed by the upper house, the Council of the Republic, on his recommendation. The president also appoints the entire Supreme Court and Supreme Economic Court, as well as all military and district judges.[47] The State Control Committee controls all the purse strings.

Transit Scams

With his power consolidated, Lukashenka had a lot of debts to repay. Consequently, the 'scourge of corruption' was soon presiding over corruption on a scale never seen under Kebich[48] – although, as Feduta puts it, Lukashenka saw 'the whole country as his household, and a good boss of the household, which Lukashenka considers himself to be, doesn't steal his own stuff'.[49] One product of the Belarus-Russia 'Union' treaties beginning in 1995 was an open border regime, which was quickly exploited to establish corrupt transit and customs rip-off schemes. Initially these mainly benefited the Belarusian side, with the Russian state budget being defrauded of billions of dollars. This was a symptom both of the price Yeltsin was prepared to pay to ease his 'Belovezhskaia complex',[50] and of the sheer chaos of the late Yeltsin era, which allowed several key Russian politicians to join the scam.

In November 1995 Lukashenka signed 'Edict Number 230', which wasn't exactly widely publicised. This set up a company called Torgexpo, supposedly to import much needed consumer goods, mainly alcohol and cigarettes, into Belarus free of tax, but they didn't stay in Belarus for long. Hundreds of millions of dollars were easily made by reexporting them to Russia, once again free of tax. Easy money invited competition. The bizarrely named 'Mahmed Esambaiev Cultural Foundation' (named after a Soviet ballet dancer),[51] and even the local Orthodox Church, made millions from 'transit income' and tax-free importing. Ivan Tsitsiankow's 'Legacy of Chernobyl' Fund was also involved, as was another shadowy businessman, Viktar Lahvinets, who ran the Konto Group, trucking contraband across Belarus, and supposedly provided Lukashenka with his new, more presidential wardrobe. Lahvinets fell foul of his attempts to take on the *siloviki* and their lucrative role in the oil business.[52] Tsitsiankow fell from grace in 1999.

Torgexpo and the other schemes made an estimated $320 million, 11 per cent of national income, in 1995–6.[53] Together with off-budget arms sales, Lukashenka's circle netted an estimated $4.5 billion in his first term in office; with the 'unofficial' budget rivalling the 'official' budget in size.[54]

Lukashenka also provided privileges to the Yeltsin 'Family', especially Boris Berezovskii,[55] despite his oft-professed 'hatred of Russian oligarchs'.[56] As well as Berezovskii's interest in BMZ, Pavel Borodin, the head of the Russia-Belarus 'Union State' after 2000, was involved in oil export. The Russian Communists and Duma chair Gennadii Seleznev have both used Belarus as a 'reserve aerodrome' (safe haven) for their and their supporters' business interests.[57] However, Russian funding for Lukashenka's 2001 campaign (and the arguably more important delivery of the Russian media) was conditional on his opening doors for Russian capital – a promise that he conspicuously failed to fulfil. This, plus his past association with Berezovskii, was a key reason for the frosty relations that developed under Putin.

The Lord of War

In the postwar era, Belarus developed a sizeable military-industrial complex. After the German invasion in 1941 and Operation Bagration in 1944, the Red Army's top brass saw Belarus as a crucial theatre of war, and the more troops and equipment that were stationed there, the greater the need for a local service industry that was relatively hi-tech by Soviet standards. As a fairly small republic, Belarus accounted for only 5 per cent of Soviet arms production, but it had many areas of expertise, including anti-missile, air-defence, communications and control systems. The MZKT factory in Minsk produced military tractors and armoured personnel carriers (APCs). BelIOMO, established in 1971, made electronic optical instruments. Many parts of the Belarusian military sector could therefore temporarily survive on their own, even after the end of the USSR disrupted so many chains of production in 1991.[58]

Nevertheless, in the early 1990s, Belarusian arms 'exports' amounted to little more than a gigantic yard sale, as everything inherited from the Soviet armed forces – on one count 3,100 tanks, 3,400 APCs and 378 jets – was sold before it could be reclaimed. In 1993 a specialist export company, Beltekheksport, was set up, which already seemed to have many shady contacts, from the KGB front firm Nordex and alleged Russian mobster Georgii Luchanskii, to notorious international arms dealers like Dmitrii Steshinsky, who ran arms to Croatia via Ukraine, and to the Austrian company SEN, overseen by a native Belarusian, Uladzimir Peftsiew (Peftiev).

Lukashenka, the 'scourge of corruption', immediately reached a private modus vivendi with Peftsiew, inviting him back from Austria in September 1994 to head Beltekheksport. Viktar Sheiman now oversaw the arms trade,[59] to make sure the lion's share of any profits went to the shadowy 'presidential fund'. Soviet S–300 surface-to-air missiles were sold to the US for $6 million, rather than $60 million, in 1994.[60] (In 2010 Belarus was accused of selling S–300s to Iran.) In 1996–8, 18 Mig–29s were sold to Peru, which was squaring off with Ecuador at the time, for an estimated $400 million, but $120 million may have been raked off.[61] According to one source, Sheiman was worth $900 million by 2006 and Peftsiew $397 million.[62] An intensified sweep of remaining assets produced sales of $500 million in 1997, making Belarus temporarily the world's ninth largest arms exporter, but this was a one-off. Lukashenka had decided he liked the business, however. It provided handy revenue, some of which could be siphoned off, some of which was vitally necessary for funding his new state machine and preventing the emergence of rival centres of power. It helped grease the shadowy Russian–Belarusian nexus that was the main source of his international power. He could even do geopolitical 'favours' for Russia, and underpin his 'anti-mondialist' foreign policy. And he could dress it all up as helping to restore Soviet might. His Russophile supporters quite liked to see him dress up in uniform, and Lukashenka certainly enjoyed it.

Nevertheless, by the late 1990s the local arms industry had to move on if it was to survive. Belarus developed a niche market in servicing old Soviet weaponry, and by the 2000s was able to make real capital investments in its more advanced sectors. It also gained extra money by helping Russia channel unseen exports to 'rogue states', often through the safely provincial airport at Machulishchi, 80 km west of Minsk. By 2004 two new companies operated alongside Beltekheksport: Goskomvoenprom and Belspetsvneshtekhnika.

Lukashenka had no qualms about the people or organisations he sold to. He sold ten thousand rifles to Sudan in 1995, which were later used in Darfur. He sold all over the Middle East. Yemen was a particularly good client after the USA imposed an arms embargo as a punishment for its support of Saddam Hussein's invasion of Kuwait in 1990, which lasted until 2004. He sold rifles to Iran and Syria, portable rocket launchers to Lebanon and Syria, forty-eight T–72 tanks to Morocco in 2001 to use against insurgents in the Western Sahara, and armoured vehicles and anti-aircraft systems to Libya before its rapprochement with the West in 2003. According to the *Wall Street Journal*, Belarus supplied over $500 million worth of arms to Palestinian militants.[63] Kebich's Belarus facilitated Russia's support for Christian Armenia which helped it win its war with Muslim Azerbaijan in 1992–5. Mines and light arms were delivered to Muslim Albania and the Kosovo Liberation Army in the late 1990s, via the Croatian arms dealer and former deputy defence minister Libo Rojs. In the wake of the Rose Revolution, Lukashenka toyed with the idea of arming the rebel Adjara region against the new Georgian leadership after its long-term leader Aslan Abashidze sent a delegation to Minsk in March 2004, shortly before his downfall that May. Light arms, grenade launchers, anti-tank missiles and APCs reached Tajikistan's civil war and allegedly even the Taliban in Afghanistan via a burgeoning relationship with authoritarian Turkmenistan. An alternative route to the Taliban is said to have been via the United Arab Emirates, helped by another shady arms dealer Viktar Bout.

Lukashenka enjoyed a meeting of minds with Saddam Hussein. According to the Iraq Survey Group Final Report which investigated Saddam's sources of arms before 2003, 'Belarus was the largest supplier of sophisticated high-technology conventional weapons to Iraq from 2001 until the fall of the regime' in 2003. 'Relations between Belarus and Iraq were so strong that an Iraqi-Belarusian Joint Committee was formed to promote illicit trade.' Lukashenka's close ally Uladzimir Zamiatalin 'was in charge of the special military cooperation with Iraq and functioned as a secret envoy between President Lukashenka and Saddam'.[64] Beginning in 2001–2, Belarus supplied air-defence, radar and electronic-warfare technology to Iraq, which was used against coalition air forces, as well as spare parts and PN–5 and PN–7 night-vision devices. Around $114 million was paid to Belarus via Syria into Infobank, Systemtech and BelarusianMetalEnergo. An estimated $7 million in kickbacks were parked in Infobank when the USA imposed sanctions against it for money laundering in 2004. Wilder accusations have been made that Iraqi chemical weapons were hidden in Belarus after 2003 (it has also been rumoured that Radovan Karadžić was flown by a Russian aircraft to hide for several months in Belarus in 1997).[65] Ivan Safronov, the defence correspondent of Kommersant, the Russian paper, who 'fell out of' a Moscow window in March 2007, was working at the time on a story about the sale of Su–30 fighters to Iran and S–300V missiles to Syria via Belarus.

Deals with more respectable countries tended to be one-offs. T–72 tanks were sold to Hungary in 1995, electronic sights to Sweden in 1996. China, India and Pakistan were also occasional markets.

According to the US administration's report to Congress in March 2006:

There have been numerous reports of Belarusian sales or delivery of weapons or weapons-related technologies to states of concern, including state sponsors of terrorism. In April and September 2004, the United States imposed sanctions on a Belarusian entity, Belvneshpromservice, pursuant to the Iran Nonproliferation Act of 2000 for the transfer to Iran of items on a multilateral export control list or items having the potential of making a material contribution to WMD or cruise or ballistic missile systems. According to the U.N. Register of Conventional Arms for 2004, the most recent year available, Belarus exported a number of Russian-origin armoured combat vehicles to Sudan. According to information Belarus provided to the Register, in 2003 Belarus sold such vehicles and large-calibre artillery systems to Sudan, and in 2002 sold large weapons systems to Iran.[66]

Many of these deals were channelled through the notorious arms dealer Viktar Bout, a native Belarusian who controlled the world's largest private army in the Sudan and was the model for Nicholas Cage's character, Yuri Orlov, in the film *Lord of War* (2005). According to Polish media reports, Igor Sechin was Bout's Russian patron,[67] and Sechin and Sheiman were personally close. Bout was arrested in a sting operation in Thailand in March 2008 and extradited to the US in 2010, on both occasions to understandably muted Russian protests. The Belarusians were even quieter.

The 1999 Shadow Election

Meanwhile, politics continued at home. Lukashenka was not yet strong enough to squeeze all opposition out of the system. The opposition attempted to regroup in 1999, when Lukashenka was due to face a new election in May after the five years allotted him by the constitution under which he was elected in 1994. The organiser was Viktar Hanchar, the head of the Central Election Commission until November 1996, who had returned from exile in Latvia to run the campaign. Behind him allegedly stood some liberal Russians who had links through Valentin Yumashev, Yeltsin's future son-in-law, to Anatolii Chubais.[68]

Finding candidates to stand in the 'election' was more difficult. Politicians like Uladzimir Hancharyk and Siamion Domash, who would contest the 2001 election, thought this venture rash. The regime seems at one time to have toyed with the possibility of inserting the secretly loyal Siarhei Haidukevich, who was now the leader of the Liberal-Democratic Party of Belarus, as a 'spoiler';[69] but he had no one to oppose after Henadz Karpenka came under pressure to pull out. Hanchar's shadow campaign therefore ended up with Lukashenka's first prime minister, Mykhail Chyhir, who had been absent in prison since March, running against Zianon Pazniak, who had been absent abroad since 1996. Hanchar stretched all credibility by claiming that 53 per cent had voted on 16 May using flimsy ballot boxes that were carried by hand from place to place. Surveys indicate as few as 5 per cent admitting to having voted.[70] Other sources estimate one million votes, or 14 per cent.[71] Ludicrously, 'Hanchar could not name the victor',[72] though he indicated Pazniak was probably ahead.[73]

Hanchar pressed on. Plan B was to reconvene the old parliament on 19 September and declare that Lukashenka's term was legally at an end. If a popular vote couldn't remove Lukashenka, then maybe this would spark an 'apparat revolution' that could.[74] Hanchar disappeared three days before the meeting.

The Disappearances

The 1999 election 'campaign' may have been a failure on the ground, but it seems to have seriously spooked Lukashenka, as it questioned his legitimacy and prestige, and revealed threatening splits within the elite. Lukashenka's perception that he needed to head off this threat came at a bad time. Since 1996, the power of the 'shadow state', its parallel budget and role in arms sales had grown ever larger. Viktar Sheiman played the key role in this increased 'securitisation' of the state, and it was also he who had played the key role in frustrating the 1999 campaign. From his position as head of the National Security Council from 1999 to 2006, Sheiman controlled the State Control Committee, the Procuracy, the audit agencies, the police and the courts. He was able to use these powers to keep Lukashenka's political rivals in check and prevent challenges to the state's economic monopoly. At the same time, Sheiman ran his own lucrative arms-trading and retail empire. In Belarus the KGB still proudly retained its name. But it was not yet part of Sheiman's empire or *siloviki* group (from the Russian for 'men of force'). In fact, some saw Uladzimir Matskevich, head of the local KGB from 1996, as a possible good cop or 'Belarusian Putin' in the late 1990s.[75]

But Sheiman was playing with fire. The years 1999 and 2000 became known as the years of the 'disappearances', as Lukashenka's opponents suddenly went missing. Moreover, the disappeared were not from the BNF, although many of its leaders were in exile. Someone seemed to be targeting Lukashenka's more dangerous opponents, who came from within the elite, particularly those who had defected from his original entourage in 1994.

The first to disappear was the former interior minister Yury Zakharanka on 7 May 1999, whom Lukashenka had fired in October 1995. Zakharanka had stood up to Lukashenka as an 'honest cop' in 1994–5, had tried to expose his shadow budget and had gone over to the United Civic Party, before organising Chyhir's campaign in 1999. Then Hanchar, the prime mover of the 1999 'election', and his business associate Anatol Krasowski vanished on 16 September 1999. Rather later Zmitser Zavadzki, a Belarusian cameraman who worked for ORT, disappeared on his way to Minsk airport to meet Pavel Sharamet, on

7 July 2000. This was assumed to be a personal vendetta. In Lukashenka's first three years as president, Zavadzki was the only cameraman allowed to film him at official events.

To this list could be added the death of Henadz Karpenka in mysterious circumstances in March 1999. Karpenka, the former head of the centrist Party of Popular Accord, who had been trying to reunite the fractured opposition since 1996, had been the prime mover in the attempt to impeach Lukashenka in 1996 and had toyed with the idea of standing in the 1999 'shadow election'. Tamara Vinnikava, the 'black orchid' of Belarus, and head of the National Bank from 1995 to 1997, was also initially included among the disappeared (she fled on the day of Karpenka's funeral), but it later emerged she had gone abroad shortly after giving an interview about illegal arms sales.

Lukashenka liked to talk about 'order' (*poriadok*), but never really about 'law and order': with good reason. It later transpired that a secret 'death squad' had been in operation in Belarus since the late 1990s. It started with actual mafiosi. According to Feduta, 'this scheme succeeded ideally, and the group started to be charged with more and more serious "orders" – political ones'. More than thirty people were killed.[76] Five were shot dead in one day.[77]

According to a detailed report prepared by a Cypriot MP, Christos Pourgourides, for the Council of Europe Parliamentary Assembly in 2004,[78] the chain of command started with Viktar Sheiman, who controlled the information flow to Lukashenka and was always whispering danger in his ear.[79] Then came the Russia-born Yurii Sivakov, minister of the interior, who 'borrowed' the official state execution pistol. Dzmitry Pawlichenka, head of the 'Special Rapid Reaction Unit' Almaz, did the deed. Other information came from the head of death row in Minsk's main prison, Aleh Alkaew, who defected to Germany in 2001 and described how the pistol was signed out by Sivakov in both May and September 1999.[80]

In November 2000, the 'good cops' rebelled. An unsigned email emerged with full details of the investigation, including information about a shovel with Zavadzki's blood on it. Pawlichenka was detained on the basis of a handwritten accusation by the chief of criminal police, Mikalai Lapatsik, but released after Lukashenka personally intervened. Sources close to the KGB chief Uladzimir Matskevich and the prosecutor general Aleh Bazhelka claim that the two had requested permission to arrest Sheiman for ordering the killings. Lukashenka had refused, and instead dismissed them both on the same day, 27 November 2000. Bazhelka was replaced by Sheiman, which meant that Sheiman was now in charge of the investigation.

The 'Ihnatovich gang' were tried in camera in October 2001. Valer Ihnatovich was another officer of Almaz, but the gang were framed with a story about carrying out a revenge killing after Zavadzki had helped produce an ORT documentary that accused Almaz of fighting for the rebels in Chechnia. No explanation was offered as to why the other victims 'disappeared'. No one higher up the chain of command was ever put in the frame.

The 2000 Election: The Failure of Boycott Politics

In 2000, it was the opposition's turn to be faced with an election it did not want. Four years after it was created in 1996, 'new elections' were due for Lukashenka's puppet parliament. Knowing that they wouldn't be allowed to win, most of the opposition decided on a boycott. The result was a new 'parliament' dominated by independents and members of the pro-Lukashenka virtual parties. Not a single real opposition deputy was elected.

Elections to the Belarusian Palace of Representatives, October 2000 (Number of Seats Achieved)

'New' Communist Party of Belarus (Chykin/Zakharchanka)	6
'New' Agrarians (Shymanski)	5
Republican Party of Labour and Justice	2
Liberal-Democratic Party of Belarus (Haidukevich)	1
Social-Democratic Party of Popular Accord	1
Belarusian Socialist-Sporting Party	1
Independents	81
Vacant/invalid	13
Total	110

Source: www.electionworld.org/belarus.htm.

Conclusion

Lukashenka's first term ended as it began, in controversy. But there were signs of strain at the top between 1999, when the president should have faced reelection, and 2001, when he chose to do so. The 'disappearances' involved people uncomfortably close to the old post-Communist elite. In his second term Lukashenka would gradually give that elite more leeway. Ultimately, that would lead to populism taking more of a back seat. Ironically, as Balazs Jarabik and

Vitali Silitski write, 'Although Lukashenka originally portrayed himself as the champion of "clean" government, an anti-corruption crusader fighting crooked state bureaucracy, he was eventually forced to reconcile himself with the nomenklatura and offer them increased opportunities for enrichment.'[81] By the end of Lukashenka's second term in 2006, they would be pressing for even more.

CHAPTER 10

BUILDING AN AUTHORITARIAN STATE: LUKASHENKA'S SECOND TERM

In 2001 Lukashenka was not yet as secure in office as he would become in later years. Relative isolation from the West was a relatively new thing, dating from 1997. Domestic opponents still existed, and there were signs of dissent at the very top. The opposition had not yet grown used to thinking of the new regime as somehow permanent. Lukashenka therefore used 'political technology' to win reelection without looking like a total autocrat – whereas he would act with less restraint at subsequent elections in 2006 and 2010. The other factor shaping the 2001 election was that all sides thought in terms of a 'Serbian scenario'. Slobodan Milošević had been toppled from power in Belgrade a year earlier, in October 2000, and many on both sides thought Lukashenka could be next.

The West and the Opposition Fight the Last War

In 2001 the 'Bulldozer Revolution' in Yugoslavia was not even a year old, but Belarus was different. Not all the 'lessons learnt' in one place could simply be applied in another. In Yugoslavia no fewer than eighteen candidates for the Democratic Opposition of Serbia had eventually united behind the supposedly more moderate Vojislav Koštunica, who had duly triumphed, rather than Zoran Đinđić, who ended up being assassinated in 2003. In Belarus there was a similar push for a single opposition candidate, and it was assumed that 'moderate' meant non-BNF and specifically not anyone like Pazniak. With encouragement from Hans Georg Vik, head of the Organisation for Security and Cooperation in Europe (OSCE) group in Minsk, and Michael Kozak, the

US ambassador who was of Belarusian émigré stock, Uladzimir Hancharyk, the leader of the Trade Union Federation, was picked in July 2001 over the protests of the divided and discredited BNF, who preferred Siamion Domash, a native of western Belarus and leader of the NGO coalition Regional Belarus. Arguably, Domash might have stood a better chance. His opinion poll ratings were on the up, rising from 8.1 per cent to 12 per cent from April to June 2001, while Hancharyk was stable at 10.1 per cent and 10.3 per cent.[1] Certainly, many hardcore opposition activists from the BNF and its milieu now stood back from the campaign. More importantly, the opposition's Western backers didn't realise that, to the vast majority of ordinary Belarusians, the official trade unions were a remnant of the old Soviet days of privilege and Party control. Their leader was not likely to be seen as a tribune of the people.

The West made another mistake by assuming that Belarus needed an equivalent of the youth movement Otpor ('Resistance'), which had prepared the ground for the protests in Belgrade in 2000. Well, maybe it did, but the Belarusian version, Zubr ('Bison'), which was 'more of a political technology attempt to imitate Otpor',[2] was full of government agents. The authorities made sure that it was under complete control, 'maybe not from the very beginning, but soon enough'.[3] Zubr leaders like Dzmitry Bandarenka became the villains of the piece, accused of diverting Western funding.[4] The US grew disillusioned after the election, but the Dutch and Norwegians kept giving to Zubr. It became 'a very successful tool for attracting money'.[5] The Belarusian KGB even supposedly developed its own department for writing NGO grant applications.

Western support in general was a double-edged sword, as it encouraged 'donor-seeking'. Up to a third of the aid, mainly from the USA (totalling $50 million over two years), may have gone missing, particularly that given to the nebulous NGO sector, but parties (the splintered Social Democrats, parts of the BNF) and opposition politicians were also accused of graft, including Hancharyk and Chyhir.[6]

The potential for violence in the 'Yugoslav scenario' also helped the regime. The remaining real opposition was now roundly abused – with the campaign once again led by local 'media-killer' Yury Azaronak. The PR onslaught ignored the choice of Hancharyk over Domash and depicted the moderate opposition as simply a cover for the same old fanatical nationalists as in the early 1990s, and behind them the Americans, who were supposedly planning to bomb Minsk, just as they had bombed Belgrade.

Milošević had been 'softened up' by the bombing campaign in 1999 and the economy crashed before recovering slightly in 2000; but Belarus was doing well economically. GDP growth had resumed in 1996 and was 6.6 per cent in 2001. Russia lent Belarus 4.5 billion roubles (about $160 million) just before the election, officially to help stabilise the Belarusian currency. Salaries were rising. A pattern was set. Lukashenka fixed elections, but still spent money on his compaign as if he were part of a real contest.

Political Technology

The regime also benefited from the use of so-called 'political technology' – the local euphemism for a whole industry of highly cynical manipulation techniques, alongside cruder methods where necessary. The disappearances of 1999–2000 meant that many of Lukashenka's potentially most dangerous opponents, like Henadz Karpenka, Tamara Vinnikava, Yury Zakharanka and Viktar Hanchar, were no longer around. Lukashenka topped off his victory with simple fraud, adding about 20 per cent of the vote to his winning margin.

Nevertheless, relatively subtle manipulation techniques were important to the campaign. According to private polls, Lukashenka was popular enough to win, but he 'felt that his rating was not yet where it should be'.[7] He led any likely opposition candidate by around 30–35 per cent to 15 per cent; but that did not guarantee victory, the key to which was to prevent the opposition moving onto the as yet unclaimed middle ground.[8] Lukashenka therefore privately sponsored 'centrist' candidates to prevent any real opposition claiming that ground – then made sure they pulled out of the race at the last minute. This was very much a home-grown campaign. 'The strategic aspects of Lukashenka's election campaign were developed in Minsk and not in Moscow.'[9] Moscow nonetheless chipped in with support.

Russia's Locomotive

If Russia and the West wanted to fight over Belarus, Lukashenka's political technologists may have obtained some private amusement by covertly running both an artificial 'Western candidate' and an artificial 'Russian candidate'.[10] Some Gazprom money allegedly reached Leanid Sinitsyn, Lukashenka's former chief of staff; but the winner of the Russophile 'primary' was Natallia Masherava, also known as 'Petrovna', her patronymic from her famous father, Piotr Masheraw, the genuinely popular head of the Communist Party of Belarus from 1965 to 1980, when he died in a suspicious car accident (see page 116). Masherava was all over official TV,[11] supposedly sponsored by the Russophile deputy head of the Presidential Administration, Uladzimir Zamiatalin.[12] Russian broadcasters added their help, particularly NTV, recently acquired by Gazprom, as did the newspaper *Izvestiia* ('News') and the new internet sites.[13] Ultimately, however, Lukashenka wished to keep the 'myth of Masheraw' to himself, and worried about a Masherava bandwagon he could not control. She was therefore leaned on to withdraw before her campaign had even really begun. Just to make sure, noises were made about her family's health and safety.[14] Russia backed off. At this time, new president Putin still deferred to the Kremlin's 'collective thinking' that only Lukashenka could serve Russia's interests in Belarus.[15]

If Project Petrovna had uncertain backers, Mikhail Marynich, the former minister for foreign economic ties and ambassador to Latvia, Estonia and Finland, was also allegedly a creature of the regime.[16] Behind him stood the 'Minsk Group' of Uladzimir Yarmoshyn, prime minister since February 2000, and head of the Presidential Administration Mikhail Miasnikovich. Leanid Sechka, whose past record included hijacking the Party of Popular Accord in a pro-presidential direction, was his campaign head.[17] Marynich was designed to be Masherava's mirror image, occupying the niche for a liberal pro-Western candidate that might otherwise have gone to a genuine liberal like Karpenka or Hanchar. In many ways, Marynich spoke the language of reform more convincingly than the wooden Hancharyk, but he failed to get enough signatures to stand and ended up backing Hancharyk. Marynich may therefore have taken his role too seriously. He was arrested on trumped-up charges of carrying counterfeit hard currency – later changed to misappropriating office equipment in 2004. His former backers Yarmoshyn and Miasnikovich were also moved on after the election.

The final part was played by Siarhei Haidukevich, leader of the Liberal Democratic Party of Belarus. The Belarusian party was named after its Russian equivalent, led by Vladimir Zhirinovskii, and Haidukevich's allotted role was similar to that of the notorious Russian provocateur. Haidukevich was prominent on Belarusian TV, constantly making over-the-top comments that distracted attention from the real opposition. In reality, he was deeply involved in shadowy business, such as providing security at the Zhdanovichi market on the western fringes of Minsk – and in Belarus nearly all shadowy business was somehow connected to state elements. His party was named as a recipient of Saddam Hussein's covert oil payments in 2004, as was Zhirinovskii's, with Haidukevich's allegedly receiving one million barrels.[18] Like Zhirinovskii, Haidukevich was far from serving up a plague on all houses and spent most of his time, as he was instructed, attacking Lukashenka's opponents, in this case Hancharyk, with one of his attacks, only days before the election, featuring suspiciously prominently in the state media.[19]

Significantly, only Lukashenka's most convenient opponents survived until election day on 9 September 2001. Masherava and Marynich were forced out, or jumped when they were asked. Hancharyk remained as a sacrificial lamb, and Haidukevich for entertainment value and last-minute attacks. On the official figures, Lukashenka won a massive victory, garnering 75.7 per cent of the vote to Hancharyk's 15.7 per cent. The independent pollster IISEPS estimated a much narrower margin, with Lukashenka on 57–58 per cent and Hancharyk on 28–29 per cent, which was roughly in line with Lukashenka's rising trend in the polls.[20] Hancharyk himself claimed to have lost by 41 per cent to 47 per cent.[21] The difference came from 'administrative resources', which in Belarus, given the paucity of election observers, often just meant rewriting local election counts behind closed doors and from inflating the turnout, which was supposedly an extremely high 84 per cent (IISEPS had predicted 76 per cent).[22]

There was no Yugoslav-style revolution after the vote. Officially Lukashenka had only won the city of Minsk by 57.3 per cent to 30.5 per cent – but the regime was already practising its 'preemptive authoritarianism'. Activists were blocked from travelling to the capital. Mobile-phone and internet communications were switched off on the night. Only a few thousand – maybe two or three thousand – gathered in October Square on 9 September to protest,[23] with the key demonstration coming four days after the election, on 13 September 2001. Unfortunately, only two days after 9/11 on the other side of the Atlantic, there was little chance of the world taking much notice.

Belarusian Presidential Election, 2001 (by Percentage)

Aliaksandr Lukashenka	75.7
Uladzimir Hancharyk	15.7
Siarhei Haidukevich	2.5
Turnout: 83.9.	

Source: www.rec.gov.by/elect/prb2001/prb2001res.html.

Permanent Election

According to Feduta, 'the third election campaign of Lukashenka began literally immediately after the end of the second in 2001'.[24] Lukashenka's tactics for dealing with his domestic opponents were now predictable, but relations with Russia proved much more turbulent in his second term. First, they took a dramatic turn for the worse in 2001–4, then recovered, temporarily as it turned out, in 2004–6. Cause and effect are difficult to work out. Lukashenka began paying much more attention to building up his own local power base, which also alienated Russia. It's hard to say which came first. More likely, and more exactly, the two processes fed into one another.

Lukashenka's 'Russian project' was, if not yet totally redundant, now seen as an impudence, as Russia already had a saviour in office. Lukashenka, moreover, broke a private promise he had made, to open up the Belarusian economy to Russian capital in return for Russian media support and in order to help secure a preelection loan of 4.5 billion roubles to help stabilise the Belarusian currency.

Lukoil was the key suitor, having been in the Belarusian market since the 1990s, building up a network of filling stations. Its main target was the Naftan refinery at Navapolatsk, a highly profitable eyesore outside the old town of Polatsk. Lukoil's boss, Vagit Alekperov, who had hoped for the creation of a joint venture or full privatisation, quietly promised to invest $100 million.[25] According to Margarita Balmaceda, 'it has been argued that Lukoil supported Lukashenka's 2001 reelection campaign, in exchange for promises that Naftan would be privatized, but that this promise was not kept by the Belarusian president'.[26] Alekperov had to be content with supplying oil and taking a cut from the Belarusian reexports. Since 2002, 42.5 per cent of the Mazyr refinery has been controlled by a Russo–Belarussian joint enterprise 'Slavneft' – behind which stands TNK and Gazprom Neft. The rest is owned by the Belarusian government (42.7 per cent) and a shadowy management front (originally 14.8 per cent).

Two other Russian companies to be rebuffed were Siberian Aluminium (Sibal), which thought it had an understanding to win a controlling share in the Minsk Car Factory (MAZ), and the Baltika brewery, which wanted to take over the leading Belarusian brand Krynitsa, and invested $10.5 million before the plug was pulled.[27] Sibal's Oleg Deripaska was a new-model oligarch close to Putin, as was Baltika's Teimuraz Bolloev, a friend from Putin's days in the St Petersburg mayor's office. Both were soon complaining bitterly about getting their fingers burnt.[28] On the other hand, the one Russian oligarch who did have a strong position in Belarus, Boris Berezovskii, had just fallen out with Putin, and linked the Belarusian president too closely to the old Kremlin 'Family' as far as Putin was concerned. Berezovskii allegedly encouraged Lukashenka's geopolitical 'reorientation' away from Russia.[29] Moscow mayor Yurii Luzhkov and his wife Yelena Baturina's Inteko company quietly invested in the local construction business.[30]

The steel company Severstal's Aleksei Mordashov also claimed to have been cheated. Most importantly, 'Gazprom's significant informal help in

Lukashenka's campaign . . . was predicated on the expectation that, after the elections, negotiations on the corporatization of Beltransgaz and the creation of a joint venture would go forward successfully,[31] as was the April 2002 agreement to sell gas to Belarus at the same price as in neighbouring Russian oblasts.

Russia began to apply economic pressure after 2001, as Putin attempted to 'economise' the relationship between the two 'Union states'. The new Russian president had much less interest in the original project than Yeltsin, and capped it in 2002 by suggesting the only endgame for Belarus was to add its six oblasts to the Russian Federation – an offer he knew Lukashenka would never accept. But Russia didn't want to give up its carrots completely, rather just to render the subsidy regime more instrumental and clearly calibrated to Russian interests. Putin found it hard to get a hold on Lukashenka, who was already practised in the art of balance. A second tactic, of sponsoring pro-Russian stooges to pressure Lukashenka at home, proved even less successful. The political space in Belarus was now so narrow that even Russia found it difficult to operate in it.

The first gas row between the two states came as early as 2002. Between 20 and 25 per cent of Gazprom's gas exports to Europe pass through Belarus, via the Yamal line. The Northern Lights line serves Belarus's domestic economy, which is almost 80 per cent dependent on gas for its energy, including 95 per cent of its electricity generation. As of 2002, Belarus was getting gas virtually free, at $34.37 per 1,000 m^3, as well as oil which was exempt from duty until 2007. Belarus, like Ukraine, was therefore both weak and strong. It was dependent on Russia for energy, but Russia depended on Belarus for export revenues. The first Russian cut-off in April 2002 led to Gazprom attempting to take over Beltrangaz, which controls the local pipeline; but the sale of 50 per cent of the latter's shares was only agreed in principle in 2006 and finalised in 2010, at a price of $2.5 billion. Further gas rows followed in January 2004, August 2007 and June 2010. There were also two 'oil wars', in January 2007 and June 2010. A regular cycle of tit-for-tat exchanges developed. Belarus usually ended up the loser, but only marginally so. The price for gas went up, albeit slowly, reaching $169.20 per 1,000$m^3$ in the first quarter of 2010 (Ukraine was paying over $300).

Meanwhile, Anatol Liabedzka, chair of the United Civic Party, sought to play the role of Russia's new man in Belarus. In September 2002 transcripts of a secret conversation between Liabedzka and Boris Nemtsov, one of Russia's leading oligarchs, were published in which Nemtsov boasted that 'I have persuaded the Kremlin to start associating with the opposition in Belarus', and that, due to his links with Putin and the Kremlin *éminence grise* Vladislav Surkov, 'the attitude to Lukashenka has completely changed there, thanks to my endeavours'. Liabedzka backed Nemtsov's proposals to develop political integration, with Belarus's formal sovereignty preserved.[32] In October 2002 Nemtsov, Irina Khakamada and Kremlin 'political technologist' Sergei Markov were detained at Minsk airport and expelled from Belarus. Liabedzka himself was subject to a 'prophylactic' arrest in November, and warned to drop his contacts. Ironically, at the time he was leaving the US embassy, where he was posing as leader of the pro-Western opposition.

Similar intrigue swirled around and eventually destroyed the twelve-strong 'Republic' opposition faction that briefly flared into life in the pocket parliament in 2002. The group was led by Russian-speakers like the former general Valer Fralow and the former Olympic sportsman Uladzimir Parfianovich, who were both Russia- and business-friendly and cared little about the cultural politics of the BNF. Lukashenka set another precedent by dealing with 'Republic' particularly harshly.

Tightening the Screws

Lukashenka responded to the worsening relations with Russia by talking more about ideology as he tried to develop a story to justify his hold on power (see below). He also played divide-and-rule with the local nomenklatura as well as with the opposition in order to prevent a Russia faction emerging around him. Bureaucrats were never allowed to settle into cosy sinecures. Yahor Rybakov, former head of Belarusian TV, was sentenced to eleven years in prison in February for grand larceny; Halina Zhurawkova, former head of the Presidential Administration's Property Management Department, got four years in 2004. Institutions were also set against one another: the Interior Ministry versus the KGB, and the KGB versus Lukashenka's own mini-security service. Kimitaka Matsuzato has ably demonstrated how Lukashenka also shuffled regional officials to prevent the formation of the type of regional clans seen in Ukraine.[33] This in turn made it more difficult for the opposition to build bridges with rebel factions among the elite, as Viktor Yushchenko was doing with elements in the Kuchma regime in the build-up to the Orange Revolution in Ukraine in 2004.

The Belarusian regime also became more straightforwardly authoritarian. In his second term Lukashenka built a fully-fledged corporate state. In August 2002 it took measures against the Russian mass media. The authorities began campaigning against independent NGOs after a semi-secret gathering at the

Presidential Administration building in March 2003. 'In all the government shut down 157 NGOs from 2003 to 2005 and 190 others were closed "on recommendations of justice departments",' reports one analyst. 'As many as 347 NGOs . . . were struck off the government's register in those years. A huge segment of civic society had to go underground.'[34]

The authorities then extended the same 'cloning' tactics they had used against parties like the Communists to the NGO sector, replacing genuinely independent organisations with 'GONGOs' (the bizarrely oxymoronic Government-Organised Non-Governmental Organisations') or, in Lukashenka-speak, 'state civic organisations'. For example, the troublesome Belarusian Union of Writers was replaced by a loyal clone the 'Union of Writers of Belarus', in August 2006. In this case the powers-that-be had to wait until after the death in 2003 of the country's greatest living writer, Vasyl Bykaw, both a Soviet and a Belarusian figure, who still carried enormous moral authority. Lukashenka failed to attend his funeral, fearing he would be booed, and chose to humiliate himself instead by saying he had never read any of Bykaw's 'poetry' (he only wrote prose).

Trade unions were turned into government 'transmission belts', returning to the role they had played in the Soviet era, Lukashenka having violently suppressed a strike of underground workers at the start of his first term in January 1995. The main Soviet successor organisation, the FTUB, was purged after 2001 and was now led by Leanid Kozik. 'Yellow unions' sprang up after 2001, particularly in giant state enterprises like MAZ, the Minsk Auto Factory. In 2003 Lukashenka ordered a clampdown on Aliaksandr Buchvostaw, who headed one of the two main independent unions, ASM, based in car and tractor production, and led the Belarusian Party of Labour, and on Hennadz Fiadynich of another union, REP, based in the electronics industry. The two unions attempted to merge in 2005, but essentially functioned underground, as did the tattered remnants of the Belarusian Congress of Democratic Trade Unions (BKDP), which first emerged as an alternative to the successor organisation during the strike wave of April 1991 (see page 149). The Party of Labour was banned in 2004.

The Belarusian Komsomol (the youth wing of the old Communist Party) was revived as the 'Lukamol' in 2002 (technically, the Belarusian Republican Youth Union), which had a massive 355,000 members in 2006; its younger wing, the neo-Soviet Scouts or Pioneers (Belarusian Republican Pioneer Organisation) had 482,000.[35] The All-Belarusian Assembly continued to meet every five years as a forum for this new type of state-sponsored corporatism.

Creole Nationalism

In his second term, Lukashenka also decided he needed a state ideology. Significantly, he wasn't particularly interested in what the ideology actually *said*; it was just important to have one. And it was even more important to have an ideology machine, with ideology commissars who would teach the population to be loyal.

The process started with an official 'ideological seminar' in March 2003. The regime's new 'ideology team' were a pretty gruesome bunch of hacks. Aleh Pralaskowski was the 'chief ideology officer'. Stanislaw Kniaziew headed the Management Academy of the President, the main training centre for ideology cadres, particular those involved in debasing education. Anatol Rubinaw was deputy head of the Presidential Administration responsible for ideology, and a man of 'openly Stalinist political views'.[36] Lev Kryshtapovich was head of the ominous-sounding Institute of Socio-Political Research Attached to the Presidential Administration of the Republic of Belarus. A 'State Ideology' course was introduced into the school curriculum from September 2003, fed by a steady stream of turgid official texts.

If an 'ideological revolution' took place,[37] it was unclear what its end product would be. Soviet nostalgia and pan-Russism were now less important than they had been at the start of Lukashenka's presidency, though they were still significant. The cultural festival 'Slavianski bazar', which had been running in Vitsebsk since 1992, for example, became a prestige annual project, attracting musicians from all over the Slavic world. But the emphasis was now on 'the ideology of the Belarusian state'. Essentially, this was an adjectival project. Everything was 'Belarusian': the 'Belarusian model of development', the 'Belarusian way', the 'Belarusian economic model', etc. Lukashenka debuted the slogan 'For Belarus!' during the 2004 parliamentary elections. It was patriotic but vague, the perfect empty box for whatever he wanted to put in it.

The new ideology was, of course, also state-centred. If Lukashenka had formerly behaved as if Belarusian history had begun in 1941 – or 1994 – the past was now valuable if it could demonstrate previous eras of state-building. And that could be any past: that of the USSR obviously, but also of the Grand Duchy of Polatsk. In that sense, the new 'ideology' was radically eclectic. The most noteworthy idea that Lukashenka's new propagandists came up with was the bizarre slogan that Minsk was the 'fourth Rome'.[38] Fifteenth-century Moscow had claimed to be the 'third Rome', the only true centre of true religion after the apostasy of Rome itself and the fall of

Constantinople in 1453. The monk Filofey's famous letter in 1510 had declared Moscow's eternal rise: 'Two Romes have fallen. The third stands. And there will be no fourth.' The Belarusian argument was that Russia had now fallen into sin – particularly in the Yeltsin era. 'At heart, in the east Slavic and (if we calculate the other peoples living on our space) in the Eastern European world, we remain the only country openly preaching our loyalty to our traditional civilisational values,' opined Lukashenka.[39] 'Multiple processes suggest that Russia today, regretfully, is no longer a spiritual and cultural pillar of the Eastern Eurasian civilisation.'[40] Russia is dominated by 'self-centred financial interests'.[41]

> Belarus, by history, fate and location, was evidently chosen to fulfil a great role as the spiritual leader of east Slavic civilisation . . . realising this destiny can propel our nation to great feats. Many people in Russia, in Ukraine, as well as other countries, look to Belarus as an example of consistent and independent politics. . . . Belarus must draw together the patriotic forces from the entire post-Soviet space. It is precisely here that these people will find a platform for expressing themselves, free from neo-liberal terror and persecution.[42]

Unfortunately, the fourth Rome was not a particularly good metaphor for Minsk, which is not exactly a shining city on a hill. It has few remaining churches, but plenty of triumphantly Brutalist Soviet architecture. Lukashenka's prestige building projects, particularly the new National Library, have added a new layer of kitsch. The president has also said the Belarusians are the 'most international people in the world'.[43] By the time the 'philocatholicist' Kirill was elected patriarch of 'All Rus' in January 2009, the concept had burnt out. Lukashenka suddenly switched to depicting Belarus as a 'bridge' between the Catholic and Protestant worlds, visiting the pope in April 2009. But Belarus found itself squeezed: Kirill had no need for Lukashenka's mediation and proved a strong supporter of the Russian Church, increasing its role among the Russian-speaking population of the former USSR. This has produced the intriguing long-term possibility of Lukashenka one day becoming an ironic convert to the idea of a more autocephalous (independent) Belarusian Orthodox Church.

Lukashenka also famously remarked that 'Belarusians are just Russians, but with the sign of quality'.[44] The idea of the Belarusians as the purest and the best Slavs segued with Lukashenka's ongoing flirtation with various members of the anti-Western movement: at one time Iraq, now Venezuela,

Iran and China. Belarus the buffer, defending east Slavic civilisation from attacks by the West, was always a part of the Soviet project.[45] According to Lukashenka's convoluted logic this was one reason for Belarus's current isolation: in his words, 'why the rest of the world falls upon us – both in the West and among some political circles – [to] hide their sins, in brotherly Russia'.[46]

But the Belarusian state's uniqueness was only partially defined by its civilisational and foreign-policy role. Belarus also stood isolated, if not alone, in its commitment to maintaining a post-Soviet paternalist economy and welfare state. The official ideology therefore codified in part the earlier unofficial 'social contract' (see pages 242–3). Natalia Leshchenko called this 'Belarusian egalitarian nationalism'.[47]

The 'ideology of Belarusian statehood' was therefore radically new. Some have sought to define it as a type of 'creole nationalism',[48] following Benedict Anderson's definition of creole states (New World colonies) as communities formed and led by people who shared a common language and common descent with those against whom they now rebelled.[49] West-Russism was an oft-quoted source, but although it helped underpin the anti-Western 'civilisational' myth, its clerical conservatism was not an obvious answer to the problems of building Belarusian statehood and a 'special Belarusian path' in the 2000s.

Culturally, it was much less clear what the formula of statehood plus homeland stood for, though it facilitated a rapprochement with some members of the intelligentsia. As one Belarusian critic puts its, 'the regime does not want the Belarusians to be loyal to the nation . . . it wants them to be loyal to the president'.[50] Lukashenka therefore liked to emphasise grand, practical, but culturally neutral prestige projects. The National Library, opened in June 2006, was supposed to look like a diamond, but was quickly nicknamed 'the spud'. Lukashenka flirted with the idea of a role in space, before a satellite rocket disaster in 2006, when the first Belarusian Earth exploration satellite, BelKA, crashed seventy-four seconds after take-off from the old Soviet launch site at Baikonur, now in Kazakhstan. Lukashenka's acolytes have also tried to sell the idea of a new Silicon Valley in the suburbs of Minsk – an 'Eastern European Bangalore' for IT outsourcing. Despite the legacy of Chernobyl, Belarus has continued to pursue the dream of its own nuclear-power station (see page 248); although financial disputes with the Russian company Atomstroieksport led to Lukashenka claiming he could finish the project with the assistance of the French or Chinese instead.

Sport under Lukashenka has been hugely important to national prestige, despite the occasional disaster, such as the national team's defeat at soccer by tiny Luxembourg in 2007. The national ice hockey team came fourth in the 2002 Winter Olympics. At the previous Olympics in 1998 at Nagano, Japan, Lukashenko's noisy support had caused a minor diplomatic incident. The 2014 ice hockey world championships were due to take place in Belarus. Yulia Nestsiarenka won the women's 100 metres at the 2004 Athens Olympics with many of her rivals banned for doping. The gymnast Vitalii Shcherbo, who won six medals at the Barcelona Olympics in 1992, was a true national hero. Olga Korbut, his predecessor from the Munich Olympics in 1972, was also discreetly celebrated. Lukashenka himself played ice hockey, and by some accounts played it reasonably well – though his special presidential team normally expected easy victory.

The 2004 Referendum

Lukashenka's relations with Russia hit a low point in 2002–3. Vladimir Putin was a totally different proposition from Yeltsin. Not only was he committed to a more rigorous assertion of Russian self-interest, he also had no need of Lukashenka as 'Russia's saviour', since he had reserved that role for himself. Moreover, Kremlin-connected businessmen were angry at the broken promises made during the 2001 election compaign, while Lukashenka's own business connections with the old Yeltsin 'Family', and with Boris Berezovskii in particular, were now a liability, particularly after Berezovskii fled Russia to the UK in November 2000. Putin's patience with Lukashenka was therefore wearing thin. Their personal relationship was not good. Putin regarded the Belarusian president as a hick who had served in the lowly position of a KGB border guard. More exactly perhaps, as Putin had not been that high up in the KGB himself, Lukashenka offended his amour-propre. Nor did Putin have time for Lukashenka's discursively expressed folk wisdom. Putin barely bothered to conceal his contempt for him, even during joint appearances on TV.

Change came from an unexpected quarter, when terrorists of presumed Chechen origin seized School Number One in Beslan, southern Russia, in September 2004. After a botched and brutal 'rescue', 396 people were killed, even on the official figures. Lukashenka addressed his nation three days later, on 7 September, and made a brazen reference to the tragedy: 'May God protect us – over these ten years no Belarusian has become a victim of a terrorist act, or an armed conflict. We have guarded our country against involvement in international adventures which could threaten your lives and security even to the smallest degree. This is our greatest achievement .... A tranquil and cosy home, where peace and harmony reign.'[51] Lukashenka used the same television broadcast to announce a referendum on abolishing the clause from his own 1996 constitution that presidents could only serve for two consecutive terms, and fast-forwarded the vote to coincide with the parliamentary elections already scheduled for 17 October, calculating correctly that Russia would be too busy to protest or interfere. Nor would the divided domestic opposition have much time to mobilise. And so it proved. Official turnout was 90.3 per cent, after 13.7 per cent took advantage of four days of early voting. Lukashenka's proposal was supposedly backed by 88 per cent of voters.[52] This meant that 79.4 per cent of the total electorate had voted 'yes'. However, according to an IISEPS poll, only 49 per cent of respondents claimed to have backed the proposal, and 29.2 per cent claimed to have voted against, with 9.5 per cent saying they had not voted and 12.3 per cent giving no answer.[53] Half of all voters needed to back the proposal for it to be valid, so on this evidence it should have narrowly failed. Not surprisingly perhaps, IISEPS was closed down in April 2005, after which it relocated to the Baltic States.

The authorities tried out a new technology of their own. Exit polls were becoming increasingly common in the region – not, as more often in the West, as a means of predicting the election night result for an impatient TV audience, but as a means of limiting the authorities' freedom of manoeuvre for plausible fraud. The exit poll in the 2002 Ukrainian parliamentary elections, for example, clearly seems to have helped to reduce the amount of fraud compared to the previous election in 1999. In 2004 Belarus debuted the neophyte organisation 'EcooM', whose exit poll contradicted that of IISEPS and just happened to coincide with the Central Election Commission's official result. Public opinion was sufficiently confused, though the tactic also confirmed the artificiality of a CEC 'result' prepared in advance.

Nor were the parliamentary elections to the puppet 'Palace of Representatives' created in 1996 too much of a problem for Lukashenka. Twelve seats went to the fake pro-government parties, including Siarhei Haidukevich for the Liberal-Democrats. The real opposition was grouped in two coalitions, neither of which won a single seat, despite the main alliance, dubbed Five Plus, managing to bring together the BPF Party, the opposition Communists and Anatol Liabedzka's United Civic Party. Mikalai Statkevich's Social-Democrats ploughed a lonely furrow with a few other minnows as the 'European Coalition'. The new parliament would be even more controlled than the old, without even the troublesome 'Republic' faction.

Elections to the Belarusian Palace of Representatives, October 2004
(Number of Seats Achieved)[54]

Pro-government	
Communist Party of Belarus	8
'New' Agrarians	3
Liberal-Democratic Party of Belarus	1
Opposition	
People's Coalition 5-Plus	–
Euro Coalition	–
Independents	98
Total	110

Lukashenka's third manoeuvre to strengthen his position was a purge of the local KGB to remove those who were thought to be too close to Russia, including the head, Leanid Yerin (who was the Moscow district FSB chief before 1995), and Ural Latypaw, the head of the Presidential Administration. Nevertheless, the 'security faction' or *siloviki* stayed in charge, but in its domestic variant, led by Viktar Sheiman, who was also made head of Lukashenka's campaign headquarters for the 2006 election. The supposedly more pragmatic, economy-first faction led by Anatol Tozik, the head of the State Control Committee, and his protégé Siarhei Sidorski, who served as prime minister after July 2003, and Siarhei Martynow, the foreign minister from March 2003, remained on the sidelines. But Lukashenka also issued a pair of decrees in late 2005 hinting that he might embrace privatisation after the election – which was an important signal to keep the younger generation of nomenklatura on board.

Conclusion

Lukashenka's paradoxical second term was both the golden age of the *siloviki* and an era of practical state-building. Sheiman and the *siloviki* saw their influence wane after the 2006 election was safely out of the way and Moscow renewed its demands, as early as March 2006, that Belarus pay market prices for energy. But even Russia underestimated the degree to which Lukashenka had built up his power base in just five years.

CHAPTER 11

THE THIRD TERM: THE EDIFICE CRUMBLES

In our country, there will be no pink or orange – or even banana
– revolution.
—Aliaksandr Lukashenka, 2005[1]

President Lukashenka successfully reinvented himself twice in his second term. He survived a difficult transition in Russia from Yeltsin to Putin by bolstering his position at home. The Orange Revolution in Ukraine was doubly fortunate in its timing. Lukashenka had managed to hold the referendum on abolishing term limits for the presidency in October 2004, just before the events in Ukraine began in November. He had already survived the threat of a repeat 'Bulldozer Revolution' in 2001. Now the threat of 'colour revolution' spreading to Belarus – amplified by the Belarus Democracy Act, signed by President Bush in October 2004 – provided him with a new lease of life. Lukashenka sold himself to the Kremlin as both a bulwark against the fear the Kremlin had sold itself of US-inspired colour revolution and as a testing ground for 'counter-revolutionary technology'. Russia was happy to loan money, media support and the services of its 'political technologists' to stop the virus spreading. The notorious political fixer Gleb Pavlovskii was suddenly a particularly frequent visitor to Minsk.[2]

The 2006 Election: Orange 2?[3]

The presidential election in Belarus was expected in July 2006. The Orange Revolution had demonstrated the importance of opposition unity. As in 2001, a single candidate was the opposition's aim for the upcoming presidential election, but not a 'parachutist' like Hancharyk five years before. Five Plus and the European Coalition had united after the 2004 elections and decided to select a single candidate between them. The process was closed to the wider public, and party-based, but was perhaps the only way of achieving minimum consensus in Belarusian conditions. Politicians who refused to abide by the rules were excluded from the process. Unfortunately, these were mainly candidates who might appeal to Russian-speaking voters: for instance, Valer Fralow and the venerable Aliaksandr Vaitovich, born in 1938, president of the Academy of Sciences from 1997 and chair of Lukashenka's 'pocket parliament' from 2000 to 2003. Lukashenka, on the other hand, weeded the field, as with Hanchar in 2001. This time he deemed his most dangerous potential opponent to be none other than Mikhail Marynich, who had served as a Lukashenka 'technical candidate' in 2001. Such a development was not as weird as it sounded in the looking-glass world of Belarusian politics. Marynich was arrested in April 2004, and released after the election two years later.

The 'united' opposition's preparations were lackadaisical, however. Plans to hold a 'unity congress' in, first, May and, then, July 2005 came and went. Fortunately, one of its leader's Anatol Liabedzka's proposal to wait until February 2006 was ignored,[4] Lukashenka having caught the opposition on the hop by bringing the vote forward to March 2006. The so-called Coordinating Council of Democratic Forces eventually met in October 2005 to decide between four leading candidates: Liabedzka, supposedly on the right; Siarhei Kaliakin, leader of the Party of Communists of Belarus (i.e. the real Communist Party, the one in opposition); the former chair of parliament Stanislaw Shushkevich; and Aliaksandr Milinkevich, a Belarusian-speaker from the western town of Hrodna whose ancestors had fought in the Kalinowski rebellion in 1863 (see pages 68–9), but a moderate from the civic sector. The veteran Shushkevich dropped out; then the first round vote went 383 to Milinkevich, 263 to Liabedzka, and 152 to Kaliakin. The second round was much closer. Liabedzka had strong support from BNF veterons who. The latter said they would never support a Communist candidate and thereby gave Milinkevich the victory by handing him the votes of Kaliakin's supporters. The result was 399 votes to 391, with a theoretically decisive sixteen votes blank or invalid.[5] Liabedzka refused to back the victor, causing many activists in his United Civic Party to drop out of the 'united' campaign.

Both elections in 2001 and 2006 encapsulated the opposition's dilemma: only the 'national movement' had well-motivated activists, but its social base among the electorate was too narrow. An activists' favourite might get less than 10 per cent of the vote, while a theoretically 'more electable' candidate would fail to find practical grassroots support. A 'National Committee' was set up, but 'as a matter of form only and not properly staffed, [and] was little involved in the presidential campaign'. There were also disagreements over tactics. 'Within the opposition there were many members who hoped to create an illusion of victory without hard work. They suggested a victory could be won by creating a "presence effect" (by encouraging supporters to wear the same colours and badges), staging campaigns of resistance and blindly copying the Ukrainian, Georgian, Kyrgyz and Serbian experience.'[6] Just as importantly, 'Plan A' – collecting a million signatures in support of Milinkevich, assembling a ten thousand-strong campaign team, placing a representative on every election commission and winning the election for Milinkevich after a leisurely campaign for a summer vote – had already given way to 'Plan B', which was 'to rally the support of at least 30% of voters', and protest against the inevitable fraud in March.[7]

The opposition's biggest problem, however, was its lack of a clear campaign theme, despite receiving advice from a Belarusian-Slovak working group.[8] It opposed Lukashenka and, in the words of its key slogan, was 'For Freedom!', but had to cope with the reality that when 'focus groups were held in March and May 2005 with representatives from various walks of life . . . the researchers found that Belarus lacked a single social group capable of spearheading changes. Belarus also lacked a single thorny issue that could be used to rally support for an opposition candidate.'[9] 'The 'campaign theory' the opposition hit on instead was the idea of a 'Denim Revolution'. The recent wave of 'coloured' or 'flower' revolutions had all had brand names: the 'Orange Revolution' in Ukraine, the 'Rose Revolution' in Georgia, even, least plausibly, the 'Tulip Revolution' in Kyrgyzstan. 'Denim' was chosen for Belarus because it was common anyway – it would be difficult for the repressive local police to victimise people for wearing it. But denim was an invisible brand. When the international media did eventually show pictures of post-election demonstrations, they just showed a lot of people dressed in denim, like normal Eastern Europeans, or most crowds anywhere.

'Project' Kazulin?

Despite its increasingly authoritarian tendencies and preference for cruder methods of political control, and despite becoming a testing ground for 'counterrevolutionary technology' in 2006 (see below), the Lukashenka regime hadn't given up on 'political technology'. As in 2001, Siarhei Haidukevich was allotted the role of fake opponent. The authorities had rescued him from a revolt in his party in September 2003, when even his fellow travellers had decided he was just too venal, and had reimposed him as the 'legitimate' leader of the Liberal Democratic Party. But after Ukraine's Orange Revolution in 2004 there were more serious possibilities to forestall.

Nevertheless, the role of the fourth candidate in the race, Aliaksandr Kazulin, rector of Belarusian State University from 1996 to 2003, was far from clear. In January 2005 Kazulin appeared, apparently from nowhere, never previously having been a politician, let alone a Social Democrat, to take over the Belarusian Social-Democratic Party, which had long sought to play the role of a 'third force' between the authorities and traditional opposition parties like the BNF.[10] But the party also had a long history of being manipulated by the authorities, so the suspicion now arose that it was being hijacked once again. Party leader Mikalai Statkevich was forced out and received a prison sentence in 2005. The revolt was led by the shady figure of Uladzimir Nistsiuk, who had been Lukashenka's press secretary in 1994, while a parallel move in the Belarusian Social-Democratic Hramada, the power base of veteran politician Stanislaw Shushkevich, was orchestrated by Aliaksei Karol, who had previously split from no fewer than three other parties. In April 2005 the two groups merged to form a new party, now called the BSDP(Popular Hramada). The new party was recognised as 'official'.

Kazulin's robust Russophilia led many to suspect he had Kremlin support. Kazulin was certainly supported by other Russophiles, such as Valer Fralow and Siarhei Skrabets, who had once belonged to the Republic group in Lukashenka's 'pocket parliament'. The newspaper *Narodnaia volia* ('People's Will') and the journalists Pavel Sharamet and Svetlana Kalinkina, who set up the website www.belaruspartisan.org, all reportedly linked to Russian circles close to Boris Nemtsov and the Union of Right Forces, also backed Kazulin. Rumours circulated of money coming from the mayor of Moscow, Yurii Luzhkov, and Gazprom.[11] According to other sources, however, Kazulin was mainly financed, to the tune of $1 million, by Viktar Lahvinets, the émigré Belarusian businessman now resident in Russia – not to create a Russian fifth column, but to cause 'some unpleasantness for Lukashenka'.[12] Milinkevich was supported by the West, but Kazulin's supporters 'couldn't get anybody in Moscow seriously interested. They only managed to get as far as the offices of the third echelon of Russian power.'[13]

Milinkevich tried to be respectable and moderate. Kazulin was happy to be intemperate and populist. In his own mind at least, he was a 'cooler, more urbanised version of Lukashenka', which is perhaps why the latter was so wary of him.[14] On occasion, Kazulin 'tried to play the national card' and outflank Milinkevich on the right (for example, by flirting with the unregistered Belarusian Autocephalous Orthodox Church). But, although he was nominally an expert in mathematics, his dissertation was actually on teaching mathematics in secondary schools. He had trouble writing basic Belarusian.[15]

Russia Struggles to Exert Influence

One thing that was certain, however, was that Kazulin represented the long-standing split between the Russian-speaking opposition and the Belarusian-speaking opposition, which backed Milinkevich. The outpouring of conspiracy theories showed that the latter were still inclined to distrust the Russian-speaking intelligentsia. But since Lukashenka had introduced the 'ideology of Belarusian statehood' after 2001, Belarus's Russophiles had been cut somewhat adrift. In fact, they had made the shocking discovery that the Russian-speaking intelligentsia was just as small as the Belarusian-speaking intelligentsia. Its would-be candidates were also from a narrow circle: Vaitovich, Fralow, Skrabets, Parfianovich and Sinitsyn. Siarhei Skrabets was reasonably well organised, so Lukashenka had him put in prison for the duration, on a charge of obtaining bank loans by fraud.

Russia provided some financial support, but could not seem to find the right candidate. Pavlovskii and Sergei Karaganov had invited Russophile activists to their conferences on 'Democracy in Eurasia', and channelled money to locals to employ Russian political technologists like themselves. Some intellectual projects also seemed to have Russian support, like the Belarusian Department at the CIS Institute, www.materik.ru, www.politboz.com and www.imperiya.by, where Yurii Baranchik liked to talk about how Belarus had helped construct the Russian Empire. But the Kremlin seemed to trust only ethnic Russians for its schemes in Belarus, just as it had after 1863.

The 'Polish Plot'

The Belarusian authorities learnt the apparent lessons of Ukraine's Orange Revolution better than the opposition. In 2006 the regime ran several 'special operations' to disable what it saw as the potential triggers of an 'electoral revolution'. The priority was to control the narrative in order to isolate the main opposition candidate, Milinkevich, from a hinterland of broader social support by depicting him as a foreign stooge bent on social chaos.

Belarusian strategists had clearly learnt from the Yanukovych campaign in Ukraine in 2004, which had been too narrowly anti-American (as had the Belarusian campaign in 2001, but the world had moved on). Even the leading Russian technologist Sergei Markov admitted after the debacle in Ukraine in 2004, 'I told them [the Yanukovych team] to use anti-Polish rhetoric'.[16] Milinkevich's key weakness was that 'he was [seen to be] a Polish project'.[17] He spoke fluent Polish and hailed from Hrodna. His popularity in foreign capitals was a double-edged sword, as was the competition between the two main candidates in the closely fought Polish presidential election decided in October 2005, Lech Kaczyński of Law and Justice and Donald Tusk of the Civic Platform, to commit to the Polish diaspora in the east. Milinkevich was therefore a gift to Lukashenka's by now finely tuned propaganda machine – Lukashenka having for a long time referred sarcastically to BNF activists as *pan* (Polish – and Belarusian – for 'Mr', but also 'Sir' – the old Polish ruling class).

An artificial conflict was provoked with the Union of Poles (ZPB), the second-biggest NGO in Belarus, with a claimed membership of twenty thousand out of an official Polish population of just under 300,000. Warsaw traditionally funded the ZPB with around $200,000 a year paid through its main diaspora organisation, the Polish Community Association (*Stowarzyszenie Wspólnota Polska*).[18] In March 2005 Tadeusz Kruczkowski, the Uncle Tom leader of the ZPB since 2000, was replaced by a young schoolteacher, Andzelika Borys who promised to take a real stand in defence of local Poles, but the authorities reimposed their man with an armed assault on the ZPB's Hrodna offices on 27 July, resulting in Warsaw recalling its ambassador from Minsk. (The authorities' *kompromat* – compromising materials, used for blackmail and control – on Kruczkowski was alleged to include fraud and relations with female students.)[19] The same trick was pulled on the organisation's newspaper, *Glos znad Niemna* ('Voice on the River Neman', the far north-west corner of Belarus where the Polish minority is now concentrated), which was closed and then turned into a loyalist paper. Two Polish diplomats were kicked out. Another Polish NGO, the Scientific Society 'Dialogue' was suspended.

Meanwhile the parallel allegations by the KGB chief Stsiapan Sukharenka that Lithuanian, Georgian and Ukrainian activists were being trained for 'provocations' apparently had some substance.[20] The more radical central and eastern European states wanted to be rid of their awkward neighbour. Lithuania in particular felt that the Lukashenka regime brought Russia too close to home – and was wary of the export of the 'Belarusian model' across its borders. Its ambassador to Belarus Petras Vaitekunas was promoted to foreign minister in July 2006. The allegations worried Milinkevich enough for him to pay a visit to the Lithuanian embassy two days before the vote, even though the embassy was known to be bugged.[21] According to Zygimantas Pavilionis of the Lithuanian Foreign Ministry, 'we wanted to make a revolution in Belarus, but it didn't work'.[22] In April 2006 Mikhail Leontiev on Russia's First Channel broadcast an alleged tape of Givi Targamadze, the chair of Georgia's Defence and Security Committee, making derogatory comments about Milinkevich to unnamed Lithuanians and one 'Irina' in Washington.[23] Whether this was authentic or not, there were soon rumours that Lithuania would switch its support to the supposedly more resolute Liabedzka.

Youth

Photogenic youth movements had captured a lot of media attention in Serbia in 2000 (Otpor), Georgia in 2003 (Kmara) and Ukraine in 2004 (Pora) with their brand image, irreverent slogans, Situationist instinct for the spectacular, and young and attractive activists. It had almost become the conventional wisdom that an effective youth movement could be the battering ram of change in Belarus as well.

Belarus had three youth movements, all with their local specifics. None was a carbon copy of the likes of Pora. Zubr was still around from 2001, though its ranks were much diminished and its remaining membership full of regime agents. According to one source, Zubr was always more 'externally inspired. Its activities were mainly based on money from US foundations.' But 'US money was destructive in the long term. When the flow of money ended, they [Zubr] disappeared.'[24]

More prominent this time was the Youth Front, which had actually been around longer, since 1997. The Youth Front received relatively little outside money, apart from some early subventions from the remnants of the BNF. Its leader, Paval Seviarynets, who was born in 1976 and was therefore only fifteen when the USSR collapsed, pushed strongly for the Christianisation, more exactly the Protestantisation, of the movement (its symbol was the Cross of Euphrosyne). The leftist, anticlerical wing of the Youth Front was opposed to this, and drifted away. The Youth Front was therefore not a postmodern movement of satirical protest in the manner of Pora in Ukraine – though at least its members were well motivated to survive repression. Zubr had been much more eclectic: being anti-Lukashenka was enough. The Youth Front believed the regime could only be overcome by moral strength. In any case it was thought necessary to organise more covertly. Seviarynets provided the example after his arrest in 2005 (he had been detained on a scarcely credible forty previous occasions), sending 'Letters from the Forest' (the title of a later book) from his place of internal exile in the north.[25] Other leaders such as Zmitser Dashkevich were arrested when they took his place – though, ironically, it would later be argued that KGB chief Stsiapan Sukharenka was dismissed in July 2007 for having failed to eradicate the Youth Front completely.

The third 'movement' was Khopits! ('Enough!'), which was born among a younger generation of activists (twenty to thirty-five years old) out of a determination to sidestep Milinkevich's caution and demonstrate in numbers after the election. Its leaders were again mostly young, like Ales Mazur, who emerged as the key coordinator of the short-lived Minsk 'tent camp' after the election.[26]

NGOs

The Belarusian NGO sector was already much weakened by constant 're-registration' campaigns. A first attempt to diminish its influence after Lukashenka came to power, in 1994–5, was only a dress rehearsal. Belarus still had a relatively large number of NGOs: 2,191 in April 1998.[27] A second anti-NGO campaign began in 1999, but the 2001 election proved a major turning point. There had been too much election monitoring for the authorities' liking, and many NGOs sided with the opposition. A third re-registration campaign in 2003–5 therefore led to the closure of 347 NGOs, including nearly all the 'politicals' – all those involved in elections in any way, and all leading think tanks.[28] Revenge was taken on the trade unions, with the apparently loyalist Leanid Kozik ultimately replacing Hancharyk after his impudence in standing against Lukashenka in the 2001 election. A new religion law in 2003 led to another crackdown in this sector.

'Sukharenka's law' (the KGB chief introduced it personally in parliament) finalised in December 2005, launched a more general crackdown. Article 193 of the Criminal Code now threatened up to two years in jail for working with an unregistered NGO. Article 293 promised up to three years for those involved in the training of persons involved in 'mass upheaval'. The provision of 'false information' abroad and the 'discrediting of the Republic of Belarus' carried another two years.

As of January 2006, there were 2,247 officially registered NGOs, but the vast majority of these were the newer, tamer 'state civic organisations' set up by the government itself. The Assembly of Pro-Democracy NGOs estimated that an almost equal number of NGOS now operated unregistered, 'underground'.[29]

In sharp contrast to the success of Ukrainian NGOs like Znaiu and the Committee of Voters in 2004, the 2006 Belarusian equivalent, *Partnerstva* ('Partnership'), was constantly harassed. In February the group was discredited by means of a 'special operation' which saw fake-fake polls planted in its office: that is, police claimed to have found leaflets due for distribution on election night, claiming that Lukashenka had lost the 'real' vote by 41.3 to 53.7 per cent, intended for use as a 'technology' to promote demonstrations – and that these bulletins had been printed abroad. Arrests and a trial followed in August 2006.

The Vote

The authorities' tactics for the election itself were to ramp up turnout to a level high enough to demoralise the opposition, use their administrative resources and social control to deliver the vote, and then fiddle the count itself inside the election commissions. Belarus didn't bother with the euphemistically named vote-fixing 'technologies' – 'cookies', 'electoral tourism', the 'carousel' – used in Ukraine in 2004. Lukashenka's vote was simply adjusted upwards in the privacy of the election commissions. In fact, it is open to question to what extent the vote was actually 'counted' at all.

The first key 'technology' was early voting, particularly for 'directed populations' like students and hospital in-patients, who could be more easily controlled. Only 3.2 per cent had voted early in 1994. By 2001 the figure was 14.6 per cent, rising to 17.4 per cent for the referendum in 2004. This time the figure was a massive 31.3 per cent, almost a third of all voters.[30] Given the pressure to 'mobilise' the vote, the extremely high turnout of 92.6 per cent seems to have been genuine. Independent polls estimated the turnout to have been 90–92 per cent.[31] An estimated 30–40 per cent of factory workers and 80–90 per cent of students voted early, whether they wanted to or not.[32] Rolling one-year contracts were introduced in January 2004, making it harder for workers to escape the system of social control. Students were closely monitored by 'prophylactic' interviews with their deans. Though once they had voted early, they were arguably freer to protest later.

State TV (ANT, LAD, NTV, Belarus and STV) pumped out the official message. The State Committee for Information Control was now directly under the president rather than the KGB. Local internet service providers had to operate by means of the state-owned Beltelecom.

Belarusian Presidential Election, 2006 (by Percentage)

Aliaksandr Lukashenka	83
Aliaksandr Milinkevich	6.1
Siarhei Haidukevich	3.5
Aliaksandr Kazulin	2.2

Turnout: 92.6; early voting: 31.3.

Source: www.rec.gov.by/elect/indexprb.html#prrb2006.

Another key 'technology' that had been refined since 2004 was the use of fake exit polls designed to chime with the eventual official results, and deprive potential protesters of the moral high ground. The technique was still somewhat unrefined – both of the principal fake organisations released their results before noon, when most people were entering polling stations rather than leaving them, and a full eight hours before the polls closed. The shadowy organisation EcooM was rolled out once again, and gave Lukashenka 82.1 per cent and Milinkevich 4.4 per cent. This time, EcooM actually had a flesh-and-blood spokesman, a certain Sergei Musiienko, but it had no office or end-of-the-telephone existence. Inappropriately for a virtual organisation, it didn't even exist on the internet. So some tricks were still missed. No one was even sure what EcooM stood for. But it was soon being quoted by the likes of ABC in the US.[33] One other phantom pollster, the Belarusian Committee of Youth Organisations – obviously a highly qualified sociological organisation – had Lukashenka on 84.2 per cent and Milinkevich on 3.1 per cent.[34]

Obstacles were placed in the way of real polling organisations. The Moscow Levada Centre ran into trouble with its poll. More than 30 per cent of voters refused to reply to its interviewers, so its claim of 47.4 per cent for Lukashenka and 25.6 per cent for Milinkevich involved attributing answers to people who hadn't spoken.[35] IISEPS attempted to conduct a retrospective poll between 27 March and 6 April, and attempted to do so from Lithuania. It estimated that Lukashenka won 63.6 per cent and Milinkevich 20.6 per cent,[36] later refined to 64.9 per cent and 21.4 per cent. A second face-to-face, but again necessarily retrospective, poll conducted on 16 April gave Lukashenka 54.2 per cent, Milinkevich 15.8 per cent, Kazulin 6 per cent and Haidukevich 4.4 per cent.[37] Kaliakin claimed Milinkevich had won 32 per cent and Lukashenka no more than 50 per cent. In late April the Polish newspaper *Gazeta Wyborcza* (Election Gazette) reported receiving a letter from 'patriots' in the Belarusian KGB claiming that Lukashenka had won only 49 per cent of the vote.[38] Crucially, however, Milinkevich was unable to claim a stolen victory; an exaggerated defeat was much less likely to put people on the streets.

If the Orange Revolution had attracted hundreds of thousands of relatively apolitical protesters with its strong moral stance and colourful style, the Belarusian authorities planned to make their own appeal to the undecided masses first. Their rival campaign 'For Belarus!' aped the style of colour revolutions. A six-week pop tour covered the country, with eight set-piece concerts in the major regional centres.[39] Since 2002–4 the authorities had insisted that 75 per cent of music on radio be Belarusian in origin – primarily to the benefit of conformist artists such as Angelika Agurbash rather than underground bands like Lavon Volski, NRM, Zet and Neuro Dubel. By 2006 the bizarrely incomplete slogan 'For . . .' was thought to work just as well as 'For Belarus'.

Protests, But No Revolution

As with the Orange Revolution in Ukraine, the opposition, if not the regime, was intent on non-violent protest. The Christian leadership of the Youth Front was also committed to moral rather than physical protest. Moreover, Milinkevich was naturally cautious: 'some members of his team thought that the campaign headquarters should not be involved in staging mass protest, in particular as people in charge of separate mobilisation campaigns promised to do the job', although ultimately most 'sought to coordinate various groups working towards the same goal'.[40] If Milinkevich was too passive, Kazulin was too rash. On 2 March the latter tried to gatecrash Lukashenka's traditional pre-election People's 'Assembly', and was supposedly beaten up by none other than Dzmitry Pawlichenka, the organiser of the 'disappearances' in 1999–2000.

Nobody really expected a rerun of the mass protests that had produced Ukraine's Orange Revolution, but many hoped for a 'revolution of the spirit' at least.[41] On the evening of the election a crowd of five to ten thousand people were attracted (not that many in a population of 1.7 million) to October Square in central Minsk by fliers and text messages.[42] Some claimed as many as 35,000.[43] But new technology had its drawbacks too. According to the native Belarusian internet expert Evgeny Morozov:

> The emergence of new digital spaces for dissent also led to new ways of tracking it. Analogue activism was pretty safe: if one node in a protest network got busted, the rest of the group was probably OK. But getting access to an activist's inbox puts all their interlocutors in the frame, too . . .

After the first flash mob, the authorities began monitoring By_mob, the LiveJournal community where the activities were announced. The police started to show up at the events, often before the flashmobbers did.[44]

In Kiev in 2004 some critics have claimed that over-elaborate preparations were evidence that the opposition never planned to accept the vote; by contrast, in Minsk the organisation was woefully poor. There weren't even any loudspeakers in October Square. The crowd couldn't hear Milinkevich, who was nervous of supporting the 'civic initiative' of a protest camp. He 'didn't want confrontation to happen – or anything to happen'.[45] He knew of the rumours that Lukashenka was having a mini-breakdown holed up in a military camp near Hrodna, ill from stress or heavy drinking; but still he told people to go home (Lukashenka disappeared for three weeks; even his inauguration was delayed until 8 April). 'KGB' letters about Lukashenka's health turned out to be from Kazulin's HQ.[46]

Kazulin's actions were once again contradictory. He allegedly 'toured Western embassies on the Friday before the election trying to get them to persuade Milinkevich to stand down with him'.[47] But on the second night of post-election protests, he surprised many by calling on the crowds to disperse.

So the second phase of protests, which began three days later on 21 March, was largely organised by youth activists who set up a small 'tent city' in October Square. The authorities initially avoided the kind of heavy-handed response that could have given the protests extra stimulus. Salami tactics thinned protesters' numbers: people were arrested *leaving* the square, so they could be picked off in small groups – though between five hundred and a thousand were eventually arrested, and 392 sentenced.[48] The authorities prevented practical supplies (food, blankets) from being brought in large enough amounts to support the protests – having previously made sure the election was held in cold March weather rather than in the summer. Portable toilets were taken away. Nearby shops were closed to stop people using their facilities. A manhole was made available for the desperate, then welded shut, but not before state TV had pictures of 'vandals' 'poisoning' the city's water supply.[49] Drunken provocateurs were also prominent on state TV. On Friday the protests briefly stopped, and the international media shifted its attention to Ukraine, where key parliamentary elections were due on Sunday 26 March. Most reporters and TV crews left town. The police therefore swooped on the tent city in the early hours of Saturday morning, and another four hundred people ended up in jail

A final, decisive rally was held later on Saturday 25 March, the highly symbolic day on which the BNR had declared independence in 1918 (a fact unknown to most departing Western journalists). An estimated fifteen thousand demonstrators were blocked by none other than Pawlichenka again, whose sinister presence was obviously designed to intimidate, alongside the KGB head, Stsiapan Sukharenka. Kazulin suddenly called on the demonstrators to march on Minsk's main detention centre (actually a long way out of town) and free those already detained, which led straight to confrontation. Kazulin allegedly brawled once again with Pawlichenka. He was arrested and imprisoned until 2008, which at least ought to put to bed the theory that he was a secret tool of Lukashenka. Rubber bullets and tear gas were used. Eight policemen were 'injured'; TV highlighted their slightly ruddy cheeks. They were later shown in a hospital with 'obviously non-hospital furniture'.[50] 'The last summer of the opposition' was over.[51]

The Aftermath

Despite all of the efforts of government and opposition during Lukashenka's second term (2001–6), underlying political patterns hadn't shifted that much. In both 2001 and 2006, Lukashenka won a slim majority or near-majority of the vote, and then falsified a heavy majority. On both occasions, the opposition won a minority vote that was not big enough as a base for further protests. Officially, the three opposition candidates in 2006 won 11.8 per cent between them, less than two candidates' combined 17.1 per cent in 2001. However, Milinkevich had at least gained a much higher international profile than Hancharyk had five years earlier, and was warmly received in Brussels and Warsaw, to the point that even many EU politicians began to think he should spend more time at home. But the opposition campaign was rightly criticised for 'romantic sentiments and symbolic gestures' – candles and denim. 'In the end, numbers matter more than gestures.'[52]

There was never much chance the Belarusian opposition could overthrow Lukashenka on its own. It was thoroughly infiltrated and ineffective. According to one official involved in the aid effort: 'Partners are either not reliable, lazy or controlled. Revolution from within is not feasible at all.'[53] All donor lines were tracked. Milinkevich had run the Belarus Resource Centre for ten years, so the authorities knew all his financial comings and goings. And, temperamentally, he was simply not a revolutionary.

Even hard-won relative opposition unity was soon lost. Milinkevich squandered momentum after the election. Renewed arguments within the opposition camp broke out distressingly quickly, some no doubt fanned by regime agents or the long arm of Moscow. Kazulin was soon in prison. There was strong pressure on the Party of Communists of Belarus to 'merge' with the pro-government Communist Party of Belarus, after Siarhei Kaliakin, the leader of the opposition Communists, served as Milinkevich's campaign manager and then immediately switched to touting for Moscow money. Kaliakin's launch of a new Union of Left Parties had to be held over the border in Chernihiv, northern Ukraine, in December 2006.

The EU at least followed up on the principles of the US Belarus Democracy Act by imposing sanctions after the election. Lukashenka and thirty-six other officials, mainly those responsible for the 'disappearances' in 1999–2000 and for election fraud, were subjected to a travel ban, and attempts were made to seize their assets, when they could be found.

An EU non-paper or 'shadow Action Plan' addressed to the Belarusian people in December 2006 set out an unofficial road-map of steps that Belarus could take to improve relations with Brussels, and finally stirred some reaction from Minsk in 2008 (see pages 226–7).[54]

But developments within the regime now seemed more important in determining Belarus's future direction. Lukashenka himself quickly bounced back. He was soon showing off his illegitimate son Kolia, born in 2004, whose mother was thought to be Lukashenka's personal doctor Irina Abelskaia, who also had alleged influence over the president through control of various medications. He has also been linked to the pop singer Irina Dorofeieva, the officially sanctioned ideal Belarusian woman, whose face is featured on sweet wrappers.

Russia Seeks Better Value for Money from Minsk

Even if the stories about his temporary breakdown after the election were true, Lukashenka was apparently more secure than ever from direct domestic challenges to his rule. But powerful pressures built up quickly during his third term. First, Russia continued to recalibrate the price of its support.[55] It did not want to end the subsidies regime, but it made its financial and other support more conditional. In fact, the speed with which Russia moved to raise gas prices to force Minsk to surrender 50 per cent of Beltransgaz as soon as the March 2006 elections were out of the way came as a real shock in Minsk – as it was intended to do. Lukashenka's links with Russian *siloviki* like Sergei Ivanov and Igor Sechin (through past oil deals) also proved a double-edged sword once Putin chose Medvedev rather than a silovik as his successor.

Second, the balance shifted within the Belarusian elite from the local *silo-viki*, who were essential to Lukashenka's survival in 2006, to the technocrats, who wanted to enrich themselves via nomenklatura privatisation (see below).

After the election, realising that Belarus's dependence on Russia had become a major problem, the president launched a quest for new foreign partners (and markets) under the slogan 'Foreign Policy with a Second Wing'. China, Iran and Venezuela were among the countries that Belarus courted. Their money was doubly welcome in Minsk because, unlike the EU or Russia, they did not meddle in Belarusian politics. During a 2010 Beijing visit, Lukashenka stated in his usual forthright style that 'China's investment has never had any political strings attached; therefore we are more than willing to see China speed up its investment in Belarus on a larger scale.'[56] Lukashenka's outreach, however, further soured relations with Russia, which did not want him to become an ironic role model for other autocratically independent leaders in the CIS.

Belarus Copies Russia's '*Siloviki* Wars'

The internal pressures produced by these multiple balancing acts were already apparent by the summer of 2007. In Russia, the *siloviki* controlled the state. As Putin neared the end of his second term as president, there was a clan struggle for power and economic assets. At the same time in Belarus, Lukashenka was about to show the *siloviki* that they were servants of the state. Lukashenka's moves against the KGB in 2007 demonstrated a 'clear trend to weaken the force in Belarus which is pro-Russian'[57] now that it was no longer so crucial to the defence of the regime against 'colour revolution'. Lukashenka also had to accommodate the interests of the rising clan of so-called 'technocrats'.

The first sign of the struggle for influence below the surface came when Zianon Lomat, head of the State Control Committee, was subjected to an extraordinary public beating in Mahilew in July 2007 by people posing as Interior Ministry officials. The attack led to the fall of KGB chief Stsiapan Sukharenka and his ally Henadz Niavyhlas, head of the Presidential Administration. This signalled the waning influence of the coalition of inter-ests around Viktar Sheiman representing certain Russian oligarchs and the domestic oil business, as well as larger retail outlets and much market trade – not just a hard line in domestic affairs. The simultaneous management purges at Belneftekhim in May 2007 and Beltransgaz and the Belarusian Oil Company in July also weakened the *siloviki*. But the removal of Sheiman, Lukashenka's long-term number two, was a dramatic and potentially risky step, as he knew where many bodies were buried – both literally, given his role in the 1999–2000 'disappearances', and metaphorically, as he had long been at the centre of the local web of *kompromat* – not to mention the truth about the attempt on Lukashenka's life apparently staged by him in 1994. Sheiman's removal seems to have been engineered by the bizarre affair of the July 2008 Minsk bombings, when fifty people were injured by a home-made bomb during an official Independence Day concert. Sheiman was made the fall-guy, but was only kicked upstairs, becoming head of the Belarus-Venezuela High-Level Commission to protect his own and the president's interests in the oil and arms trades.

The decline of one clan was matched by the rise of another. The successor of the Tozik clan (see page 208) now centred around the president's eldest (and official) son, Viktar Lukashenka, who had quietly built up a strong position in construction and property development. The reshuffles also showed that clan politics mattered more than competence, as the alliance between Viktar Lukashenka and the 'technocrats' pushed its men forward: both Sukharenka's temporary replacement at the KGB, Yury Zhadobin, who was moved on to head the National Security Council in July 2008, and Zhadobin's successor, Vadzim Zaitsaw, were born in Ukraine and lacked direct security experience. Zhadobin had previously headed the Presidential Guard Service. Zaitsaw was a protégé of Ihar Rachkowski of the State Border Committee, another ally of Viktar Lukashenka. Niavyhlas was replaced at the Presidential Administration by Uladzimir Makei, who was a long-term associate of both Lukashenkas, father and eldest son – though it was less clear just who was riding on whose coattails. Makei was an arch-manipulator, but no liberal (though he studiously read the opposition press), and not particularly young either, unlike his glamorous deputy, Natallia Piatkevich, who was put in charge of developing the regime's 'ideology' – such as it was.[58]

The net effect of this protracted game of musical chairs was, however, clear enough. The 'old guard' was down and almost out. The *silovik* interior minster Uladzimir Naumaw was ousted in April 2009, and Prime Minister Sidorski was now in the technocrats' camp. But the new technocrats were just as self-interested as a group as the old Sheiman clan. They wanted to enrich themselves in the same fashion. They did not want Belarus to learn from the mistakes of Russia and Ukraine in the 1990s – Lukashenka's line in public – quite the opposite. They wanted Western support, but they didn't want too much Western capital. They wanted control of key economic assets for themselves, seeing the West as a useful counterweight to Russian incursions, which came with too many strings attached. Russian oligarchs like Roman

Abramovich were already hovering over the juiciest Belarusian assets.[59] The children of the new bureaucratic elite were now reaching their twenties, and Viktar Lukashenka had been at school and university with them all. In President Lukashenka's third term semi-conspicuous consumption became possible. Big houses started to go up in the nicer suburbs of Minsk (not where Lee Harvey Oswald used to live). Building them and living in them were equally pleasant and profitable activities – the real-estate business was almost as lucrative as arms sales. In 2008 it cost $350 to $500 per square metre of floor space to build an apartment in Minsk, but the average market price was closer to $2,000 per square metre. Elite housing was marketed at $3,500 per square metre.

In 2007–8 Lukashenka announced a series of measures to ease the nomen-klatura's path to self-enrichment, including a flat 12 per cent rate of income tax, an expanded privatisation programme, some loosening of red tape and hints at easier access for foreign investors. In March 2008 the National Bank announced that bankers could acquire up to 20 per cent of shares in banks and other companies (i.e. hard assets in manufacturing enterprises that had previously been off-limits – the nomenklatura already controlled most trade and service enterprises). In April 2008 it was announced that the moratorium on the sale of stakes in stock companies would be phased out over three years to January 2011 (just before the then-expected date of the next election). The State Property Management Committee ruled that presidential permission was not needed for deals of less than $16.5 million.

But Lukashenka had no intention of opening the floodgates. He didn't want to encourage the rise of powerful oligarchs who might ultimately challenge his monopoly of political control, as in Russia in the 1990s. Some 'technocrats' may have been deluding themselves that they could use Lukashenka the younger as a 'battering ram' to win power, just as the Young Wolves (the would-be equivalents of Russia's shock-therapy liberals of the 1990s) tried to do with Lukashenka the elder in 1994.[60] However, President Lukashenka was unlikely to be so easily outmanoeuvred; nor was he likely to let his son Viktar monopolise power. One indicative sign was Lukashenka's reluctance to sanc-tion the establishment of a ruling party (due to be called Belaia Rus) which would bind him more closely to the new elite, despite a 'founding congress' that claimed 82,000 members in October 2008.[61]

Ironically, not long after Lukashenka had introduced a 'state ideology' in 2003, many of its key tenets were now being ditched. But Lukashenka's long-standing rhetoric against oligarchs and corrupt privatisation would be diffi-cult to abandon completely. He wanted to preserve the state factories, with mass workforces and welfare-through-the-workplace, that were the bedrock of his social contract. Twenty per cent stakes are not full control. The introduction of limited curbs on state welfare in May 2007 (pensioners' health subsidies, free student travel) was a significant milestone, but so was the partial backtracking almost immediately afterwards. Cultural policy, on the other hand, moved in the opposite direction, as some mild and eclectic Belarusianisation measures suited the state-building strategy of the new elite. Pavel Latushka, the new culture minister after July 2009, switched regional news programmes to the Belarusian language in October 2009, and talked of one state TV channel going all-Belarusian. Legislation was increasingly printed in both Russian and Belarusian. A propaganda campaign with the snappy title 'Belarus Is Us' emphasised selective points of ancient history like the Battle of Grunwald.[62]

For their part, the nomenklatura still depended on Lukashenka's ability to reach a deal with Russia on cheap energy supplies and market access, and on Russian government orders for the output of Belarusian enterprises. There was no sign of the technocrats bringing about regime change from the inside.

2008: A Tentative Opening

Meanwhile, the West was simultaneously deciding that its isolation policy wasn't working. Brussels had been under no real pressure from member states to change its isolationist approach between 1997 and roughly 2004. After EU enlargement, Poland made the running in setting the strategy towards Belarus for the 2006 election, but ultimately realised that its one-shot policy of pushing Milinkevich was counterproductive, allowing Lukashenka the propaganda gift of a 'Polish plot'. Lithuania had been tempted to promote a colour revolution in Minsk in 2006, which also played into Lukashenka's hands, but Vilnius became more pragmatic after the election of new president Dalia Grybauskaitė in 2009. Germany was the biggest Western investor in Belarus and sponsored the annual business-friendly 'Minsk Forum' every November which became an important lobby for pragmatic engagement. A broader spectrum of EU member states was keen to rethink the strategy of placing all bets on a weak and divided opposition, as was the special Belarus Task Force under former Polish president Aleksander Kwaśniewski, which produced its report on 'A European Alternative for Belarus' in October 2008.[63] The US was pushing sanctions at this time (see below), but was not a constant hawk.

In this more optimistic world – before the war in Georgia and before the global economic crisis later in 2008 – it was assumed or hoped by many that Belarus would be the sixth member of the EU's embryonic 'Eastern Partnership' – eventually launched in 2009, alongside Ukraine, Moldova, Georgia, Armenia and Azerbaijan – and indeed that it was somehow the missing geo-political piece, which, after a bit of special treatment, would fall in line with the other five.

Georgia Shock

In March 2008 agreement was reached to open an EU Delegation in Minsk, though real change was not anticipated until after the September 2008 parliamentary elections in Belarus. But after the war in Georgia in August 2008, Lukashenka shrewdly sold himself to the West not as an unlikely introducer of democracy, but as a more plausible defender of Belarusian sovereignty, calculating that this now suited Western realpolitik. Milinkevich helpfully chipped in, saying that securing the country's independence from Russia took precedence over all other objectives, and that there was therefore 'no alternative to a policy of dialogue' with the current regime.[64] The EU therefore produced a new, watered-down set of five conditions for dialogue, but Lukashenka sidestepped them by releasing all political prisoners, including Kazulin, within days of the war in Georgia. US officials insisted that Lukashenka's climb-down was actually the result of the sanctions introduced by Washington against the main refining company Belneftekhim – a key financial prop for the regime – in November 2007, and heightened in March 2008, when Lukashenka had reacted furiously by expelling the US ambassador and forcing the US mission to downsize from thirty to five.[65]

The September 2008 parliamentary elections saw only cosmetic improvements. Allowing in OSCE observers was an important step, but one that was predicated on maintaining a system that would not allow them to see very much. The presence of fifty to sixty opposition candidates led to unseemly speculation, even bargaining, over just how many opposition victories would be necessary for the elections to 'count' – hence the obvious disappointment when not a single seat was won. Even the regime parties were poorly represented: the loyal version of the Communist Party had six deputies and the Agrarians one, leaving a massive 103 regime-loyal 'independents'. The traditional processes of candidate registration weeded out most significant opponents; the opposition was largely excluded from the election committees (and there were no real observers at the higher levels where the votes were actually counted); a punitive new media law and criminal code were approved in June 2008 (on top of the restrictions from 'Sukharenka's law' dating from before the

2006 elections); 'active measures' were used to split Kazulin's Social Democratic Party, the United Democratic Front and others; in June state media soured the atmosphere with a propaganda film, 'The Network', pitching the now-traditional message of a foreign-financed and frankly treasonous opposition. And as the subsequent report by the OSCE's election monitors made clear,[66] 'transparency' disappeared in the actual counting process.

It seemed that Lukashenka's amour-propre was so profound he would prevent his own 'many-winged' foreign policy from actually taking flight. Wherever the EU pressed for a signal or a symbolic step, Lukashenka pushed back. For example, NGOs like Amnesty International had campaigned hard to get the EU to persuade Belarus to drop the death penalty. A few countries like Russia technically only had a moratorium on its use in place (since 1996), but Belarus was the last European state to embrace the death penalty openly, so if it fell into line, this would, in the words of an Amnesty report, amount to 'Ending Executions in Europe'.[67] Lukashenka toyed with the idea, then held two executions of convicted murderers in March 2010, Soviet-style, with a bullet to the back of the head. The Union of Poles of Belarus was also subjected to seemingly counter-productive renewed repression, probably because Lukashenka wanted to make it difficult for Poland to take the lead in setting Belarus policy within the EU, and just because the Union of Poles was the biggest remaining NGO in Belarus.

The Polish–Russian rapprochement, given extra momentum by the tragic plane crash in Smolensk in April 2010 that killed President Lech Kaczyński and ninety-five other members of the Polish elite, was also bad news for Belarus. The Tusk government in Warsaw had in any case long buried the Kaczyńskis' ideological eastern policy and was lining up with the business-friendly pragmatists: Waldemar Pawlak, deputy prime minister and minister of the economy, represented the Peasants' Party, a remodelled hangover from the Communist era whose members traditionally sold much of their produce to the east, favoured good relations with Belarus, as did the Polish magnate Jan Kulczyk, who wanted to build a 'traditional' 'dirty' power station using lower-grade Polish coal out of reach of the EU over the border in western Belarus. But the rapprochement also reduced Poland's interest in the east. Lukashenka made things worse with his crass response to the Smolensk tragedy: saying that pilots would always obey his orders.[68]

Belarus complained about not being a full and equal member of the new Eastern Partnership, but broke its spirit by expelling an activist, Tatsiana Shaputska, from her home university after she attended the Civil Society Forum of the Eastern Partnership in Brussels. Nothing could have been better

designed to provoke the protests of EU foreign ministers like Carl Bildt and
Radosław Sikorski, but to no avail.

A small businessman, Mikalai Awtukhovich, was charged with firearms
offences and subjected to a show trial, presumably because he was undermining the regime's claim to be pro-business. He got five years in May 2010.

Local elections were held in the same month with even less regard to due
procedure than normal. Only ten deputies from anything resembling the opposition were elected in the whole country, leading the Parliamentary Assembly of
the Council of Europe to suspend high-level contact with Belarus.

By the spring of 2010 the putative 'opening' was no more. Lukashenka
seemed deliberately to avoid taking the simple steps required of him. Makei
and Foreign Minister Martynow reportedly got a private dressing-down for
pushing the policy in the first place. It is important to note that the tentative
'opening' to the West came before the economic crisis. If Lukashenka had been
motivated by economic desperation, then his struggle for resources would
probably have made him carry it further. But his real motive was to rebalance
his relationship with Russia. He wanted just enough Western support, ironically, to allow him to maintain the authoritarian system and keep Russia
paying for his social model. He therefore took it so far and no further.

Recession Shock

As mentioned above, all of this was just before the global economic crisis.
Belarus was not initially as directly exposed as many of its neighbours. The
banking sector was small; there had been no mortgage boom and consequent
property bubble. Belarus even went ahead with an Investment Forum in
London in November 2008, though the timing was poor and the event was
hardly a success. But the economy swiftly deflated over the winter, and only
survived 2009 (official growth was 0.2 per cent) on state orders and foreign
loans (see Chapter 12). Exports – both of manufactures to Russia, and energy
and raw materials to the West – collapsed and the state bought up inventories.
Factories were on a four- or three-day week. Lukashenka tried every planning
trick he could think of, but the most telling statistic was the balance of
payments. Despite the crisis hitting demand for imports, this actually got
worse, going from 6.7 per cent of GDP before the crisis in 2007 to 14 per cent
in 2010, which was over $7 billion.[69] External debt almost doubled, reaching
a record 52 per cent of GDP in 2010. However successful Lukashenka was in
raising funds from unlikely sources, he would surely find it impossible to
produce $7 billion a year. So Russia decided to hit him when he was down.

Russia Shock

No doubt it was Lukashenka's exaggerated sense of his own importance that left him disappointed when Europe failed to welcome his 'opening' with open arms, when he himself had sabotaged it at every turn. But by 2010 Russia seemed to have run out of patience with him too. Before the 2001 election Lukashenka had won Russian backing with what became broken promises of insider privatisations for Russian capital; in 2006 he had posed as a bulwark against 'coloured revolution'. But it wasn't clear what cards he had to play in 2010. On the contrary Russia was increasingly irritated by his 'many-winged' foreign policy – particularly his refusal to recognise Abkhazia and South Ossetia after the war in Georgia in 2008, and his constant feet-dragging on Putin's pet project of a Customs Union between Russia, Belarus and Kazakhstan. Even the moderate Russian foreign policy doyen Fiodor Lukianov declared in 2010 that 'Lukashenka has for some time been trying to establish himself as a systemic opponent of Russian policy'.[70]

A new gas war between Russia and Belarus broke out in June 2010. Prices were increased to $194 per 1,000 m^3; prices of between $220 and $250 loomed in 2011. On the Russian side, the powerful *éminence grise* of the *siloviki*, Igor Sechin, railed against what he saw as open-ended subsidies for little return. Finance minister Aleksei Kudrin estimated those subsidies to have amounted to $50 billion over the past fifteen years.[71] Russia did not want to subsidise Lukashenka's by now traditional round of pre-election social spending, though the Kkarkiv deal that gave a gas discount to new Ukrainian president Viktor Yanukovych undermined the drive to commercialise Russia's relations with the 'near abroad'. Lukashenka's response to the revolution in Kyrgyzstan in April 2010 was both personal and emotional. He took in the fugitive Kyrgyz president, Karmanbek Bakiyev, and promised an 'armed response' to anyone trying anything similar in Belarus. The Russian elite even believed that Lukashenka had helped foment the trouble in Osh against the new Kyrgyz authorities.

In July 2010 a four-part series on Russian TV called *The Godfather* portrayed Lukashenka as a dictator maintained at Russian expense, and revived the issue of the 'disappearances', as well as his 1995 comments praising Hitler. It accused him of smuggling, and even questioned his mental health.[72] It was surely no accident that the show aired on NTV, which was controlled by Gazprom. Russian money also backed the new NGO campaign 'Speak the Truth!', albeit indirectly via Viktar Rakhmanka, former boss of Belarusian Railways before his arrest in 2001, who was now one of many Belarusian businessmen in exile in Moscow (he was also head of the Transport Division of the Investment and Building Department at Gazprom). Lukashenka responded by publishing Boris Nemtsov's accusations about Putin's corruption in the official Belarusian media.[73]

Russia knew it couldn't remove Lukashenka but wanted to take him down a peg nonetheless. Its new policy was relatively flexible. It could back post-election protest if Lukashenka suddenly looked vulnerable. It sought to encourage a more fractious elite, and hoped for part of it to swing its way if it saw which direction the wind was blowing (significantly, *The Godfather* attacked no one other than Lukashenka and his eldest son, Viktar). But it didn't want to put pressure on the general population, or allow Lukashenka to pose as the defender of national sovereignty. One theory about Russia's behaviour was that Putin was particularly sensitive about apparently successful authoritarian competition on its doorstep, so what it called 'democracy promotion' in Belarus meant promoting pluralism that it thought would make Lukashenka weaker.[74] But Russia's two-step also involved a last-minute offer by President Medvedev to cut oil tariffs if Belarus became a member of the Single Economic Space, which is supposed to be stage two of Russia's Customs Union project. (The small print revealed the deal was also to Russia's benefit, as it would control any export tariff from oil refined at Mazyr and Novapolatsk.)

The Biggest Shock: The Crackdown

Lukashenka's fourth presidential election was brought forward to December 2010 rather than March 2011, to make sure the vote came before looming economic problems and another potential winter energy war with Russia. The EU hoped the tentative rapprochement would continue and set the bar low: the European Council in October 2010 calling for 'clear and visible progress on the conduct of elections', not a free and fair election per se.[75] The Polish and German Foreign Ministers Radosław Sikorski and Guido Westerwelle went to Minsk in November 2010 and produced a vague promise of $3 billion in potential assistance out of an unknown hat.

Some cosmetic improvements were duly made to the election process. No fewer than nine other candidates were eventually allowed to stand, the signature collection process that had previously been used to filter out awkward opponents having been somewhat eased. TV debates between the 'political' candidates – not, of course, including the President himself, who was beneath such grubby politicking, were introduced, in addition to personal ad slots. Facing seven-plus dwarves suited Lukashenka perfectly well, however. The absence of a single strong opposition leader meant there would be no single

focal point for protests after the vote. Most importantly, however, no significant changes were made to the counting process – i.e. the votes didn't have to
be counted; they would be fixed at the level of administrative diktat, safe from
the scrutiny of domestic and foreign NGOs.

Russia, however, had its own deal in mind. Although Russia had been piling
on the pressure for two years, the most likely reason for reversing its previous
policy is that the Russians thought it had worked. The Kremlin had failed to tie
Lukashenka down to his promises after previous elections in 2001 and 2006,
but now presumably calculated that his tentative opening to the West had run
its course and that Belarus's dire economic situation gave Moscow much more
leverage (see pages 249–53). On 10 December, nine days before the vote, the
two sides produced a spectacular *volte face* on a new energy deal. Putin promised that it would be worth $4.1 billion a year as Belarus could resume duty-
free supply of 21.7 million tons of oil and revive its key cash-cow refineries.
Belarus would also have $500 million to $700 million (1.7 million tons) for its
own use and the petrochemical industry could regain solvency with access to
duty-free oil. Russian oil companies, even those closest to the Kremlin, understandably chafed at the threat to their profits. A three-week dispute in January
eventually led to the addition of a $46 premium per ton.

An increasingly confident Lukashenka was therefore already back-pedalling
before the vote. Viktar Sheiman re-emerged as the head of Lukashenka's reelection 'strategy': possibly because the *siloviki* were worried that even minimal
'liberalisation' was losing control, or because they wanted to widen their piece
of any post-election privatisation pie, or because the partial restoration of oil
money on election eve had played into their hands. The head of the Presidential
Administration Uladzimir Makei accused the opposition of 'preparing provocations' and armed insurrection, while hiding behind 'beardless lads'.[76]

But none of the new opposition candidates were front-line politicians. Most
were running more to occupy a particular niche than hoping actually to win
the race. Others were alleged to be 'regime candidates' such as Viktar
Tsiareshchanka, the head of an association of small- and medium-size enterprises. Another businessman, Dzmitry Us, took a more independent line.
They served as 'sparring partners' to keep the race alive if the real opposition
decided on a boycott, and as attack dogs to criticise the opposition, particularly during the TV debates, when Lukashenka was loftily absent.

Without Aliaksandr Milinkevich, who withdrew from the race as he lacked
both money and Polish support, the traditional rightist opposition was split
between marginal figures: Vital Rymashewski, Ales Mikhalevich and Ryhor
Kastusiow, all from the old Belarusian Popular Front, Christian Democratic

Party or satellite groups. The one prominent new face was the famous poet Uladzimir Niakliaew who headed a new NGO Tell the Truth, allegedly funded by Belarusian émigrés in Russia,[77] which was an ironic contrast to 2006, when the West was accused of backing Milinkevich. Niakliaew competed with Andrei Sannikaw (in Russian Sannikov) for the leadership of this new-style opposition, which targeted the new middle class and those threatened by the economic crisis. Sannikaw was backed by the remnants of the youth group Zubr, but was seen by many as a divisive force, as he had also refused to support Milinkevich as the united opposition candidate in 2006.[78] His critics snidely referred to 'Sannikov land' – a group of non-existent islands that Russian explorers thought they had discovered in the Arctic Circle in the nineteenth century, which is also a satirical term for the chimerical or imaginary. But Sannikaw, like Kazulin in 2006, was the one candidate who was not afraid to criticise Lukashenka on a personal level.

Another candidate, Yaroslaw Ramanchuk from the United Civic Party, had hoped to work more closely with Niakliaew but his campaign suffered from a lack of resources and many of his supporters left to join Niakliaew's camp. The purpose of Mikalai Statkevich's candidacy remained unclear – his party was unregistered and although he was one of the 'oldest' opposition figures in the race, he lacked the money and activists to mount a serious campaign.

Official Result of the 2010 Election (by Percentage)

Aliaksandr Lukashenka	79.7
Andrei Sannikaw	2.6
Yaroslaw Ramanchuk	2.0
Ryhar Kastusiow	2.0
Uladzimir Niakliaew	1.8
Vital Rymashewski	1.1
Ales Mikhalevich	1.0
Mikalai Statkevich	1.0
Viktar Tsiareshchanka	1.1
Dzmitry Us	0.5

Against all: 6.5.
Turnout: 90.7.
Early voting: 23.1.

Source: www.rec.gov.by/pdf/prb2010/sved20.pdf

An independent opinion poll in September had indicated that Lukashenka could win 35–45 per cent in a free election.[79] But on the day he claimed an implausible 79.7 per cent, having in October mentioned a target of at least two-thirds of the total vote.[80] 'Exit polls' released before the real poll had closed confirmed Lukashenka's victory; the fake sociologists 'EcooM' predicted a traditionally resounding and almost perfectly accurate 79.1 per cent for Lukashenka.[81] The total official vote for the 'opposition' was only 13 per cent – barely changed from 2006. Apart from Sannikaw, all the candidates got fewer votes than signatories on their nomination papers (minimum 100,000). It was impossible to judge the real result. Other exit polls on the day were of questionable provenance. One by TNS gave Lukashenka 42.2 per cent, with Niakliaew on 17.7 per cent and Sannikaw on 13.2 per cent.[82] An underground poll by the Ukrainian group SOCIUM had Lukashenka on only 38.4 per cent, later refined to 40.2 per cent.[83] A post-election poll carried out by the more respectable IISEPS from Vilnius had 58 per cent saying they voted for Lukashenka, with Niakliaew on 9.7 per cent and Sannikaw 7 per cent.[84]

But the pre-election atmosphere had stoked expectations; mass demonstrations were provoked on election night by the crudity of the fraud. Initially some 7,000 to 10,000 went to October Square, the scene of the rallies after the 2006 election; but no speeches were possible as the authorities had turned the square into an ice rink with deafening Russian pop blaring out. So the crowds paraded down the old Skaryna Avenue through the centre of Minsk, with thousands more joining from side-streets. By the time they reached Independence Square numbers had risen to an estimated 30,000. The atmosphere was peaceful and curious, with no drinking. An informal rally took place bedside the Red church (see pages 64–5), big Lenin statue and main government buildings. The demonstration initially passed peacefully, albeit with no clear leadership. Niakliaew had the sound equipment and the guys to work it; but he was attacked by special forces and his van was taken by the police. Some opposition leaders seemed to play the same role as Kazulin in 2006, making wild claims that the 'government had fallen'. But trouble did not start until about 11.30 p.m., when one group of OMON police actually escorted unknown young men with iron bars that Makei had warned were about to attack the Government House. Another group of OMON then attacked the peaceful demonstrators,[85] who had no Plan B – not really having had a Plan A. There were no tents or supplies for a long stint. Paranoia about infiltrators led to fear of making plans.

The crack-down had to have been pre-planned. A total of 639 were arrested.[86] NGOs were raided overnight. The OSCE office was closed. Almost all the opposition candidates ended up in jail. Ramanchuk and Tsiareshchanka were the only ones never arrested, Us and Kastusiow were released relatively early, but Niakliaew, Sannikaw, Kastusiow and Rymashewski were beaten up. Niakliaew was seized by police in hospital. Mikhalevich claimed he was tortured in prison and fled the country once he was released. Trials in the spring handed out some shocking sentences: Aliaksandr Atroshchankaw, a spokesman for Sannikaw, was sentenced to four years.

The crackdown seemed deliberately designed to wreck any hopes of rapprochement with the West. One theory was that Lukashenka had panicked at reports that his real vote was somewhere near the level reported by the IISEPS poll. The size of the crowd had also shocked him, particularly because it was swelled by large numbers of ordinary, even new middle class, Belarusians, who were not subject to traditional methods of control (all the opposition parties being riddled with agents) – confirming that the limited liberalisation in late 2010 had had real effect and was threatening to get out of control. Though Lukashenka had been lucky again: in the same way as he had managed to fix a referendum on abolishing term limits for the presidency in October 2004, just before the 'Orange Revolution' in neighbouring Ukraine in November-December 2004, the crackdown in Belarus in December 2010 came just before the 'Arab Spring' in early 2011 which might have given Belarusian demonstrators extra impetus.

Other explanations looked to the *siloviki* seeking to win back power from the technocrats, if only to bolster their chances in the new privatisation process. The government reshuffle a week after the election seemed to be Lukashenka's attempt to balance these factions: it brought back some of the 'old guard', though several reformers retained their positions, not least Lukashenka's oldest son Viktar. The new Prime Minister Mikhail Miasnikovich was considered the doyen of the Belarusian bureaucracy and could act as honest broker in the upcoming privatisation process.

A third explanation was that the authorities were clearing the ground of opposition before the difficult economic times ahead. In fact, the pain post-poned until after the election was not postponed for very long. Before any Russian money materialised utility prices were raised by 10 to 15 per cent in January; Lukashenka signed a new law on privatisation; $800 million was raised in a Eurobond issue, but at a punitive 8.95 per cent. Meanwhile, the government's reserves continued to drain away, falling by $1 billion in the first two months of 2011 to a low of $4 billion.

Lukashenka also seemed to assume that the West would not react, that western politicians were just like him, and only thought of realpolitik. Foreign Minister Martynow was sent to Brussels to ask for aid as if nothing had happened – and blame the crackdown on the Russians. But the West did react, albeit still not as toughly as some would have liked. In January the EU revived and extended a visa ban to include Lukashenka and one hundred and fifty seven others. The USA restored sanctions on Belneftekhim and its subsidiaries and raised the possibility of financial sanctions against key individuals in line with a Presidential Executive Order originally passed under George Bush in 2006. But both the EU and the US backed a twin-track approach leading to a donors' conference in Warsaw in February 2011 which produced $120 million in commitments to aid Belarusian civil society. The USA promised to increase its support from $11 million to $15 million, the EU to quadruple its efforts to $21.5 million and Poland to double to $14 million.

Conclusion

If the election was supposed to signal renewed liberalisation, it had clearly not served its purpose. Belarus was threatened with renewed isolation or over-dependence on Russia. But even dictatorships are never static. Would Lukashenka try to return to a policy of outreach once the cycle of repression was finished? Would the new elite finally make its presence felt in Lukashenka's fourth term? The next chapter looks at Belarus's economic dilemmas. The book then concludes with an examination of some of Belarus's more general future dilemmas – not including the unlikely possibilities that Lukashenka might be defeated at the polls or removed by some Russian-backed Act of God.

CHAPTER 12

THE MYTH OF THE BELARUSIAN ECONOMIC MIRACLE

For most of their history, the territories that are now Belarus based their occasional prosperity on trade with the Baltic littoral or down the river Dnieper to the south. In the modern era, however, they have been an economic backwater, until the Second World War at least. As late as 1940, only 21.3 per cent of locals lived in towns.[1] Belarus was one of the Tsarist Empire's poorest regions, lacking even Ukraine's natural strength in agriculture. The interwar Soviet republic built some islands of industry, but Belarus was rightly thought vulnerable to invasion and was not then a target for the kind of breakneck Soviet industrialisation seen in Ukraine with the coal industry and the Dnieper dams, or in the Urals with the new industrial megatowns like Magnitogorsk. To make matters worse, Belarus was decimated in the Second World War (see page 110). Postwar production was only 20 per cent of the prewar level.[2] Some 80 per cent of Minsk was destroyed. The capital was rebuilt as the quintessential Soviet city, with wide boulevards and identikit Brutalist architecture – which is why tourist guides always show the same row of colourful prewar houses by the river Svislach; it's the only photogenic architecture to have survived the Nazi occupation.

Belarus benefited disproportionately from belated postwar reconstruction, particularly under the 'partisan' leaders Mazuraw and Masheraw (mainly after the beginning of the USSR's seventh Five-Year Plan in 1961). From the 1960s to the 1980s Belarus was rebuilt practically from scratch – and was one of the few areas of the USSR to receive any investment at all after the Soviet planning system burnt itself out with the last-gasp showcase of the 1980 Moscow Olympics. Overall output increased ninefold. Belarus was geographically westerly and near European markets, but politically loyal, unlike the Baltic republics and western Ukraine, where cities like Vilnius and Lviv grew increasingly dowdy after 1945. Soviet planning and the benefits of westernmost geography also made Belarus a key energy transit state. Twenty per cent of Soviet, now Russian, gas exports to the EU passed through Belarus via the Northern Lights and Yamal pipelines, and 37 per cent of its oil through the Druzhba ('Friendship') pipeline. As crude oil is best refined near to final markets, two giant refineries were built in Belarus, at Mazyr and Novapolatsk. Gazprom now owns the newer gas pipeline, Yamal, which carries 63 per cent of gas going through Belarus. Beltransgaz controls the older Northern Lights system (and has nominal oversight of Yamal), but 50 per cent of Beltransgaz was painfully ceded to Gazprom between 2007 and 2010. Belarus also became a key Soviet manufacturing centre: 60 per cent of the computers sold in the last years of the USSR were made in Belarus. The Horizont factory where Lee Harvey Oswald once worked churned out exploding TVs. Although further north than the green fields and black earth of Ukraine, Belarus had a dairy industry and pig farms, which employed the young Aliaksandr Lukashenka in the 1980s – the agricultural sector still produced 24 per cent of GDP in 1991.

As president, Lukashenka has therefore been lucky. He has been able to free-ride on a capital stock that, unlike most of the rest of the Soviet Union, benefited from actual investment in the Soviet Union's twilight years. Until the global economic crisis in 2008, he was also able to free-ride on Russian aid (see below). But many in the West have bought into the idea of Lukashenka overseeing a specific 'Belarusian economic model', and even of a 'Belarusian economic miracle'.[3] On the left, the myth has grown up that Belarus is some kind of Cuba of the East, maintaining planning and strong social solidarity, and avoiding 'gangster privatisation' and oligarchs.[4] In reality, the Belarusian economy has gone through several periods since independence in 1991. First was an unconsummated search for a relatively liberal approach in 1992–5, which included Lukashenka's first few months in power after the 1994 election. Economic recovery in the late 1990s was not due to some unique 'Belarusian model', but to a generous subsidy regime from Russia and to the restoration of the Russian export market under the cover of the 'Union State'. Lukashenka proved adept at using his pivotal political position with Russia to extract rents and resources – while also presiding over a variety of blatant scams. These subsidies were wound down a little after his reelection in 2001 and the economy slowed down, before another mini-boom began from late 2003 as Belarus exploited the increasingly lucrative subsidy of cheap Russian crude and high global oil prices to become an 'offshore oil state'. The true

Lukashenkist left-populist model was funded by these two expansions, in the late 1990s and mid-2000s. But after Lukashenka's second reelection in 2006 Russia began to recalibrate the subsidies it paid, leading to an eclectic search for alternatives, segueing with the beginnings of authoritarian liberalisation in 2007–8. This proved badly timed. The global economic crisis hit Belarus with particular force in late 2008, and called into question the entire economic model built since 1995.

'Belarusian Liberalism', 1992–5

Belarus's economic problems in the early 1990s were little different from those of most other post-Soviet states. The country was dominated by former Communist apparatchiks, who parroted reform slogans but were profoundly ignorant of and hostile to the realities of a true free market. Like most post-Soviet states, Belarus managed to combine rampant inflation and a collapse in output in the first few years after independence, although the cumulative 37 per cent decline of GDP was not as bad as in Ukraine (more than 50 per cent) or war-torn and earthquake-blighted Armenia (60 per cent in four years). Belarus's particular contribution to the popular infamy of post-Soviet penury was its new currency. The original plan was to show local animals – a safer option than picking controversial historical figures (though under Kebich the Pahonia was shown on the reverse). The new money was therefore known as the *zayets* after the hare that appeared on the one-rouble note. Increasingly large animals featured on the larger notes, culminating in a *zubr* or bison on the hundred-rouble notes – but rampant inflation meant that the Belarusians soon ran out of even larger animals. The authorities settled for showing buildings instead.

As well as inflation, corruption and the first stirrings of 'nomenklatura privatisation' generated intense popular dislike of the elite. In truth, Kebich did do some things to liberalise prices and grapple with the rudiments of monetary control, and Lukashenka, it is easily forgotten, kept the momentum of quasi-liberal reform going for several crucial months after his election in the summer of 1994 (see page 170) – 'enough for the economy to start reviving slowly'.[5] Nascent market relations allowed Belarus to make much better use of Russian subsidies once they started flowing – though restored state control dissipated their impact soon enough. Back in the early 1990s, Belarus even had the seal of approval of the IMF, which gave the country three loans, in July 1993 and in January and September 1995, to a total of $190.2 million.[6]

Nevertheless, the eventual recovery of the economy from 1996 was due much more to Belarus learning how to exploit its strategic position and its symbolic importance to President Yeltsin, who was keen to appease Communist and nationalist critics of his role in the dissolution of the USSR. That said, Kebich's April 1994 agreement with Russia on currency union and soft loans failed to save him, as it was never implemented. Lukashenka's timing was better, particularly given Yeltsin's desperate need to win reelection in 1996.

Lukashenka's First Boom

After his brief flirtation with liberal reform, Lukashenka reverted to 'socialism in one country'. There was no mass privatisation; elaborately cross-subsidised state enterprises generated 75 per cent of GDP and 64.8 per cent of state budget revenue.[7] Lukashenka re-created a mini planned economy, with nineteen 'production indexes' established at the start of every year. Belarus has 4.4 million employees, and half a million accountants. But planning was only possible because of five strategic favours provided by Russia. According to Yaroslaw Ramanchuk: 'For ... ten years Russia has paid Belarus $45–50 billion for nothing. Since Russia is a rich country, nobody cares about losses.'[8]

First was the initial attempt at a customs union in May 1995, which led to a strong recovery in export demand, until Russians began switching to better products in the late Putin era. Belarus also sold goods to Russia on excessively generous barter terms. For example, Russia paid it more than the world price for sugar. The politics of the 'Union State' set up with Russia in 1995–9 *did* make a difference, winning back markets for many Belarusian products, though often these 'markets' came from state procurement by Russian local authorities after political lobbying by Lukashenka (Belarus has ten 'consulates' in the Russian provinces) and 'administratively secured demand for Belarusian finished goods on Russia's market (including trade preferences, barter deals and simply smuggling)'.[9] Much Belarusian–Russian trade depended on a complex system of tariffs and non-trade barriers, and the kickbacks set up for waiving those barriers. Its fortunes restored, the bright red 'Belarus' tractor much beloved of Socialist Realist painters in Soviet days acquired a certain iconic status.

Trade between Russia and Belarus grew strongly in Lukashenka's early years in office. Total turnover (i.e. trade in both directions) rose from $5.2 billion in 1995 to $12.5 billion in 2003 and $26 billion in 2007 (though Russia's exports were double those of Belarus, $17.2 billion to $8.9 billion in

2007).[10] Even after the global economic crisis, in the first half of 2010 Belarus accounted for 4.4 per cent of Russia's trade, only just behind Ukraine on 5.7 per cent,[11] and Ukraine has a population five times the size. Belarus had a dual export model, but was doubly dependent on Russia. Industrial exports (tractors and trucks, 77 per cent of all consumer goods) and some agricultural products went to Russia; raw materials (processed oil and potassium), chemicals and fertilisers went to the EU, but their production depended on cheap Russian energy. Exports to the rest of the world actually overtook those to Russia in 2005; by 2007 exports to Russia stood at $8.9 billion, non-CIS exports at $13.1 billion.[12] The traditional route to the Baltic was therefore still important, and Lukashenka has played off Klaipėda in Lithuania against Ventspils in Latvia as trade routes. Despite periodic political problems with Lithuania, and Lithuania's EU membership after 2004, trade through Klaipėda has continued to grow rapidly. In 2006 Belarus sent 4.5 million tons through the port, 19.1 per cent of its total business. There has even been talk of reverse use, that is, of one day supplying Belarus with oil through the port to reduce its dependence on Russia.[13]

So long as the country's current account remained near balance, the export boom also allowed a new consumer economy to develop on the import side. But the strain was showing before 2008. A small trade surplus of 1.4 per cent of GDP in 2005 had become a deficit of 8.4 per cent by 2008.

A second Russian favour was to write off $1.3 billion of energy imports in March 1996 (then 8.2 per cent of GDP).[14] This began a decade of subsidised oil and gas, though the relative difference only really began to add up after the 1999 Union State Treaty and the boom in global energy prices after 2003. Among the CIS states, Belarus paid least in relative terms from 2002 to 2006: that is, not just a low price, but a lot lower than the world price (Belarus was paying $22–25 per 1,000 m³ in 2002, then $46.68 in 2005–6). Even after 2006, prices rose relatively slowly, not much beyond $100, when Ukraine was paying $360. According to the IMF, such subsidies were worth a minimum of 10 per cent of GDP, two-thirds from subsidised gas and a third from oil. In 2007 Russia estimated they were worth $5.8 billion.[15] Belarus kept all the revenue from oil duties until January 2007, despite an original agreement to split them 50–50 (after 2007, 85 per cent went to Russia, only 15 per cent to Belarus). Cheap energy made Belarusian manufactures competitive, at least in Russia, which paid for them twice. Most Belarusian exports, especially tractors, trucks and fertilisers, have energy-intensive production.

Another significant factor was contraband, which added an estimated $1.5–2 billion a year (9–12 per cent of GDP) until Russia introduced proper border posts in October 2000. Finally, proxy arms sales for Russia were worth hundreds of millions a year (see pages 186–9).[16]

According to one Belarusian analyst, Alexei Pikulik, 'Adding gas and oil rents, the administratively stimulated demand for domestic goods on Russia's market, the profits from barter dealings (exchanging overpriced finished goods, due to the fixed exchange rate for under-priced energy) and the rents from the loopholes existing in the border, due to the imperfect design of the first Customs Union, we may actually approach a shocking figure of 40 per cent rents in GDP [making] Belarus [like] Qatar.'[17]

The combined effect of all these favours allowed Belarus to return to growth more quickly than many of its neighbours, and to have a relative cushion from the ups and downs of the global economy. GDP first grew by 2.8 per cent in 1996, a year before Russia (temporarily) returned to growth (1997) and four years before Ukraine (2000). GDP growth in Belarus accelerated to between 8 and 11 per cent in 1997–8, and Belarus avoided the worst effects of the 1998 Eastern European financial crisis, with growth still of 3.3 per cent in 1999.

Lukashenka's Social Contract

Having campaigned in his only shabby jacket in 1994, Lukashenka spent his first term (1994–2001) in populist mode. In 2001 foreign-registered cars were often stopped on the street and required to pay on-the-spot 'contributions' to the sowing season. In 2003 factory directors had their pay fixed at no more than 3.5 times that of the average worker.[18] It was only in Lukashenka's second term (2001–6) that serious money began to accumulate in the country, with a new class of potential oligarchs emerging from the lucrative Russian oil trade and from domestic construction.

The standard of living in Belarus has undoubtedly gone up since the mid-1990s, after falling catastrophically in the previous five years. The Gini Coefficient, which measures the unevenness of the distribution of income, was relatively low, at 0.217 in 1998 and 0.262 in 2006 (0 is a society of perfect equality, 1 perfect inequality, or the theoretical extreme of one person receiving all of national income).[19] According to the World Bank, only 19 per cent of the population were below the national poverty line in 2007 – just below Russia.[20] Unlike many other post-Soviet states, which suffered catastrophic falls in population, figures in Belarus held up much better through the 1990s, going from 10.18 million in 1995 to 9.69 million in 2007.[21] Public health, particularly HIV-AIDS, was less of a problem in the 1990s, though

8,737 people were registered as HIV-positive by 2008. Most were in regional centres like Homel, where boredom and drugs were a problem.

Belarus is not Cuba. Even Cuba isn't as Cuban as Western fellow travellers like to think it is. Some Russian subsidies *were* diverted, but they have also made an impact on the ground. Real wages increased 3.5-fold between 1996 and 2005; welfare and public works accounted for 61.1 per cent of the budget in 2006,[22] though very little went on capital investment. Credit growth has outstripped production growth – i.e. credits have been used to keep the less productive parts of the economy afloat. Engineering's share of total industrial production declined from 34.2 per cent in 1990 to 20.3 per cent in 2008, while that of raw materials and woefully inefficient agriculture went up.[23]

Oligarchs

Lukashenka has also promised that 'oligarchs' will not take over the economy – and they certainly haven't on the scale of Russia or Ukraine. Lukashenka can therefore claim that living standards for the general population are not depressed by the corruption of the super-rich. Not that Belarus doesn't have plenty of rich men, and even a few rich women. 'Minigarchs' like Aliaksandr Pupeika and Ivan Tsitsiankow were beginning to emerge in the early 1990s (see pages 164–5), and many more would no doubt have done so if Kebich or Shushkevich (or even Pazniak) had won the 1994 election. But soon after 1994 Lukashenka brought them under his control; his inner circle could still make money, but only on the president's terms. Most money was made either off-budget (oil and arms sales) or by controlling income flows rather than through actual enterprise ownership – which under Lukashenka has never been secure. The biggest oligarchs are Lukashenka himself and his oldest son, Viktar. Lukashenka is not personally ostentatious, though he is not frugal either and is alleged to have large sums of money in the Lebanon, Austria and elsewhere. The Belarus Democracy Act passed by the US Congress in 2004 requires an annual report on the personal wealth of Lukashenka and other senior officials. Nonetheless, even US analysts could only provide guestimates regarding the president's wealth, starting at over $1 billion; one unsourced estimate claims Lukashenka has a personal fortune of $11.4 billion.[24] In 2007 the US both extended visa sanctions and froze the overseas assets of the petrochemical conglomerate Belneftekhim, one of Belarus's top hard-currency earners and reportedly a personal fief of Lukashenka himself.

Semi-conspicuous consumption by the ruling elite's 'underground million-aires' began to take off towards the end of Lukashenka's second term.

Uladzimir Peftsiew and Viktar Sheiman are thought to have made money from arms sales; Mikhail Miasnikovich from proximity to the president. Metropolitan Filaret, the head of the local Orthodox Church, which is still a branch of the broader Moscow Church, has supposedly made millions from alcohol imports of all things, though he still has to devote some of his time to his duties as head of the Church. In recent years 'rich lists' have become popular, if not comprehensive. They tend to figure those who have made fortunes from oil and gas transit, like Yury Chyzh and Anatol Tsernawski, or from the construction boom of the 2000s, like Viktar Shawtsow.[25]

Those who didn't play by the president's rules were forced out of business or out of the country. A significant class of Belarusian businessmen in Russia therefore began to develop: men like Viktar Lahvinets and Viktar Rakhmanka, who funded the opposition back home as a form of revenge (see pages 212 and 230).[26] An early trailblazer in this regard was Ivan Tsitsiankow, the former heard of Lukashenka's powerful 'presidential affairs department', who moved to Moscow to work for the gas company Itera in 1999, then set up his own business.

Russian oligarchs were a different matter. From the very beginning, Lukashenka has built his regime in close cooperation with the Russian oligarchy, constantly chopping and changing allegiances to ensure his economic and political survival. Moscow mayor Yurii Luzhkov was a constant presence until he was fired by Medvedev in September 2010, getting involved in the construction and restaurant business in Minsk alongside his wife, Yelena Baturina. In the 1990s Lukashenka leant heavily on Boris Berezovskii (see page 199) and on 'patriotic' business groups close to the Russian defence industry, veteran Communist leader Gennadii Ziuganov and former Patriarch Aleksei. In the Putin era Lukashenka switched to the new power brokers, the so-called *siloviki* like Sergei Ivanov and Igor Sechin of Rosneft, 'one of the major beneficiaries of the previous oil deals'.[27] Nor was the election of Dmitrii Medvedev as Russian president in 2008 in itself a fatal blow to Lukashenka's policy, so long as he maintained good links with presidential foreign policy aide Sergei Prikhodko, who is the key 'gatekeeper' in the Kremlin.

Belarus Becomes an 'Offshore Oil State', 2003–6

Belarus and Ukraine are the two key transit states for Russian energy exports to the EU. Unlike Ukraine, Belarus has no real gas storage facilities, so cannot hoard it; but its two oil refineries are relatively modern. Nevertheless, the main reason that Belarus became an 'offshore oil state' under Lukashenka was that the 'oil barons' in both Russia and Belarus developed a scheme for making vast amounts of money using 'the union state and the customs union as a political cover or "legend"'.[28] Belarus received crude oil from Russia so cheaply it was able to add a massive mark-up on refined products and still undercut others on world markets. The Russian partners also made big profits until 2007 at least, so long as the Russian state was happy to turn a blind eye to the loss of export revenue. The key beneficiaries were Vladimir Bogdanov's Surgutneftegaz with 30 per cent of the trade, Igor Sechin's Rosneft with 25 per cent, Gazpromneft with 13 per cent, Lukoil with 11 per cent, Slavneft with 10 per cent and finally Rusneft with 6.5 per cent.[29]

Cheap gas was more important for the economy as a whole – gas makes up 80 per cent of the domestic energy mix – but Russian crude oiled the system, providing Lukashenka with enough ready cash to keep the elite happy and certain favoured projects financed. Oil profits peaked at $5.4 billion in 2006, and became a major source of cross-subsidisation for the rest of the economy.[30] According to Alexei Pikulik, the money funded 'a) upholding generous social spending via employment and bail-outs of inefficient enterprises; b) supporting the quasi-socialist system of cross-subsidies, price controls and productive targets for enterprises; c) limiting the development of the private sector in order to foreclose the "exit" strategy for the state-dependent electorate and d) growing the autocratic muscles of the illiberal state'.[31] The cash-rich energy sector was the biggest single taxpayer, followed by the newly profitable mobile-phone sector and the always profitable alcohol sector. The biggest employers, however, were the machine-building sector. Until the global economic crisis, big enterprises like the Minsk Tractor Factory served as a bulwark of social stability, underpinning the authorities' informal social contract by employing hundreds of thousands of the semi- or narrowly skilled who had doubtful prospects anywhere else.

After a slowdown in the early 2000s, Belarus enjoyed a second growth spurt from late 2003 thanks to the rise in the world price of oil. More than 60 per cent of Belarusian exports to the EU were now refined oil products.[32] From 1999 to 2009 the share of oil and oil products in exports to non-CIS markets went up from 12.5 to 56.2 per cent,[33] and the volume of oil product exports rose from 7.8 million tons in 2000 to 15.1 million tons in 2007.[34]

Fingers in the Dyke, 2006–7

Yeltsin subsidised Belarus for largely political reasons, while a variety of Russian oligarchs made hay. Putin then took a back seat to the Russian oil lobby, until the Belarusian election in 2006. The Russian president could still be persuaded when necessary to put politics before economics and keep some subsidies flowing. In December 2007 Russia handed over a $1.5 billion 'Stabilisation and Transition Fund'. But, other things being equal, Putin wanted to save money and to recalibrate Russian support to make Belarus a more pliable partner and push Minsk to yield Gazprom's key target: control of Beltransgaz. Russia had grown tired of the 'virtual integration' games Belarus had played since the mid-1990s. Plans for monetary union were constantly put off – the Belarusian rouble switched to being pegged against the dollar in 2008 – and Belarus dragged its feet on the idea of a customs union. Gazprom wanted to shift the burden of supporting Belarus onto the Russian state budget.

Meanwhile, Belarus's booming trade with Russia had moved into serious deficit by 2007–8. Russian GDP increased by 70 per cent while Putin was president (2000–8). Russian consumers became more discerning and began to switch away from Belarusian goods. Belarus also suffered as Russia shifted away from the state procurement system. In 2005 exports to Russia fell 10 per cent; and this was the last year Belarus recorded an overall trade surplus. By 2007 the current account deficit was 6.7 per cent of GDP. The balance of trade with Russia was -$10 billion by 2008. Gross external debt rose, from $4.2 billion at the end of 2003 to $12.5 billion at the end of 2007, and $14.8 billion by the end of 2008 (though this was still only 24.6 per cent of GDP).[35]

As soon as the 2006 election was out of the way, Russia was finally ready to raise energy prices. The gas subsidy alone was worth an estimated annual $2 billion.[36] Russo–Ukrainian gas spats were fast becoming an annual winter event, with a particularly bitter dispute in January 2006; but the next winter it was suddenly Belarus's turn – after dress-rehearsal rows in 2002 and 2004 (see page 200). In the face of drastic supply reductions in freezing temperatures, Belarus was forced to concede that it would pay 'European prices' by 2011. Its long-standing price of $46.68 per 1000 m^3 went up to $100 in 2007 and an average of $150 by 2009. In June 2010 another crisis saw an increase to $194 and the threat of between $220 and $250 in 2011. Lukashenka was also forced to cede 50 per cent of Beltransgaz, the company that ran the gas pipelines across Belarus, to Gazprom. A price of $2.5 billion and a three-year delay to 2010 were scant compensation for losing a key strategic asset.

Just as damaging was a second agreement in January 2007 that sharply squeezed the profit margin of Belarus's lucrative oil-refining industry by introducing customs duties on Russian crude oil exports to Belarus and forcing Belarus to raise its own export tariffs to the Russian level. According to IMF calculations, this change alone took 5.5 per cent off Belarusian GDP in 2007.[37] The threatened elimination of the subsidy was delayed; but after the global economic crisis hit the Russian oil industry hard, Igor Sechin decided to call time on this particular scam, which no longer served to benefit his company, Rosneft. After another confrontation in January 2010, Russia finally raised the tariff from 35 per cent to 100 per cent. Belarus imported 21.5 million tons of Russian crude oil in 2009. Russia calculated that Belarus needed 6.3 million tons for domestic use, which would still be duty-free (and was still equivalent to a $1.3 billion subsidy). But it was the export profit that Belarus had relied on. In the first half of 2010 Belarusian crude oil exports dropped by half, exports of petroleum products were down by 40 per cent and the output of Belarus's oil industry fell by 36 per cent.[38] Even this was only possible because Belarus diverted some of the duty-free crude to export.

Even Belarus's status as an energy transit country was now under serious threat. Work on the Nordstream gas pipeline from Russia to Germany through the Baltic Sea finally began in April 2010, with the first pipeline scheduled for completion in late 2011. Work on the Baltic Pipeline System, or BPS-2 oil pipeline, bypassing Belarus from Druzhba to the Gulf of Finland started in June 2009; it could open in 2013.

Lukashenka's first response to this Russian pressure was to look for a series of stopgap measures. As early as May 2007 he toyed with the idea of trimming the large-scale (although highly inefficient) system of social privileges and subsidies, but quickly backed down. A limited number of privatisations began in 2007, when the state still controlled an estimated 80 per cent or more of the economy. In January 2008 Heineken bought Belarus's second biggest brewery, Siabar (and a smaller company, Rechitaspivo), via its Cypriot holding company, for around €130 million. Telekom Austria, again via third parties based in Cyprus, bought 70 per cent of the second-largest Belarusian mobile operator, MDC (or Velcom), then with 2.9 million subscribers, in October 2007 for about €730 million. In November 2008, 80 per cent of the next-largest operator, BeST, along with its Chinese loans, went to the Turkish mobile operator, Turkcell, without any bidding or tender process for $500 million. (Both deals were suspected to be nomenklatura privatisations in elaborate disguise.) Russian banks began moving in. Vneshtorgbank bought control of Belarusian Slavneftbank, Vneshekonombank (VEB) bought its counterpart, BelVneshekonombank, and Alfa Group bought Mezhtorgbank for $27.7 million. By the time the global economic crisis hit in late 2008 the share of foreign capital in Belarusian banks had risen to 22 per cent – though this was still a lot less than the 40 per cent and more in Ukraine and over 60 per cent in Latvia.

The south of Belarus is still suffering from the after effects of the Chernobyl accident in 1986. There was therefore a genuine sense of shock when Lukashenka announced the building of a nuclear power plant in 2007 (originally near Mahilew, then near the Lithuanian border in the west). This was an option much more in keeping with continued statism, but there were serious doubts whether such a white elephant would actually save on energy bills or reduce energy dependency on Russia. The government originally estimated the plant would cost $4–5 billion, others nearer $8–12 billion, though it could save $400 million a year on the national energy bill in the long-term. In June 2009 a Russian company was chosen to build the plant, backed by a Russian loan of $6 billion – but Minsk wanted $9 billion. In any case, Belarus would therefore simply be swapping dependency on Russian gas for dependency on Russian nuclear fuel and nuclear waste disposal facilities.

External props were a better idea, hence Lukashenka's announcement of a new 'many-winged' foreign policy in 2006. Initial results were modest – and expensive. Belarus took a series of loans from Western banks, but they were only prepared to offer short-term ones, for between six and twenty-four months. Foreign debt almost doubled in 2007 from $6.8 billion to $12.5 billion, but 60 per cent of that were short-term loans.[39] So when Russia began to squeeze harder after the onset of the economic crisis in late 2008, Lukashenka began a serious, even desperate, search for alternative sources of support abroad (see page 223).

Authoritarian Liberalisation, 2008

The authorities began contemplating limited liberalisation measures in 2007 and implementing some of them in early 2008. Most of the measures were introduced before, and therefore not because of, the global economic crisis. If the changes had been motivated by the global economic crisis, they might have been more profound. In fact, they were introduced because Russia began turning the screws after the 2006 election, and Lukashenka was looking for ways to tinker with the system to ensure its survival. He was happy to make minimal concessions to the new would-be nomenklatura oligarchs (see pages 223–5), but not for them to develop into a new class that might ultimately seek to displace him from power.

Lukashenka hoped to exploit the fact that the rest of the world now considered its isolation policy wasn't working. Western business saw a potential market. Indeed, the authorities won surprisingly enthusiastic international reviews just for their tinkering in 2007–9. The 'golden share' rule that gave the government carte blanche to interfere in any business was abolished in March 2008. Compulsory declaration of bank deposits was abandoned. A flat-rate income tax was introduced in January 2009 at 12 per cent, carefully set 1 percentage point below Russia's rival flat rate of 13 per cent (the old progressive system went up to 35 per cent). Corporate profit tax at 24 per cent and VAT at 18 per cent were the same as in Russia. One hundred and fifty companies were listed for privatisation in a Lukashenka decree issued in November 2008, including 25 per cent of the country's two largest banks, Belarusbank and Belahroprombank. Unfortunately, this was just as the global economic crisis was scattering would-be investors. Almost none of the enterprises slated for sale in 2009 were sold (BPS-Bank eventually went to Russia's Sberbank for around $281 million). In September 2008 the government allowed the registration of a Belarusian Bank for Small Businesses, funded by the European Bank for Reconstruction and Development (EBRD) and others.

According to the World Bank, Belarus rose in the global league table for 'ease of doing business' from 115th in 2007 to 85th in 2008 and 58th out of 183 in 2009.[40] To the regime's planning mentality, rising into the survey's 'top thirty' became a target in itself. Unfortunately, Belarus slipped back down to 68th in 2010.[41]

But there was an important paradox: because the mini-reform began early, Belarus had repaired relations with the IMF before the crisis hit and was thus able to secure a life-saving loan. On the other hand, the government's response to the crisis was short-term and superficial, only postponing problems for later. Lukashenka was able to scale the reforms down once the system seemed more stable around late 2009.

The Global Economic Crisis

The global economic crisis hit Belarus particularly hard, from the fourth quarter of 2008 – if not through the same channels as elsewhere. Belarus's banking system was small, its stock market almost nonexistent, its foreign borrowing up to that point manageable. Belarus was not like neighbouring Latvia, several years into an Anglo-Saxon-style credit boom which left it particularly vulnerable to the crisis. But Belarus under Lukashenka had become quite an open trading economy – in part because of the president's skill in exploiting various schemes and scams and in parleying Belarus's limited economic resources for political favours.

Declining profits in the energy sector as oil and gas prices collapsed (plus other commodity prices, potash in particular) and declining Russian demand for Belarusian exports led to a sharp and unexpected deterioration in the balance of payments. The fact that the crisis initially hit nearly all of Belarus's neighbours worse, apart from Poland, was little comfort once their demand for Belarusian exports began to collapse. Belarus needed $6–7 billion annually to close the gap in the short term, but unlike Russia had no large accumulation of reserves to spend or resource nationalism to exploit. In short: 'The crisis exhausted the previous growth model based on preferential access to the Russian market and preferential conditions of Russian energy supplies'.[42]

The economic crisis affected the different sectors of the Belarusian economy in different ways.[43] The energy sector was severely hit by declining profits in the refining industry. Machine-building was hit by collapsing Russian demand for its traditional mainstays, trucks and tractors, exports of which fell by 80 per cent – nobody else was going to buy them. Chemicals were also badly hit, with the privatisation of the nitrogen plant HrodnaAzot placed in doubt and only kept afloat by diverting some of Russia's duty-free gas, designed for domestic consumption. The previously booming construction sector was also hit hard. Private loans for buyers and builders were drying up; most credit in Belarus was state-allocated, and there was no real domestic venture capital for risky projects. On the other hand, there was a natural floor under declining demand for the Belarusian food industry – assuming people didn't stop eating, that is.

Strong GDP growth of 8.6 per cent in 2007 carried the economy through most of 2008, when the official figure for growth was still 10 per cent. Only in the first quarter of 2009 did the economy start to shrink, by a dramatically sudden 4.5 per cent. Given the highly controlled nature of the Belarusian economy, the authorities had many short-term options to try and keep it afloat – although these also stored up problems for later. As so often, Belarus was also lucky, in terms of timing at least. Tentative authoritarian liberalisation in 2008 meant that Belarus had reestablished the dialogue with the IMF broken off after 1995, and was able to secure a loan much more quickly than would have been the case even a year or two earlier, with an agreement for the provision of $2.46 billion in December 2008. But the terms of the deal with the IMF meant the government had little room for fiscal loosening (see below). A government surplus of 1.4 per cent of GDP in 2008 rapidly became a deficit of 0.7 per cent in 2009. Although this was hardly huge by global standards, this was because in relative isolation, Belarus previously had no real government bond market, so couldn't really borrow. The budget deficit grew to at least 3 per cent in 2010.[44]

So Minsk used administrative measures and political stopgaps to support the economy instead, and fought a running battle to sneak them past the IMF.

Temporary import restrictions were imposed and factories were ordered to keep producing and allow stocks to rise. Big investments in agriculture were made in early 2009 to compensate for declining manufacturing exports, followed by a temporary shift of resources to construction (in the second quarter of 2009 its share in GDP soared from 1.9 to 11.9 per cent), backed by cheap 1 per cent home loans to families with three children or more. Wage creep was allowed to continue, at 0.1 per cent in 2009 – which was hardly massive, but was extremely generous in a time of collapsing demand, and an onerous burden on state firms facing disappearing markets.[45] And 2010 was then an election year, with further populist wage increases.

In total Belarus was burning $0.5 billion a month. But because the authorities kept production and domestic demand relatively high, spending on imports did not collapse as it did in some neighbouring countries like Latvia and Ukraine. Belarus was almost the only country in the region where the current account deficit not only failed to close, but actually grew, despite the crisis and much weaker domestic demand. During the worst moments of the crisis, in the first and second quarters of 2009, it ballooned to a record-breaking 18.6 per cent and 17.7 per cent of GDP.[46] According to the IMF, the overall annual current account deficit was 6.7 per cent of GDP before the crisis in 2007, and it was forecast to be 14 per cent in 2010, which would be over $7 billion.[47] In October 2010 official foreign exchange reserves stood at a mere $5.9 billion. The interest and repayments would obviously rise fast: Belarus was scheduled to pay $695 million in 2011.[48] Belarus cannot afford $7 billion a year with its current social contract and without significant privatisation. The government was forced into a de facto public sector wage freeze, and devalued the Belarusian rouble by 20 per cent in January 2009.

The government survived in the short term by borrowing. A formal soft landing meant that GDP still grew by 0.2 per cent in 2009, but at the cost of a massive leap in state debt which reached a record 52 per cent of GDP in 2010. There was no recovery in domestic investment, and foreign investment hopes had dried up for the time being. At least Lukashenka was relatively successful in touting for international loans: in addition to the IMF money, Moscow lent Belarus $2 billion in November 2008 and Minsk unsuccessfully asked Moscow for 100 billion roubles ($2.77 billion) more in February 2009. The IMF loan led to help from other International Financial Institutions (IFIs), including a $200 million development loan from the World Bank. A Eurobond issue in summer 2010 raised $600 million, increasing within weeks to $1 billion, at an initial 9 per cent. Lukashenka also borrowed $0.5 billion from Russian banks, indicating that he wasn't completely out of favour with the Kremlin.

But mainly Lukashenka looked to the other 'wings' of his newly eclectic foreign policy. Azerbaijan provided Belarus with a $200 million twelve-day loan in June 2010 to help Minsk to pay its debt for Russian gas deliveries.[49] India agreed to buy potassium. But China was the most generous. In 2010 Beijing agreed a credit line of $5.7 billion from its Import-Export Bank to finance investment projects with Chinese companies, and a potential $8.3 billion credit line to the Belarusian Ministry of Finance. China also agreed a $3 billion 'currency swap' in March 2009.[50] A visit by Lukashenka to China in October 2010 led to $3.5 billion of contracts in energy, construction (including a long overdue revamp of Minsk airport), transport and the Belarusian petrochemical sector (sulphates).[51] Venezuela chipped in with a handy $0.5 billion. The grandest scheme of all was unveiled during President Chavez's bizarre visit to Minsk, also in October 2010, when he promised his country would supply Belarus with some thirty million tons of oil over a three-year period, starting in 2011. The deal was worth an estimated $19.4 billion; Chavez talked wildly of supplying Belarus for two hundred years. The Venezuelan president had probably not looked at the map; but real supply experiments began soon enough, after a long tanker journey to Ukraine's underused pipeline from Odesa on the Black Sea to Brody in western Ukraine and onto Mazyr in southern Belarus by rail. A promise was also made to supply 2.5 million tons per annum via the Lithuanian port of Klaipėda (and a new LNG terminal) starting in January 2011. This would be a dramatic reordering of the energy map, which meant it was almost certain not to happen. Lukashenka was no doubt trying to indicate to Russia that he had other options.

This was a lot of money, but it wasn't enough. Moreover, Lukashenka's impressive record in winning foreign support did not necessarily produce hard cash. According to the Polish Institute for Eastern Studies (OSW):

> the search for financial and raw-material support outside Europe, which has been so widely publicised by the Belarusian government, has failed to provide any real alternative to relations with Russia as yet. The multi-billion Chinese loans are linked to concrete investment projects, and are granted on condition that Chinese technologies, equipment and workforce are employed. For this reason, they may be helpful in the implementation of several investment projects, but cannot resolve the country's key macroeconomic problems. In turn, the supplies of Venezuelan oil by sea via Ukrainian and Baltic ports which have been carried out since this April are still a political

demonstration of independence from Moscow, rather than a viable alternative to Russian supplies [after travelling half way round the world, Venezuelan oil was estimated to cost $95 more than its nearer Russian equivalent].[52]

Lukashenka was forced to pick up the pace of reform again in late 2010. In August of that year he announced a programme to end cross-subsidisation in the energy sector. In September a decree announced the abolition of sixteen types of licensing – though, strangely enough, not in newspapers or publishing. In part this was because Belarus's limited number of foreign investors were already demanding clearer structural conditions. But real change would have to wait until after the election in December 2010, as would dealing with a post-election hangover after a 35 per cent increase in public sector wages and a 25 per cent splurge in the money supply (cash, or MO).

Conclusion

A moment of truth seemed likely at some point after the 2010 election. Lukashenka could yield to Russian pressure and sell off major assets like the refineries, steel and chemicals. The money would fund the social contract, but the shrinkage of the state sector would quickly narrow his power base among the elite. Or he could begin to dismantle the 'Belarusian model' by embarking on widespread structural reform and privatisation; in which case the personal consequences were unpredictable. He would lose his reputation as a guarantor of stability; nomenklatura privatisation would allow the elite to cut free; a boom in foreign investment would increase the pressure to open up the political system. The third and probably most likely strategy was small-scale reform to trim both the social contract and the most inefficient heavy industries, while trying to keep the crown jewels in the state sector, borrowing more and privatising small parcels here and there – like the 25 per cent of the Belarusian Potassium Company apparently offered to the Chinese in 2010.[53]

There was as yet, however, no new ideological formula to explain any policy shift. Lukashenka was prepared for the damage to his popularity after the one-off devaluation in January 2009, but baulked when it became clear that further measures would be needed. The persistent trade deficit was clearly structural. Slashing domestic demand wasn't Lukashenka's style and probably wouldn't work anyway. In the long term Belarus needed to move to a different economic model, with more hi-tech and high-value exports. A relatively well-educated workforce was an asset; but there were also some signs that Belarus might concentrate on more esoteric markets, such as offshore banking and cyber-crime.

Lukashenka may have wanted Belarus to be the new China, but it wasn't economically important enough to achieve this. The risks for potential investors were high, and the potential gains middling at best. There was no giant outsourcing manufacturing miracle about to take off. The diaspora is small, so the economy is not supported by remittances. A business-friendly Belarus would be difficult to construct without political change, particularly the introduction of a rule of law in a country where even the Russians got robbed.

Belarus used to be an outlier in Eastern Europe, but by 2010 it was becoming more of a test case. States that thought they could not afford to adopt the whole body of EU law, the *acquis communautaire*, were toying with low-tax, low-regulation economic policies instead. Belarus could easily fit into this model of soft authoritarian rule and Singaporean economics, except that its past authoritarianism had often been quite hard. Or Belarus might have its '1989 moment' more than twenty years late.

CHAPTER 13

THE 2010s: LUKASHENKA'S JUGGLING ACT

Chapter 11 was the final narrative chapter of the first edition of this book and takes events up to the election in 2010. Its title is 'The Edifice Crumbles' because at the time the economy was in serious difficulty, a brief cosmetic political liberalisation for the 2010 election had ended in fraud and mass arrests, and the West had imposed sanctions against the regime. Nevertheless, Lukashenka survived.

I stand by the judgement implied in the title, however. Not only was the edifice crumbling, Lukashenka's following decade in power produced a systemic crisis in 2020 rather than a mere disputed election, 'bringing down the load-bearing structures of the system that Lukashenka so lovingly built for almost three decades'.[1] The events of 2020 were a detonation of accumulated problems. A now-predictable political cycle of pre-election loosening and post-election crackdown was easy to see through. Moreover, the authorities couldn't keep the two elements in balance: elections didn't provide accountability, but they were destabilising nevertheless. Economically, the regime lived hand-to-mouth. The 'social contract' grew threadbare. Economic difficulties also undermined Belarusian foreign policy. After the war in Ukraine began in 2014, Belarus knew that it had to protect itself against similar Russian offers of 'enforced friendship'; but its attempts at foreign policy diversification were always hampered by the need for Russian subsidies.

The regime's support base was clearly shrinking, but in a dictatorship, which is what Belarus remained, it can be hard to tell how seriously. Moreover, a dictatorship can survive for a long time with the use or threat of force.

The 'Clapping' Protests

The protests after the 2010 election led to hundreds of arrests, including no fewer than seven of the electoral candidates. Andrei Sannikaw, Mikalai Statkevich and Dzmitry Us received prison sentences of five to six years. They and others were tortured in prison. The EU and US responded with coordinated asset freezes and travel bans. In the summer an arms and instruments of coercion embargo was added, as well as targeted sanctions against companies linked to Lukashenka ally Uladzimir Peftsiew.

But Lukashenka's domestic crackdown did not go as planned. A still unexplained bomb on the Minsk metro in April 2011 killed fifteen. Two suspects were arrested within two days, who were supposedly also behind previous attacks in 2005 and 2008, but their motives were unclear. A lot of the evidence didn't add up. They were not Islamists or nationalists. The authorities accused the two of seeking political destabilisation, but they were also accused of being drunk and mentally ill. There were suspicions that the whole thing was an invention, but if so, it didn't shift the blame on to anybody. The standard dictator's ploy of creating a problem that only the dictator can solve was also doubleedged, given Lukashenka's boast in 2004, after the deaths of hundreds of schoolchildren at Beslan in Russia, that Belarus was a 'tranquil and cosy home' (see pages 206–7) compared to other parts of the former USSR. In March 2012 the two accused received the death penalty, with a bullet in the back of the head.

Furthermore, the unprecedented domestic crackdown only worked in the short term. A new and more global protest wave reached Belarus within months of Lukashenka's crackdown. Demonstrations began again in the summer of 2011, inspired by the Arab Spring, tutored by new social media methodologies and ignited by a post-election economic collapse. The protests were ambitiously dubbed the 'Revolution through Social Networks', and quickly amassed more than 215,000 followers online. First there was an experiment with 'silent protests', then isolated protests (to avoid restrictions on freedom of assembly), and finally ironic clapping protests to try and avoid arrests. The regime didn't understand or appreciate the irony. A total of 1,900 were detained and almost 500 given hefty fines and prison sentences on charges of 'hooliganism'.[2]

Countries that have a revolution often have another. Belarus's neighbour Ukraine has had at least three, in 1990, 2004 and 2013–14, plus several close calls, largely because none was fully successful, but also because each built on its predecessor. Belarus had no real attempted 'revolution' before 2020, but protest was common. First were the 'Denim protests' in 2006 (pages 211 and

219–22). Then there were protests in 2010, in 2011 and later in 2017 (see below). 2020 didn't come out of nowhere.

The Economy

Before 2010, Belarus outperformed its neighbours economically; after 2010 the opposite was true. The standard of living was stagnant. According to IMF figures, Belarus GDP per capita was the sixty-first highest in the world at

GDP Growth in Belarus

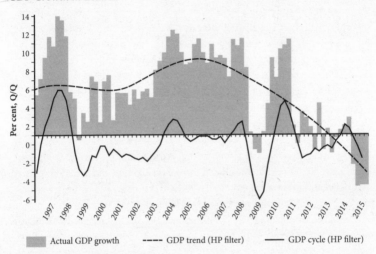

Actual GDP growth   ---- GDP trend (HP filter)   —— GDP cycle (HP filter)

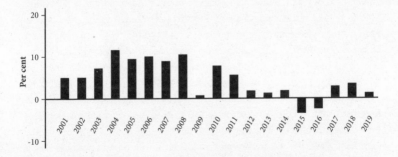

Sources: Uladzimir Akulich, Sierž Naŭrodski and Aleś Alachnovič, 'The Belarusian Economy is Currently Experiencing Both Cyclical and Structural Recessions', *CASE Belarus*; data supplied by Dzmitry Kruk.

market exchange rates in 2013. But by 2015, it was only eighty-first. Belarus was suffering from 'both cyclical and structural recessions'.[3] It had three major cyclical recessions in ten years: the first with the global economic crisis in 2009; then in 2011; and then with the local economic crisis caused by the Ukraine war and sanctions in 2014–15. But Belarus was also stuck in a low-growth trap; even years of recovery saw only small gains. And economic policy mistakes were engendered by the political cycle and the rapidly changing foreign policy situation after the war in Ukraine began in 2014.

Lukashenka's first big mistake was to stoke the economic fires before the 2010 election – almost as if he were actually facing a real competition – which was too soon after Belarus's weak recovery from the 2007–9 global economic crisis. Public sector wages were increased by 35 per cent: the economy grew by 10.2 per cent in the fourth quarter of 2010. Low productivity in the still-dominant state economy meant a ballooning balance of trade deficit, which reached a massive 16 per cent of GDP by 2010. Servicing the gap meant an annual hard cash bill of $3 billion upwards, often substantially more, as Belarus has no real domestic capital market. The government's reserves drained away, falling below $4 billion in the first half of 2011, but were effectively almost zero, their true level hidden by complex swap schemes with local state banks. Official statistics still showed growth in 2011, but the Belarusian rouble lost 60 per cent of its value in three devaluations, and inflation topped 108 per cent, hitting savings and salaries hard. Lukashenka's pride in meeting his key target of $500 average monthly salaries did not last long.

The old economic model had broken down. Belarus had received $3.6 billion in IMF assistance in 2009–10, but Lukashenka had no wish to make real reform and ended the programme in April 2010. A Russian bailout was agreed in November 2011: $1.2 billion for foreign reserves, cheaper gas and a $10 billion loan to build a nuclear power plant. But this only bought time. More importantly, Russia was never again as generous with its subsidy regime as it had been in the 2000s. Russia itself was entering a decade of lower growth and severe recessions in 2008–9 and 2014–16, exacerbated by sanctions and a lower oil price after Russia's aggression against Ukraine in 2014. This resulted in shrinking export markets for Belarus, only worsened after Russia's unilateral decision to save itself with rouble devaluation in 2014. Russia's import substitution also hurt Belarus, which used to do well from Russian state contracts. Belarus's only gain from the crisis was becoming a producer of salmon and parmesan, as it smuggled banned products to Russia under fake labels.

Belarus joined the Russia-led Eurasian Economic Union (EEU) in 2015, but it produced few economic gains, apart from yet more loans. Membership certainly did not provide a way out of Belarus's economic dilemmas. For Russia, the EEU was a geopolitical instrument, but Belarus, Kazakhstan, Armenia and Kyrgyzstan had joined in the expectation of gains from trade. These proved fleeting. So even did free trade; Russia continued its habitual trade bans, usually on spurious health and safety grounds, with friends and foes alike, EEU members and non-members, Belarus included. The smuggling of EU goods was always a problem, even if Russia was secretly happy to receive them; dairy products were banned in 2017, oil supplies were disrupted in 2010 and 2019. Belarus had hoped to access oil and gas at domestic Russian prices, but Russia said no.

Belarus began borrowing heavily, from anywhere it could. International lending was minimal before 2010; it surged thereafter. Debt as a percentage of

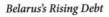

Belarus's Rising Debt

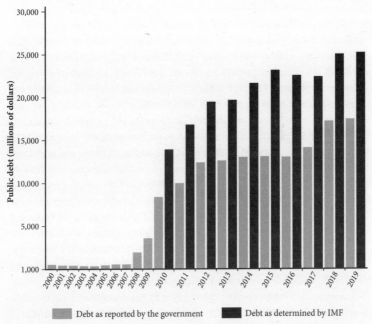

Debt as reported by the government   Debt as determined by IMF

Source: https://lossi36.com/2020/06/21/lukashenkos-last-stand-part-1-the-rise-and-fall-of-post-soviet-belarus/.

GDP rose from 8.4 per cent in 2005 to 47.8 per cent in 2018[4] – not a huge amount, but, as already stated, the government's minimal foreign exchange reserves made any debt hard to service. A 2011 Eurobond issue looked like a one-off, with investors wary thereafter; but due diligence or ESG (Environmental, Social and Governance) checks were minimal when the government raised $1.4 billion in 2017 and $1.25 billion as late as June 2020.

The big bet was on China. Statistics were contradictory. One Chinese source counted $7.6 billion in loans by 2014;[5] others much less. But many credit lines were long term, and many offers were not taken up. Great hopes for hi-tech manufacturing investment were placed in the China–Belarus Great Stone Industrial Park near Minsk airport, which was also planned to be a key onward site for the Belt and Road to the EU, and the main site for cross-border transactions in yuan in the EEU. China did not impose political conditions, but it was toughly mercantilist. Chinese loans led mainly to the import of Chinese goods and a ballooning bilateral trade deficit of nearly $3 billion.

The explosion of debt was periodically stabilised, but was growing again in 2020, peaking at $41 billion in the second quarter. The Belarusian authorities resorted to shuffling the pack: in 2019 Belarus was seeking Chinese loans to pay off Russian loans. The authorities rechannelled their international borrowing to keep the state economy afloat with directed loans, which maintained structural problems of soft budgets, capital misallocation and low productivity. At least fire sales were minimised. The gas transit network, Beltransgaz, was sold in November 2011, and one of Belarus's two main oil refineries at Mazyr was 42.6 per cent owned by Slavneft, but on the whole Belarus kept hold of its 'crown jewels'.

There was increasing talk of a new generation of economic pragmatists in government. The National Bank was professionalised. There was a rational economic strategy under the government of Siarhei Rumas from 2018 to 2020. State sector burdens were diminished; private sector growth was encouraged, especially in the IT sector. Three special economic zones grew in importance: the China Park, the Minsk High-Technologies or IT Park, and one in Arsha in eastern Belarus, for trade with Russia.[6] Some Belarusian IT companies were global brands, like Wargaming and Grammarly. The Google parent company Alphabet acquired AIMatter, a Belarusian start-up that used artificial intelligence to transform selfies on Android and iOS apps.

Lukashenka tried to confine the changes to macroeconomic policy while keeping his basic socioeconomic model – big state enterprises, subsidised employment and directed lending – intact. But there was a slimming process, with significant cumulative effects. There were some reforms to help small businesses; local bureaucracy was reasonably competent and less corrupt than in

Russia or Ukraine. In the decade after 2010 Belarus went up to thirty-eighth in the Ease of Doing Business Index. The private sector workforce in Belarus grew to outnumber the SOE equivalent, producing almost half of GDP. Belarus's biggest employer was now a private company, the retail and trading conglomerate Yevrotorg, with 40,000 employees. The new private sector expected a different kind of relationship with the state and was already often resentful that 'its' taxes were paying for keeping the bloated public sector afloat.[7]

The Rumas government also pursued a 'third-third-third' export strategy: seeking gradually to shift away from one-sided dependence on Russia, cutting its share of trade from a half to a third, and growing trade with the EU and the rest of the world to the same share. This was symbolised by Lukashenka's visit to Austria in November 2019, his first official visit to an EU state since 1996. Austria was Belarus's leading economic partner in the EU. Russia still accounted for more than 40 per cent of exports, but it was trade with the EU that was booming, mainly in services, up by 20.6 per cent in 2018 to €10.93 billion.[8] The IT industry alone already accounted for over 5 per cent of GDP by 2018.[9]

Experiments with energy diversification grew more common after 2010. The first attempts with Venezuela and Azerbaijan brought limited results, given basic facts of geography. Belarus exports some oil to Ukraine, but the idea of importing oil from Odesa up through Ukraine seems impractical. In 2020 there was talk of reverse oil supply via Poland, possibly of American exports. Another possibility was a link from Homel to Horki to connect the southern and northern routes of Druzhba, on Belarusian territory. The new nuclear power station at Astravets, opened in November 2020, would make Belarus a potential electricity exporter; but it only shifted Minsk's dependency away from gas and towards the debt for the project and the Russian nuclear fuel Astravets now needed.

Nascent Oligarchy?

Lukashenka had long made a virtue of accentuating that there would be no oligarchy in Belarus. In 1995 he said 'They [the new post-Soviet business elite] must be shaken off like lousy fleas!'[10] In 2004, on a visit to a chocolate factory, after praising the fact the product was entirely made in Belarus, he opined 'there are no glittering skyscrapers or "ragged" oligarchs [here]. Maybe it would be nice if there were, but not at the expense of the bulk of the population, as is the case in the post-Soviet republics, when 10 per cent own the entire country, and 90 per cent are beggars. This will not happen in Belarus.'[11]

The old 'red directors' were incorporated into his system in the late 1990s and early 2000s; they grew rich but were basically service providers. An interlocking network of little-known institutions kept the economy under the government's 'manual control'. The Committee for Government Control (KGK) oversaw the bureaucracy and a network of semi-autonomous businesses. The Presidential Business Administration (UDP) and its Property Management Division acted as leaseholders for almost the entire economy. Notorious strongman Viktar Sheiman headed the UDP, but was present at most government 'security' meetings (see page 190). The off-budget Presidential Fund was allegedly used to control key income streams from oil and arms sales. The new private economy, especially in the digital sector, may have been the engine of growth, but had to make 'accommodations' with these institutions. The prominent tech entrepreneur Viktar Prakapenia of VP Capital was subject to a typical 'prophylactic' arrest in 2015–16. No one could yet operate independently; but many wanted to. Conversely, state elites or 'court capitalists', including Lukashenka's eldest son Viktar, were increasingly manoeuvring to give themselves more freedom, investing in property, football clubs and the service economy. The Bremino Group was behind the Arsha scheme. The Sohra Group traded with the Gulf States and made headlines when one of its assets, the football club Dynama Brest in south-west Belarus, briefly appointed Diego Maradona as honorary chairman – he only turned up once in the town.[12] Some balanced their accommodations with Lukashenka's system with operations abroad. Large parts of the IT economy were registered in Malta or Cyprus. Prakapenia moved to London.

But nascent Belarusian oligarchs could easily make alliances with their Russian counterparts. Many Belarusian businesspeople were resident in Moscow anyway.[13] They formed a lobby for maintaining good relations; but Lukashenka's old partners, the likes of Boris Berezovsky and former Moscow mayor Yurii Luzhkov, were gone, and new players like the Khotin family depended on Russian contacts. Conversely, Russian oligarchs like Igor Makarov and Mikhail Gutseriev were active in Belarus. Lukashenka allowed them to expand in growing sectors such as construction, hotels and retail, without engaging in a zero-sum war over the 'crown jewel' state assets. Gutseriev had eyes on Naftan, Rosneft's Slavneft had a minority stake in Mazyr, Dmitrii Rybolovlev's Uralkali eyed Belaruskali ('Kali' means 'potash'). All three Russian state banks, Sberbank, VTB and Gazprom Bank, operated in Belarus.

The War against Ukraine

The Belarusian authorities were spooked by the Russian invasion of Georgia in 2008. Not because of the reversal for Western-backed reform forces, but because if Russia could so easily ignore the sovereignty of one neighbour, then

Belarus could be next. Belarus refused to recognise the 'independence' of South Ossetia and Abkhazia, despite massive Russian pressure.

The war in Ukraine was an even bigger security shock. The appearance of 'little green men' (Russian special forces, pro-Russian proxies) in Belarus was a serious threat. There was a worrying uptick in the activity of small or dormant 'Cossack organisations, unions of Afghan war veterans, Orthodox youth camps, patriotic military clubs, and others'.[14] Several hundred Belarusian citizens had fought in the Donbas war on the Russian side – and smaller numbers on Kiev's side; plus one of the first three killed in the Maidan protests in Kieiv was a Belarusian – but 'volunteers' were only subject to minimal supervision on their return.[15] *Belarusian Donbas*, a book by two Belarusian journalists published in 2020, argued that the Belarusian security services were far from even-handed, and covertly supported the traffic to and from the Donbas.[16] Conversely, however, the use of Belarusian territory to attack Ukraine was a real possibility, as was the fact that some passing Russian forces might choose to stay. Overspill and embroilment could easily happen in many ways; Belarus took in around 100,000 Ukrainian migrants,[17] including some high-profile figures from the former Yanukovych regime.

Direct fears of military pressure were revived during the *Zapad* military manoeuvres in 2017. Russian and Belarusian troops practised repelling an 'invasion' from the West. Many commentators feared that the Russian troops might manufacture an excuse to stay, or that protests or provocations might lead to a 'request' from the Belarusian authorities to help 'maintain order'. In the end, the Russians went home; but a similar script was used in 2020. Russia constantly pressured Belarus to house a new air base on its territory. The two existing facilities were not proper bases, but a radar and naval communications centre, and their lease expired in 2021. Lukashenka, however, didn't want any local equivalent of the Russian Black Sea Fleet, based in Crimea – a bridgehead for possible direct military options against Belarus.

Conversely, Lukashenka was also worried that protests and demands for democratisation could spread from Ukraine. Around two-thirds of Belarus's public sided with the Russian mass media's propagandist view of events in Ukraine, but the remaining third could be dangerous. In a summer 2014 poll, in response to the unfortunate local habit of sociologists asking leading questions, 26.9 per cent of Belarusians agreed that what happened in Crimea was 'imperial seizure, annexation' compared to 62.2 per cent who opted for 'the return to Russia of Russian lands, the restoration of historical justice'. When asked to assess the situation in east Ukraine, 65.5 per cent endorsed the chosen wording that 'it is a popular protest against illegitimate power', as against 23.2 per cent who opted for the description of the events as 'rebellion (*miatezh*), organised by Russia'.[18]

But Russia was now a threat to the sovereignty of all its neighbours, friend or foe. The very basis of Belarusian foreign policy thinking had to adjust. Previously, it was satirised as 'oil for kisses'. 'Oil' meant cheap oil and gas, and the broader Russian subsidy regime. 'Kisses', as Margarita Balmaceda has put it, involved playing up to Russia's collective self-esteem and selling the idea of Belarus as the 'ally of last resort'.[19] Plus selling nostalgia for the USSR and its great power status – as Belarusian analyst Dzianis Melyantsow has said, 'selling anaesthesia to Russia's fake missing limbs'.[20] These strategies were predicated on there being only one axis of hostility, between Russia and the West. Then, according to Balmaceda, 'a certain regularity could be observed: every time relations between Russia and the West worsened, the relative value of Belarus as an ally increased'.[21] But now there were two lines of tension – between Russia and the West and between Russia and its neighbours. So the old foreign policy position of maximum advantage for Belarus – positioning Belarus as a pro-Russian power with autonomy to act in its own interests – was now seen in Moscow as the position of an insufficiently enthusiastic ally and a potential defector. And Belarus could not simply return to the position of 'ally of last resort' because it had to think about its own national security first.

Belarus began sharing security information with Ukraine, even on Russian troop movements, immediately in 2014, and continued to do so. Lukashenka met acting President Turchynov, whom Russia viewed as illegitimate. The two countries' National Security and Defence Councils held a joint sitting. According to officials on the Ukrainian Council, 'Lukashenka has always promised he would not allow Belarusian territory to be used for an attack on Ukraine, but we do not think he could refuse a direct request'.[22]

The 2015 Election

Despite mounting economic problems since 2010, Lukashenka was largely spared a contest at the presidential election in 2015. Because the war in Ukraine was raging, security arguments disabled the opposition. Some saw Russia threatening Belarusian sovereignty just as it had the sovereignty of Ukraine; others didn't want to get dragged into somebody else's war. It was not, then, the time to protest. This was especially fortunate for Lukashenka as this was his first election without economic pump-priming. In fact there were post-election spending cuts – one reason for the 'parasite tax' protests in 2017 (see below).

The authorities had by this time settled on a '1+3' formula. Lukashenka lined up his traditional fake sparring partner, Siarhei Haidukevich, the Belarusian equivalent, literally, of Vladimir Zhirinovskii, as he headed the Liberal-Democratic Party of Belarus. Haidukevich's real job was to attack the opposition (as also with Mikalai Ulakhovich of the Patriotic Party). In 2001, 2006 and 2015 he had come third. Then there was the opposition, but never the same candidate. The risks of standing were high. No opposition candidate ever survived to the next election; most ended up in exile. The fourth candidate was the one everybody talked about: were they covertly supported by the regime? This served two purposes: one, as in Russia, was to blur the very idea of principled opposition; the other was to fuel debate among the opposition about whether to boycott the election or not. In 2015, Tatsiana Karatkevich of Tell the Truth! was the candidate nobody could define. Her colleague Andrei Dzmitryew was accused of cooperating with the KGB to secure his release from prison in 2011 to run a moderate and peaceful campaign, and in return receive help with collecting signatures.[23] In 2010 the blurred candidate had been Uladzimir Niakliaew of Tell the Truth!, whom some suspected of being pro-Russian. In 2006 it had been Aliaksandr Kazulin, although he ended up serving two years in jail. That said, Belarus under Lukashenka did not use Russian-style 'political technology' (puppet parties, GONGOs, astroturfing online) so much. Methods were cruder. The regime was too personalised. There was no oligarchy seeking to fund political proxies to defend their interests, as in Ukraine.

Once again, massive fraud exaggerated the size of Lukashenka's victory. He was incapable of settling for an honest figure, claiming 84.1 per cent, and storing up problems for the future. A record 36 per cent were prompted or forced to vote early. IISEPS numbers showed between 34 and 47 per cent prepared to back Lukashenka, representing 50–60 per cent of the actual turnout. An IISEPS poll in December asking people to remember how they voted in the election two months earlier recorded only 50.8 per cent for Lukashenka, 22.3 per cent for Karatkevich, 7.4 per cent for Haidukevich and

Official Result of the 2015 Election (by Percentage)

Aliaksandr Lukashenka	84.1
Tatsiana Karatkevich (Tell the Truth!)	4.5
Siarhei Haidukevich (Liberal-Democratic Party)	3.3
Mikalai Ulakhovich (Patriotic Party)	1.7
Against all: 6.4	
Turnout: 87.2.	

Source: www.rec.gov.by.

2.7 per cent for Ulakhovich.[24] Moreover, public opinion was souring more generally. Just over 50 per cent thought that 'in general the state of things in our country is developing in the wrong direction' versus 37 per cent who were optimistic for the future. Over 35 per cent of respondents thought that 'our society needs serious reforms (structural and system changes)', 41.6 per cent that 'our society needs gradual reforms which would preserve [the] current system' and only 22.1 per cent that 'our society needs protection against forces which try to change [the] current order'.

Unusually, there was little post-election protest. The regime then felt safe enough to allow two, but only two, opposition MPs to be elected to parliament in 2016. The West, and to a lesser extent the domestic opposition, was easily impressed. Lukashenka began floating the idea of constitutional change before the next elections, talking of shifting some powers away from the all-mighty presidency. But such plans were pushed into the background whenever there was unrest elsewhere in the former Soviet space, such as in Armenia in 2018.

The 2017 Protests

The authorities managed to keep kicking the economic can down the road, but they also made mistakes under financial pressure. An unprecedented five weeks of protests in February and March 2017 were triggered by the imposition of what the government itself dubbed a 'social parasite' tax. If that was not bad enough, official pronouncements used the much stronger Soviet-era term *tuneiadets*, meaning 'scrounger'. The tax was an ill-judged attempt to reduce the costs of state support for the welfare state, the provinces and the declining parts of the public sector. It resulted in 450,000 of the economically 'inactive' (in a workforce of 4.5 million), which included young mothers and those caring for the infirm, receiving demands for steep payments of about $250. Unlike previous protests, average Lukashenka supporters, not just the urban elites, now took to the streets, turning out in large numbers in usually quiet regional towns.

The root cause of the protests was the substantial worsening of the socioeconomic situation over the previous three years, exacerbated by declines in construction and seasonal labour in Russia – normally a vital source of support for regions in the east of Belarus. The average monthly salary nationally had crept back up to around $450, but in the regions it could be as low as $150. Without adequate foreign exchange reserves, the government had adopted a deflationary policy, high interest rates and a floating exchange rate. Consumer prices were higher than in supposedly unstable Ukraine. There was suddenly talk of 'two Belaruses', or even three: the first comprised those covered by Lukashenka's social contract, but was shrinking; the two new poles were the people falling through the traditional social safety net, and workers in the new economy who resented state controls – though in 2017 IT workers happily showed solidarity with those who had to pay the 'parasite tax'.

Lukashenka was caught out by the protests, and lacked the funds to buy the protesters off. He was also hamstrung by the fact that Western sanctions had only just been lifted, in 2016, and he didn't want them to be immediately reimposed if he cracked down too heavily. The protests were not the beginning of a 'Belarusian Maidan'; they were not about geopolitical orientation or national identity, despite the traditional opposition's attempts to radicalise them. But they made Lukashenka's social support rhetoric ring hollow. The authorities did nothing initially, then suspended the 'social parasite' decree for a year, but they also detained hundreds of protesters in two waves of arrests. They made much of the arrest of two dozen members of a nationalist 'White Legion' group, on the grounds of preparing armed riots, in a bogus case to justify the crackdown (the group, always semi-mythical, had disbanded in the early 2000s). Since 2014, the authorities had used the 'Ukrainian scenario' and the spectre of violent revolt as a means of scaring the public and as an asset when negotiating with Russia (seemingly successfully) by posing as a bulwark against the spread of revolution. Lukashenka was lucky that his crackdown at home coincided with a sudden wave of anti-corruption demonstrations in Russia – increasing the force of this argument to the Kremlin.

But on closer inspection, all sides behaved differently compared to 2010. The authorities trod a line between using enough force to end the protests, but not enough to threaten the country's rapprochement with the West, or to give Russia an excuse to intervene. Most protesters were released the same day as their arrest; two-thirds of the remainder received only administrative fines. The members of the White Legion were released by the summer, although the cases against them were not closed. For the protesters, 'objectively there was less violence, but emotionally it felt intimidating'.[25] The protests were mainly organised on social media. They didn't produce new leadership or ideas but they did garner new solidarity networks and crowdfunding successes. The human rights NGO Viasna raised $30,000 for the families of those arrested. The same would happen on a larger scale in 2020.

In April 2017 Lukashenka and Putin met in St Petersburg, agreeing yet another sticking plaster deal, providing only short-term economic relief. If anything, it highlighted the fact that Russia no longer had the resources to bail out Belarus. Belarus needed Russian money to survive, but Russia could not provide enough for it to prosper.

Even after the protests were over, the regime looked nervous. Media controls were tightened. The outstandingly dull presidential newspaper *Belarus Today* closed its online comments section in February 2018, 'apparently due to an increase in negative comments'.[26] From December, internet users had to prove their identity before posting online, and website owners were obliged to set up ID systems. Major General Ihar Siarheyenka, deputy head of the KGB for counter-intelligence activities, was appointed as the head of the presidential administration in December 2019, despite his only recently having been removed from the EU sanctions list. Siarheyenka was previously responsible for 'internal state security . . . the fight against extremism and terrorism, counterintelligence support of government bodies and law enforcement agencies (i.e. ensuring their loyalty)'. He was expected 'to deal with these [same] issues in his new position. Obviously, only using different tools.'[27]

New Foreign Policy Strategies

According to Foreign Minister Uladzimir Makei, in the past Belarusian authorities 'spoke about a multi-vectored foreign policy, but in reality we were oriented to Russia'.[28] After 2014 the aim was to make Belarusian foreign policy genuinely 'multi-vectoral', or, in Lukashenka's clumsy phrase, 'many-winged' (more than two wings being unlikely). One think tank in Minsk began producing something called the 'Minsk Barometer' aiming to quantify relations with Russia, the EU, the US, Ukraine and increasingly China to show relations improving with all sides.[29] Official foreign policy discourse began to fill up with terms like 'balance', 'proportion', 'strategic hedging' and the correct 'algorithms' of relations. This did not mean 'balance' in the literal sense, with Belarus halfway along some metaphorical plank between Russia and the West. Belarus's primary strategic, economic and security relationships were still with Russia. Rather, Belarus was manoeuvring to preserve its freedom of manoeuvre. It was making sovereign choices to stress its sovereignty, or to build up its effective sovereignty.

According to leading Belarusian foreign policy analyst Yawheni Preiherman, small states in asymmetrical relations need sovereignisation strategies to avoid being policy-takers. His preferred term is 'hedging': a mix of diversifying, minimising threats and vulnerabilities, maximising engagement with others, bandwagoning, pacifying and opposing, even utilising some elements of neutrality, or at least avoiding forced choices. Contradictory moves were inherent in such a complex strategy. So was opponents or partners misreading your intentions.[30] The new strategy was, Preiherman said, 'an exercise in minimising risk, but it's risky in itself'.[31] The first risk was Russian reaction, or rather over-reaction; Russia wanted Belarus to remain a client state rather than an independent actor. The second risk was being misunderstood.

Crucially, Belarus now had a 'brand'. For strategic reasons, it preferred not to be dragged into a conflict not of its own making, still less a general conflict between Russia and the West. It could also point to the first line of the national anthem, 'We Belarusians are peaceful people'. Belarus was keen to promote its image as a 'security donor' and Minsk as a venue for diplomatic discussions. Most important was the ongoing Normandy Format, the main venue for peace discussions in Ukraine, after two Minsk Agreements were signed in September 2014 and February 2015. They weren't great agreements: Ukraine signed under duress, Russia pretended not to be a party to the conflict; but from Belarus's perspective it both made Minsk a new diplomatic hub and made it easier for Belarus to pose as neutral in the conflict. Other hostings included the OSCE Parliamentary Assembly and the Munich Security Core Group. Belarus took the chair of the Central European Initiative in 2017 – the first time in its history it had chaired an organisation outside of the post-Soviet space. There was also Belarus's own initiative from 2015 onwards, the annual Minsk Dialogue forum.

Foreign Minister Makei and President Lukashenka launched the grandiose idea of a 'Helsinki 2' security dialogue. Unlike then Russian President Medvedev's ill-fated European Security Treaty initiative in 2010, this would give all European countries a voice. Lukashenka has said that 'it doesn't matter what this process is called or where it is held',[32] but he would clearly like to host the process in Minsk. According to Makei, 'Belarus is the only place where people from different regions can meet'. [33]

Not every diplomatic initiative was a positive contribution to regional security, or substantive. Like many autocracies, Belarus was also keen on 'sportswashing'. Minsk was never likely to land the football World Cup, but hosted the 2019 European Games, a multi-sport imitation Olympics first held in Azerbaijan in 2015, and the International Ice Hockey Federation Championship in 2014 and planned for 2021 (as co-host) but then moved due to security concerns.

Soft Securitisation

Belarus was Russia's closest military ally. Its armed forces cooperated closely with Russia's and were under joint command during frequent joint exercises. But the threat to Ukrainian sovereignty since 2014 led to a rethink. Again, the

emphasis was on preserving and protecting sovereignty. The Belarusian security services were still proudly called the 'KGB'. They still had strong links with
Russia. The last tentative rapprochement between Belarus and the West was
ended by widespread repressions initiated by the KGB after fraudulent elections
in 2010. This did, however, lead Lukashenka to diversify the security agencies
to balance one another and provide alternative sources of information, to avoid
being 'bounced' in the future. The process gained extra momentum after the
war in Ukraine began in 2014. By one count, there were fourteen security agencies by 2017.[34] The most important, the innocuous-sounding Information
Analytical Centre and Operational-Analytical Centre, were reportedly under
the control of Lukashenka's eldest son Viktar. His empire also included the State
Security Committee (responsible for 'counter-intelligence'), the Financial
Investigation Department of the Committee for Government Control (KGK;
see page 262) and the Investigation Committee – all key bodies for controlling
the nascent oligarchy, or allowing Viktar to head it.[35] The Presidential Security
Service had existed since the 1990s without legal or judicial oversight.

Economic problems in the 2000s led to modest cuts in KGB personnel, but
it was still powerful enough to act as a brake on too diversified a foreign policy,
or too much domestic liberalisation, and even too many changes in economic
policy. In the words of one Belarusian commentator, 'everybody ends up like
[Vadzim] Zaitsaw', head of the Security Services from 2008 to 2012 – initially
appointed to nationalise the service and reduce Russian influence, but eventually presiding over yet more repression.[36] Above all, the continuing power of
the KGB 'limits the possibility of moving further away from Russia'.[37]

Nevertheless, Lukashenka changed the military doctrine in 2015 to guard
against any appearance of 'little green men' in Belarus. As it now read, the
'sending of armed groups, irregular armed forces, mercenary groups, or
regular armed forces who use arms against the Republic of Belarus by a
foreign country or countries or on behalf of a foreign country or countries'
will trigger a declaration of war.[38] In 2016 a revised version talked of the dual
threat of 'hybrid warfare' and 'colour revolutions', but with the implication that
Russia would launch the former or exploit the latter.

Defence spending went up, albeit from a low level, but towards 2 per cent
of GDP. Belarus was noticeably more transparent and cooperative with
Western observers than Russia when it hosted the *Zapad* exercises in 2017.
The new defence minister Andrei Rawkow spoke of building a 'people's army',
with large-scale civilian mobilisation to bolster national defence. In 2006
Belarusian law enforcement units had 50,000 personnel, and the army had
48,000. A decade later the army was bigger.[39]

Soft Belarusianisation

Logically, Belarus could have shifted its priorities toward sovereignty much earlier, in the 2000s. Lukashenka was first elected president in 1994, and he spent his first term as a neo-Soviet nostalgist, defeating the local nationalist opposition and playing a role in all-Russian politics. The West was then the enemy; true sovereignty for Belarus could only be found under the umbrella of the 'Union State' negotiated with Russia in 1999. But the election of Vladimir Putin as Russian president in 2000 meant that the job of Russia's saviour was already taken. The two men did not get on personally. Lukashenka withdrew a little and oversaw the writing of a fairly vacuous, but still neo-Soviet, 'state ideology' of Belarus in 2003. But, as he said in 2014, 'To be honest, I gave instructions, tried to invent something myself, this state ideology. But it didn't lie well with my soul. Well, yes, patriotism, but this is understandable even without ideology, and so on . . . what is needed is such an incendiary thing that would be accepted by the entire society and who would strive for this.'[40]

The time was still not right in the 2000s. The defeat of the Belarusian Popular Front in the 1990s was too recent. Belarus was too alienated from the West. Russia's economic boom years of high oil prices, from the Iraq war in 2003 until the global economic crisis in 2008, kept Belarus close. The leading figure in the new 'West-Russism' (page 205), Yakaw Trashchanok, who had actually been Lukashenka's university history teacher, died in 2011. But it was Russia's wars against Georgia in 2008 and Ukraine beginning in 2014 that led to 'soft Belarusianisation' measures, accompanied by the 'soft securitisation' measures described above. The regime needed extra props of support – not just for statehood as an abstract principle, or the social contract, expectations for which had to be adjusted downwards – but also cultural and identity props. The other lesson from Ukraine in 2014 was that internal divisions between regions or languages make you vulnerable, especially to Russian leverage.

President Lukashenka's primary motives were regime survival and personal survival. He was pushing for changes for instrumental reasons. But the changes that had been building up since 2010 had been delayed by political factors, and so after 2014 they came in a rush. There was also a push from below. As nearly all political NGOs were banned, energy was channelled into cultural policy. The new private economy often sponsored cultural initiatives. The old and often troubled relationship between civil society and the Belarusian state was now embryonically trilateral, with the regime allowing relations between private business and NGOs to develop, including support for some of the new patriotic campaigns.[41] Soft Belarusianisation was also useful for national branding – just as branding Minsk as a centre of diplomacy, and Belarusians as a 'peaceful people', had helped with foreign policy diversification. Many originally civic initiatives were then taken up by the state. All of this was done slowly. But the cumulative change was potentially great and could take Belarus just as far away from Russia as Ukraine in the long run.

In 2018 one of the iconic symbols of the nationalist movement, the short-lived Belarusian People's Republic of 1918, was granted centenary celebrations – an inconceivable event even only a year or two previously.[42] The other two pillars of traditional Belarusian nationalist historiography were gradually reintroduced. One was deconstructing the idea of a common east Slavic origin at the time of Kievan Rus by stressing the separate local history of Polatsk. The other was reviving the idea of the medieval Grand Duchy as a quasi-Slavic and therefore quasi-Belarusian state rather than a time of Polish repression. The publication from 2018 of a new official *History of Belarusian Statehood* – note the title – did both.[43]

All of this was 'soft' or 'slow', piece by piece. According to Piotr Rudkowski, head of the Belarusian Institute for Strategic Studies, the old 'east Slavic unity' formula has 'never been *directly* deconstructed by Belarusian ideologues, but it was gradually marginalised by a number of indirect measures. Direct deconstruction of the east Slavic idea would be too costly. First, it would make a strong impression of inconsistency (discontinuity) of the regime (there was a time when this idea played an important role in the official discourse). Second, it would directly offend pro-Russian opinion within the establishment. So, the indirect way of marginalisation [was] politically "cheaper".'[44]

Soft Belarusianisation also ironically used neo-Soviet propaganda methods. Successive campaigns to raise awareness of, and increase commitment to, national history and culture were splashed across public billboards, including 'Be Belarusians!', 'The taste of national language' and pushing 2018 as the 'Year of local homelands', celebrating the idea of Belarus as a patchwork of local identities. *Vyshyvanka* (embroidered shirt) day and a more 'national' team kit for the Rio Olympics came in 2016. The 500th anniversary of Skaryna's Bible was celebrated in 2017. One of the most interesting initiatives was 'Belarus Remembers', a nationalised local version of Russia's Immortal Regiment, with local symbols instead of the St George Ribbon. A new state emblem was introduced in February 2020. The old version had a globe in the centre, with Belarus next to Eurasia; the new one was tilted to Europe.

By 2018, there was more popular support for the key markers of the *Nasha Niva* view of national identity (see pages 83–5), but neo-Soviet ideas remained strong, and views were eclectic or hedged. Roughly equal numbers supported the celebration of the centenary of the BNR as were opposed to it, 18.5 per cent to 17.5 per cent; but most, 61 per cent, claimed to know 'too little to judge'. Only 7 per cent saw it as a 'source of Belarusian statehood': more went further back, 30.4 per cent to the Grand Duchy and 15.9 per cent to the Principalities of Polatsk and Turaw, while 21.8 per cent saw the origins of Belarusian statehood in the BSSR, and 9.3 per cent in the post-1991 Republic. 86.1 per cent agreed that the Belarusian language is 'the most important part of our culture and it should be preserved', if only for their children to learn. On the other hand, only 13.2 per cent supported the white-red-white flag and Pahonia as national symbols; 69.4 per cent backed Lukashenka's neo-Soviet symbols (see page 174).[45] The rehabilitation of the former would have to wait until 2020.

But there were foreign policy consequences too. In repeat polls asking the question 'In which union would Belarusians live better: the European Union, or a Union State with Russia?', the Russian option had a clear advantage over the EU – in January 2018 by 63.9 per cent to 20.2 per cent, but by December 2019 by just 40.4 per cent to 32 per cent. 74.6 per cent thought that Belarus and Russia should be 'independent, but friendly countries, with open borders and no visas or custom duties'.[46] However, much of this support was instrumental: only 24.9 per cent agreed it was important 'to preserve the sovereignty of Belarus even at the cost of lowering the living standards of citizens'; 51.6 per cent thought the opposite.[47]

Did Soft Belarusianisation Reach its Limits?

This type of Belarusianisation was called 'soft' to distinguish it from the two earlier periods, in the Soviet 1920s and in the early years of independence in 1991–4, when state support for Belarusian language and culture was rather more wholehearted. To be sure, it involved a more eclectic approach to national identity than Lukashenka's earlier neo-Soviet, Slavophile period, rehabilitating certain symbols of national identity, particularly if less political, and campaigns for native language, regional pride, etc.[48] But in 2018 Belarus also celebrated the centenary of the Red Amy and the KGB. The predecessor of the KGB, the Cheka, was founded in 1918 by Felix Dzerzhinsky, who was born in Belarus. There is still a Dzerzhinsky Street and statue in Minsk.

Lukashenka did not want to empower the opposition. He didn't want it setting the agenda. Nor did he want to provide too many easy targets for Russian propaganda. In 2017–19 Lukashenka stopped opposition campaigns over the Kurapaty forest, a mass grave of Stalinist victims and a potential mobilising symbol (see pages 105 and 144), and vetoed plans for a Belarusian language university that would potentially produce a lot of rebellious students. In 2019 when the remains of Kastus Kalinowski and his allies (see pages 68–9) were found and solemnly reburied in Vilnius, the regime left the commemoration to civil society. The event was something of a joint Belarusian-Lithuanian 'Litvinist' celebration (see pages 61 and 78–80), with scores of white-red-white flags.

West-Russism or Belarusian Eurasianism did not go away, however. It was less common in state circles, but easy to find online, where it overlapped with Russian propaganda: Trashchanok's main successor, Lev Khristapovich, wrote for teleskop-by.org, and similar sites included sonar2050.org and imhoclub. by. In 2020 Aliaksei Dzermant published a book *Belarus-Eurasia: Borderlands of Russia and Europe*.[49] But in December 2016 pro-Russian bloggers linked to *Regnum.ru* were actually arrested. The three were given five years in jail, with three years suspended.

Religious identity is weak in Belarus, leaving the field relatively free for the well-funded Russian Orthodox Church. One 2020 book, for example, traced the parallel lives of Euphrosyne of Polatsk (see page 11) and other 'princess-saints' from Ukraine and Russia to tell the story of east Slavic unity.[50] The Roman Catholic and Protestant Churches, however, increasingly served as ancillary channels for Belarusianisation.

The Return of Litvinism

The abovementioned *Zapad* ('West') exercises in 2017 involved thousands of troops doing manoeuvres on the borders of the Baltic States and Poland. The scenario was to defend against an imagined invasion of Belarus by foreign-backed extremists. One of the fictional enemy states, 'Vesbaria', was a thinly disguised Lithuania; the other, 'Lubenia', looked a lot like Poland. There were the usual low-level provocations, with Russian planes buzzing borders, which made the whole passive-aggressive show of strength look more like an invasion of the West than the other way around. The exercises were staged in the north-west of the country, given the name of another fictional state, 'Veishnoria'. But this was the historical heartland of real Belarusian nationalism, where Belarusian activists in the early twentieth century competed with Poles, Lithuanians and Jews to claim the old Tsarist administrative region of Vilna. Unfortunately for the Belarusians, much of this became Vilnius, the capital of modern-day Lithuania. But the rest remains in the north-west of modern Belarus, with the division testament to the long-standing love-hate relationship between Baltic peoples and Belarusians. Hence the Baltic-style spelling of Veishnoria. The region also voted for Lukashenka's main opponent, the nationalist Zianon

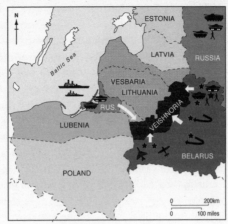

Map 7. *Zapad* military exercises, 2017.

Pazniak, the last time Belarus had a real competitive election, back in 1994. So *Zapad* was directed as much against an 'internal enemy' as against NATO powers – the same scenario that Russia claimed to detect in Ukraine in 2014.

Some Belarusians had fun with this.[51] Veishnoria soon got its own Twitter account, T-shirts and mugs. Some 7,000 people applied for its passports.[52]

Russia's Integration Push

Russia was of course not standing idly by. It changed the terms of engagement with Belarus after its war against Ukraine began in 2014, demanding a higher level of loyalty. At the same time, sanctions and the collapse in oil prices in 2014 meant that Russia could no longer subsidise Belarus so generously; one faction sought to save money, getting the same loyalty for less. These aims were to an extent contradictory: Russia could not afford to pay Belarus more to be a closer ally. To complicate things still further, many Russian attacks on Belarus were sponsored by oligarchs eyeing up Belarusian assets.[53]

A 'hybrid' campaign began to soften up Lukashenka, starting with ramped-up propaganda. According to a report by iSANS, 'Many of the media involved in the information attack on Belarus are sponsored and promoted by "patriotic businessmen" close to Vladimir Putin or associated with the Presidential Administration.' The Telegram channel 'Game of Thrones' was linked to *Regnum. ru*, Tsargrad TV and promoters of pro-Russian separatist forces in Ukraine.[54]

Russia attacked soft Belarusianisation as hard 'Ukrainianisation' or dismissed it as *mestechkovyi natsionalizm* ('small-town nationalism').[55] The more popular online term was *Zmagarism*: in Belarusian *zmagar* means 'fighter', as in freedom fighter. Belarusian nationalists were mocked as *Bat'kiny natsisty* ('*batka*'s Nazis' – see page 294).[56] Foreign Minister Makei was a frequent target, accused of plotting to sell Belarus to the West or create 'a second Switzerland, where officials rule the quiet people and capitalise their political and bureaucratic assets'.[57] But Russia suffered from a lack of what might be called 'negative culture capital'. In Ukraine, Russia could attack 'Banderites' (the followers of wartime nationalist leader Stepan Bandera) or west Ukrainians, former citizens of the Habsburg Empire, as alien and artificial 'other' types of Ukrainian. But there was no real equivalent in Belarus. Nor was there the opposite: there was no Belarusian Donbas or Crimea. There was no Belarusian equivalent of Viktor Medvedchuk, who was Russia's chief propagandist in Ukraine, but also had immunity from being a major player in Ukraine's oligarchy.

Direct propaganda was still pumped out through *Regnum.ru* (1.2 million visitors daily) and *Eurasia Daily* (400,000), *Zapadrus.su* and *Sputnikipogrom.com*. But Russia also began targeting the Belarusian regions with political messaging hidden behind local news.[58]

In December 2018 Russian Prime Minister Dmitrii Medvedev issued an 'ultimatum': financial support was now contingent on Belarus unfreezing the process towards making a true Union State. In September 2019 the Russian newspaper *Kommersant* published claims that Russia and Belarus planned to establish an 'economic confederation', with a common currency, customs union and supranational institutions.[59] Moreover, the paper claimed that the plan would be unveiled at a special summit on 8 December 2019, which was the twentieth anniversary of the original 'Union Treaty' between the two countries, signed in 1999 (page 241). To ramp up the pressure, Russia reduced oil supplies and pulled a 'tax manoeuvre' on oil exports to Belarus that cost Minsk between $330 million and $400 million. Belarusian businessmen like the Khotin family in Moscow saw their real estate empire attacked. Russia put forward more and more 'roadmaps' for deeper integration, by one count no fewer than thirty-one,[60] and no fewer than twelve supranational bodies. Lukashenka stalled, talking of an overall package agreement.

Conclusion

The juggling strategy could have continued if Lukashenka had been able to organise a quieter election in 2020. He would likely have tried to preserve some elements, even if forced to move closer to Russia. But all the underlying dilemmas were still there, as both cause and consequence of the crisis in 2020.

CHAPTER 14

THE REVOLUTION WITHOUT A NAME

After the war in Ukraine began in 2014, Belarus as a country was less secure, but Lukashenka thought he was more secure in his own self-appointed role as president for life. He reinvented himself as the defender of Belarusian sovereignty, with Russia defined *sotto voce* as the threat to that sovereignty. Only six months before everything went wrong in August 2020, Belarus's Nobel Prize winner Svetlana Aleksievich (in Belarusian, Sviatlana) could say 'I don't know who could resist Moscow like Lukashenka.'[1] The Minsk Process that began in September 2014 – diplomatic negotiations to try and end the war in Ukraine, based in Minsk as 'neutral ground' – didn't actually bring much peace to Ukraine, but it made Belarus a regional diplomatic hub, with Lukashenka boasting about the country being an all-round 'security donor'. The West began to reframe its Belarus policy to include supporting Belarusian sovereignty as well as human rights, and the regime liberalised just enough – but no more – to support its foreign policy aims and blunt criticism of the fact that it was still a dictatorship. Most international sanctions against Belarus were lifted in 2016.

But problems were accumulating in Lukashenka's backyard, as the previous chapter has made clear. The 2017 'parasite tax' protests were in many ways a dress rehearsal for what happened in 2020 – just as the Ukrainian 'Orange Revolution' in 2004 was preceded by smaller protests in 2001, and the Orange Revolution was itself a prelude to the Maidan Revolution in 2013–14. The Belarusian regime survived the 2017 protests; but did little to reinvent itself. It tightened control, but its governing formula looked increasingly threadbare.

Business as Usual?

Elections to the puppet Belarusian parliament were due in the same year as the next presidential election, in 2020. Lukashenka separated the two, bringing the rehearsal vote forward to November 2019 to try and minimise protests. He also hoped to benefit from the PR of the second European Games hosted in Belarus in the summer (see page 269). 'Sportswashing' can be expensive, however: the reported bill was $260 million, leading to mockery of the 'Hunger Games'. Attendance was low.[2] The regime was clearly nervous. It reversed the decision in 2016 to allow two – yes, 2 out of 110 – carefully screened opposition candidates to win seats. Zero was thought to be a more comfortable number, because the two MPs had been able to travel the country during the 2017 protests with constitutional immunity from arrest. But over-control only increased the gulf between Lukashenka and the public. The elections also showed a tentative step, not towards democracy, but towards 'managed democracy'. Only five MPs were elected as representatives of political parties in 2012. The regime allowed the number to go up to fifteen in 2016 and to twenty-one in 2019. But all were members of 'loyal' parties, in a lazy imitation of the four 'Kremlin parties' in Putin's Russia. More than eighty MPs in the old puppet parliament and exactly sixty-eight MPs in the new one belonged to the vague organisation Belaia Rus, set up in 2007. It chimed with the country's name, almost, and wanted to be the local equivalent of Russia's United Russia, the ruling patriotic party supporting whatever Lukashenka's latest definition of patriotism might be (just as United Russia supported whatever Putin threw its way). But it was an amorphous structure. Lukashenka reportedly said to its leaders, 'Guys, I understand why you need me, but I am not sure why I need you.'[3] He didn't want a formal party structure that would encourage elite consolidation over his own personal rule.

But it made more sense to create peripheral satellite parties that were modelled on Russian equivalents – because they were only satellites, window-dressing. The fake Communist Party of Belarus (see page 177) won eleven seats in 2019, the Republican Party of Labour and Justice won six, the Patriotic Party won two, and the 'Agrarians' and Haidukevich's Liberal-Democratic Party won one each. All were artificial creations, but could serve Russia just as easily as they served the local regime.

Coronavirus

The parliamentary elections were designed to show that Lukashenka was back in control, in advance of the real election, the presidential vote due in 2020.

Harassment of independent media was stepped up once the first vote was out of the way. Ihar Siarheyenka from KGB counter-intelligence was made head of the Presidential Administration in December 2019. The government of Siarhei Rumas, which included some pragmatists, technocrats and reformers, was removed in June 2020. The new prime minister, Raman Halowchenka, had previously been head of the State Military-Industrial Committee, and he was surrounded by *siloviki*, (nearly all) men with a security or heavy industry background. Lukashenka was standing in the election just to survive, without any real social or economic programme.

But the coronavirus hit Belarus just as Lukashenka was beginning his campaign and his campaign PR. Clearly frustrated, Lukashenka played his normal populist game, calling the virus a 'psychosis'. 'There are no viruses here,' he said after an ice-hockey game, still in kit. 'Did you see any of them flying around? I don't see them either.'[4] State TV grew increasingly unreal: it 'used a dozen manipulative tricks to convince the population of the insignificance of the coronavirus and the brilliant conduct of the Belarusian authorities. TV hosts repeatedly stated that no one died from the coronavirus in Belarus, cited absurd comparisons of mortality from other causes such as road accidents, and argued that world politicians were following Lukashenka's wise actions.'[5]

There was no lockdown. Shops and restaurants stayed open. The only significant measure was slightly longer school holidays. Belarus was the only country in Europe whose football league was still active. Lukashenka showed no sympathy for victims, even though the virus hits vulnerable populations harder, calling them 'fatties' and 'old folks'.[6] Health workers were forced onto a *subbotnik* in April (Lukashenka maintained the Soviet tradition of unpaid collective labour days), with hardly anyone wearing masks.[7] Lukashenka suggested tractor driving, vodka and visits to the sauna as remedies for or insurance against the virus. He took positive pleasure in organising his own Second World War Victory Day parade in May, despite the danger to veterans, after Putin had had to cancel his in Moscow. In April various Twitter accounts began encouraging users to imagine what careless cliché the president would use about them if they had the virus.

Lukashenka's non-policy had unintended effects. People had to band together to protect themselves. Large sums were crowdfunded online by the likes of #bycovid19 to provide respirators and basic safety equipment for the embattled health service. One hundred and fifty businesses made donations.[8] Solidarity demonstrations for health workers were held, with proper social distancing. People turned to independent media, particularly online and social media, for more reliable information on the pandemic. Lukashenka was unwittingly fostering social cooperation and cohesion.

The coronavirus crisis also had diplomatic and economic effects. The ongoing row between Belarus and Russia over oil subsidies flared up again when Moscow unilaterally closed the border in March. Lukashenka reacted disdainfully, pointing out that Russia had more cases than Belarus, and that he would create a 'green corridor' for transit trade to Russia through Belarus. But by April all borders were closed. Although that kept infection numbers down, the world price of oil collapsed, which is always bad news for Belarus, as oil refining is the country's most profitable business.

Belarus had 71,843 cases by the end of August and 681 deaths. This put the country on a par with laissez-faire Sweden, which had a population of only a million more and 84,379 cases. But the fact that Sweden had 5,821 deaths, more than eight times that of Belarus, supported the suspicions of many that coronavirus cases in Belarus were being reclassified as 'influenza' and so on.[9] The high number of cases among medical workers was another indication that statistics were rigged. Per capita, Belarus was the seventh worst case in Europe; Sweden was fifth.[10] Lukashenka was even evasive on whether he had had the virus himself, claiming he was 'asymptomatic'. Numbers began shooting up again in September, to over 100,000 cases.

The virus undermined Lukashenka's image as the provider of social goods. According to the commentator Artyom Shraibman, it also focused attention on the drawbacks of autocracy when the autocrat makes the wrong decisions; it was, he said, 'a powerful indicator of how autocracy doesn't work. Ordinary people began to see the consequences that one-man rule can have.'[11]

The 2020 Election Campaign

The 2015 election most likely gave Lukashenka the impression of another easy ride in 2020. But none of the conditions from 2015 applied in 2020. First, the coronavirus affected timing and planning. Four days before polling was due there, neighbouring Poland delayed their presidential election scheduled for May to June/July. Belarus, on the other hand, moved its election day forward by three weeks to 9 August. The regime's primary motives were not public health but political: holding the elections in the holiday period, when fewer would be watching globally, would hopefully yield a lower (real) turnout, in which directed voting and the presumed loyalty of Lukashenka's traditional supporters would carry more weight. But an early election meant less time to prepare and to deal with the tensions caused by the coronavirus.

Fifteen initiative groups registered for the election by the 15 May deadline. By the next deadline on 19 June the potential candidates needed to collect 100,000 signatures to gain a place on the ballot, which is a lot in a country of fewer than 10 million people. An early sign of trouble was that the authorities were unable to repeat the '1+3' formula. Siarhei Haidukevich was replaced by his son Aleh; their Liberal-Democratic Party had turned into a family business, with Aleh reprising his father's act. But he was pulled from the race in May as he was proving more likely to take votes off Lukashenka than off the real opposition. The closest equivalent to the Haidukeviches was Siarhei Cherachen, a businessman with a background in pro-Russian NGOs, who took over an old party, the Social Democratic Assembly, in unclear circumstances in 2018. 'Moderate' candidates included Andrei Dzmitryew from the Tell the Truth! Movement, and Hanna Kanapatskaya, one of the two oppositions MPs who were allowed to win seats in the 2016 parliament, an experience that had left her rather shop-worn. The 'traditional opposition' – Belarus's old pro-European parties – tried to hold primaries for a unity candidate in spring, only to descend into arguments over whether to delay the election campaign because of the virus. Volha Kavalkova, Yury Hubarevich and Mikalai Kazlow stayed in the race but were never likely to get the 100,000 signatures they needed.

But this time there were three candidates the government could not control, tolerate or ignore – all of whom could reach a broad audience. The biggest initial impact was made by a vlogger, Siarhei Tsikhanowski, whose YouTube channel 'A Country for [real] Life' offered 'real news that they don't show on state TV', talking to ordinary Belarusians and airing their grievances. By the summer it had 311,000 subscribers.[12] Tsikhanowski was a cross between Lukashenka in 1994, when he first won the presidency through an anti-corruption campaign, and the new breed of social-media populist. His campaign slogan was 'stop the cockroach' – meaning Lukashenka – and at rallies he brandished a slipper, the normal method for killing cockroaches indoors, hence his call for a 'slipper revolution'. Hardly enamoured with the idea of someone stealing and updating Lukashenka's act, the regime targeted Tsikhanowski first, in May: a sequence of short prison sentences on trumped-up charges (related to public order and the organisation of rallies, and the implausible discovery of $900,000 in his home) ensured that he was in jail on registration day. But in a twist that accumulated in importance over time, Tsikhanowski's wife Sviatlana Tsikhanowskaya agreed to take his place, first campaigning against her husband's multiple arrests, and then formally replacing him on the ballot paper.

The Tsikhanowskis represented the left-behind half of the 'two Belaruses' (see page 266). But this was also the first election in which high-profile regime insiders, representing the most dynamic parts of the economy, entered the race. With its traditional state-owned manufacturing sector in decline, Belarus was increasingly reliant on a booming information technology industry, which had special legal and tax privileges. Valer Tsapkala had been on Lukashenka's team in 1994, before serving as ambassador to the United States; he brought back ideas from Silicon Valley to found the IT Park in Minsk in 2005, which he headed until 2017. Tsapkala campaigned rather awkwardly, as a businessman rather than a politician, so the authorities left him relatively unmolested in the first half of the campaign. He easily collected 158,683 signatures. But the authorities crudely rejected 53 per cent, at odds with the miniscule share of rejections for the moderate or fake opposition candidates, leaving him with only 75,249 signatures.

By then, Tsapkala's campaign had been eclipsed by another businessman, Viktar Babaryka, the twenty-year head of Belgazprombank, Belarus's fourth biggest bank, and a subsidiary of Russia's Gazprom and Gazprombank. Babaryka represented a more radical version of the economic strategy of the Rumas government from 2018 to 2020. There was therefore widespread speculation about whether he represented the would-be Belarusian oligarchy,[13] and/or Russian interests. Babaryka was prominent in some Russian media.[14] He supposedly 'discussed' his candidacy with the Kremlin.[15]

But Babaryka, from Smilavichy near Minsk, was also a major art collector and sponsor of Belarusian culture, owning works by Chagall and the Expressionist Chaïm Soutine (a favourite subject of his friend Modigliani). This made Babaryka the potential sweet-spot candidate, acceptable to all sides, though it was unclear if Russia saw this as an actual advantage. Overall, Russia was giving no obvious steer,[16] although Babaryka was obviously better than a populist like Tsikhanowski, as the Kremlin would be extremely averse to any local Russian equivalent. Babaryka collected 435,000 signatures – an astonishing number given that there were only 7 million voters in Belarus – and submitted the best 361,654. The election commission chucked out as many as it could, but eventually had to accept 165,744 of them. So the authorities banned Babaryka from the election for 'receiving financial aid from abroad' – apparently his campaign team included Belgazprombank employees who had used their work phones – implying a link with Russia. More seriously, but without much evidence, Babaryka and leading bank bosses were arrested on corruption charges and accused of laundering $430 million. Belgazprombank was effectively nationalised on 15 June.

The authorities backed up the exclusions with escalating repression. In early June, Lukashenka scandalously referred to how 'former President Karimov suppressed a coup in Andijan by shooting thousands of people'.[17] (In 2005 hundreds were indeed killed in Uzbekistan, but the causes of the unrest remained under-investigated.) The threat was plausible, albeit left in the background. The authorities tightened the screws, but not enough to stamp out the groundswell of opposition. By 8 June, 275 people had been detained, fined and imprisoned in the previous 40 days.[18] In big cities, voters organised impressive 'solidarity chains' that maintained social distancing. Although the events were entirely peaceful, the authorities detained another 360 people during 18–21 June,[19] and 280 more on 14 July.[20] By mid-July over 700 people had been detained.[21] According to local NGOs, Belarus now had at least 25 political prisoners.[22]

The Feminisation of the Campaign

There were five candidates on the final ballot paper: Lukashenka and Tsikhanowskaya, plus the moderate/murky candidates Kanapatskaya, Dzmitryew and Cherachen. The regime was confounded in its attempts to divide and rule when the Tsapkala and Babaryka campaigns threw their weight in with Tsikhanowskaya. Resources were pooled. Tsikhanowskaya now campaigned with Tsapkala's wife Veranika Tsapkala and Babaryka's campaign manager Maryia Kalesnikava. Lukashenka referred to them dismissively as the 'girls'. Tsikhanowskaya was told to stay at home and 'Fry your cutlets'. Lukashenka boorishly declaimed that 'our constitution is not [right to be placed] under a woman. And our society is not ripe to vote for a woman'.[23] The burden of the presidency, he claimed, would cause Tsikhanowskaya to 'collapse, poor thing'.[24]

Lukashenka was wrong. And anyway, 53.5 per cent of the population was female. The three women ran a powerful campaign. They attracted huge crowds with warm and simple, positive messaging. There was no detailed manifesto, just the demand for a free and fair election – not this one but the next. A lowest common denominator campaign made it easy to opt in. Music and the message of a better country helped set the tone. The campaign theme song deconstructed Lukashenka's Soviet nostalgia by revisiting the Gorbachev-era classic 'I Want Changes' by Kino ('Cinema') and their charismatic singer Viktor Tsoi. Also popular were the folk songs 'Pahonia' (written in 1916, evoking old Litva)[25] and 'Kupalinka', a favourite of Aliaksandr Rybak, the Belarusian-Norwegian (not Russian, although he sang for Russia) winner of the Eurovision Song Contest in 2009,[26] and the 'unofficial national anthem' 'Almighty God', from the 1943 poem by the émigré poet Natallia Arseneva.[27]

The regime's response was flat-footed and old-fashioned. There were no real counter-rallies. These came late and were fake, organised after Russian 'political technologists' took over Lukashenka's fightback campaign. Traditional state TV propaganda reached a declining audience, and with 79 per cent of Belarusians online by 2018–19, the regime gifted dominance of social media to the opposition. According to Sławomir Sierakowski, 'the independent media have become mainstream . . . a kind of second media sphere has arisen online'.[28] Online sites like *Nasha Niva*, *Radio Liberty* and *TUT.by* saw a three- to four-fold increase in readership. Most important was the Telegram channel *NEXTA*, pronounced 'Nekhta', which is Belarusian for 'someone',[29] run by a young Belarusian émigré in Warsaw, which accumulated a huge 2.5 million subscribers, a world record, and 30 per cent of Belarus's entire population.

The 'Result'

The authorities could have claimed a smaller win for Lukashenka, and recognised the appeal of the Tsikhanowskaya campaign. Instead it claimed a 'traditional' result: Lukashenka was awarded over 80 per cent of the vote. Early voting reached another record high, 41.7 per cent. Voter turnout was supposedly 84.2 per cent.

This was egregious fraud. The point often made that Lukashenka could have won previous elections without fraud no longer applied. Tsikhanowskaya was detained at the Central Election Committee and forced to make a 'hostage video' conceding and calling for calm. It was actually filmed in the office of Lidziya Yarmoshyna, the unwittingly frank head of the Central Election Committee (prone to claims such as that queues to vote were opposition

Official Result of the 2020 Election (by Percentage)

Aliaksandr Lukashenka	80.1
Sviatlana Tsikhanowskaya	10.1
Hanna Kanapatskaya	1.7
Andrei Dzmitryew	1.2
Siarhei Cherachen	1.1

Against all 4.6
Invalid 0.01.

Source: www.rec.gov.by.

'sabotage'. Yarmoshyna, a twice-divorced woman prominent in Belarusian public life, also said that prominent women in public life were 'bad wives' and 'bad mothers'. In 2010 she managed to win a 'Sexist of the Year' anti-award).[30] Threats were made against Tsikhanowskaya's children and she fled to Lithuania.

We will never know the exact, true result, because there wasn't one. Votes were miscounted, and in many cases not counted at all. There was massive evidence of fraud, given how crudely it was done. Discrepancies were collected at the website *Partizan-results.com*.[31] At many polling stations the evidence showed Tsikhanowskaya received ten times her official result.[32] A small number of honest officials published actual results.[33] At one factory, when someone shouted 'Who voted for Tsikhanowskaya?'[34] everybody stood up. Many polling stations reported suspiciously identical figures.[35] Ballot paper piles and protocols were simply swapped from one candidate to another.[36]

Previous patterns of fraud had been taken to wildly implausible extremes. An analysis of earlier elections in 2006, 2010 and 2015, with the pertinent title 'Mathematics against Yarmoshyna', showed 'absurd results' that 'contradict mathematical laws and cannot exist in principle'. The statistical impossibilities included huge variations in the vote 'against all', turnout at over 100 per cent, more votes cast than ballot papers received, implausible differences in the number of invalid votes between regions and between elections, and figures that were added up incorrectly. All of which was evidence of mass fraud via 'manual control'.[37] Other countries like Russia were experimenting with more sophisticated methods of fraud, trying to avoid obvious 'tells', but in Belarus things had not moved on since Lukashenka's first fraudulent wins in the 2000s.

After the election, 565,743 Belarusians uploaded pictures of their ballot papers to a special online platform, the Voice or *Golos* (*Belarus2020.org*). Over a million, 1,047,933 voters, confirmed how they had voted to *Golos* by either verifying their phone number or submitting a verification code. In total *Golos* digitised the details of 1,875,998 voters, almost a third of all the votes cast, from 1,310 polling stations. The sample over-represented Minsk and those with mobile phones, and anti-Lukashenka voters were more likely to contact the site. Nevertheless, there were extrapolations. Analysts calculated that, after removing mass early voting and suspiciously high turnouts, 'the result of Tsikhanowskaya in Minsk is estimated at 55–65%'.[38] And Boris Ovchinnikov stated: 'In regional centres and other cities with a population of one hundred thousand – clearly more than 50%, maybe more than 55%. If we add to this my estimate of 44% for Tsikhanowskaya in the rest of Belarus, then in the country as a whole she gets about 49–53%. Winning in the first round or on the verge of winning in the first round.'[39]

The Chatham House Post-Election Survey (by Percentage)

Sviatlana Tsikhanowskaya	52.2
Aliaksandr Lukashenka	20.6
Other candidates	3.9

Against all 9.2

Refused to answer 13.7.

According to another data cruncher, Aleksei Zakharov, in relatively homogenous cities like Minsk turnout varied implausibly by 35 per cent between districts. Early voting favoured Lukashenka, but for every extra vote for Lukashenka, Tsikhanowskaya went down by *more than one* – indicating that in these voting districts ballot stuffing and fake counting went together. In a fifth of Minsk districts, Tsikhanowskaya's reported vote was crammed into the narrow range of 14.5–15.5 per cent, as ordered from above. Extrapolating from the honest results gave '30–35% for Lukashenka and 50–55% for Tsikhanowskaya' in Minsk. And 'the same is true in other cities'.[40] An analysis by the Russian paper *Novaya Gazeta* and a Ukrainian count both concluded that stripping out all the falsifications would leave Tsikhanowskaya ahead, in the case of the latter analysis by 47.9 per cent to Lukashenka's 40.5 per cent.[41]

In the week of 22–28 September Ryhor Astapenia from Chatham House managed to conduct a survey by Computer Assisted Web Interview (CAWI). One of the questions was 'Who did you vote for in the 9 August presidential election?'[42] The answers are tabulated above. CAWI samples are of course biased towards the 80 per cent of the population who are internet users; moreover, the sample only 'corresponds to the general structure of Belarus's urban population', and 21 per cent still live in the countryside.

Sociologist Oleg Manaev estimated that nobody won 50 per cent.[43] Leaked data in the spring showed Lukashenka's rating was 24 per cent in Minsk and around 30 per cent nationally. One rumour of a 3 per cent rating gave Lukashenka the nickname of 'Sasha 3%'. Such a low level was unlikely; Lukashenka's 'old' (pensioners, the countryside) and 'new' (the government payroll) electorate was decayed, but could be assumed partially intact, Manaev opined.

The final *Golos* report could not say what the result might have been, but could say with certainty 'since at least 30% of the final ballot reports were falsified, the elections were not legitimate. [Lukashenka] is not a legitimate president of Belarus.'[44]

The 'Three Nights of Terror'

The regime's post-election response to protests was even cruder. This time Lukashenka was thinking of the 2010 election, not 2015. As in 2010, he assumed protesters would go home after a day or two of savage repression. Viktar Sheiman (see pages 190 and 232) was reportedly a key figure in urging a tough response.[45] During 'three nights of terror' from election day on 9 August, 6,000 were detained, with another 700 on 12 August.[46] State hospitals reported 200 admissions,[47] undoubtedly a huge underestimate as protesters knew that hospitals were not a safe haven. The Belarus Free Theatre made *The Okrestina Sisters*, a shockingly simple film of detainees' testimonies from the most notorious detention centre.[48] Other video blogs showed police brutality in broad daylight.[49] The first official fatality, Aliaksandr Taraikowsky, occurred on the second night of protest. Scores were unaccounted for, many presumed dead. By 1 September there were 450 documented cases of torture and ill-treatment in detention.[50] Interior Ministry officials were accused of taking part.[51] Screams were audible on video taken outside detention centres.[52]

The police violence was much worse than in Ukraine a week into the Maidan protests on 30 November 2013, when the demonstrations first grew in size after police attacked young protesters. But it had the same effect: moral outrage sparked further protest, particularly a crucial women's march on 13 August when there was some danger of protests dying down.

The authorities tried to shut down internet and social media access, using equipment purchased from US network equipment company Sandvine. 'People found ways around these barriers, however ... [via] proxy servers, VPNs, and [the censorship circumvention tool] Psiphon, as well as private ISPs that are outside government control.' IT experts helped 'the opposition ... counter the regime. Hackers are constantly switching off the government websites or adding Lukashenka's name and face to official lists of criminals.'[53]

The Developing Repertoire of Protests

There was no Maidan in Minsk, in the sense of putting up barricades and occupying public space in the manner of the Ukrainian Revolution of 2013–14, although on the night of 10 August police used the 'tsunami specials' – water-cannon trucks – to destroy barricades being erected near the Universam Riga shopping mall, north-east of the city centre.

But mass protests became both regularised and diverse. There were special days for the old, for students, for women and for those with special needs. The biggest women's event was 'The Loudest March' on 12 September. The pensioner Nina Bahinskaya became something of a celebrity, cleverly exploiting the authorities' patriarchal reluctance to arrest her.[54] A 'Grandmothers versus OMON' (the militia) march was held on 4 October. The women's march became a regular Saturday event. The 'March of Heroes' on 13 September included an attempt to march on Drozdy, where Belarusian officials lived. *Minsk Courtyard Chats* was a shared Google document that provided links to local groups and Telegram channels for micro-mobilisation. Another Telegram channel *Belarus Main Brain* discussed the presence of provocateurs and how demonstrators might protect themselves. An overall opposition 'Victory Plan' included six 'fronts' against Lukashenka: protest, economic, information, political, judicial and international.[55]

IT specialists were prominent in the demonstrations. They also put their skills to use. Many were already in the diaspora, which had been minimal in size in 1991 but was now an important political factor, numbering according to some estimates over a million.[56] Political repression at home had created émigré groups in Warsaw and Vilnius. The IT industry was used to working partly 'offshore'. *The Black Book of Belarus* on Telegram[57] published the identities of the militia. *NEXTA* successfully perfected a 'deanon' strategy – de-anonymising the identities of political and security officials. On 19 September it published the personal data of over a thousand militia, provided by the hacktivist group Belarusian Cyber Partisans. Belarusian IT specialists based in the US claimed to have developed software that could identify police even if they were wearing a mask and only part of their face was visible.[58] But there was scepticism as to whether this really worked. Attacks on state websites were certainly effective.[59] In the last week of September hackers got into the state TV website and replaced its propaganda with images of police violence.[60] Many of the above groups appropriated the names and mythology of wartime partisans (pages 110–12), flipping Lukashenka's love of neo-Soviet nostalgia into a tool against him. This implied the regime were the true 'fascists' (see below); but it also implied a long struggle to come. Efforts to encourage the militia and others to defect had some symbolic successes, but mainly at the foot of the pyramid of power. Lukashenka had always paid his police. He also deliberately sought to make as many as possible complicit in his survival.

Formal opposition political structures were less successful. On 14 August Tsikhanowskaya set up the Coordination Council (for the Transfer of Power). It represented her campaign but also the breadth and civic ambitions of the post-election protests. Business and workers were included and at least one regime defector, former Minister of Culture Pavel Latushka. There were ten working groups, including Christian, trade unions, business and human rights.[61] But Lukashenka refused to negotiate with the Council and treated its very existence as a crime. Its Presidium of seven was an easy target and was soon arrested and dispersed. In late October Latushka set up a 'People's Anti-Crisis Administration'; it wasn't clear how that related to the Coordination Council, or whether it was capable of functioning as a shadow government.

Subjects into Citizens

Following the 'three nights of terror', Lukashenka was heckled at a factory visit on what he thought was his natural territory, the workers bursting into a spontaneous chant of 'Leave!'[62] The event was symbolic of the idea of emancipation: that Lukashenka's neo-Soviet, paternalist society of subjects were becoming self-assertive citizens.[63]

The protest movement was also noteworthy for protesters' civic behaviour. Non-violence was not just a tactical principle, it permeated every aspect of behaviour. People cleaned up after themselves. Unlike Ukraine, Belarus has no real Cossack tradition (see page 43), no previous history of anarchic rebellion. The opening line of the national anthem is 'We Belarusians are peaceful people'. There was also the more recent history of dealing with a repressive state: caution was ingrained. But so was the opposite; people had grown used to greater freedom since the lifting of (most) sanctions in response to the government's tactical easing of coercion since the mid-2010s. 'Soft Belarusianisation' also had an effect. The white-red-white flag removed after the 1995 referendum (pages 173–4) was back, but less as a historical symbol and more a reminder of pre- (and post-) Lukashenka Belarus. But the idea of 'One Nation, Two Flags' was built in: Lukashenka's neo-Soviet flag was also a part of the new civic nation. It in turn welcomed, but was not based on, the Belarusian language, as it was Russian-speaking.[64]

Unlike the Maidan protests in Ukraine in 2013–14 there was no controversy around, or even mention of, foreign policy orientation or geopolitics. There were no sharp regional divides: there was no equivalent of Crimea or the Donbas in east Belarus; neither Hrodna in the west nor the remnants of the old Vilna guberniia in the north-west were nationalist strongholds like Ukrainian Galicia. The revolution was, however, about 'dignity' in the same sense as Ukraine's 'Revolution of Dignity' in 2014. The desire for a 'normal life' was also about yearning for *la vie européenne*.

But the new nation wasn't infinitely broad. The sociologist Oleg Manaev argued that 'Lukashenka's Belarus didn't disappear on 9 August; it's still there.

They were not the ones protesting, as they were "broadly satisfied with life" ... The disagreeing Belarus was more visible."[65] But Lukashenka's supporters weren't turning up to counter-demonstrations either. Such passive loyalty was nevertheless an asset for the incumbent president.

The most intriguing question related to working-class attitudes to the protests. Many Belarusians looked to the Polish paradigm: the intelligentsia protested alone in 1968, the workers in 1970, and both were defeated; but that led to worker-intelligentsia cooperation via the Workers' Defence Committee in 1976 and Solidarity in 1980. In Belarus during the 'parasite tax' protests in 2017 crowdfunding had helped various informal groups support one another.[66] But the researcher Oksana Shelest concluded from her interviews of protesters in August 2020 that 'the current actions remain a protest of the intelligentsia and new groups – teachers, university professors, the creative class, culture workers, media, a lot of IT people. At first we did not see people from factories at all, but now they began to appear as the strike movement developed.'[67] Vladimir Socor argued that 'the social mainspring of this protest movement is primarily members of the Minsk-based "bourgeois".'[68]

The counter-argument to the idea of a 'bourgeois revolution' was that there was plenty of worker sympathy for the protests, but the costs of striking were much higher than the costs of marching – not just losing your job, but arrest, the harassment of your family. There was a severe collective action problem. The regime was highly vulnerable if the giant factories of the neo-Soviet economy all went on strike at once; but until that tipping point was reached, the big state-owned enterprises were also an effective means of social control. They still directed many welfare services, and the short-term contract system (page 217) meant workers were easy to fire.

But the new civic nationalism reached the most unlikely of places: the Orthodox Church. The Orthodox majority in Belarus are not particularly religious – one consequence of the legacy of the Soviet era. Metropolitan Pavel, head of the Church since 2013, was even a native Russian. The Holy Synod of the Russian Orthodox Church, trying to orchestrate a pan-Orthodox campaign against the new Orthodox Church of Ukraine, made a point of convening in Minsk to cut off relations with the Ecumenical Patriarch in October 2018 (Patriarch Bartholomew I, head of world Orthodoxy, who had approved the creation of the Ukrainian Church). Pavel initially congratulated Lukashenka on his 'victory', but then allegedly withdrew his statement, and 'highlighted that it was Lukashenka's duty to ensure that the rule of law prevailed and that the security officials did not attack innocent bystanders.'[69] After visiting victims of state violence, he was instantly replaced by Bishop

Veniamin of Borisov and Martina Horka, who was Belarusian, but a loyal supporter of the regime. Bishop Artemii of Hrodna more explicitly condemned regime violence. The Roman Catholic Church, led by its Metropolitan Archbishop Tadeusz Kondrusiewicz, and the Protestant Churches played an important mobilising role. Kondrusiewicz prayed outside Okrestina detention centre.

Ironically, the Orthodox faithful could now outgrow their Church. In the long run a push towards autocephaly – the creation of a national Church separate from Moscow – on the Ukrainian model was now imaginable, albeit against the fierce resistance of a very conservative hierarchy. Before 2020 such an outcome had been inconceivable[70] – unless Lukashenka had decided to try and construct a state Church from above. Now bottom-up autocephaly was a possibility. However, the moment for historical reunion with Kiev was gone, despite Metropolitan Epifaniy of the new Orthodox Church of Ukraine encouraging the Belarusians to follow his path.[71] It is worth pointing out that when the Orthodox Church of Kiev and all Rus' was dissolved uncanonically in 1686 (pages 44–7) it included the two dioceses of Polatsk and Mahilew, in what is now Belarus. Many 'West-Russian' thinkers like Mikhail Kaialovich (page 70) had seen the Ukrainians as part of their 'west'.

Lukashenka Turns to Russia

Lukashenka continued to make threats. On Monday 17 August he stated coldly, 'You know my harsh side'.[72] Police began to use rubber bullets, stun grenades or flashbangs, and water cannons, the so-called 'tsunami specials'.[73] But the regime's domestic coercive capacities were limited. Between 14 and 16 August Lukashenka and Putin spoke on the phone several times. The Russian National Security Council met more than once to discuss Belarus.[74] Russia's hybrid intervention was launched on 17–18 August. 'Two groups of Russian political, military, security, and media advisers arrived in Minsk from Moscow to take control over the situation in Belarus in key public and governing areas (media, social and political sector, army and security agencies). The operation was partially disguised as a celebration of [the] Russian ambassador's birthday party'.[75] Full-on military intervention was too risky, but an FSB plane arrived on 18 August carrying FSB personnel and equipment. Rumours of a special Russian intervention force proved unfounded, but were a useful means of intimidating protesters by signalling there were no limits to which domestic coercion, backed by Russia, could go. An unknown amount of Russian equipment allegedly bolstered the local militia.

Lukashenka shocked observers with a performative video on 24 August.[76] In a bulletproof vest he flew over protesters in a helicopter, claiming 'they ran away like rats'. He then brandished a Kalashnikov, accompanied by his son Nikolai, then fifteen, also in army gear. The message was clear: Lukashenka wasn't going anywhere and would do what it took. The whole episode was designed to show that Lukashenka was the exact opposite of Viktor Yanukovych, the Ukrainian president who filled his helicopter with art and money before fleeing in the middle of the night in February 2014.

On 25 August Dzmitry Pawlichenka, the man named in a Council of Europe report as responsible for the 'disappearances' of Lukashenka's opponents in 1999–2000 (page 191), re-emerged in central Minsk, swearing profusely at protesters. (In 2019, police conscript Yuri Gavraski, a member of Pawlichenka's unit, repeated the allegation that Pawlichenka had shot the victims himself.)[77] In September, Chief Prosecutor Aliaksandr Kaniuk and Chair of the National Security Council Andrei Rawkow were removed for insufficient zeal. New tactics of targeting leaders and snatch-and-grab arrests meant that the NGO Viasna calculated that by the end of August 12,000 had been arrested, 7,500 had been detained, there were 500 cases of torture and 41 political prisoners,[78] up to 121 by early November.[79]

Direct Russian assistance came mainly in the form of propaganda and 'political technology'. On 19 August Russians began arriving at state TV. Belarusian TV had long been dominated by Russian channels but had its native 'media-killers' (the Russian term for attack-dog presenters). Most seemed unwilling to do the job anymore. Yawhen Perlin resigned on 13 August. Dzmitry Siomchanka, one of the main presidential cheerleaders and presenter of the *Antifake* programme at the main state TV channel ONT, was arrested in September. Ihar Marzaliuk, one of the leading spokesmen for Lukashenka's ever-changing 'ideology', was seen staggering home dead drunk on 14 August.[80]

The Russian takeover of Belarusian TV involved both attack dogs and technicians, mainly from RT. Russian oligarch Mikhail Gutseriev provided the finance. Many of those taking up a whole floor of the Renaissance Hotel were veterans of the anti-Lukashenka *Godfather* campaign of 2010 (page 230).[81] 'Propagandists and conspiracy theorists'[82] who had worked on anti-Ukrainian propaganda for years were now expected to do the same thing for Belarus. But this was more than just Russians working on Belarusian TV; they imported the baroque paranoia and aggressive big-lie culture of Russian TV, belligerent and aggressive, with dramatic music. Fake 'experts' populated the screen, the same stable of talking heads as on Russian TV. Professional troll and promoter of Russian 'concert of chaos' Alexander Malkevich,[83] president of Yevgenii

Prigozhin's Fund for the Protection of National Values, became a frequent interviewee.[84] Ukrainians were enlisted to talk about how terrible the 2013–14 Maidan protests had been, but they were either actors or from pro-Russian circles, such as the émigré vlogger Anatolii Shariy and Yanukovych cronies like former Prime Minister Mykola Azarov, then in Moscow exile. The 'famous German political scientist' Alexander Sosnovsky appeared to talk about '$6 billion' in foreign funding for the protests.[85] People had already switched off state TV, but anonymous Telegram channels like *Trikatazh* and *BeloRusskii Dialog* added to the disinformation.[86] The propaganda was echoed by a growing network of pro-Russian NGOs in Belarus,[87] which seemed to be competing for potential sponsorship.

According to the Russian expert on political technology Maksim Katz, old-style Belarusian 'propaganda is similar to the Soviet one. It's an alternative reality on TV and is not worried about anyone believing it. Then the Russian one is a mixture of political technologies and social engineering. It clings to real events, emotions, feelings and tries to promote them. The goal is for people to stop their resistance, quarrel among themselves, doubt their leaders, each other, believe that nothing can be achieved and there is no need to even try.'[88] A fake news campaign against Tsikhanowskaya accused her of plotting the withdrawal of Belarus from the Union State and the Russia-led Collective Security Treaty Organisation, leaving the country defenceless, and planning a hard border, banning Russian TV and 'a creeping ban on the Russian language.'[89] She was a foreign puppet, mocked as *Sveta Litovskaya* ('Lithuanian Svetlana'), or a likely candidate for 'Guaidisation' (the West would use her to plunder Belarus, just as they had supposedly done with Juan Guaidó in Venezuela).[90] Tsikhanowskaya had even called for her foreign supporters to bomb Belarus.

Konstantin Pridybailo was in charge of the Russian propaganda, in partnership with Lukashenka's PR person Natalya Eismont.[91] She almost certainly writes Lukashenka's thoughts on the Telegram channel *Pul Pervogo* ('The Pool of the First', i.e. the president's pool of wisdom, though *pul* with an added soft sign means 'bullets'). However, even after expanding its audience during the protests, it had only 85,000 readers, compared to over 2 million for *NEXTA*.[92] *Trikatazh* had 40,000. Eismont had boasted back in 2019 that 'Dictatorship is now our brand.'[93] 'I don't know if you'll agree with me here,' she continued, 'but today, in 2019, the word "dictatorship" is gaining a certain positive connotation. We see what's happening around us. We see the chaos and sometimes the disorder. And, you know maybe I'm about to say something paradoxical or surprising, but sometimes it seems to me that someday soon there may be a demand for dictatorship in the world. Because when we think about dictatorship today, we see discipline and an absolutely normal, quiet life, first and foremost.'[94] When a major accident disrupted Minsk's water supply Lukashenka quipped, 'Dictatorship is bad, but it's good when we solve an extreme problem overnight.'[95] Eismont and others had supposedly built a 'safe space' around the president, controlling his information supply; in which case, so much for supposedly diversifying his sources of security information.

That said, the attempts to redeploy the Ukraine formula from 2014 would not necessarily work in Belarus. There were too many paper tigers. A fake story of Lithuanian attack was unlikely to inspire fear[96] – modern Lithuania not exactly being a major military power. On 27 August Lukashenka said that 'the country has to spend huge money to stabilize the situation at its western border, where some military units were dispatched'. In the same government meeting, Lukashenka also said, 'You see these statements saying that if Belarus falls apart, Hrodna Oblast will become part of Poland. They are already saying it openly, they are dreaming about it.'[97] Other themes were also retreads: a 'colour revolution' orchestrated by the West, the threat from NATO and of Belarus being dragged into NATO, the nationalist threat to the Russian language and Russian Orthodox Church, the Nazi origins of the white-red-white flag, Russian protection and the heroic restraint of the security forces.[98] The internal enemies – the *zmagary* (see page 276) and the *svyadomyye*, a mocking term for the nationally 'conscious' – were also too obviously artificial.[99] However, the danger of a Belarusian Maidan, a 'Belomaidan', the increasing violence of protesters and the fear of chaos, had more potential traction, as in the government video *Belarus Never Wavers*.[100] But the drift away from state media towards online sources continued after August, with increasing distrust of an obviously politicised message.[101]

Counter-demonstrations, known in Russia as *Putingi* (pro-Putin meetings), small in number but visually necessary for TV propaganda, were belatedly organised. Plans for bigger meetings – bigger than opposition protests – were regularly abandoned. The slogans for the mini-meetings, *Za Bat'ku* and *Yabatki* (supporters of *batka* – Lukashenka's nickname in less traumatic times), were absurd.[102] On 17 September a big copycat forum *Women for Belarus!* was held.

Try-out projects for new political parties began to compete. Aleh Haidukevich set up the People's Patriotic Movement of Belarus on 18 August ('patriotic' in this context meant pro-Russian). The Souiz ('Union') party featuring Lev Khristapovich and veteran Russian nationalist Sergei Baburin campaigned for Russia-Belarusian union. Rodina ('homeland') was set up in October, working with *Zapadrus.by*. Its platform of Orthodox nationalism may have historical resonance but little contemporary appeal. The synchroni-sation of existing Belarusian and Russian 'Kremlin parties' (see page 278)[103] was likely to be used to try out how competitive the Belarusian 'court' parties might be: the Communists, Liberal-Democrats and the Republican Party of Labour and Justice. All of these parties could be pro-Lukashenka; they could be pro-Russian; they could be both; or they could diverge if Russia decided Lukashenka was not delivering.

Russia's Changing Plans

One other reason for cautioning against a full Russian takeover was that Russia didn't know exactly what it wanted. In the first few days after the election there was a variety of stories on Russian media, even some criticism of police brutality. There was initial talk of an 'Armenian scenario' – that Russia would accept a transfer of power as it had in Armenia in 2018, given the assumption that any Armenian or Belarusian leader was likely to be Russia-friendly – though this soon proved to be a flimsy analogy. Yes, any Armenian leader would need Russian help from real existential security threats, surrounded as it was by Azerbaijan backed by Turkey. But when renewed war broke out in September 2020, it seemed that Russia was happy to leverage it to weaken Armenia's reformist leader Nikol Pashinyan. It was far from clear that a successor to Lukashenka would be boxed in in the same way in the long term.[104]

The stakes for Russia were huge. Its official red line was Belarus moving to the West. But Russia was also existentially fearful of a real election in a kin country which could inspire protest at home. A few Russians, like Andrei Kortunov of the Russian Institute of International Affairs, worried that the 'Russian iceberg' would melt not long after the 'Belarusian ice-floe': 'Sooner or later the Belarusian scenario in one or another of its modifications will become a very real prospect for Russia too.'[105] Russia had to move from *Krym nash* to *u nas nyet* – from the expansionist slogan of 2014, 'Crimea is Ours', to 'it won't happen here'. The Kremlin would also be mindful of the dangers of mass fraud. Russia's referendum on constitutional change in 2020 was also marked by huge numbers of falsified votes; but that was before events in Belarus. The Russian authorities claimed a 'Yes' vote of 77.9 per cent on a turnout of 68 per cent; independent calculations put 'Yes' at 65 per cent, but turnout much lower at between 42 per cent and 45 per cent.[106] The Kremlin would have to think carefully about how it would manage its next election cycle: for the Duma in 2021 and the presidency in 2024. 'Manage' is the key word. It's not that there wouldn't be fraud, but that the regime would hide it better, and there would likely be a roster of new parties and candidates to draw the sting of protest votes.

Another red line was exposing just how dysfunctional its neighbourhood policy actually was. The Crimean model couldn't easily be replayed in Belarus – using a military base as a bridgehead, staging a 'responsibility to protect' invitation. There was no dense urban network like the Ukrainian Donbas where Russia could count on or manufacture some base of support. And the Donbas was a mess – too much responsibility, too many bills. Russia was keen to chalk up some apparent victories in the dying days of the Trump administration, in Armenia as well as Belarus, but it was far from clear that they would last.

Moreover, if Russia wanted to replace Lukashenka, it was not clear what Russia wanted. Lukashenka could claim to be a new man anyway. Did Russia want a Gomułka? The USSR invaded Hungary in 1956, but not Poland, despite parallel unrest, and was persuaded to accept the return to power in Warsaw of Władysław Gomułka instead. Gomułka was sufficiently loyal to Moscow but had a domestic base of support. He removed his pro-Soviet defence minister but stayed in power until 1970. A Belarusian Gomułka would be more likely to be Babaryka; Lukashenka's domestic support base looked too narrow after August 2020. Lukashenka was more likely to sell himself as a version of another Polish Communist leader Wojciech Jaruzelski, who did the USSR's dirty work for them by suppressing the Solidarity movement in 1980, to forestall the threat, he claimed, of Soviet invasion. Or Lukashenka could play the part of East Germany's post-war leaders, who had spent the war years in Moscow and were prepared to see the USSR asset-strip their economy. Lukashenka could claim to be all three, though Gomułka only minimally, insofar as he could continue, implausibly, to be the defender of Belarusian sovereignty. A covert takeover of Belarus could be financed by such asset-stripping, but Russia still faced the dilemma of more control meaning more bills to pay.

Russia's and/or Lukashenka's immediate plan was the implementation of constitutional reform by 2022 via a stage-managed 'national dialogue', with media control and political technology would manage the process. One possibility was Lukashenka giving constitutional status, and the power to change the constitution, to the All-Belarusian People's Assembly – the stage-managed gatherings he had held every five years since 1996, sonorous and soporific affairs resembling the Communist Party Congresses of old (see pages 180 and 202). Changing the constitution by referendum and another mass fraud would likely be too risky. On 10 October Lukashenka visited some of his political prisoners. Yury Vaskrasenski from the Babaryka campaign and

PandaDoc director Dzmitry Rabtsevich were released. Vaskrasenski was charged with 'dialogue' and drawing up changes to the constitution (his name, Voskresensky in Russian, means 'Resurrection'). But he was only a minor figure from Babaryka's campaign, a 'coordinator of a group of volunteers'.

Putin and Lukashenka supposedly discussed Babaryka's long-term fate when the two men first met after the election in Sochi on 14 September. Russia promised a $1.5 billion loan, but most of the money would go on servicing existing debts. There was little mention of the Union State 'roadmap' – but only because it was now an assumed given. There was little money up front because there was so much to discuss. The price of Lukashenka's survival was likely to be high. Conversely, it was far from clear that he could deliver on the full range of Russia's expanded ambition.

International Reaction

The EU, on the other hand, found it difficult to react. Although trade and other forms of linkage had been growing, especially since 2014, leverage was limited. The US was preoccupied with the 2020 presidential election. When Secretary of State Mike Pompeo had visited Minsk in February 2020, the talk had not been about human rights, but about possible US contracts for reverse energy supply. The West in general was reluctant to intervene in Belarus in any way that confirmed Russia's propaganda narrative that this was a geopolitical tug-of-war.

An emergency summit of heads of European foreign ministries on 19 August did not recognise the elections as valid. But there was no agreement on sanctions until a Cyprus veto – unrelated demands for support regarding a dispute with Turkey over territorial waters – was overcome on 2 October. By then the Baltic States had imposed their own sanctions on 31 August against thirty Belarusian officials, including Lukashenka. On 10 September the Lithuanian parliament recognised Tsikhanowskaya as the only elected leader of Belarus. The initial EU sanction list of forty individuals did not include Lukashenka, so as to keep 'dialogue' open. The list was also short; before 2016 the sanctions regime had named 240 individuals and 32 companies.

On 9 September, the Council of Europe's Parliamentary Assembly called for an international body to collect information and preserve evidence of crimes against human rights. The 'Moscow Mechanism' was invoked on 17 September, an OSCE procedure that seeks to bypass Russian veto power by allowing groups of OSCE states, in this case seventeen, to mandate an expert mission to report on human rights violations. But little more could be done in the face of Belarusian intransigence.

Self-Inauguration

The expiration of Lukashenka's term was originally due on 5 November. Instead he inaugurated himself in secret on 23 September. The mini-ceremony was not broadcast on state media as constitutionally required. Guests didn't know where they were going, but were asked to be smartly dressed for a museum visit.[107] The Russian ambassador wasn't informed. Lukashenka was trying to show that any 'transition' process would be on his terms, so it wouldn't really be transition. But in doing so he bounced EU states, including Germany, into not recognising his legitimacy. The expected regime crackdown was not unleashed immediately, however, despite the regime threatening to use arms against demonstrators. Interior Minister Yuryi Karaew was replaced with the hard-line Minsk boss Ivan Kubrakow, who was already on the EU and UK sanctions list.

Peaceful protests stayed peaceful, but there were signs of frustration. In Kyrgyzstan, another post-Soviet state, rigged election results were overturned in a matter of days in early October. Some complained that 'Belarusians have been protesting for two months, but the regime has not collapsed . . . The Kyrgyz, on the other hand, disposed of the powers they were fed up with virtually overnight. On social networks, voices sounded: that is who we need to learn from.'[108] But quite rightly, the differences between the two cases were stressed: in Kyrgyzstan unlike in Belarus there were regular clan-based political coups capable of overcoming minimal local security forces, a president who promptly resigned, and relative Russian indifference. The Belarusian opposition was aware that the most likely explanation for the regime not yet unleashing further mass violence was that they were waiting for protest numbers to fall to levels that were more 'dispersible'. The opposition therefore sought to keep numbers up.

Tsikhanowskaya managed to have a public phone conversation with her husband, still in detention, which was notable for one word: his urging her to act *zhestche* – 'more toughly'.[109] This was not a deep planning process, but Tsikhanowskaya responded by issuing a People's Ultimatum from exile with three demands that, within thirteen days, by 25 October, 'Lukashenka must announce his departure', 'Violence on the streets must stop completely' and 'All political prisoners must be released'.[110] The weekend that the ultimatum expired saw the last big demonstration, again with increased numbers. But the call for a general strike once more met with only a limited response, apart from at universities and the fertiliser plant Hrodna Azot.

The point was to maintain momentum, appease radicals, show that the protests had their own logic, and buy some time. But the move also signalled weakness. After this last hurrah, and following ninety days of protests, numbers finally began to drop. On 8 November central Minsk was locked down and police numbers rose dramatically. More than 1,000 were arrested, a level last seen in August, and 1,300 the following weekend. New laws were introduced threatening protesters with years in jail, rather than fifteen days. Raman Bandarenka, a children's art teacher, died from his beatings on 12 November. The EU finally added Lukashenka, his eldest son Viktar and thirteen others to its sanctions list on 6 November, indicating that hopes for dialogue were dead.

Conclusion

Even on official figures, 18,000 Belarusians had been arrested in total during the protests, which per capita was the most severe repression anywhere in Europe in forty years[111] – far more than the 10,000 interned during the repression of Solidarity in Poland in the 1980s. Leaked Interior Ministry documents indicated the real figures were 25,800 by 3 November and 30,000 a week later.[112] That level of repression would be difficult to replicate next time. The new Belarus could not be bottled up for long; a new civic nation had been born. Its numerical strength had been tested on the streets, and partially demonstrated at the election. Lukashenka's short-term survival would segue soon enough into controversy over whether the constitutional transition process would be real or fake. Russia thought it had the leverage to remove Lukashenka if it wanted. The People's Ultimatum had a sting in its tail: Lukashenka's departure was entirely possible before his five-year term was up.

CONCLUSIONS: LUKASHENKA'S RISE AND FALL

The history of Belarus has been a series of false starts under different names. Various parts of its various territories have been 'Krywia', Polatsk, Litva, Ruthenia, Uniate-land, West-Russia, the *krai*, Soviet Belarus and finally independent Belarus. A similar pattern of reinvention was also for a time true of Lukashenka himself. He first stood for office as a pan-Russian nationalist in 1994, and seriously tried to play the role of Russia's saviour during Yeltsin's declining years. In the 2000s he became first a 'creole' as he shifted to building up his own bailiwick instead, and then also a bulwark against 'coloured revolution' after 2004. After 2006 he tentatively experimented with a minimal version of economic liberalisation and a more 'multi-winged' foreign policy as Russia cut back its previously generous subsidy regime. In 2015 he was able to reinvent himself as the defender of Belarusian sovereignty.

Lukashenka was clearly an opportunist. Ironically, he learnt much of his original populist style from Russian models, mainly Boris Yeltsin and Vladimir Zhirinovskii, though Lukashenka also originally wanted to be Putin before Putin took the job. But Lukashenka was also a great survivor, and like all survivors he is a chameleon when he has to be. Some observers have stressed his malleability,[1] some his skill at addressing his local audience.[2] Others tread a middle route, stressing Lukashenka's skill at exploiting some opportunities and blindness in missing others.[3] In 2020 the blindness looked extreme, as his dictatorial instincts threatened to destroy the whole direction the country had taken since 2014. The brutal post-election crackdown left Lukashenka persona non grata to many at home and abroad.

Lukashenka's Rise

Lukashenka also failed to quit while he was on top. The former Polish President Aleksander Kwaśniewski lamented in September 2020, 'If you had left five years ago, people would remember you as a good president, a person who changed their lives, raised their standard of living.'[4] One of Lukashenka's leading critics, the political scientist Vitali Silitski, also chose to edit a book back in 2009 called *Social Contracts in Contemporary Belarus* to try and understand why Lukashenka originally had some base of support.[5] Others have called the social contract 'distributional authoritarianism', examining the regime's spending on social goods to maintain baseline popularity and keep the level of coercion lower than it would be otherwise.[6] A 2019 study talked of 'adaptive authoritarianism', as the regime was able to mix various strategies at different times: façade elections, performance legitimacy, patrimonialism and managed pluralism, alongside coercion and what Silitski called 'preemptive authoritarianism' (see page 198).[7]

The truth about 'social contracts', however, is that they are rarely actually contracted: there are no formal negotiations and agreement, no signing ceremony, no written promises. The truth about adaptation is that it is a skill set that constantly needs updating. But for his first two decades in power, through all these transformations, economic growth allowed Lukashenka to maintain the base of support that he first won in 1994, when he received 44.8 per cent of the vote in a more or less free and fair first round. His rating hovered between 30 and 50 per cent thereafter, though never near the 75.7 per cent or 83 per cent that he claimed at the elections in 2001 and 2006, nor the 79.7 per cent in 2010 and 84.1 per cent in 2015.

The relatively open 1994 election tells us much more about electoral geography (see pages 165–7), when Lukashenka's original vote base was heavily skewed to the east. Conversely, the most oppositional areas were in the west, in the areas that were part of interwar Poland and had a shorter experience of Soviet rule, and in the north-west, the remnants of the old Vilna guberniia (see pages 126–7), now in the corner of Hrodna region. The east, the old White Russia, was more amorphous. The antipole to the north-west therefore shifted over time. In the 1994 election the heaviest vote for Lukashenka (86.5 per cent) and the lowest vote for Pazniak of the BNF (4.7 per cent) was in Mahilew; whereas Lukashenka scored highest in 2001 in Homel (85 per cent) and in 2006 in Homel (90.3 per cent). There is no Belarusian equivalent of Crimea or the Donbas in Ukraine.

But as Lukashenka increased his control over the country, his vote became more homogenous in all regions. Elections that are fixed provide limited

INDEPENDENT BELARUS

Lukashenka's Support by Region, West to East, 1994–2020 (by Percentage)

Lukashenka's Vote	1994	2001	2006	2010	2015	2020
Hrodna	78.1	77.0	83.8	81.4	85.9	78.7
Brest	84.7	76.2	82.6	81.5	86.2	81.9
Minsk	82.4	76.6	83.5	80.7	85.7	79.2
Minsk City	69.6	57.4	70.8	67.6	66.7	64.5
Vitsebsk	80.0	77.4	83.1	82.5	87.3	83.6
Mahilew	86.5	83.0	88.5	85.0	88.3	88.1
Homel	77.3	85.0	90.3	82.3	87.8	85.4
National	**80.1**	**75.65**	**83.0**	**79.7**	**84.1**	**80.1**

Source: for the second round in 1994, Marples, *The Lukashenka Phenomenon*, p. 24, quoting *Radiefakt*, 1 July 1994; for 2001 to 2020, www.rec.gov.by.

evidence, apart from the obvious manner in which Lukashenka's winning margins have been uniformly exaggerated across the country. But there was no longer much of an east–west split.

According to a poll undertaken by BISS and IISEPS in February 2010, which put his overall rating at 39 per cent, Lukashenka's support base now varied less by region and more by the three key factors of town-versus-country, age and education: it was strongest in the countryside and among the elderly and less educated.[8] Lukashenka scored 37.3 per cent in regional centres (including only 32.1 per cent in Minsk) and 50 per cent in villages. His support varied even more by age, rising steadily from a low of 29.6 per cent among late teens to 73.3 per cent amongst the over-60s. Pensioners gave him 74.2 per cent support. Among those with higher education Lukashenka scored only 26.8 per cent, but a massive 88.8 per cent among those with only elementary schooling. Women gave him 43.7 per cent, men only 33.3 per cent. IISEPS methodology was criticised, however, for accepting nominal support for Lukashenka at face value, and not digging deeper beyond what was socially acceptable in an autocracy.[9]

Three overlapping explanations suggest themselves for Lukashenka's support base in these constituencies. Authoritarian saviour figures are popular in all the three east Slavic states, but they exist in different forms. Putin is the tub-thumping chekist, Ukraine's Viktor Yanukovych briefly the proletarian everyman. Lukashenka was *batka*, which is Belarusian for 'father', but in the sense of a strict Victorian dad, and has increasingly seen himself as a proper 'father of the nation'.

Being *batka* required Lukashenka to balance various roles. First was maintaining the informal social contract promised by his quasi-ideology of 'Belarusian egalitarian nationalism'.[10] According to official figures, real wages reached $503 a month by the end of 2010, and had risen 4.9 times since 1996.[11] The IMF estimated that GDP per capita, adjusted for PPP, had reached $13,865 in 2010,[12] which interestingly enough is above the oft-cited 'threshold' of $10,000 for democracy-supporting relative prosperity. Spending on welfare and on education and health were both maintained at high levels of 11–12 per cent of GDP.[13]

Second was maintaining the supply of authoritarian public goods. The 'tranquil and cosy home' that he described in 2004 was valued by many. Corruption was not so much absent as kept behind closed doors, but Belarus was spared the street crime and mafia disorder that plagues Ukraine and Russia. The streets of Minsk were also clean, the snow cleared in winter, albeit by the type of press-gang labour common in the Soviet era.

Belarus is not Russia – it does not have the same great power complex. After the massive losses of the Second World War, the absence of foreign entanglements is a real asset. And delivery was what mattered to Lukashenka's core constituency. In the September 2010 IISEPS poll, 44 per cent still thought that Lukashenka's concentration of power was good for the country (though 38.5 per cent were against); but the figures were reversed (43.2 per cent to 38.2 per cent) when people were asked if they would vote for a president who supported 'cardinal changes in the country's present course'.[14]

Lukashenka's third role as *batka* was building a new nation on his own terms. The BNF's version of national identity, like that of the Nashanivtsy after 1905, remained marginal. Lukashenka's version of Belarus was more of a pot-pourri, but was therefore more mainstream, like most Belarusians themselves. The Belarusian language nationalists of the BNF could provide part of that mixture, but only a small part. Lukashenka was more concerned to maintain the aspects of Soviet Belarusian identity that supported his rule, particularly the myth of the Second World War, but he was increasingly necessarily eclectic. His presidential website, for example, had sections on history and culture, which included more or less any and every famous Belarusian.[15] The new nation called 'Belarus' that began to emerge after the end of the USSR was, initially at least, Lukashenka's Belarus. According to Natalia Leshchenko, 'the Popular Front got nationalism wrong in the 1990s, Lukashenka got it right'.[16]

But whatever his baseline popularity, Lukashenka was also a serial election stealer. Although his original election in 1994 was more or less free and fair, albeit disfigured by dirty tricks on all sides, at every election since he has converted plausible pluralities into fraudulent super-majorities. Precisely because his baseline of support was stable at around 30–45 per cent, the level of fraud had to be considerable to claim 75.7 per cent in 2001, 83 per cent in

2006 and 79.7 per cent in 2010. Lukashenka's favourite method of control was to keep the upper reaches of the counting process away from the prying eyes of observers from the OSCE-ODIHR or domestic NGOs, so it seems likely that the final result was obtained by his personal order, rather than any actual counting process.

Lukashenka's Fall

As I argued in Chapter 11, 'The Edifice Crumbles', all three factors were being eroded after 2010, partly in opposition to Lukashenka's survival strategies, partly as a consequence of them. Many of the triggers of the 2020 protests were short-term – sudden sparks and Lukashenka's mistakes – but there were longer-term factors involved. Some commentators focused on the coronavirus as the single cause of the protests. It was clearly one among many, most important for rekindling the sense of neglect and discontent felt by ordinary Belarusians since at least the 'parasite tax' protests of 2017. But the nearest thing to a single cause, clearly related, was the long-term state of the economy and the decline of the social contract. By the time of the 2017 protests it was common to talk of 'two Belaruses', the old and new economy, the neo-Soviet state sector and the emerging private economy. Lukashenka had an unequal stake in both. His previous popularity had been based on maintaining the old economy, though he, or those around him, also hoped to hold the reins of the new. But the 2020 campaign threw up dynamic candidates for both Belaruses too. Tsikhanowski campaigned for the left-behinds, Tsapkala and Babaryka for the new economy and new middle class. Tsapkala represented the IT economy, Babaryka the bureaucracy that wanted to be an oligarchy.

A second long-term cause was that the era of creole nationalism and the ideology-that-wasn't had been succeeded by the politics of 'soft Belarusianisation'. Initially, this was mainly for *raison d'état*: to bolster Belarusian sovereignty after the war against Ukraine began in 2014. Increasingly, however, it became a bottom-up and horizontal reality.

Third was the decline of what Vitali Silitski called 'preemptive authoritarianism'.[17] To bolster its 'sovereignisation' strategies in foreign policy, the regime was forced to relax domestically after 2014, resulting in the lifting of most sanctions in 2016. This was always tactical: the screws were tightened after the 'parasite tax' protests in 2017 and over the winter of 2019–20. Atavistic instincts returned brutally in August 2020. But by then society had changed. Preemptive authoritarianism clearly failed this time: the regime was unable to prevent serious challengers emerging.

Silitski's other key idea was an 'authoritarian international':[18] authoritarianism can spread in waves, just like democratisation. Authoritarian regimes can copy one another and pool resources. But how does a preemptive authoritarian state react when its main threat comes from its supposed partner in the authoritarian international – i.e. Russia? The 'coloured revolution' era had been about collective defence of local autocracies against a heavily mythologised threat from the West. But the main threat to Russia's neighbours was now from Russia. Russia has a 'frenemy' complex, undermining even the countries who are supposed to be its allies. So, instead of a preemptive authoritarianism in 2020, there was belated and crudely savage coercion, with the regime struggling to respond to both a Russian threat and a vitalised domestic opposition. But a belated, or retrospective, authoritarianism is likely to want to close the gap ceded to pluralism, not partially but completely – striving vainly for the status quo ante. A first round of savage repression wasn't enough to shut down the protest movement. The belated invocation of the authoritarian international led to crude copying of Russian counter-revolutionary technology.

More broadly, the world had moved on. The dictators' skill set had changed since 1994. So-called 'smart authoritarian' states relied more on media propaganda and political manipulation than on crude coercion. Lukashenka's regime looked old-fashioned. The props of the regime were weak. State media had a declining audience. Pro-regime institutions like Belaia Rus and the BRSM youth league had no real social depth. There was no real national ideology.[19] Conversely, Lukashenka's repression had ironically 'privatised' civil society. A lot of subterranean networks existed below the formal NGO level, and have knitted together during the campaign and during the protests.

But there was still Lukashenka's 'new electorate' (see page 286), the state apparatus that he had built during his twenty-six-year rule. 'State people' included not just the militia but the central state bureaucracy, the military, all police forces, directors of state enterprises or 'court' businesses, schools, hospitals and universities. All were appointees. All had families. Perhaps a million all told. And 'Lukashenka fed them very effectively, not just salaries, but legal and social privileges'.[20]

It was difficult to tell how much Lukashenka's 'old' and 'new' electorates had shrunk since 2010. Elections were fixed. Sociology had replaced psephology. IISEPS's last poll was in June 2016; they weren't able to measure the impact of the events of 2017 and 2020. Oleg Manaev, the former head of IISEPS, points out that some survey work was still possible, but 'not the whole picture we could get when IISEPS was in Belarus'. But extrapolating from changes already apparent before 2016, he thinks it most likely that change was slow; his estimate was that Lukashenka's broader electorate was maybe still a third of the population.[21] But the power of symbolic events to shift opinion was another matter: the regime clearly lost support during the 2017 protests and during the coronavirus first wave. And brutal coercion after the election on 9 August 2020 shifted opinion, as Manaev willingly admits.

Sovereignisation

If Lukashenka originally wanted to be a serious player in Russian politics in his first term at least, he had increasingly played a game of diversification and hedging in foreign policy, trying to position his fiefdom as 'a transit country, aimed at obtaining as much as it can from both the East and the West'.[22] To some extent this began with the war in Georgia in 2008, but more decisively after the war in Ukraine in 2014. Lukashenka sought closer relations with the West, with China and the Middle East, not for real dialogue, but as an 'attempt to change the geopolitical supplier of rents'.[23] The main aim of this game was personal and regime survival, but for a time it was close to the mean voter's position. Support for integration with Russia slipped in the 2000s, and support for hedging grew. Though cause and effect was not clear, Lukashenka may have sensed the change in the air or Belarusians may have taken their cue from their leader's changing policies. In the September 2010 IISEPS poll the number supporting integration with Russia was down to 24.5 per cent, while 39.1 per cent favoured closer ties with the EU – but 34.6 per cent dodged the question.[24] According to similar IISEPS polls in the past, 41.8 per cent had supported the creation of a single state with Russia in 1999, and 53.8 per cent had done so in 2002.[25] Given the rise when Lukashenka was already into his second term, and Putin had been Russian president for two years, there is some evidence for Lukashenka shaping opinion rather than the other way around. Belarusians also view foreign policy options in instrumental terms, assessing what resources they will bring – satirised as Lukashenka's 'oil for kisses' policy.

Both Russia and the West grew increasingly irritated with this foreign policy style, but for different reasons. Russia has bemoaned what Finance Minister Aleksei Kudrin considered to be $50 billion of subsidies over the years for insufficient result. Russia had an unfinished agenda. Its venal elites eyed almost every potentially profitable asset in the country. Politically, Russia wanted a more reliable satrap – which it certainly hadn't got. But even the Kremlin didn't know how to get a handle on Lukashenka. It couldn't outflank him with 'political technology'. Political parties, real or fake, weren't yet important actors in

Belarus: it couldn't empower an opponent; it couldn't penetrate his court. Putin's dislike of Lukashenka used to be simply personal – he couldn't stand him. Then Putin couldn't stand the fact that he had no alternative to dealing with him.

The EU and the US wanted Belarus to transform its society and be a joiner not a hedger. But Lukashenka never sought an 'opening' with the West per se, just a means of enlisting the West in his own survival games. Hence the West had dilemmas of its own. The isolation policy decided in 1997 after Lukashenka's original constitutional coup d'état in 1996 had limited effect, and meant a loss of leverage over Minsk. The window of opportunity for improved relations that seemed to open in 2008 closed in 2010. Belarus was only a minimal member of the EU's Eastern Partnership policy launched in 2009. Constructive engagement with Belarus after 2016 helped support the country's sovereignty, but brought only limited domestic liberalisation. It allowed the growth of a private economy and a new civic nation to begin to mature. But after 2020 the West was back to partnership with civil society on its own, as after 1997.

The Price of Survival

In a dictatorship, the dictator's decisions make a big difference. Belarus had changed a lot since 2010, and even more so from 2014 to 2020. The 2020 protests were the result of these changes, many of which were supported by Lukashenka or which he was unable to oppose. One possible outcome was the maturation of these changes, and the birth of a very different Belarus. But another possible outcome was a dramatic handbrake turn, with Lukashenka prepared to reverse everything to ensure his own survival. A third, middle way would be Lukashenka preserving some semblance of sovereignty in a satellite state.

What might the price of Lukashenka's survival be? Foreign policy concessions might include recognising the annexation of Crimea and the independence of Abkhazia and South Ossetia. Russia would likely renew its push for a military base. Conceivably, Lukashenka could ditch all the sovereignisation, security and foreign policy gains since 2014. Andrei Savinykh, chair of the parliamentary international affairs committee, was already arguing that foreign policy 'multi-vectorism' was dead, and that Belarus's future was in the emerging Eurasian macroregion.[26] Post-2014 'soft securitisation'[27] and 'soft Belarusianisation' policies could be reversed. Russia could press for the sale of the key state enterprises that earned 70 per cent of Belarusian export revenue – the potash refinery Belaruskali, the MTZ tractor factory, the truck maker BelAZ, the MAZ car plant, the Polimir chemical works, BMZ steel, the tyre manufacturer Belshina, the oil refinery at Naftan and the fertiliser plant Azot. Russia was pressing for the rerouting of exports from the Baltic States to Russia, despite Belarusian investments in one of the terminals in Klaipėda and in the Lithuanian ship charter company Fertimara UAB. The weakness of the economy might enforce such sales. But the economy could also crash overnight, disrupting all of Lukashenka's survival plans.

The three months of protest after 9 August 2020 were almost certainly only the first round – the end of Act One, but not the final denouement. After Solidarity in Poland was repressed in 1980, it came back with a vengeance nine years later, winning every contested seat but one in the 1989 elections. Time moves more quickly in the twenty-first century.

APPENDIX: THE BELARUSIAN ECONOMY SINCE INDEPENDENCE

	GDP, Growth Rate, %	CPI Inflation (%)	Current Account Balance ($ million)	Current Account Balance (% of GDP)	Budget Deficit or Surplus (% of GDP)
1991	−1.2	83.5			
1992	−9.6	970.3	220	1.8	
1993	−7.6	1190.0	−430	−3.9	
1994	−11.7	2220.0	−440	−2.9	
1995	−11.1	709.3	−460	−4.5	
1996	2.8	52.7	−520	−3.7	−2.0
1997	11.4	63.8	−866	−6.3	−2.0
1998	8.4	73.0	−1020	−7.0	−1.4
1999	3.4	293.7	−190	−1.7	−2.8
2000	5.8	168.6	−460	−3.6	−0.6
2001	4.7	61.1	−530	−4.3	−4.9
2002	5.0	42.6	−330	−2.2	−8.1
2003	7.0	28.4	−460	−2.6	−7.0
2004	11.4	18.1	−1190	−5.2	−7.3
2005	9.4	10.3	460	1.5	−6.9
2006	10.0	7.0	−1390	−3.8	−8.0
2007	8.6	8.4	−3010	−6.7	−8.1
2008	10.2	14.8	−4960	−8.2	11.3
2009	0.2	13.0	−6130	−12.1	−7.2
2010	7.8	7.7	−8280	−14.5	−4.2
2011	5.5	53.2	−5050	−8.2	−2.8
2012	1.7	59.2	−1860	−2.8	0.4
2013	1.0	18.3	−7570	−10.0	−1.0
2014	1.7	18.1	−5230	−6.6	0.1
2015	−3.8	13.5	−1830	−3.3	−3.0
2016	−2.5	11.8	−1610	−3.4	−1.7
2017	2.5	6.0	−0950	−1.7	−0.3
2018	3.1	4.9	20	0.0	1.8
2019	1.2	5.6	−1170	−1.8	0.6
2020	−3.0	5.1	−1890	−3.3	−4.7

Sources: 1992–6 GDP, EBRD Transition Report 2001, p. 59; 1996–2004 GDP and prices, OECD Belarus; http://belstat.gov.by/homep/en/indicators/prices.php; 2004–20, www.imf.org/en/Countries/BLR#countrydata. According to critics, GDP figures were routinely exaggerated by 4–5 per cent.[1]

NOTES

Introduction to the New Edition

1. Lucia Kubosova, 'Rice Condemns Belarus as "Last True Dictatorship"', *EUobserver*, 21 April 2005, https://euobserver.com/foreign/18907.
2. Timothy Heritage and Richard Balmforth, 'Lukashenko: "I am the Last and Only Dictator in Europe"', *Atlantic Council*, 28 November 2012, www.atlanticcouncil.org/blogs/natosource/lukashenko-i-am-the-last-and-only-dictator-in-europe/.
3. Ryan Chilcote and Aliaksandr Kudrytski, 'Belarus Strongman Balances Between Ukraine War, Putin, EU', *Bloomberg*, 2 April 2015, www.bloomberg.com/news/articles/2015-04-02/belarus-strongman-balances-among-war-in-ukraine-putin-eu.
4. See the data at www.eiu.com/topic/democracy-index and https://freedomhouse.org/countries/freedom-world/scores. Assuming the EIU score was 2.88, occasionally it appears as 2.48.

Chapter 1 Polatsk

1. Serhii Plokhy, *The Origins of the Slavic Nations: Premodern Identities in Russia, Ukraine and Belarus* (Cambridge: Cambridge University Press, 2006), p. 47.
2. Aleh Latyshonak, *Natsyial'nas'ts' – Belarus* (Vilnius: Institute of Belarusian Studies/Belarusian Historical Society, 2009), pp. 34–47; *Saxonis Gesta Danorum*, vol. 1, p. 38 (II, 1:8), 46 (II, 3:8).
3. Henadz' Sahanovich, *Narys historyi Belarusi ad starazhytnastsi da kantsa XVIII stahoddzia* (Minsk: Entsyklapedyks, 2001), p. 25.
4. Uladzimir Arlow, *Taiamnitsy polatskai historyi* (Minsk: Belarus, 1994).
5. Simon Franklin and Jonathan Shepard, *The Emergence of Rus 750–1200* (London: Longman, 1996), p. 152.
6. Usevalad Ihnatowski, *Karotki narys historyi Belarusi* (Minsk: Belarus' 1st edn, 1991–26), p. 37.
7. Wladyslaw Duczko, *Viking Rus: Studies on the Presence of Scandinavians in Eastern Europe* (Lieden and Boston: Brill, 2004), pp. 126–7; Oleg Łatyszonek (Aleh Latyshonak) and Ales' Bely, 'On the Scandinavian Origin of Rahvalod', *Annus Albaruthenicus*, 2005, pp. 49–64, available at http://kamunikat.net.iig.pl/pdf/annus/annus2005.pdf.
8. Samuel Hazzard Cross and Olgard P. Sherbowitz-Wetzor (trans and eds), *The Russian Primary Chronicle: Laurentian Text* (Cambridge, Mass.: Mediaeval Academy of America, 1973), p. 91.

9.   Jonathan Shepherd, 'The Origins of Rus' (c. 900–1015)', in Maureen Perrie (ed.), *The Cambridge History of Russia. Volume 1. From Early Rus' to 1689* (Cambridge: Cambridge University Press, 2006), pp. 47–72, at p. 71.

10. *Ibid.*

11. From the *Russian Primary Chronicle: Laurentian Text*, the year 1128.

12. Sahanovich, *Narys historyi Belarusi*, p. 27.

13. Cross and Sherbowitz-Wetzor, *The Russian Primary Chronicle*, p. 144.

14. Arnolds Spekke, *History of Latvia: An Outline* (Riga: Jumava, 2006 – originally published in Stockholm in 1948), pp. 112–13.

15. Cross and Sherbowitz-Wetzor, *The Russian Primary Chronicle*, pp. 145–6.

16. V. N. Tatishchev, *Istoriia rossiiskaia* (Moscow: Academy of Sciences, 1962), pp. 199 and 247.

17. Ihnatowski, *Karotki narys historyi Belarusi*, p. 35.

18. Franklin and Shepard, *The Emergence of Rus*, pp. 250–1. Names changed from the Russian versions in the original.

19. Omeljan Pritsak, *The Origin of Rus'. Vol. 1. Old Scandinavian Sources Other than the Sagas* (Cambridge, Mass.: HURI, 1981), p. 137.

20. Cross and Sherbowitz-Wetzor, *The Russian Primary Chronicle*, p. 139.

21. Martin Dimnik, 'The Rus' Principalities (1125–1246)', in Maureen Perrie (ed.), *The Cambridge History of Russia. Volume 1. From Early Rus' to 1689* (Cambridge: Cambridge University Press, 2006), pp. 98–126, at pp. 101–2.

22. Franklin and Shepard, *The Emergence of Rus*, p. 255.

23. Leonard Magus (ed.), *The Tale of the Armaments of Igor* (Oxford: Oxford University Press, 1915), p. 17

24. Latyshonak, *Natsyial'nas'ts' – Belarus*, pp. 56–7.

25. Sahanovich, *Narys historyi Belarusi*, p. 57.

26. L.R. Kazlow (ed.), *Istorychny atlas Belarusi* (Minsk: Arty-Feks, 2002), p. 3.

27. Andres Kasekamp, *A History of the Baltic States* (Houndmills: Palgrave/Macmillan, 2010), p. 12.

28. Sahanovich, *Narys historyi Belarusi*, pp. 56–7.

29. Yan Stankevich, *Krywia-Belarus' u minulas'tsi* (Vilnius: Institute of Belarusian Studies, 2010), a collection of writings originally produced between 1930 and 1978.

30. Latyshonak, *Natsyial'nas'ts' – Belarus*, p. 56.

31. Sahanovich, *Narys historyi Belarusi*, p. 35.

32. Cross and Sherbowitz-Wetzor, *The Russian Primary Chronicle*, p. 91.

33. Sahanovich, *Narys historyi Belarusi*, p. 36.

34. Viacheslav Nosevich, 'Belorusy: stanovlenie etnosa i "natsional'naia ideia"', in Dmitrii Furman (ed.), *Belorussiia i Rossiia: obshchestva i gosudarstva* (Moscow: Prava cheloveka, 1998), pp. 11–30, at p. 17.

35. Ioffe, 'Belarusian Identity', pp. 1261–2.

36. Kasekamp, *A History of the Baltic States*, p. 9.

37. Karski's main work was the three-volume *Bielorussy*, published in six editions between 1903 (Warsaw) and 1916 (Moscow). The edition *Belarusy: Vvedenia k izucheniiu yazyka i narodnoi slavenosti* (Vilnius, 1904) was reprinted as Efim Karskii, *Belarusy* (Minsk: Belaruski knihazbor, 2001).

38. V.I. Picheta, *Istoriia belorusskogo naroda* (Minsk: BDU, 2003); *idem*, *Historyia Belarusi* (Minsk: BDU, 2005).

39. M.V. Dovnar-Zapol'skii, *Istoriia belorussii* (never fully published in the 1920s, but issued in Minsk by Belarus' in 2003).

40. M. Ya. Grynblat, *Belorusy: ocherki proiskhozhdeniia i etnicheskoi istorii* (Minsk: Nauka i tekhnika, 1968; reprinted 1991).

41. Cross and Sherbowitz-Wetzor, *The Russian Primary Chronicle*, pp. 56–7.

42. *Ibid.*, p. 55.

43. M.F. Pilipenka, *Vozniknovenie Belorussii: Novaia kontseptsiia* (Minsk, 1991); *idem*, 'Kantseptsyi wzniknennia Belarusi', in I.P. Khawratovich et al., *Belarus' na miazhy tysiachahoddziaw* (Minsk: Belaruskaia Entsyklapedyia, 2000), pp. 6–16.

44. Pilipenka, *Vozniknovenie Belorussii: Novaia kontseptsiia*, p. 41.

45. Vasil' Bandarchyk, Valiantsina Bialiavina and Halina Kaspiarovich, *Belarusy. Vol. 4. Vytoki i etnichnae razvitstse* (Minsk: Belarskaia navuka, 2001), p. 29.
46. Plokhy, *The Origins of the Slavic Nations*, p. 44.
47. Ingunn Lunde, *Kirill of Turov: Bishop, Preacher, Hymnographer* (Bergen: University of Bergen, 2000); *idem, Verbal Celebrations: Kirill of Turov's Homiletic Rhetoric and its Byzantine Sources* (Wiesbaden: Harrassowitz, 2001); Alexander Nadson, 'Spiritual Writings of St. Cyril of Turaw', http://www.belarusians.co.uk/e-library/002.html; Simon Franklin, *Sermons and Rhetoric of Kievan Rus': Harvard Library of Early Ukrainian Literature*, vol. 5 (Cambridge, Mass.: HURI, 1991).
48. Serhii Plokhy, *The Origins of the Slavic Nations: Premodern Identities in Russia, Ukraine and Belarus* (Cambridge: Cambridge University Press, 2006), p. 94. Spelling of 'Kryvichy' changed.
49. *Ibid.*, p. 95.
50. The so-called *Letopis' krivichansko-polotskoi zemli.*
51. Valer Bulgakov, *Istoriia belorusskogo natsionalizma* (Vilnius: Institute of Belarusian Studies, 2006), p. 299. Tatishchev claims to have studied the lost local chronicles in the eighteenth century. See his *Istoriia Rossiiskaia* (1962), pp. 5, 49, 111, 122.

Chapter 2 Litva

1. L.S. Abestsedarskii, V.N. Pertsov and K.I. Shabunin, *Istoriia belorusskoi SSR*, 2 vols (Minsk: Academy of Sciences, 1961).
2. I.M. Ihnatsenka et al., *Historyia Belaruskai SSR* (Minsk: Navuka i tekhnika, 1972–5), especially vols 1 and 2.
3. Vasil' Bandrachyk, Valiantsina Bialiavina and Halina Kaspiarovich, *Belarusy. Vol. 4. Vytaki i etnichnae razvitstse* (Minsk: Belaruskaia navuka, 2001).
4. Yawhenii (Yawheni) Novik, Henadz' Martsul', Ihar Kachalaw et al., *Historyia Belarusi u dzviukh chastkakh. 1. Ad starazhytnykh chasaw – na liuty 1917 r.* (Minsk: Universitetskae, 2nd edn 2000), pp. 72–3, 39–40, 44–53.
5. Zigmantas Kiaupa et al., *The History of the Baltic Countries* (Tallinn: Avita, 3rd edn 2008), p. 32. The original text refers to 'Russians'.
6. Jerzy Ochmański, *Litewska granica etniczna na wschodzie od epoki plemennej do XVI wieku* (Poznań Mickiewicz University, 1981); Zinkevičius et al., *Where We Come From*, p. 107; Zigmantas Kiaupa, *The History of Lithuania* (Vilnius: Baltos lankos, 2005), p. 125.
7. Aleksander Krawcewicz, *Powstanie Wielkiego Księstwo Litewskiego* (Białystok: Wyższa Szkoła Ekonomiczna w Białymstoku, 2003), p. 76.
8. Zinkevičius et al., *Where We Come From*, p. 109.
9. Tomas Baranauskas, *Lietuvos valstybės ištakos* (Vilnius: Vaga, 2000).
10. Mart Laar (former prime minister of Estonia), *Estonia's Way* (Tallinn: Pegasus, 2006), p. 37.
11. Arnolds Spekke, *History of Latvia: An Outline* (Riga: Jumava, 2006), pp. 112–13.
12. Virgil Krapauskas, *Nationalism and Historiography: The Case of Nineteenth-Century Lithuanian Historicism* (Boulder, Col.: East European Monographs, distributed by Columbia University Press, 2000), p. 4.
13. Kiaupa, *The History of Lithuania*, p. 31.
14. *Ibid.*, p. 24.
15. Kasekamp, *A History of the Baltic States*, p. 17.
16. Kiaupa, *The History of Lithuania*, pp. 28–31.
17. V. Stanley Vardys and Judith B. Sedaitis, *Lithuania: The Rebel Nation* (Boulder, Col.: Westview, 1997), p. 10.
18. Kiaupa, *The History of Lithuania*, p. 38.
19. S.C. Rowell, *Lithuania Ascending: A Pagan Empire within East-Central Europe, 1295–1345* (Cambridge: Cambridge University Press, 1994); Albinas Kuncevičius,

Zigmantas Kiaupa and Jūratė Kiaupienė, *History of Lithuania* (Vilnius Arlila Press, 2000); Kiaupa, *The History of Lithuania*, pp. 39–56.

20. Rowell, *Lithuania Ascending*, p. 20.

21. Serhii Plokhy, *The Origins of the Slavic Nations: Premodern Identities in Russia, Ukraine and Belarus* (Cambridge: Cambridge University Press, 2006), p. 92.

22. Henadz' Sahanovich, *Narys historyi Belarusi ad starazhytnastsi da kantsa XVIII stahoddzia* (Minsk: Entsyklapedyks, 2001), p. 61.

23. Kiaupa, *The History of Lithuania*, p. 21; Zinkevičius et al., *Where We Come From* p. 106.

24. Yahor Novikaw, *Vaennaia historyia belaruskikh zemliaw da kantsa XII stahoddzia* (Minsk: Lohvinaw, 2007). An English extract is available at http://www.deremilitari. org/resources/articles/novikou.htm.

25. Ihnatowski, *Karotki narys historyi Belarusi*, p. 67.

26. *Ibid.*, p. 68.

27. *Ibid.*, p. 73.

28. Kiaupa, *The History of Lithuania*, p. 43.

29. Plokhy, *The Origins of the Slavic Nations*, p. 93.

30. Mitrofan Dovnar-Zapol'skii, *Istoriia Belorussii* (Minsk: Belarus', 2003, from the manuscript never formally published in the 1920s), p. 57.

31. Sahanovich, *Narys historyi Belarusi*, p. 72.

32. Ihnatowski, *Karotki narys historyi Belarusi*, p. 73.

33. Potašenko (ed.), *The Peoples of the Grand Duchy of Lithuania*, p. 14.

34. Kiaupa, *The History of Lithuania*, p. 45.

35. Snyder, *The Reconstruction of Nations*, p. 18.

36. Valentin Sedov, *Slaviane Verkhnego Podneprov'ia i Podvin'ia* (Moscow: Nauka, 1970).

37. Sahanovich, *Narys historyi Belarusi*, p. 17.

38. Edvard Zaikovskii, 'Baltic-Slavic Contacts in the Central and Eastern Belarus in the Middle Ages', *Acta Baltico-Slavica*, 30 (2006), pp. 47–59.

39. Kiaupa, *The History of Lithuania*, p. 18.

40. Serhii Plokhy, *Unmaking Imperial Russia: Mykhailo Hrushevsky and the Writing of Ukrainian History* (Toronto: University of Toronto Press, 2005), pp. 137–9.

41. Zinkevičius et al., *Where We Come From*, p. 110.

42. Mikalai Ermalovich, *Belaruskaia dziarzhava Vialikae kniastva Litowskae* (Minsk: Bellitfond, 2000); *idem, Pa sliadakh adnaho mifa* (Minsk: Navuka i tekhnika, 1991).

43. From President Lukashenka's speech to the Belarusian State University, 'The Historical Choice of Belarus', on 14 March 2003, at www.president.gov.by/press29279. html#doc.

44. Timothy Snyder, *The Reconstruction of Nations: Poland, Ukraine, Lithuania, Belarus, 1569–1999* (New Haven and London: Yale University Press, 2003); Karin Friedrich and Barbara Pendzich (eds), *Citizenship and Identity in a Multinational Commonwealth: Poland-Lithuania in Context, 1550–1772* (Lieden: Brill, 2009); Andrzej Kamiński, *Historia Rzeczypospolitej wielu narodów 1505–1795* (Lublin: Instytut Europy Stodkowo Wschodniej, 2000); Mathias Niendorf, *Das Grossfürstentum Litauen: Studien zur Nationsbildung in der Frühen Neuzeit (1569–1795)* (Wiesbaden: Harrassowitz, 2006).

45. Grigorijus Potašenko (ed.), *The Peoples of the Grand Duchy of Lithuania* (Vilnius: Aidai, 2002).

46. See the discussion at Krawcewicz, *Powstanie Wielkiego Księstwo Litewskiego*, pp. 124–8.

47. Kiaupa, *The History of Lithuania*, p. 46.

48. Jerzy Suchocki, 'Formowanie się i skład narodu politycznego w Wielkim Księstwie Litewskim późnego średniowiecza', *Zapiski Historyczne*, 48:1–2 (1983), pp. 31–78; Rita Trimonienė, 'Lietuvos Didžiosios Kunigaikštystės vidaus konsolidacijos ir «politinės tautos» formavimosi problema', *Lietuvos istorijos studijos*, 2 (1994), pp. 17–34; Jūratė

Kiaupienė, 'Palitychnaia natsyia Vialikaha Kniastva Litowskaha. Litowskaia perspektyva', *Arche*, 9 (2009), pp. 72–85.

49. Potašenko (ed.), *The Peoples of the Grand Duchy of Lithuania*, p. 55.
50. Stefan Gąsiorowski, *Karaimi w koronie i na Litwie w xv–xviii wieku* (Kraków: Austeria, 2008).
51. Potašenko (ed.), *The Peoples of the Grand Duchy of Lithuania*, pp. 62–3.
52. Snyder, *The Reconstruction of Nations*, p. 19.
53. Latyshonak, *Natsyial'nas'ts' – Belarus*, p. 12.

Chapter 3 Ruthenia

1. See the critique by Piotr Rudkowski of Zianon Paz'niak and others' view of the Grand Duchy in his *Pawstan'ne Belarusi*, pp. 79–91, at p. 87.
2. Viachaslaw Chamiarytski, *Belaruskiia letapisy yak pomniki litaratury (Uzniknenne i litaraturnaia historyia pershykh zvodaw)* (Minsk: Navuka i tekhnika, 1969).
3. Oleg Łatyszonek (Aleh Latyshonak), 'From White Russia to Belarus', *Annus Albaruthenicus*, 5 (2004), pp. 13–47, at pp. 33, available at http://kamunikat.net.iig.pl/pdf/annus/annus2004.pdf.
4. Potašenko (ed.), *The Peoples of the Grand Duchy of Lithuania*, p. 35.
5. *Ibid.*, p. 36.
6. Łatyszonek (Latyshonak), 'From White Russia to Belarus', pp. 33, 42.
7. Kasekamp, *A History of the Baltic States*, p. 28.
8. Christian Stang, *Die Westrussiche Kanzleisprache des Grossfürstentums Litauen* (Oslo: Norske Videnskaps-Akademi, 1935).
9. Rudkowski, *Pawstan'ne Belarusi*, pp. 89–90.
10. Author's conversation with Jan Fellerer of the Faculty of Medieval and Modern Languages, Oxford, 31 August 2010.
11. *Ibid.*
12. Barbara Skinner, *The Western Front of the Eastern Church: Uniate and Orthodox Conflict in Eighteenth-Century Poland, Belarus, Ukraine and Russia* (DeKalb, Ill.: Northern Illinois University Press, 2009), p. 19.
13. Sahanovich, *Narys historyi Belarusi*, pp. 172–3.
14. Potašenko (ed.), *The Peoples of the Grand Duchy of Lithuania*, p. 33.
15. Author's conversation with Fellerer, 31 August 2010.
16. Stanislaw Akinc'hyts, *Zalaty vek Belarusi*, at http://knihi.com/bel/zalaty.html, no date of publication.
17. On the spread of Polish in this period, see Antoine Martel, *La langue polonaise dans les pays ruthènes, Ukraine et Russie Blanche, 1569–1667* (Lille, 1938).
18. Jakub Zejmis, 'Belorussian National Historiography and the Grand Duchy of Lithuania as a Belorussian State', *Zeitschrift für Ostmitteleuropa-Forschung*, 48:3 (1999), pp. 383–96.
19. Skinner, *The Western Front of the Eastern Church*, p. 18.
20. Sahanovich, *Narys historyi Belarusi*, p. 233.
21. Andrei Katliarchuk, 'Pravaslawe w Vialikim Kniastve Litowskim i pratestanty Belarusi', available at www.belreform.org/katlarchuk_prat_i_pravasl.php.
22. Diarmaid MacCulloch, *A History of Christianity: The First Three Thousand Years* (London: Allen Lane, 2009), pp. 527, 642–3.
23. Katliarchuk, 'Pravaslawe w Vialikim Kniastve Litowskim i pratestanty Belarusi'.
24. Skinner, *The Western Front of the Eastern Church*, p. 28.
25. *Ibid.*, p. 30.
26. *Ibid.*, pp. 30–1.
27. Lavrentii Abetsedarskii, *Belorusy v Moskve XVII v.: iz istorii russko-belorusskikh sviazei* (Minsk: Belgosuniversiteta, 1957).
28. Plokhy, *The Origins of the Slavic Nations*, pp. 360–1.

29. Vital'd Biamatski, 'Pawstan'na Khmialnitskaha: Vaennyia dzeian'ni w Litwe w 1648–1649 hh.', *Arche*, 1–2 (2008).

30. Łatyszonek (Latyshanak), 'From White Russia to Belarus', p. 43.

31. Łatyshonak (Łatyszonek), 'Chas belaruskikh palkownikaw 1654–1667. Belaruski palkownik Kanstantsin Paklonski', in *Natsyial'nas'ts' – Belarus*, pp. 237–48; Sahanovich, *Neviadomaia vaina*, pp. 28ff.

32. Andrej Kotljarchuk, *In the Shadows of Poland and Russia: The Grand Duchy of Lithuania and Sweden in the European Crisis of the mid-17th Century* (Södertörn Studies in History 3, 2006), p. 196.

33. Łatyszonek (Latyshanak), 'From White Russia to Belarus', p. 46.

34. Plokhy, *The Origins of the Slavic Nations*, pp. 327–8.

35. Yurii Lypa, *Chornomorsika doktryna* (Geneva, 1947), p. 14 (quoting Lypynskyi in *Ukraina na perelomi*).

36. Henadz' Sahanovich, *Neviadomaia vaina: 1654–1667* (Minsk: Navuka i tekhnika, 1995).

37. Łatyszonek (Latyshanak), 'From White Russia to Belarus', p. 46.

38. Kiaupa, *The History of Lithuania*, p. 142.

39. Andres Kasekamp, *A History of the Baltic States* (Houndmills: Palgrave/Macmillan, 2010), p. 50; Sahanovich, *Neviadomaia vaina*, pp. 139–40.

40. Kotljarchuk, *In the Shadows of Poland and Russia*, p. 269.

41. *Ibid.*, p. 279.

42. Sahanovich, *Narys historyi Belarusi*, p. 282.

43. Katliarchuk (Kotljarchuk), 'Pravaslawe w Vialikim Kniastve Litowskim i pratestanty Belarusi'.

44. Skinner, *The Western Front of the Eastern Church*, p. 34.

45. *Ibid.*, p. 36.

46. Plokhy, *The Origins of the Slavic Nations*, pp. 186, 331, 356–9.

Chapter 4 Uniate-land

1. Plokhy, *The Origins of the Slavic Nations*, p. 315.

2. Father Alexander Nadson, 'The Belarusian Greek Catholic (Uniate) Church: A Short History', written in 1999, at www.belarusians.co.uk/catholic/history-church.html.

3. Barbara Skinner, *The Western Front of the Eastern Church: Uniate and Orthodox Conflict in 18th-Century Poland, Ukraine, Belarus and Russia* (DeKalb, Ill.: Northern Illinois University Press, 2009), p. 9.

4. *Ibid.*, p. 45.

5. *Ibid.*, pp. 223–4.

6. *Ibid.*, p. 100.

7. Plokhy, *The Origins of the Slavic Nations*, pp. 312–13.

8. Aliaksandr Ts'vikevich, 'Zapadno-russizm'. *Narysy z historyi hramadzkai mys'li na Belarusi w XIX i pachatku XX v.* (Minsk: Navuka i tekhnika, 1993), p. 8.

9. Skinner, *The Western Front of the Eastern Church*, pp. 40–1.

10. *Ibid.*, p. 65.

11. *Ibid.*, pp. 38–9.

12. *Ibid.*, pp. 66–7.

13. *Ibid.*, p. 66.

14. *Ibid.*, p. 48.

15. Jerzy Turonek, 'Between Byzantium and Rome: On the Cause of Religious and Cultural Differences in Belarus', *International Journal of Sociology*, 31; 3 (Fall 2001), pp. 46–61, at p. 51 cites figures of 15 per cent Roman Catholic and 70 per cent Uniate. Sahanovich, *Narys historyi Belarusi*, p. 404, gives figures of 18 per cent Roman Catholic and 75 per cent Uniate.

16. Sahanovich, *Narys historyi Belarusi*, p. 294.

17. Author's conversation with Fellerer, 31 August 2010.
18. Snyder, *The Reconstruction of Nations*, p. 45 and p. 48, Table 1.
19. Skinner, *The Western Front of the Eastern Church*, p. 49.
20. *Ibid.*, p. 227.
21. See Priest Aleksandr Romanchuk, 'Vossoedinenie uniatov i istoricheskie sud'by be-lorusskogo naroda', http://www.pravoslavie.ru/arhiv/050513111111, dated 13 May 2005, accessed 12 December 2006; V.A. Mel'nik, *Respublika Belarus': vlast', politika, idelogiia: Praktecheskaia politologiia* (Minsk: Tesei, 2000), p. 183.
22. E.A. Vernikovskaia, 'Rol' unii v etnokul'turnom razvitii Belorussii kontsa XVI–XVII v. v sovremennoi belorusskoi istoriografii', in B.N. Floria (ed.), *Belorussiia i Ukraina: Istoriia i kul'tura. Ezhegodnik 2003* (Moscow: Nauka, 2003), pp. 254–81.
23. Dennis J. Dunn, *The Catholic Church and Russia: Popes, Patriarchs, Tsars and Com-missars* (Farnham: Ashgate, 2004), p. 36, records Potemkin trying to persuade Cath-erine that even an independent local Uniate Church would be no real threat.
24. Skinner, *The Western Front of the Eastern Church*, p. 42.
25. Skinner, *The Western Front of the Eastern Church*, p. 179.
26. *Ibid.*, pp. 211–12; Zakhar Shybeka, *Narys historyi Belarusi (1795–2002)* (Minsk: Entsyklapedyks, 2003), pp. 17–18.
27. Shybeka, *Narys historyi Belarusi (1795–2002)*, p. 60.
28. James T. Flynn, 'The Uniate Church in Bielorussia: A Case of Nation-Building?' in J. Niessen (ed.), *Religious Compromise, Political Salvation: The Greek Catholic Church and Nation-Building in Eastern Europe* (University of Pittsburgh, Carl Beck Papers in Russian and East European Studies, no. 1003, 1993), pp. 27–46.
29. Sviatlana Marozava, *Uniiatskaia tsarkva w etnakul'turnym razvitstsi Belarusi (1596–1839 hady)* (Hrodna: University of Yanka Kupala, 2001), pp. 257, 52, 70. See also M.O. Bich and P.A. Loika (eds), *Z historyi uniiatstva w Belarusi (da 400–hoddzia Brestskai unii)* (Minsk: Ekaperspektyva, Institute of History, 1996), and P.A. Loika, *History of Belarus in the 16th–18th Centuries*, a seventh-grade textbook which provides a posi-tive evaluation of the 1596 Union.
30. Simon Sebag Montefiore, *Prince of Princes: The Life of Potemkin* (London: Pheonix, 2000), pp. 524–6; paperback edn, pp. 473–4.
31. Latyshonak and Miranovich, *Historyia Belarusi*, p. 80.

Chapter 5 Belarus Begins

1. Aleh Latyshonak and Yawhen Miranovich, *Historyia Belarusi ad siariadziny XVIII st. da pachatku XXI st.* (Vilnius: Institute of Belarusian Studies, 2010), p. 69.
2. Miroslav Hroch, *Social Preconditions of a National Revival in Europe* (Cambridge: Cambridge University Press, 1985).
3. Neither Vakar, *Belorussia: The Making of a Nation*, nor Zaprudnik, *Belarus: At a Cross-roads in History*, mentions west-Russism at all.
4. Aliaksandr Ts'vikevich, 'Zapadno-russizm.' *Narysy z historyi hramadzkai mys'li na Be-larusi w XIX i pachatku XX v.* (1929; Minsk: Navuka i tekhnika, 1993), p. 54.
5. Ales' Smalianchuk, 'Belaruski natsyianl'ny rukh: ad "kul'tutrnaha nakaplennia" da barats'by za dziarzhawnats'. Pachatak XIX st. – 1918 h.', www.autary.iig.pl/smalan-chuk/artykuly/ruch/baracba.htm.
6. Egidijus Aleksandravičius and Antanas Kulakauskas, *Cary Valdžioje: XIX amžiaus Lietuva* (Vilnius: Baltos lankos, 1996); L. Lаučkaitė, 'The Duality of Lithuanian Art', in *idem, Art in Vilnius, 1900–1915* (Vilnius: Baltos lankos, 2008), pp. 52–61.
7. Jerzy Turonek, 'Between Byzantium and Rome: On the Cause of Religious and Cultural Differences in Belarus', *International Journal of Sociology*, 31: 3 (Fall 2001), pp. 46–61, at p. 52.
8. Shybeka, *Narys historyi Belarusi (1795–2002)*, pp. 60–1.
9. Nadson, 'The Belarusian Greek Catholic *Church*'; Romanchuk, 'Vossoedinenie Uniatov'.

10. The standard Uniate interpretation is Wasyl Lencyk, *The Eastern Catholic Church and Tsar Nicholas I* (Rome and New York: Ukrainian Catholic University Press, 1966). Cf. Theodore Weeks, 'Between Rome and Tsargrad: The Uniate Church in Imperial Russia', in Robert P. Geraci and Michael Khodarkovsky (eds), *Of Religion and Empire: Missions, Conversion and Tolerance in Tsarist Russia* (Ithaca, NY: Cornell University Press, 2001), pp. 70–91.

11. Author's email conversation with the historian Sviatlana Marozava, 3 March 2009.

12. Laučkaitė, *Art in Vilnius, 1900–1915*, p. 90.

13. In the sense that the authorities politicised and persecuted Catholic identity after 1863.

14. Latyshonak and Miranovich, *Historyia Belarusi*, p. 123.

15. Turonek, 'Between Byzantium and Rome', pp. 55–6.

16. Yury Turonak (Jerzy Turonek), *Madernaia historyia Belarusi* (Vilnius: Institute of Belarusian Studies, 2006), p. 436. Paval Tereshkovich, *Etnicheskaia istoriia Belarusi XIX–nachala XX v*, p. 184, cites a much lower figure for conversions, between 30,000 and 62,000. See also V.V. Yanowskaia, *Khrystsiianskaia tsarkva w Belarusi w 1863–1914 hh.* (Minsk BDU, 2002).

17. Yaroslav Hrytsak, *Prorok u svoi vitchyzni: Franko ta yoho spil'nota* (Kiev: Krytyka, 2006), p. 137.

18. Tserashkovich, 'Social Conditions of National Revival of the Peoples in the East of Central Eastern Europe', p. 82.

19. *Ibid.*, pp. 80–1; Jan Molenda, *Chłopi, narod, niepodległość: kształtowanie się postaw narodowych i obywatelskich chłopów w Galicji i Królestwie Polskim w przededniu odrodzenia Polski* (Warsaw: Neriton/Institute of History PAN, 1999).

20. A Jesuit college was founded in 1570 and granted a charter as the Academia et Universitas Vilensis Societatis Jesu in 1579.

21. Valer Bulgakov (Bulhakaw), *Istoriia belorusskogo natsionalizma* (Vilnius: Institute of Belarusian Studies, 2006), p. 111.

22. *Ibid.*

23. On the 'Polish Project', see *ibid.*, pp. 109–40.

24. *Ibid.*, p. 118.

25. Aleksander Rypiński, *Białoruś: Kilka słów o poezji prostego ludu tej naszej polskiej prowincji i o jego śpiewie, tańcach* (Paris, 1840).

26. Latyshonak, *Natsyial'nas'ts' – Belarus*, p. 403.

27. Shybeka, *Narys historyi Belarusi (1795–2002)*, p. 34.

28. Ts'vikevich, *'Zapadno-russizm'*, p. 151.

29. Anne Applebaum, *Between East and West: Across the Borderlands of Europe* (London: Papermac, 1994), pp. 128–39.

30. Bulgakov, *Istoriia belorusskogo natsionalizma*, p. 122.

31. *Ibid.*, p. 146.

32. *Ibid.*, p. 131.

33. Sviatlana Kul'-Sialverstava, *Belarus' na miazhy stahoddziaw i kul'tur: Farmavanne kul'tury Novaha chasu na belaruskikh zemliakh (druhaia palova XVII st.–1820-ia h.)* (Minsk BDU, 2000).

34. Alexei Miller and Oksana Ostapchuk, 'The Latin and Cyrillic Alphabets in Ukrainian National Discourse and in the Language Policy of Empires', in Georgii Kasianov and Phillip Ther (eds), *A Laboratory of Transnational History: Ukraine and Recent Ukrainian Historiography* (Budapest: Central European Press, 2009). See also S. Tokt', 'Latinitsa ili kirilitsa: problems vybora alfavita v beloruskom natsional'nom dvizhenii vo vtoroi polovine XIX–nachale XX veka', *Ab Imperio*, 2 (2005), pp. 297–319.

35. Miller and Ostapchuk, 'The Latin and Cyrillic Alphabets', p. 182.

36. *Ibid.*, p. 187.

37. John Stanley, 'The Birth of a Nation: The January Insurrection and the Belorussian National Movement', in Béla K. Király (ed.), *The Crucial Decade: East Central*

European Society and National Defense, 1859-70 (Boulder, Col.: Brooklyn College Press, 1984), pp. 185–202.

38. Jan Zaprudnik and Thomas E. Bird, *The 1863 Uprising in Byelorussia: 'Peasants' Truth' and 'Letters from beneath the Gallows'* (New York: The Byelorussian Institute of Arts and Sciences/The Krecheuski Foundation, 1980). The originals of *Muzhytskaia prawda* were published in *K. Kalinovskii: Iz pechatnogo i rukopisnogo naslediia* (Minsk: Belarus, 1988).

39. Bulgakov, *Istoriia belorusskogo natsionalizma*, pp. 137, 138. See also Tereshkovich, *Etnicheskaia istoriia Belarusi XIX–nachala XX v*, p. 81, and Vakar, *Belorussia: The Making of a Nation*, p. 72.

40. Anatol' Astapenka, 'Mif pra Kastusia Kalinowskaha', *Arche*, December 2008, http://arche.by/by/9/30/222/.

41. Kastus Kalinowski, *Listy z-pad shybenicy. Za nashu volnasc: Teksty. Dokumenty* (Minsk, 1999), p. 42; Zaprudnik and Bird, *The 1863 Uprising in Byelorussia*, p. 64.

42. Latyshonak and Miranovich, *Historyia Belarusi*, p. 84.

43. Bulgakov, *Istoriia belorusskogo natsionalizma*, p. 129.

44. M.O. Koialovich (the Russian version of his name), *Chteniia po istorii zapadnoi Rossii* (Minsk: Belaruskaia Entsyklapdeyia, 2006); Valerii Cherepitsa, *Mikhail Osipovich Koialovich. Istoriia zhizni i tvorchestva* (Hrodna: Hrodna State University, 1998); O.E. Maiorova, 'War as Peace: The Trope of War in Russian Nationalist Discourse during the Polish Uprising of 1863', *Kritika*, 6: 3 (summer 2005), pp. 501–34.

45. Ales' Smalianchuk, 'Litvinstva, zakhodnerusizm i belaruskaia idieia: XIX–pachatak XX st', http://kamunikant.org/7983.html, accessed 5 June 2009.

46. Bulgakov, *Istoriia belorusskogo natsionalizma*, p. 149, n. 6.

47. Ts'vikevich, *'Zapadno-russizm'*, p. 148.

48. Mikhail Koialovich, *Istoriia vossoedineniia zapadnorusskikh Uniatov starykh vremen* (St Petersburg, 1873).

49. Bulgakov, *Istoriia belorusskogo natsionalizma*, p. 154.

50. Ts'vikevich, *'Zapadno-russizm'*, pp. 144, 172, 51 and 161. Kaialovich's call was originally in *Den'*, 39 (1863).

51. Ts'vikevich, *'Zapadno-russizm'*, p. 176.

52. Quoted in *ibid.*, p. 223. Capitals in original.

53. Pavel Bobrovskii, *Otviet na kritiku g. Koialovicha, po povodu sochineniia 'Russkaia greko-uniatskaia tserkov' pri Aleksandrie I'* (St Petersburg, 1890).

54. Bulgakov, *Istoriia belorusskogo natsionalizma*, pp. 158–9.

55. Ts'vikevich, *'Zapadno-russizm'*, p. 170.

56. Bulgakov, *Istoriia belorusskogo natsionalizma*, p. 144; Aksakov in *Den'*, June 1863.

57. Quoted in Ts'vikevich, *'Zapadno-russizm'*, p. 143.

58. F. Dobryanski, *Staraja i Novaja Vilna* (Vilna: Typografia A.G. Syrkina, 1904), pp. 10–11; as quoted in Laimonas Briedis, *Vilnius: City of Strangers* (Vilnius: Baltos lankos, 2008), p. 146.

59. Latyshonak, *Natsyial'nas'ts' – Belarus*, pp. 420–36, which includes the 'Tales'.

60. O. Turchinovich, *Obozrenie istorii Belorussii s drevneishikh vremen* (St Petersburg, 1857); Latyshonak, *Natsyial'nas'ts' – Belarus*, pp. 354, 360.

61. Mikhail Dolbilov, 'Russification and the Bureaucratic Mind in the Russian Empire's Northwestern Region in the 1860s', *Kritika*, 5: 2 (spring 2004), pp. 245–71; *idem*, 'The Stereotype of the Pole in Imperial Policy: The "Depolonization" of the Northwestern Region in the 1860s', *Russian Studies in History*, 44: 2 (Fall 2005), pp. 44–88; Alexei Miller, 'Ukrainophilia', *ibid.*, pp. 30–43.

62. Darius Staliūnas, *Making Russians: Meaning and Practice of Russification in Lithuania and Belarus after 1863* (Amsterdam and New York: Rodopi, 2007), p. 47.

63. Ts'vikevich, *'Zapadno-russizm'*, p. 48.

64. Staliūnas, *Making Russians*, p. 52.

65. Dmitrii Karev, *Belorusskaia i ukrainskaia istoriografiia kontsa XVIII–nachala 20-kh gg. XX v. v protsesse genezisa i razvitiia national'nogo istoricheskogo soznaniia belorusov i ukraintsev* (Vilnius: European Humanitarian University, 2007), pp. 182, 191, 197; Laima Laučkaitė, *Art in Vilnius, 1900–1915* (Vilnius: Baltos lankos, 2008), p. 100.

66. Ts'vikevich, 'Zapadno-russizm', p. 168.

67. Latyshonak, *Natsyial'nas'ts' – Belarus*, pp. 439–40.

68. Ts'vikevich, 'Zapadno-russizm', p. 283.

69. *Ibid.*, p. 116

70. *Ibid.*, pp. 115–16.

71. Theodore R. Weeks, 'Russification: Word and Practice, 1863–1914', *American Philosophical Society Proceedings*, 148: 4 (December 2004), pp. 471–89, at p. 478.

72. Bulgakov, *Istoriia belorusskogo natsionalizma*, p. 148.

73. Ivan Nosovich (Nasovich), *Slovar' belorusskogo narechiia* (St Petersburg, 1870).

74. Bulgakov, *Istoriia belorusskogo natsionalizma*, p. 157.

75. Ts'vikevich, 'Zapadno-russizm', p. 291.

76. Author's interview with Andrei Dyn'ko, 7 October 2007.

77. Ts'vikevich, 'Zapadno-russizm', p. 300.

78. *Ibid.*, p. 309.

79. *Ibid.*, p. 307.

80. M. Dolbilov and A. Miller (eds), *Historia Rossica: Zapadnye okrainy rossiiskoi imperii* (Moscow: New Literary Obozrenie, 2006), p. 369.

81. Latyshonak and Miranovich, *Historyia Belarusi*, p. 125.

82. Dolbilov and Miller (eds), *Historia Rossica*, p. 390.

83. Ts'vikevich, 'Zapadno-russizm', p. 310.

84. Shybeka, *Narys historyi Belarusi (1795–2002)*, p. 157.

85. Ts'vikevich, 'Zapadno-russizm', p. 338.

86. *Ibid.*, p. 335.

87. Bulgakov, *Istoriia belorusskogo natsionalizma*, p. 179.

88. Ts'vikevich, 'Zapadno-russizm', p. 199.

89. *Ibid.*, p. 337.

90. *Ibid.*, p. 219.

91. Pavel Tereshkovich, *Etnicheskaia istoriia Belarusi XIX–nachala XX v.: v kontekste Tsentral'no-Vostochnoi Evropy* (Minsk: BGU, 2004), pp. 142, 144.

92. Bulgakov, *Istoriia belorusskogo natsionalizma*, p. 41.

93. Ts'vikevich, 'Zapadno-russizm', pp. 233, 319.

94. *Ibid.*, p. 170.

95. See also Ales' Smalianchuk, *Pamizh 'kraevastsiu' i natsyianal'nai idziai: Pol'ski rukh na belaruskikh i litowskikh zemliakh. 1864–lity 1917 h* (Hrodna: Hrodna State University, 2001).

96. Snyder, *The Reconstruction of Nations*, pp. 54–5.

97. Tserashkovich, 'Social Conditions of National Revival of the Peoples in the East of Central Eastern Europe', p. 80.

98. Bulgakov, *Istoriia belorusskogo natsionalizma*, p. 149.

99. Smalianchuk, 'Belaruski natsyianal'ny rukh i kraievaia idieia', *Bialoruskie zeszyty historyczne* (Bialystock), 14 (2000), pp. 105–14, at p. 109.

100. Laučkaitė, *Art in Vilnius, 1900–1915*, p. 108.

101. Shybeka, *Narys historyi Belarusi (1795–2002)*, p. 158.

102. Michał Romer (Mykolas Römeris), *Litwa: studyum o odrodzeniu narodu litewskiego*, (Lviv: Polskie towarzystwo nakladowe, 1908).

103. Vital'd Zhukowski, *Paliaki i belarusy* (Vilna, 1907); Shybeka, *Narys historyi Belarusi (1795–2002)*, p. 158.

104. Opinion in *Vecherniaia gazeta*, 1 (1912) quoted in Smalianchuk, 'Belaruski natsyianal'ny rukh i kraievaia idieia', p. 108.

105. Ales' Smalianchuk, 'Belaruski rukh pachatku XX st. i ideia palitychnai natsyi', http://autary.iig.pl/smalanchuk/artykuly/ruch/krajovasc.htm, accessed 17 July 2007.

106. Mikhal Romer, 'Pra nash krai', *Kurier krajowy*, 50 (1913); Smalianchuk, *Pamizh 'kraevastsiu' i natsyianal'nai idziai*, pp. 253–4.

107. Smalianchuk, *Pamizh 'kraevastsiu' i natsyianal'nai idziai*, pp. 253–4.

108. *Ibid.*, p. 255.

109. Dolbilov and Miller (eds), *Historia Rossica*, p. 356; Egidijus Aleksandravičius, 'Political Goals of Lithuanians, 1863–1918', *Journal of Baltic Studies*, 23:3 (autumn 1992), pp. 27–38; and Shybeka, *Narys historyi Belarusi (1795–2002)*, p. 148 all give different figures.

110. Ts'vikevich, *'Zapadno-russizm'*, p. 304.

111. Smalianchuk, *Pamizh 'kraevastsiu' i natsyianal'nai idziai*, p. 121.

112. *Ibid.*, p. 121.

113. *Ibid.*, p. 363.

114. Ales' Smalianchuk, 'Belaruski rukh pachatku XX st. i ideia palitychnai natsyi'.

115. Smalianchuk, *Pamizh 'kraevastsiu' i natsyianal'nai idziai*, p. 122.

116. Dovid Katz, *Lithuanian Jewish Culture* (Vilnius: Baltos Lankos, 2004); Rūta Puišytė and Darius Staliūnas, *Žydų gyvenimas Lietuvoje/Jewish Life in Lithuania* (Vilnius: Leidykla Zara, 2008).

117. Gerrad Silvain and Henri Minczeles (eds), *Yiddishland* (Corte Madera, Cal.: Gingko Press, 1999).

118. Eli Lederhendler, *The Road to Modern Jewish Politics: Political Tradition and Political Reconstruction in the Jewish Community of Tsarist Russia* (Oxford: Oxford University Press, 1989); *idem*, 'Did Russian Jewry Exist Prior to 1917?' in Yaacov Ro'i (ed.), *Jews and Jewish Life in Russia and the Soviet Union* (Portland: Frank Cass, 1995), pp. 15–27.

119. Laimonas Briedis, *Vilnius: City of Strangers* (Vilnius: Baltos lankos, 2008), p. 130.

120. Benjamin Harshav, *Marc Chagall and the Lost Jewish World: The Nature of Chagall's Art and Iconography* (New York: Rizzoli, 2006), p. 11.

121. Briedis, *Vilnius: City of Strangers*, pp. 207–8.

122. Harshav, *Marc Chagall and the Lost Jewish World*, p. 11.

123. Jackie Wullschlager, *Chagall: Love and Exile* (London: Allen Lane, 2008), p. 9.

124. Alvydas Nikžentaitis, Stefan Schreiner and Darius Staliūnas (eds), *The Vanished World of Lithuanian Jews* (Amsterdam and New York: Rodopi, 2004).

125. Paval Kas'tsiukevich, *Dushpastarskiia spatkan'ni dlia diachnikaw* (Minsk: Nasha Niva, 2008).

126. Aliaksandar Smalianchuk, 'Belarusian National Idea in the Early Twentieth Century', *Annus Albaruthenicus*, 2007, pp. 55–68, available at http://kamunikat.net.iig.pl/pdf/annus/annus2007.pdf.

127. Zakhar Shybeka, *Narys historyi Belarusi (1795–2002)* (Minsk: Entsyklapedyks, 2003), pp. 135–6, 139–40.

128. Smalianchuk, *Belarusian National Idea in the Early Twentieth Century*, p. 57. First quotation's from the 1906 programme of the BSH.

129. Smalianchuk, *Belarusian National Idea in the Early Twentieth Century*, p. 62.

130. Alexander Nadson, 'Princess Magdalena Radzivill and the Greek Catholic Church in Belarus', 2004, http://www.belarusians.co.uk/e-library/001.html.

131. A. Ryttikh (Ryttykh), *Etnograficheskaia karta evropeiskoi Rossii* (St Petersburg, 1875).

132. Ye Karski, *Belorusy* (Warsaw, 1903); Karski, *Etnograficheskaia karta belorusskogo plemeni: Trudy Komissii po izucheniiu plemennogo sostava naseleniia Rossii* (Petrograd, 1917).

133. Potašenko (ed.), *The Peoples of the Grand Duchy of Lithuania*, p. 10.

134. Shybeka, *Narys historyi Belarusi (1795–2002)*, p. 160.

135. Smalianchuk, *Belarusian National Idea in the Early Twentieth Century*, p. 59, quoting Shybeka, *Narys historyi Belarusi (1795–2002)*, p. 160.

136. Łatyszonek, 'Belarusian Nationalism and the Clash of Civilizations', p. 65, quoting Uladzimir Samoila in 1929. Retranslated from the Belarusian version in *Arche*, 7–8 (2007).

137. Smalianchuk, *Belarusian National Idea in the Early Twentieth Century*, pp. 59–60.

138. *Ibid.*, p. 57.

139. Łatyszonek, 'Belarusian Nationalism and the Clash of Civilizations', p. 65.

140. Briedis, *Vilnius: City of Strangers*, p. 150.

141. Bulgakov, *Istoriia belorusskogo natsionalizma*, pp. 270–310; Pavel Tserashkovich, 'Social Conditions of National Revival of the Peoples in the East of Central Eastern Europe in the 19th–early 20th Centuries (Belarusians, Ukrainians, Lithuanians, Latvians, Estonians)', *Annus Albaruthenicus*, 2007, pp. 69–110, at http://kamunikat.net.iig.pl/pdf/annus/annus2007.pdf; Pavel Tereshkovich, *Etnicheskaia istoriia Belarusi XIX–nachala XX v.: v kontekste Tsentral'no-Vostochnoi Evropy* (Minsk: BGU, 2004); Ryszard Radzik, *Między zbiorowością etniczną a wspólnotą narodową: Białorusini na tle przemian narodowych w Europie Środkowo-Wschodniej XIX stulecia* (Lublin: UMCS, 2000).

142. Barbara Törnquist-Plewa, 'Language and Belarusian Nation-Building in the Light of Modern Theories of Nationalism', *Annus Albaruthenicus*, 2005, pp. 109–18, at p. 110, at http://kamunikat.net.iig.pl/pdf/annus/annus2005.pdf.

143. *Ibid.*, p. 111.

144. Alexei Miller, *The Romanov Empire and Nationalism* (Budapest: Central European University Press, 2008), p. 25.

145. Cf. Theodore Weeks, '"Us" or "Them"? Belarusians and Official Russia, 1863–1914', *Nationalities Papers*, 31: 2 (June 2003); Witold Rodkiewicz, *Russian Nationality Policy in the Western Provinces of the Empire (1863–1905)* (Lublin: Scientific Society of Lublin, 1998).

146. Steven L. Guthier, 'The Belorussians: National Identification and Assimilation, 1897–1970', *Soviet Studies*, 26: 1 and 2 (January and April 1977), pp. 37–61, 270–83.

147. Tserashkovich, 'Social Conditions of National Revival of the Peoples in the East of Central Eastern Europe', pp. 84–5.

148. *Ibid.*, p. 91.

149. *Ibid.*, p. 86.

150. Smalianchuk, *Belarusian National Idea in the Early Twentieth Century*, p. 59.

151. Tserashkovich, 'Social Conditions of National Revival of the Peoples in the East of Central Eastern Europe', p. 93.

152. Timothy Snyder, *The Reconstruction of Nations: Poland, Ukraine, Lithuania, Belarus, 1569–1999* (New Haven and London: Yale University Press, 2003), pp. 42–9.

153. Tserashkovich, 'Social Conditions of National Revival of the Peoples in the East of Central Eastern Europe', p. 88.

154. Bulgakov, *Istoriia belorusskogo natsionalizma*, p. 298. See also Serhy Yekelchyk, 'Nationalisme ukrainien, biélorusse et slovaque', in Chantal Delsol and Michel Maslowski (eds), *Histoire des idées politiques de l'Europe centrale* (Paris: Presses Universitaires de France, 1998).

155. Tserashkovich, 'Social Conditions of National Revival of the Peoples in the East of Central Eastern Europe', p. 74, quoting a dissertation by U.A. Lobach.

156. Bulgakov, *Istoriia belorusskogo natsionalizma*, p. 279.

157. *Ibid.*, pp. 313 and 314.

158. *Ibid.*, pp. 308–9.

Chapter 6 Belarus Begins Again: The Traumatic Twentieth Century

1. Smalianchuk, *Belarusian National Idea in the Early Twentieth Century*, p. 66.

2. Yury Turonak, 'Nezhadanaia respublika', in his *Madernaia historyia Belarusi*, pp. 66–80.

3. Briedis, *Vilnius: City of Strangers*, pp. 166–7.
4. Dolbilov and Miller (eds), *Historia Rossica: Zapadnye okrainy rossiiskoi imperii*, p. 415.
5. Tomas Balkelis, *The Making of Modern Lithuania* (London: Routledge, 2009), p. 57.
6. Smalianchuk, 'Natsyia w poshukakh historyi', www.kamunikat.org/7984.html and www.kamunikat.org/7985.html, 5 February 2009, accessed 3 June 2009.
7. Smalianchuk, 'Belaruski natsyianal'ny rukh i kraievaia idieia', p. 114.
8. Smalianchuk, *Belarusian National Idea in the Early Twentieth Century*, p. 64.
9. Smalianchuk, 'Natsyia w poshukakh historyi'.
10. Shybeka, *Narys historyi Belarusi (1795–2002)*, p. 182.
11. *Ibid.*, p. 184.
12. Tereshkovich, *Etnicheskaia istoriia Belarusi XIX–nachala XX v*, pp. 181–2.
13. Shybeka, *Narys historyi Belarusi (1795–2002)*, p. 188.
14. Smalianchuk, 'Natsyia w poshukakh historyi'.
15. Shybeka, *Narys historyi Belarusi (1795–2002)*, pp. 200–1.
16. *Ibid.*, p. 206.
17. Oleg Łatyszonak, *Białoruskie formacje wojskowe 1917–1923* (Białystok: BTN, 1995), p. 94, as quoted in Jerzy Borzęcki, *The Soviet-Polish Peace of 1921 and the Creation of Inter-War Europe* (New Haven and London: Yale University Press, 2008), p. 321, n. 63.
18. Shybeka, *Narys historyi Belarusi (1795–2002)*, p. 224.
19. Borzęcki, *The Soviet-Polish Peace of 1921*, p. 33.
20. *Ibid.*, p. 364, n. 12, and p. 157.
21. Shybeka, *Narys historyi Belarusi (1795–2002)*, p. 236.
22. See www.radabnr.org.
23. See the roundtable discussion by Lukashenka's official historians, 'BNR: poverkh bar'erov', *Sovetskaia Belorussiia: Belarus' segodnia*, 27 March 2008; www.sb.by/print/post/64919; and David Marples, 'Historians Debate 1918 Declaration of Independence in Belarus', *Eurasia Daily Monitor*, 5:58 (27 March 2008).
24. Shybeka, *Narys historyi Belarusi (1795–2002)*, p. 207.
25. As quoted in Borzęcki, *The Soviet-Polish Peace of 1921*, p. 15.
26. Shybeka, *Narys historyi Belarusi (1795–2002)*, p. 222.
27. Borzęcki, *The Soviet-Polish Peace of 1921*, pp. 29–30.
28. *Ibid.*, p. 321, n. 64.
29. See *ibid.*, pp. 134–5 for Polish discussions on the future of Minsk.
30. *Ibid.*, p. 58 and p. 330, n.77.
31. *Ibid.*, pp. 330–1, n. 78.
32. *Ibid.*, p. 132.
33. *Ibid.*, p. 46; Shybeka, *Narys historyi Belarusi (1795–2002)*, p. 215.
34. Daina Bleiere et al., *History of Latvia: The 20th Century* (Riga: Jumava, 2006), p. 183.
35. Shybeka, *Narys historyi Belarusi (1795–2002)*, p. 259.
36. *Ibid.*
37. *Ibid.*, p. 260.
38. *Ibid.*, p. 261.
39. Andrei Katliarchuk, 'Pradmova', *Arche*, 9 (2009), special issue entitled 'Lithuania (Litva) and Belarus: A Thousand Years Together', pp. 5–8, at p. 5.
40. See Yawhen Miranovich, *Belarusy w Pol'shchy (1918–1949)* (Vilnius: Institute of Belarusian Studies, 2010).
41. Turonek, 'Between Byzantium and Rome', pp. 58–9.
42. Shybeka, *Narys historyi Belarusi (1795–2002)*, p. 270.
43. *Ibid.*, p. 264.
44. *Ibid.*, pp. 264–5.
45. *Ibid.*, p. 265.
46. Borzęcki, *The Soviet-Polish Peace of 1921*, p. 119.
47. As quoted in *ibid.*, p. 186.

48. Shybeka, *Narys historyi Belarusi (1795–2002)*, p. 242.
49. *Ibid.*, p. 240.
50. *Ibid.*, p. 253.
51. *Ibid.*, p. 250.
52. Francine Hirsch, *Empire of Nations: Ethnographic Knowledge and the Making of the Soviet Union* (Ithaca, NY: Cornell University Press, 2005), p. 150.
53. *Ibid.*, p. 149.
54. S.M. Tokt', 'Dinamika etnicheskogo samosoznaniia krest'ianskogo naseleniia zapadnoi Belorussii v 1920-1930-kh godakh', in *Belorussiia i Ukraina: istoriia i kul'tura. Ezhegodnik 2004* (Moscow: Nauka, 2005), pp. 285–304.
55. Shybeka, *Narys historyi Belarusi (1795–2002)*, p. 244.
56. Hirsch, *Empire of Nations*, pp. 152–4.
57. Shybeka, *Narys historyi Belarusi (1795–2002)*, p. 244.
58. *Ibid.*, pp. 243–4.
59. Per Anders Rudling, 'The Battle Over Belarus: The Rise and Fall of the Belarusian National Movement, 1906–1931', University of Alberta PhD, 2010, p. 3.
60. Latyshonak and Miranovich, *Historyia Belarusi*, p. 168.
61. *Ibid.*, p. 173.
62. Grigory Ioffe, 'Understanding Belarus', Part III, *Europe-Asia Studies*, 56, 1 (January 2004), pp. 85–118, at p. 86.
63. Shevtsov, *Ob'edinennaia natsiia: fenomen Belarusi*, p. 22.
64. *Ibid.*, pp. 23–4.
65. Serhii Hrabovs'kyi, 'Nezolotyi veresen' 1939 roku', *Den'*, 30 September 2009.
66. Author's interview with Andrei Dyn'ko, 7 October 2007.
67. Yury Turonak (Jerzy Turonek), 'Fabiian Akinchyts – pravadyr belaruskikh natsyianal-satsyialistaw', *Madernaia historyia Belarusi* (Vilnius: Institute of Belarusian Studies, 2006), pp. 373–82.
68. Turonak, *Madernaia historyia Belarusi*, p. 529.
69. Yury Hrybowski, 'Belaruski rukh i Niamechchyna napiariedadni i w pachatku Druhoi sus'vetnai vainy', *Arche*, 5 (2009).
70. Tadeusz Piotrowski, *Poland's Holocaust: Ethnic Strife, Collaboration with Occupying Forces and Genocide in the Second Republic, 1918–1947* (Jefferson: McFarland, 1990).
71. Turonak, *Madernaia historyia Belarusi*, p. 672.
72. Jerzy Turonek, *Białoruś pod okupacją niemiecką* (Warsaw: Ksiażka i Wiedza, 1993).
73. Babette Quinkert, *Propaganda und Terror in Weißrussland 1941–1944. Die deutsche 'geistige' Kriegführung gegen Zivilbevölkerung und Partisanen* (Paderborn: Ferdinand Schöningh, 2009).
74. Martin Dean, *Collaboration in the Holocaust: Crimes of the Local Police in Belarus and Ukraine, 1941–44* (Basingstoke: Palgrave/Macmillan, 2000).
75. Per Anders Rudling, ' "For a Heroic Belarus!": The Great Patriotic War as Identity Marker in the Lukashenka and Soviet Belarusian Discourses', *Sprawy Narodowościowe*, 32 (2008), pp. 43–62; *idem*, 'The Great Patriotic War and National Identity in Belarus', in Tomasz Kamusella and Krzysztof Jaksułowski (eds), *Nationalisms across the Globe, Volume I: Nationalisms Today* (Bern: Peter Lang, 2009), pp. 199–225.
76. This was still the figure in the official history published in 1995: Kastiuk et al., *Narysy historyi Belarusi*, vol. 2, p. 324.
77. Shybeka, *Narys historyi Belarusi (1795–2002)*, p. 336.
78. Timothy Snyder, *Bloodlands: Europe between Hitler and Stalin* (London: The Bodley Head, 2010), p. 251.
79. 'Vaennyia straty', in Latyshonak and Miranovich, *Historyia Belarusi*, pp. 222–3.
80. Shybeka, *Narys historyi Belarusi (1795–2002)*, p. 316. For the latest study of the subject, see Mark Batushka, *Partyzanskaia vaina u Belarusi u 1941–1944 hh.* (Vilnius: Institute of Belarusian Studies, 2011).

81. Shybeka, *Narys historyi Belarusi (1795–2002)*, pp. 315–16.
82. *Ibid.*, p. 324.
83. Snyder, *Bloodlands*, p. 243. On the partisans in general, see pp. 233–52.
84. Shybeka, *Narys historyi Belarusi (1795–2002)*, p. 325.
85. Kastiuk et al., *Narysy historyi Belarusi*, p. 314.
86. Snyder, *Bloodlands*, p. 251.
87. *Ibid.*, pp. 241–2.
88. *Ibid.*, p. 251.
89. See the paper by Olga Baranova, 'Was Belarus a Partisan Republic? Resistance and Occupation by the Belarusian Population during the Nazi Occupation of 1941–1944', BCMH Summer Conference 2009, at www.bcmh.org.uk/archive/conferences/WebSmallWars.pdf; Olga Baranova, *Nationalism, Anti-Bolshevism or the Will to Survive? Forms of Interaction with the German Occupation Authorities, 1941–1944* (Saarbrucken: Lambert Academic Publishing, 2010); and Alexandra Goujon, 'Memorial Narratives of WWII Partisans and Genocide in Belarus', *East European Politics and Societies*, 24: 1 (February 2010), pp. 6–25.
90. Shybeka, *Narys historyi Belarusi (1795–2002)*, pp. 316, 331, 334.
91. Mark Mazower, 'Wartime Nostalgia Blinds Us to Britain's Changed Realities', *The Guardian*, 3 September 2009.
92. Timothy Snyder, 'Holocaust: The Ignored Reality', *New York Review of Books*, 56:12 (16 July 2009).
93. David Meltser and Vladimir Levin, *The Black Book with Red Pages: Tragedy and Heroism of Belarussian Jews* (Cockeysville, MD: Vestnik, 2005).
94. Snyder, *Bloodlands*, p. 350.
95. Yitzhak Arad, *The Holocaust in the Soviet Union* (Lincoln and Jerusalem: University of Nebraska Press and Yad Vashem, 2009), p. 525.
96. Emanuil Ioffe, *Stranitsy istorii Evreev Belarusi* (Minsk: Arti-Feks, 1996), pp. 107–62.
97. Barbara Epstein, *The Minsk Ghetto 1941–1943: Jewish Resistance and Soviet Internationalism* (Berkeley: University of California Press, 2008).
98. Snyder, *Bloodlands*, pp. 230, 226.
99. *Ibid.*, p. 252.
100. *Ibid.*, pp. 236, 251.
101. *Ibid.*, p. 249.
102. *Ibid.*, p. 237.
103. *Ibid.*, p. 239.
104. Nechma Tec, *Defiance: The Bielski Partisans* (Oxford: Oxford University Press, 1993).
105. Piotr Głuchowski and Marcin Kowalski, 'The True Story of the Beilski Brothers', *Gazeta Wyborcza*, 6 January 2009, http://wyborcza.pl/1,86871,6125087,The_True_Story_of_the_Bielski_Brothers.html.
106. Michael Urban, *An Algebra of Soviet Power: Elite Circulation in the Belorussian Republic 1966-86* (Cambridge: Cambridge University Press, 1989), p. 14. Italics in original.
107. Shevtsov, *Ob'edinennaia natsiia: fenomen Belarusi*, p. 77.
108. Urban, *An Algebra of Soviet Power*, p. 15.
109. See *ibid.*, chapter 7.
110. *Ibid.*, p. 132.

Chapter 7 The Building Blocks of National Identity

1. Source: the official figures at http://belstat.gov.by, especially http://belstat.gov.by/homep/ru/perepic/p5.ph p and http://belstat.gov.by/homep/en/census/main1.php.
2. See the table at http://belstat.gov.by/homep/ru/perepic/2009/vihod_tables/5.9–0.pdf.
3. See the fascinating travelogue by Andrei Dyn'ko and Andrei Skurko, *Belarus' za 10 padarazhzhaw* (Vilnius: Institute of Belarusian Studiers, Nasha Niva, 2007).
4. *RFE/RL Newsline*, 18 October 2007.

5. Shybeka, *Narys historyi Belarusi (1795–2002)*, p. 339.

6. Alexandra Goujon, 'Language, Nationalism and Populism in Belarus', *Nationalities Papers*, 27:4 (December 1999), pp. 661–77.

7. See the table at http://belstat.gov.by/homep/ru/perepic/2009/vihod_tables/5.8–0.pdf.

8. See the table at http://belstat.gov.by/homep/ru/perepic/2009/vihod_tables/5.9–0.pdf.

9. Zaprudnik, *Belarus: At a Crossroads in History*, p. 81.

10. Andrej Dynko (Andrei Dyn'ko), 'Language of Streets and Languages of the Ploshcha: Evolution and Status of the Belarusian Language after 2000', in Marta Pejda (ed.), *Hopes, Illusions, Perspectives: Belarusian Society 2007* (Warsaw and Minsk: East European Democratic Centre, 2007), pp. 52–8, at p. 53.

11. *Ibid.*, p. 56.

12. Anthony Brown, 'Language and Identity in Belarus', *Language Policy*, 4:3 (September 2005), pp. 311–32.

13. See the BISS survey at www.belinstitute.eu/images/stories/documents/pressbudzma. doc.

14. From a 2004 survey by IISEPS, see www.iiseps.by, cited by Larissa Titarenko, 'Post-Soviet National Identity: Belarusian Approaches and Paradoxes', *Filosofija. Sociologija* (Lithuania), 18:4 (2007), pp. 79–90, available at http://images.katalogas.lt/maleidykla/Fil74/fil_20074_79–90.pdf.

15. Stankevich was a deputy to the Polish Sejm in 1928–30, served under the Belarusian Central Council in the 1940s, then lived out his life in exile in Germany and the USA. For a modern collection of his works, see Yan Stankevich, *Yazyk i yazykaveda*, 2 vols (Vilnius: Institute of Belarusian Studies, 2007).

16. See the discussion in and around the pages of *Arche*, the main Belarusian-speaking intellectual journal, for example, Ihar Klimaw, 'Belaruskaia trasianka i wkrainski surzhyk vachyma navukowtsaw', in *Bulletin of the International Association of Belarusianists*, 3 (2009); and Siarhei Zaprudzki, 'Nekatoryia zawvahi ab vyvuchen'ni "trasianki", abo Vykliki dlia belaruskikh humanitarnykh i satsyialnykh navuk', *Arche*, 11–12 (2009), pp. 157–200.

17. Siarhei Astrawtsow, 'Uskhodniki i zakhodniki', *Kur"er 2000*, 2.

18. Author's interview with Andrei Dyn'ko, 7 October 2007.

19. Andrej Kazakievič, 'Regional Peculiarities in the Context of the Presidential Elections of 1994, 2001 and 2006', in Valer Bulhakaw (ed.), *The Geopolitical Place of Belarus in Europe and the World* (Warsaw: WSHP, 2006), pp. 127–38, at p. 132.

20. See http://belstat.gov.by/homep/en/census/main1.php and http://belstat.gov.by/homep/en/census/p6.php.

21. Jan Maksimiuk, 'An Unclaimed Creative Potential or the Belarusians in the Bialystok Region as a Trilingual People', http://www.pravapis.org/art_belarusian_poland.asp.

22. Andrei Dyn'ko, 'Nainowshaia historyia Yatsviahaw', *Arche*, 6 (2000), at http://arche. bymedia.net/6–2000/dynko600.html; A.D. Duličenko, 'The West Polesian Literary Language', in S. Gustavsson and H. Runblom (eds), *Language, Minority, Migration* (Uppsala: Centre for Multiethnic Research, 1995).

23. R.A Grigor'eva and M.Yu. Martynova (eds), *Belorussko-russkoe pogranich'e: Etnologicheskoe issledovanie* (Moscow: Russian University of the Friendship of the Peoples, 2005), p. 59. See also the site on 'Russia and Belarus: Ethnocultural Dialogue' (in Russian) at http://by.ethnology.ru/; and Lew Kryshtapovich, *Belarus i Rossiia: istoriosofskoe i tsivilizatsionnoe edinstva* (Minsk: Academy of Administration of the President, 2006).

24. Grigor'eva and Martynova (eds), *Belorussko-russkoe pogranich'e*, p. 59.

25. *Ibid.*, p. 69.

26. *Ibid.*, pp. 59–60.

27. Leonid Gorizontov, 'The "Great Circle" of Interior Russia: Representations of the Imperial Center in the Nineteenth and Early Twentieth Centuries', in Jane Burbank, Mark von Hagen and Anatolyi Remnev (eds), *Russian Empire: Space, People, Power, 1700–1930* (Bloomington and Indianapolis: Indiana University Press, 2007), pp. 67–93, at p. 84.

28. Staliūnas, *Making Russians*, p. 36.
29. Grigor'eva and Martynova (eds), *Belorussko-russkoe pogranich'e*, pp. 58–9.
30. *Ibid.*, pp. 60–1.
31. *Ibid.*, pp. 64, 61, emphasis added.
32. Uladzimir Arlow, *Iliustravanaia historyia kraina Belarus'* (Martin, Slovakia: Neografia/Angloproject, 2003), p. 94.
33. Grigor'eva and Martynova (eds), *Belorussko-russkoe pogranich'e*, pp. 60, 63.
34. Łatyszonek, 'Belarusian Nationalism and the Clash of Civilizations', p. 64.
35. See Aleś Uładamirski, 'Religious Diversity in Belarus', in Pejda (ed.), *Hopes, Illusions, Perspectives: Belarusian Society 2007*, pp. 24–8, at p. 24. Figures for the beginning of 2009 could be seen at www.president.gov.by/press23736.html; accessed 17 March 2011.
36. Łatyszonek, 'Belarusian Nationalism and the Clash of Civilizations', p. 72. For the English-language version of Kepel's 1991 book, see Gilles Kepel, *The Revenge of God: The Resurgence of Islam, Christianity and Judaism in the Modern World* (Cambridge: Polity, 1994).
37. Shevtsov, *Ob'edinennaia natsiia: fenomen Belarusi*, p. 46.
38. *Ibid.*, p. 48.
39. For a translation, see www.cesnur.org/2002/belarus_law.htm.
40. See F18News, 24 June 2003, http://www.forum18.org/Archive.php?article_id=89.
41. 'Lukashenko predlozhil Pape i Patriarkhu vstrechu', Russian Reuters, 5 May 2009, http://ru.reuters.com/article/oddlyEnoughNews/idRUMSE5440FU20090505?pageNumber=1&virtualBrandChannel=0.
42. Aleś' Belyi, *Khronika Belai Rusi = Chronicon Russiae Albae: narys historyi adnoi heahrafichnai nazvy* (Minsk: Entsyklapedyks, 2000); Sahanovich, *Narys historyi Belarusi*, pp. 9–11.
43. Sahanovich, *Narys historyi Belarusi*, p. 10.
44. Licwin-Hudas-Krews, quoted in Nina Barshcheuskaya (Barshchewskaia), 'The Way [the] Belarusian Emigration Treats [the] Ethnographic Borders of Belarus', *Annus Albaruthenicus*, 6 (2005), pp. 65–82, at p. 75, at http://kamunikat.fontel.net/www/czasopisy/annus/2005/04.htm.
45. Arkadz Smolich, *Heohrafiia Belarusi* (Minsk: Belarus, 1993).
46. Valer Fralow, in Valer Bulhakaw and Agnieszka Komorowska (eds), *Belarus: Neither Europe, Nor Russia. Opinions of Elites* (Warsaw: Stepan Batory Foundation, 2006), p. 121.
47. Shevtsov, *Ob'edinennaia natsiia: fenomen Belarusi*, pp. 15–17.
48. Bulhakaw and Komorowska (eds), *Belarus: Neither Europe, Nor Russia*, p. 125.
49. Paval Seviariynets, *Listy z' lesu* (Vilnius: Nasha Niva, 2007). Ihar Babkow, 'Etykapamezhzha: transkul'turnas'ts' yak belaruski dos'ved', in Valiantsin Akudovich and Aleś' Antsipenka (eds), *Antalohiia suchasnaha belaruskaha myslen'nia* (St Petersburg: Nevskii prostor, 2003), p. 68.
50. Shevtsov, *Ob'edinennaia natsiia: fenomen Belarusi*, p. 66.
51. Sviatlana Kalinkina, in Bulhakaw and Komorowska (eds), *Belarus: Neither Europe, Nor Russia*, p. 123.
52. Uladzimir Arlow and Hanadz Sahanovich, *Dzesiats' viakow belaruskai historyi 862–1918* (Vilnius: Nasha Buduchynia, 1999).
53. Zianon Pazniak, *Belaruska-Raseiskaia vaina = Belarus Is an Eastern Outpost* (Warsaw: Belaruskiia Vedamastsi, 2005). This booklet can be found on Pazniak's personal website, http://www.zianonpazniak.de/publications/creation/belarusanwar/belarusanwartext.htm, accessed 1 July 2007. Spelling adapted.
54. Andrej (Andrei) Dyn'ko, 'Chamu my prahnem u Ewropu', *Arche*, 2 (2004), translated as 'Between Brotherly Russia and Peaceful Europe', at http://www.eurozine.com/articles/2004-10-18-dynko-en.html.
55. Dyn'ko, 'Chamu my prahnem u Ewropu'.

56. Http://president.gov.by/press29279.html#doc.

57. See the essay by S.D. Laptenok on the sixtieth anniversary of victory in 2005, 'Belarus' – voennyi i nravstvennyi forpost', www.president.gov.by/press14033.html#doc.

58. As quoted in Grigory Ioffe, 'Culture Wars, Soul-Searching, and Belarusian Identity', *East European Politics and Societies*, 21:2 (May 2007), pp. 348–81.

59. Sjarhej Pan'koŭski, 'Minsk – das Vierte Rome?', *Osteuropa*, 2 (2004), pp. 8–17. Pietra (Piotr) Rudkowski, 'Pamizh Lukashyzmam i natsyianalizmam', paper presented at conference on Belarus, Warsaw, November 2006.

60. Speech of Lukashenka, *Sovetskaia Belorussiia*, 28 March 2003.

Chapter 8 Politics Either Side of Independence, 1989–1994

1. Pavel Sheremet and Svetlana Kalinkina, *Sluchainii prezident* (Yaroslavl: Niuans, 2003).

2. Lucan Way, 'Deer in Headlights: Political Skill and Authoritarian Survival after the Cold War', *Slavic Review*, 2010, quoting Lukashenka's speech in *Narodnaia hazeta*, 7 October 1994.

3. From Lukashenka's 'Lecture on the Historical Choice of Belarus' at the Belarusian State University, 14 March 2003, www.president.gov.by/press29279.html#doc.

4. Vital' Silitski, ''Uvodziny', in Valer Bulhakaw and Silitski (eds), *Belaruskaia palitychnaia stsena i prezydentskiia vybary 2006 hodu* (Vilnius: Institute of Belarusian Studies, 2007), pp. 7–14, at p. 8.

5. Way, 'Deer in Headlights'.

6. Quoted in L. Dudkov, 'Struktura i kharakter natsional'noi identichnosti v Rossiia', in *Geopoliticheskoe polozhenie Rossii* (Moscow, 1999).

7. Petr Kravchenko (Krawchanka), *Belarus' na rasput'e, ili pravda o Belovezhskom soglashenii: Zapiski diplomata i politika* (Moscow: Vremia, 2006), p. 15.

8. *Ibid.*, p. 23.

9. Though Krawchanka reckons it could have been Hennadii Bartoshevich. See *ibid.*, pp. 214–15.

10. Feduta, *Lukashenko: Politicheskaia biografiia*, p. 107.

11. Michael Urban, *An Algebra of Soviet Power: Elite Circulation in the Belorussian Republic 1966–86* (Cambridge: Cambridge University Press, 1989), p. 122.

12. *Ibid.*, pp. 118–26.

13. *Demakratychnaia apazytsiia Belarusi: 1956–1991* (Minsk: Archive of Contemporary History, 1999), available at http://slounik.oeg/demap.

14. Alexandra Goujon, *Révolutions politiques et identitaires en Ukraine et en Biélorussie (1998–2008)* (Paris: Belin, 2009), p. 29.

15. *Ibid.*, p. 29.

16. Zenon Pozniak (Pazniak) and Evgenii Shmygalev (Shmyhalow), 'Kurapaty – doroga smerti', *Litaratura i mastatstva*, 10 June 1988.

17. Aleksandr Feduta, *Lukashenko: Politicheskaia biografiia* (Moscow: Referendum, 2005), p. 26.

18. Goujon, *Révolutions politiques et identitaires en Ukraine et en Biélorussie*, p. 33.

19. *Ibid.*, p. 35.

20. *Ibid.*, p. 45.

21. *Prahrama i statut Belaruskaha Narodnaha Fronta "Adradzhen'ne"* (Minsk: No publisher, 1991).

22. Goujon, *Révolutions politiques et identitaires en Ukraine et en Biélorussie* , pp. 77–8.

23. Alexander Martynou, 'The Non-Accidental President', 2 December 2010, www.tol. org.

24. Valer Bulhakaw et al., *Palitychnaia historyia nezalezhnai Belarusi* (Vilnius: Institute of Belarusian Studies, 2006), pp. 671–2.

25. Feduta, *Lukashenko: Politicheskaia biografiia*, p. 29.

26. Bulhakaw et al., *Palitychnaia historyia nezalezhnai Belarusi*, pp. 22, 64.
27. Astrid Lorenz, *Vorwärts in die Vergangenheit? Der Wandel der politischen Institutionen in der Republik Belarus' seit 1991* (dissertation for the Humboldt University, Berlin, 2001), available at http://edoc.hu-berlin.de/dissertationen/lorenz-astrid-2001-05-09/PDF/Lorenz.pdf, p. 68.
28. Way, 'Deer in Headlights', quoting *Narodnaia gazeta*, 26 January 1991.
29. Shybeka, *Narys historyi Belarusi (1795–2002)*, p. 398.
30. Feduta, *Lukashenko: Politicheskaia biografiia*, pp. 54–5.
31. *Ibid.*, p. 51.
32. Aleksandr Lukashenko, 'Diktatura: belorusskii variant?', *Narodnaia gazeta*, 25 May 1991.
33. Feduta, *Lukashenko: Politicheskaia biografiia*, p. 21.
34. *Ibid.*, p. 65, quoting Krawchanka.
35. Kravchenko, *Belarus' na raspute*, p. 12.
36. Feduta, *Lukashenko: Politicheskaia biografiia*, p. 43.
37. *Ibid.*, pp. 35–6.
38. Viacheslav Kebich, *Iskhushenie vlast'iu* (Minsk: Paradoks, 2008), pp. 44–50.
39. Way, 'Deer in Headlights'.
40. *Sovetskaia Belorussiia*, 4 April 1990.
41. Feduta, *Lukashenko: Politicheskaia biografiia*, p. 58.
42. Goujon, *Révolutions politiques et identitaires en Ukraine et en Biélorussie* , p. 59.
43. Kravchenko, *Belarus' na raspute*, pp. 122–3.
44. *Ibid.*, p. 123.
45. *Litaratura i mastatstva*, 27 September 1991; Ol'ga Shestakova and Ol'ga Ulevich, 'GK-ChP sokhranil vlast' v Moskve, no smenil rukovodstvo v Minske', *Komsomolskaia pravda*, 10 August 2009, at http://kp.by/daily/24345/535209/.
46. Anatolii Taras (ed.), *Istoriia imperskikh otnoshenii: belarusy i russkie, 1772–1991 gg.* (Minsk: FUAinform, 3rd edn, 2010), p. 462.
47. Latyshonak and Miranovich, *Historyia Belarusi*, p. 301.
48. Kravchenko, *Belarus' na raspute*, p. 133.
49. Kebich, *Iskhushenie vlast'iu*, pp. 134–6.
50. *Ibid.*, p. 132.
51. Kravchenko, *Belarus' na raspute*, p. 133.
52. Walter Stankievich, 'The Events behind Belorussia's Independence Declaration', *Report on the USSR*, 38, (20 September 1991), pp. 24–6.
53. Kebich, *Iskhushenie vlast'iu*, p. 138.
54. Author's interview with Anatolii Mykhailov, 17 June 2008. Mykhailov was then chief foreign policy adviser to Shushkevich.
55. Kravchenko, *Belarus' na raspute*, pp. 146–7.
56. Leonid Kravchuk, *Maiemo te, shcho maiemo* (Kiev: Stolittia, 2002), p. 129.
57. Timothy J. Colton, *Yeltsin: A Life* (New York: Basic Books, 2008), pp. 205–6. Shushkevich gave his account in an anniversary interview in *Belorusskaia delovaia gazeta*, 7 December 2001. See also the interview at http://www.svaboda.org/content/article/1897868.html.
58. Kravchenko, *Belarus' na raspute*, p. 145.
59. *Ibid.*, pp. 173–4.
60. *Ibid.*, p. 162.
61. Kebich, *Iskhushenie vlast'iu*, pp. 201, 205.
62. *Ibid.*, p. 212.
63. *Ibid.*, p. 202; Kravchenko, *Belarus' na raspute*, p. 152; also referring to Anatolii Shutov, *Na ruinakh Velikoi Derzhavy, ili Agoniia vlasti, 1991–2003 gody* (Moscow: Veche, 2004), p. 44.
64. 'Sil'nuiu razvedku mozhet imet' tol'ko silnoe gosudarstvo', *Tribuna*, 12 December 2000, available at http://svr.gov.ru/smi/2000/trib20001220.htm.

65. Kravchenko, *Belarus' na rasput'e*, p. 152.
66. Feduta, *Lukashenko: Politicheskaia biografiia*, pp. 55–6; Kravchenko, *Belarus' na rasput'e*, pp. 176–7.
67. For Pazniak's views, see Zianon Pazniak, *Saprawdnae Ablichtcha* (Minsk: Palifakt, 1992).
68. Pazniak (Pozniak), 'Bilingualism and Bureaucratism', *Nationalities Papers*, 16:2 (1988), pp. 259–71.
69. Kravchenko, *Belarus' na rasput'e*, p. 367.
70. *Dokumenty svidetel'stvuiut . . . Stranitsy istorii PKB* (Minsk: no publisher, 2003).
71. Bulhakaw et al., *Palitychnaia historyia nezalezhnai Belarusi*, p. 68.
72. Feduta, *Lukashenko: Politicheskaia biografiia*, pp. 86–7.
73. Kebich, *Iskhushenie vlast'iu*, p. 337.
74. Bulhakaw et al., *Palitychnaia historyia nezalezhnai Belarusi*, p. 67.
75. Kebich, *Iskhushenie vlast'iu*, pp. 246, 255–6.
76. Kravchenko, *Belarus' na rasput'e*, p. 357.
77. Alexander Lukashuk, 'Belarus: A Year on a Treadmill', *RFE/RL Research Report*, 2:1 (1 January 1993).
78. Kravchenko, *Belarus' na rasput'e*, p. 356.
79. Quoted in Feduta, *Lukashenko: Politicheskaia biografiia*, p. 99.
80. Way, 'Deer in Headlights'.
81. Feduta, *Lukashenko: Politicheskaia biografiia*, p.79.
82. *Ibid.*, p.92.
83. *Ibid.*, p.99.
84. Kebich, *Iskhushenie vlast'iu*, p. 364.
85. Ustina Markus, 'Conservatives Remove Belarus Leader', *RFE/RL Research Report*, 3:8 (25 February 1994).
86. Quoted in Feduta, *Lukashenko: Politicheskaia biografiia*, p. 118.
87. *Ibid.*, p. 117.
88. To be fair, the Ukrainian system was stable from 1996 until 2003, when the first attempts to amend it in advance of the 2004 election began, but only because President Kuchma developed a strongly personalised system of rule.
89. Kebich, *Iskhushenie vlast'iu*, pp. 398–401.
90. Alex Danilovich, *Russian–Belarusian Integration: Playing Games behind the Kremlin Walls* (Aldershot: Ashgate, 2006), pp. 31–49.
91. Kravchenko, *Belarus' na rasput'e*, p. 358.
92. *Ibid.*, p. 359.
93. Kebich, *Iskhushenie vlast'iu*, p. 20.
94. Feduta, *Lukashenko: Politicheskaia biografiia*, p. 569.
95. Martynou, 'The Non-Accidental President'.
96. Way, 'Deer in Headlights'.
97. David R. Marples, *The Lukashenka Phenomenon: Elections, Propaganda and the Foundations of Political Authority in Belarus* (Trondheim: Trondheim Studies on East European Cultures and Societies, no. 21, 2007), p. 18.
98. Kravchenko, *Belarus' na rasput'e*, p. 363.
99. Feduta, *Lukashenko: Politicheskaia biografiia*, p. 110.
100. Kravchenko, *Belarus' na rasput'e*, p. 369.
101. Feduta, *Lukashenko: Politicheskaia biografiia*, p. 144.
102. Kravchenko, *Belarus' na rasput'e*, pp. 203–4.
103. *Ibid.*, p. 219.
104. Lucan A. Way, 'Authoritarian Failure: How Does State Weakness Strengthen Electoral Competition?' in Andreas Schedler (ed.), *Electoral Authoritarianism: The Dynamics of Unfree Competition* (Boulder, CO and London: Lynne Rienner, 2006), pp. 167–80, at p. 174.
105. Feduta, *Lukashenko: Politicheskaia biografiia*, p. 153.

106. See Tsitsiankow's (Titenkov) interview at www.charter97.org/eng/news/2001/07/17/06, dated 17 July 2001.

107. Feduta, *Lukashenko: Politicheskaia biografiia*, p. 155.

108. *Ibid.*

109. *Ibid.*, pp. 142–4, quote at p. 144.

110. Ustina Markus, 'Belarusians Elect First President', *RFE/RL Research Report*, 3:30 (29 July 1994).

111. Feduta, *Lukashenko: Politicheskaia biografiia*, p. 125.

112. Kravchenko, *Belarus' na rasput'e*, p. 367.

113. *Ibid.*, p. 381.

114. Feduta, *Lukashenko: Politicheskaia biografiia*, pp. 72, 64–6.

115. *Ibid.*, p. 73.

116. *Ibid.*, p. 136.

117. *Ibid.*, pp. 140, 128.

118. *Ibid.*, p. 161.

119. *Ibid.*, p. 568.

120. *Ibid.*, p. 110.

121. *Ibid.*, p. 130.

122. *Ibid.*, p. 176.

123. *Ibid.*, p. 16.

124. *Ibid.*, p. 140.

125. *Ibid.*, p. 161.

126. Aleksandr Feduta, 'Poslednii oligarkh', http://mignews.com.ua/articles_print/227206.html, 11 October 2006.

127. Vadim Sekhovich, '1991–2006. Itogi. Chestnyi biznes', Salidarnats', www.gazetaby.com/index.php?sn_nid=5886&sn_cat=48, 3 April 2007, accessed 18 April 2008.

128. Feduta, *Lukashenko: Politicheskaia biografiia*, p. 166.

129. *Ibid.*, p. 135.

130. Kravchenko, *Belarus' na rasput'e*, p. 365.

131. *Ibid.*, p. 372.

132. Feduta, *Lukashenko: Politicheskaia biografiia*, p. 136.

133. Bulhakow et al., *Politychnaia historyia nezalezhnai Belarusi*, p. 106.

134. Feduta, *Lukashenko: Politicheskaia biografiia*, p. 158.

135. *Ibid.*, p. 167.

136. Source: www.cec.gov.by and Bulhakaw et al., *Palitychnaia historyia nezalezhnai Belarusi*, p. 297.

137. Kravchenko, *Belarus' na rasput'e*, p. 372.

138. Feduta, *Lukashenko: Politicheskaia biografiia*, p. 170.

139. Kravchenko, *Belarus' na rasput'e*, pp. 364–5.

140. Feduta, *Lukashenko: Politicheskaia biografiia*, p. 205.

141. *Ibid.*, p. 180.

142. Way, 'Deer in Headlights'.

Chapter 9 Building Authoritarianism: Lukashenka's First Term

1. Feduta, *Lukashenko: Politicheskaia biografiia*, pp. 193–4.

2. See the press release 'IMF Praises Belarus Economic Policy, Sees September Stand-By', dated 24 August 1995, http://www.imf.org/external/np/sec/nb/1995/nb9518.htm.

3. Quoted in Feduta, *Lukashenko: Politicheskaia biografiia*, p. 201.

4. *Ibid.*, p. 197.

5. *Ibid.*, p. 201.

6. *Ibid.*, p. 202.

7. *Ibid.*, p. 175.

8. *Ibid.*, p. 339.

9. Andrei Kazakevich, 'Kul'turny fon belaruskai palityki', in Bulhakaw et al., *Palitychnaia historyia nezalezhnai Belarusi*, pp. 446–54.
10. Kryshtapovich, 'Istoriosofskii imperativ obshchestvennogo razvitiia', and *idem*, 'Ob adekvatnoi interpretatsii mezhdunarodnykh i vnutripolititicheskikh problem', in Matusevich, Pashkovskii and Krishtapovich (eds), *Belarus' i Rossiia: imperativy obshchestvennogo razvitiia* (Minsk: ISPI, 2002), pp. 30–9, 181–206, at pp. 36, 35, 38.
11. Krishtapovich, 'Ob adekvatnoi interpretatsii mezhdunarodnykh i vnutri-polititicheskikh problem', p. 206.
12. Piotra Rudkouski, 'Belarusian National Ideology: Contemporary Utopia', in Pejda (ed.), *Hopes, Illusions, Perspectives. Belarusian Society 2007*, pp. 46–51, at p. 49.
13. David Brandenberger, *National Bolshevism: Stalinist Mass Culture and the Formation of Modern Russian National Identity, 1931–1956* (Cambridge, Mass.: Harvard University Press, 2002).
14. Aleksandr Dugin, *Osnovy geopolitiki: geopoliticheskoe budushchee Rossii* (Moscow: 1997).
15. Yawhenii Novik, Henadz' Martsul', Ihar Kachalaw et al., *Historyia Belarusi u dzviukh chastkakh. 1. Ad starazhytnykh chasaw – na liuty 1917 r.* (Minsk: Universitetskae, 2nd edn, 2000), pp. 72–3, 39–40, 44–53. See also Vasil' Bandrachyk, Valiantsina Bialiavina and Halina Kaspiarovich, *Belarusy. Vol. 4. Vytaki i etnichnae razvitstse* (Minsk: Belaruskaia navuka, 2001).
16. See the video 'Notre Damme de Lukashenka', www.youtube.com/watch?v= pjRxV0mqtec.
17. *Narysy historyi Belarusi*, vol. 1 (Minsk, 1994), p. 228, quoted in Grigor'eva and Martynova (eds), *Belorussko-russkoe pogranich'e*, pp. 58–9.
18. Feduta, *Lukashenko: Politicheskaia biografiia*, p. 594.
19. Author's interview with Anatolii Mykhailov, 17 June 2008.
20. Timothy J. Colton, *Yeltsin: A Life* (New York: Basic Books, 2008), pp. 385–6.
21. Feduta, *Lukashenko: Politicheskaia biografiia*, p. 615.
22. *Ibid.*, p. 230.
23. *Ibid.*, p. 232.
24. *Ibid.*, pp. 245, 248.
25. Source: www.rec.gov.by/refer/ref1995respr.html.
26. See www.gesis.org/en/data_service/eastern_europe/data/questionnaire/2817que.pdf.
27. Feduta, *Lukashenko: Politicheskaia biografiia*, p. 266.
28. *Ibid.*, p. 267.
29. Author's interview with Aliaksandr Feduta, 12 September 2003.
30. Drakokhrust, Drakokhrust and Furman, 'Transformatsiia partiinoi sistemy Belarusi', p. 120.
31. Valer Bulhakaw (ed.), *The Political System of Belarus and the 2001 Presidential Election* (Minsk and Warsaw: East European Democratic Centre, 2001), p. 216.
32. Nelly Bekus, *Struggle over Identity: The Official and the Alternative 'Belusianness'* (Budapest: CEU Press, 2010), p. 115.
33. Feduta, *Lukashenko: Politicheskaia biografiia*, p. 283.
34. Bulhakaw et al., *Palitychnaia historyia nezalezhnai Belarusi*, p. 133.
35. Feduta, *Lukashenko: Politicheskaia biografiia*, p. 300.
36. Ustina Marcus, 'A War of Referenda in Belarus', *Transition*, 2: 25 (13 December 1996), pp. 11–15, at p. 15,
37. Bulhakaw et al., *Palitychnaia historyia nezalezhnai Belarusi*, p. 148.
38. Feduta, *Lukashenko: Politicheskaia biografiia*, p. 316.
39. *Ibid.*, p. 271.
40. *Ibid.*, p. 272.
41. Bulhakaw et al., *Palitychnaia historyia nezalezhnai Belarusi*, p. 142.
42. Feduta, *Lukashenko: Politicheskaia biografiia*, p. 321; Bulhakaw et al., *Palitychnaia historyia nezalezhnai Belarusi*, p. 287.

43. Yegor Gaidar, *Collapse of an Empire: Lessons for Modern Russia* (Washington, DC: Brookings Institution Press, 2007), p. 248, and p. 313, n. 72.
44. *Narodnaia volia*, 109 (1996); *Svaboda*, 29 November 1996.
45. As quoted in Bulhakaw et al., *Palitychnaia historyia nezalezhnai Belarusi*, p. 87.
46. *Ibid.*, pp. 136–7.
47. The Lukashenka constitution can be found at www.president.gov.by/en/press10669.html.
48. 'Wallet for Lukashenko', *Belorussky chas*, 9 August 2001; Feduta, *Lukashenko: Politicheskaia biografiia*, pp. 578 ff.
49. Feduta, *Lukashenko: Politicheskaia biografiia*, p. 418.
50. *Ibid.*, p. 570.
51. *Ibid.*, p. 581.
52. *Ibid.*, pp. 416–17.
53. Balhakaw, *The Political System of Belarus*, p. 98.
54. Interview with Tamara Vinnikava, 'U prezidenta sosredotochena ogromneishaia summa', *Kommersant*, 3 September 2001, available at www.kommersant.ru/doc.aspx?DocsID=281285; Pavel Sheremet and Svetlana Kalinkina, *Sluchainyi prezident* (Yaroslavl': Niuans, 2003), pp. 50–8.
55. Feduta, *Lukashenko: Politicheskaia biografiia*, p. 583.
56. *Ibid.*
57. Sheremet and Kalinkina, *Sluchainyi prezident*, pp. 52–3.
58. See the series of articles by Simon Araloff, beginning with 'Europe's Black Hole', www.axisglobe.com/article.asp?article=207, July 2005, accessed 30 April 2007.
59. Feduta, *Lukashenko: Politicheskaia biografiia*, p. 403.
60. Mikhail Shchipanov, 'Sekrety na kryl'iakh', *Rossiiskaia gazeta*, 27 December 1994.
61. Jan Maksymiuk, 'Belarus: EU to Freeze President's Assets', *Radio Free Europe/Radio Liberty*, 18 May 2006, http://origin.rferl.org/content/article/1068494.html.
62. Vladimir Matikevich, 'Dollarovye millionery Belarusi', www.bat'ke.net, 15 July 2006.
63. Mark Lenzi, 'Selling Guns to Terrorists, from the "Heart of Europe"', *Wall Street Journal Europe*, 26 April 2002.
64. See www.globalsecurity.org/wmd/library/report/2004/isg-final-report/isg-final-report_vol1_rfp–05.htm, accessed 2 May 2007.
65. Florence Hartmann *Paix et châtiment: Les guerres secrètes de la politique et de la justice internationale* (Paris: Flammarion, 2007); John Lichfield, 'Russia and the US Accused of Secret Deal to Protect Karadzic', *The Independent*, 8 September 2007.
66. 'Report on Belarus, the Last Dictatorship in Europe, Including Arms Sales and Leadership Assets', 16 March 2006, at www.state.gov/p/eur/rls/prsrl/63297.htm.
67. Witold Gadowski, 'Ślady baronów śmierci', *Gazeta Polska*, 11 March 2008.
68. Feduta, *Lukashenko: Politicheskaia biografiia*, p. 522.
69. *Ibid.*, pp. 488–9.
70. Elena A. Korosteleva, Colin W. Lawson and Rosalind J. Marsh (eds), *Contemporary Belarus: Between Democracy and Dictatorship* (London: Routledge Curzon, 2003), pp. 52, 30.
71. Feduta, *Lukashenko: Politicheskaia biografiia*, p. 510.
72. Bulhakaw et al., *Palitychnaia historyia nezalezhnai Belarusi*, p. 202.
73. Feduta, *Lukashenko: Politicheskaia biografiia*, p. 510.
74. *Ibid.*, p. 527.
75. *Ibid.*, p. 464.
76. *Ibid.*, p. 531.
77. *Ibid.*, p. 539.
78. See http://assembly.coe.int/Main.asp?link=/Documents/WorkingDocs/doc04/EDOC-10062.htm.
79. Feduta, *Lukashenko: Politicheskaia biografiia*, p. 535.
80. Oleg Alkaev, *Rasstrel'naia komanda* (Moscow: Partizan, 2006).

81. Balazs Jarabik and Vitali Silicki (Silitski), 'Say Hallelujah: How Lukashenka's Survival Instinct Moves Belarus toward the EU', in Michael Emerson and Richard Youngs (eds), *Democracy's Plight in the Eastern Neighbourhood: Struggling Transitions and Proliferating Dynasties* (Brussels: CEPS, 2009), pp. 130–8, at p. 133.

Chapter 10 Building an Authoritarian State: Lukashenka's Second Term

1. Bulhakaw et al., *Palitychnaia historyia nezalezhnai Belarusi*, p. 303.
2. Author's interview with Andrii Dyn'ko, 7 October 2007.
3. *Ibid.*
4. Author's interview with Lithuanian officials involved in supporting the Belarusian opposition, 17 June 2008.
5. *Ibid.*
6. Vital' Silitski, 'Hrantavy skandal', in Bulhakaw (ed.), *Miastsovyia vybary w nainowshai paliitychnai historyi Belarusi*, pp. 109–14; *Christian Science Monitor*, 10 September 2001; Ian Traynor, 'Belarussian [sic] Foils Dictator-Buster . . . for Now', *The Guardian*, 14 September 2001.
7. Feduta, *Lukashenko: Politicheskaia biografiia*, p. 549.
8. Dmitrii Vereshchagin and Sergei Lozhkin, 'Rabota nad oshibkami', *Belorusskaia delovaia gazeta*, 13 November 2001; also available at http://bdg.press.net. by/2001/11/2001/_11_13.1064/index.htm.
9. Bulhakaw et al., *Palitychnaia historyia nezalezhnai Belarusi*, p. 287.
10. Feduta, *Lukashenko: Politicheskaia biografiia*, p. 550.
11. Davis and Grigorian (eds), *Polls Apart: Media Coverage of the Parliamentary Elections, Belarus, October 2000* (Vilnius: Institute of Belarusian Studies, 2006), pp. 49–50.
12. Bulhakaw et al., *Palitychnaia historyia nezalezhnai Belarusi*, pp. 284–6; Bulhakaw, *The Political System*, p. 215.
13. Bulhakaw et al., *Palitychnaia historyia nezalezhnai Belarusi*, p. 284.
14. Feduta, *Lukashenko: Politicheskaia biografiia*, p. 552.
15. *Ibid.*, p. 553.
16. Bulhakaw et al., *Palitychnaia historyia nezalezhnai Belarusi*, p. 286.
17. *Ibid.*, p. 216.
18. *RFE/RL Newsline*, 5 February 2004.
19. See, *inter alia*, *Zviazda*, 31 August 2001.
20. See the analysis by Oleg Manaev (Aleh Manaew), head of IISEPS, 'Pobediteli ne poluchaiut nichego', *Belorusskii rynok*, 46 (19–26 November 2001), also available at www. br.minsk.by/index.php?article=8247&year=2001; Bulhakaw, *The Political System*, p. 224.
21. Bulhakaw *The Political System*, p. 250.
22. *Ibid.*, pp. 226–7.
23. Korosteleva, 'Was There a Quiet Revolution?', p. 325.
24. Feduta, *Lukashenko: Politicheskaia biografiia*, p. 567.
25. Bulhakaw et al., *Palitychnaia historyia nezalezhnai Belarusi*, p. 310.
26. Margarita Balmaceda, *Belarus: Oil, Gas, Transit Pipelines and Russian Foreign Energy Policy* (London: GMB Publishing, 2006), p. 30.
27. Feduta, *Lukashenko: Politicheskaia biografiia*, pp. 368, 589.
28. Bulhakaw et al., *Palitychnaia historyia nezalezhnai Belarusi*, pp. 310–11; Feduta, *Lukashenko: Politicheskaia biografiia*, pp. 588–90.
29. Aleksei Paramonov, 'Khvost viliaet Lukashenko', www.ng.ru/cis/2007-02-22/7_hvost. html, 22 February 2007.
30. See Mikhail Stelmak, 'Luzhkov zagovoril po belorusskii', 19 June 2007, www.rosbalt. ru/2007/06/19/299485.html.
31. Balmaceda, *Belarus*, p. 23.
32. 'Bespokoit priemnaia Nemtsova . . .', *Sovetskaia Belorussiia*, 4 September 2002, http://sb.by/post/20677.

33. Kimitaka Matsuzato, 'A Populist Island in an Ocean of Clan Politics: The Lukashenko Regime as an Exception among CIS Countries', *Europe-Asia Studies*, 56:2 (March 2004), pp. 235–61.

34. Jury Čavusau, 'Belarus' Civic Sector', in Pejda (ed.), *Hopes, Illusions, Perspectives: Belarusian Society 2007*, pp. 6–15, at p. 9.

35. Pavał Usau, 'Pro-Government Associations in Belarus', in Pejda (ed.), *Hopes, Illusions, Perspectives: Belarusian Society 2007*, pp. 16–19, at p. 17.

36. Andrej Dynko, 'Language of Streets and Languages of the Ploshcha: Evolution and Status of the Belarusian Language after 2000', in Pejda (ed.), *Hopes, Illusions, Perspectives: Belarusian Society 2007*, pp. 52–8, at p. 54.

37. See the essay by Andrei Kazakevich, 'Kul'turny fon belaruskai palityki', in Bulhakaw et al., *Palitychnaia historyia nezalezhnai Belarusi*, pp. 446–55; Natalia Leshchenko, 'A Fine Instrument: Two Nation-Building Strategies in Post-Soviet Belarus', *Nations and Nationalism*, 10:3 (July 2004), pp. 333–52; and *idem*, 'The National Ideology and the Basis of the Lukashenka Regime in Belarus', *Europe-Asia Studies*, 60:8 (October 2008), pp. 1419–33.

38. Sjarhej Pan'koŭski, 'Minsk – das Vierte Rom?', *Osteuropa*, 54:2 (February 2004), pp. 8–17.

39. Lukashenka, as quoted in Stanislav Kniazev (Kniaziew) et al., *Osnovy ideologii belorusskogo gosudarstva: Istoriia i teoriia* (Minsk: IVTs Minfina, 2nd edn, 2006), p. 179.

40. Pavał Usau, ' "Ideology of Belarusian State": Propaganda Mechanisms', in Pejda (ed.), *Hopes, Illusions, Perspectives: Belarusian Society 2007*, pp. 40–5, at p. 41, quoting Lukashenka at the March 2003 seminar, *Materialy, postoianno deistviushchego seminara rukovodiashchikh rabotnikov respublikanskikh i mestnikh gosudarstvennikh organov* (Minsk: East European Democratic Centre, 2003), p. 19.

41. Usau, ' Ideology', p. 42, quoting Anatol Rubinov (Rubinaw), 'Tupiki krestovogo pokhoda za demokratiiu', *Belarus' segodnia*, 27 October 2006.

42. Lukashenka, quoted in Pietra Rudkowski, *Pawstan'ne Belarusi* (Vilnius: Nasha Niva, Institute of Belarusian Studies, 2007), p. 59.

43. *Sovetskaia Belorussiia*, 22 May 2001.

44. Feduta, *Lukashenko: Politicheskaia biografiia*, p. 604.

45. V. Mel'nik, *Tsivilizatsionnye osnovaniia ideologii Belorusskogo gosudarstva* (Minsk: BIP-S Plius, 2005).

46. See www.president.gov.by/eng/president/speech/2004/obr.html.

47. Leshchenko, 'The National Ideology and the Basis of the Lukashenka Regime in Belarus', pp. 1419–33.

48. Uladzimir Abushenka, 'Kreol'stva i problema natsyianal'na-kul'turnai samaidentyfikatsyi', in Ales' Antsipenka and Valiantsin Akudovich, *Antaliehiia suchasnaha belaruskaha mys'len'nia* (St Petersburg: Nevskii Prostor, 2003), pp. 216–34.

49. Benedict Anderson, *Imagined Communities* (London: Verso, 1983), p. 47 ff.

50. Andrej Dynko, 'Language of Streets and Languages of the Ploshcha', p. 56.

51. The speech can be read at www.belarusembassy.org/news/digests/pr090704.htm, dated 7 September 2004, accessed 2 May 2007.

52. The official results are at www.rec.gov.by/refer/refer2004.html.

53. See www.iiseps.org/ebullet04-4.html. See also 'Sociological Research in the 2004 Political Campaigns', in Bulhakaw et al., *Palitychnaia historyia nezalezhnai Belarusi*, pp. 534–43.

54. See Stephen White and Elena Korosteleva-Polglase, 'The Parliamentary Elections and Referendum in Belarus, October 2004', *Electoral Studies*, 25:1 (March 2006), pp. 155–60.

Chapter 11 The Third Term: The Edifice Crumbles

1. Reported by *Belapan*, 8 January 2005.

2. See the account of Pavlovskii's press conference in Minsk on 10 February 2006, at http://viperson.ru/wind.php?ID=266405&soch=1. Vitali Silitski, in Valer Bulhakau

(ed.), *The Geopolitical Place of Belarus in Europe and the World* (Warsaw: WSHP, 2006), p. 87; *idem*, 'Different Authoritarianisms, Distinct Patterns of Electoral Change', in Pavol Demeš, Joerg Forbrig and Robin Shepherd (eds), *Reclaiming Democracy: Civil Society and Electoral Change in Central and Eastern Europe* (Erste Foundation, German Marshall Fund, 2007), pp. 155–75.

3.   Joerg Forbrig, David Marples and Pavol Demeš (eds), *Prospects for Democracy in Belarus* (Washington, DC: German Marshall Fund, 2006), available online at www.gmfus.org/doc/Belarus%20book%20final.pdf. Valer Bulhakaw and Vital' Silitski (eds), *Belaruskaia palitychnaia stsena i prezydentskiia vybary 2006 hodu* (Vilnius: Institute of Belarusian Studies, 2007); Vitali Silitski, 'Has the Age of Revolutions Ended?', www.tol.cz, 13 January 2005; Gerald J. Bekkerman, 'The End of the Last Dictatorship in Europe: Four Keys to a Successful Color Revolution in Belarus', www.kentlaw.edu/perritt/courses/seminar/jerry-bekkerman-BELARUS%20THE-SIS.htm; Vitali Silitski, 'Preempting Democracy: The Case of Belarus', *Journal of Democracy*, 16: 4 (October 2005), pp. 83–97; *idem*, 'Still Soviet? Why Dictatorship Persists in Belarus', *Harvard International Review*, 28: 1 (spring 2006), pp. 46–53; *idem*, 'Contagion Deterred: Preemptive Authoritarianism in the Former Soviet Union ('The Case of Belarus)', *CDDRL Working Papers*, 66 (June 2006), at http://iis-db.stanford.edu/pubs/21152/Silitski_No_66.pdf; Elena Korosteleva, 'Was There a Quiet Revolution? Belarus after the 2006 Presidential Election', *Journal of Communist Studies and Transition Politics*, 25: 2–3 (June–September 2009), pp. 324–46. Also online is a book produced by the Kazulin camp, Daria Tsyvanchik (ed.), *Vybory Prezidenta Respubliki Belarus' v 2006 godu: Fakty. Kommentarii* (Minsk, 2006), at www.kozylin.com/kniga.

4.   Viktar Karniajenka, 'Analysis of the 2006 Campaign', in Pejda (ed.), *Hopes, Illusions, Perspectives: Belarusian Society 2007*, pp. 84–92, at p. 86.

5.   Marples and Demeš, *Prospects for Democracy in Belarus*, p. 55.

6.   Karniajenka, 'Aspects of the 2006 Political Campaign', pp. 88, 89.

7.   *Ibid.*, p. 88.

8.   Jury Čavusau, ' "For Freedom!" Campaign', in Pejda (ed.), *Hopes, Illusions, Perspectives: Belarusian Society 2007*, pp. 93–6, at p. 94.

9.   *Ibid.*, p. 93.

10. Pavel Usaw, 'Rasiia, satsyial-demakratyia i "praekt Kazulin" ', *Arche*, 7–8 (2006). Kazulin had dabbled with intellectual support in 2001; now he needed a serious party.

11. I am grateful in this section for information and opinion provided by the Swedish analyst Tobias Ljungvall in two emails dated 16 and 17 March 2006.

12. Author's interview with Andrei Dyn'ko, editor of *Nasha Niva*, 21 May 2007.

13. See the critique of Usaw's piece, posted 5 January 2007, accessed 3 May 2007, at www.afn.by/news/docview.asp?id=821.

14. Author's interview with Natalia Leshchenko, 24 July 2007.

15. Author's interview with Andrei Dyn'ko, 21 May 2007.

16. As cited in Francesca Mereu, 'Spin Doctors Blame Yanukovych', *The Moscow Times*, 30 November 2004.

17. Author's interview with Anatolii Mykhailov, 17 June 2008.

18. See www.wspolnota-polska.org.pl.

19. Jan Maksymiuk, 'Authorities Set to Rein in Polish Organisation', *RFE/RL Belarus, Ukraine and Moldova Report*, 7: 23 (22 June 2005), http://www.rferl.org/reports/pbu-report/2005/06/23-220605.asp.

20. *Zviazda*, 7 February 2006.

21. Author's interview with Andrei Dyn'ko, 21 May 2007.

22. Author's interview with Zygimantas Pavilionis, 16 June 2008.

23. Christina Tashkevich, 'Influential Georgian MP Dubiously Accused of Murder Conspiracy by Russian Newsman', 19 April 2006, www.data.minsk.by/belarus-news/042006/215.html.

24. Author's interview with Andrei Dyn'ko, who helped set up the Youth Front.

25. Paval Seviarynets, *Listy z' lesu* (Vilnius: Institute of Belarusian Studies, Nasha Niva, 2007).

26. Ihar Lalkou, 'The New Generation of Opposition', in Pejda (ed.), *Hopes, Illusions, Perspectives: Belarusian Society 2007*, pp. 99–101.

27. Jury Čavusau, 'Belarus' Civic Sector', in Pejda (ed.), *Hopes, Illusions, Perspectives: Belarusian Society 2007*, pp. 6–15, at p. 6; V. Chernov, *Tretii sector v Belarusi: problem stanovleniia i razvitiia* (Minsk, 2004).

28. Čavusau, 'Belarus' Civic Sector', p. 9.

29. *Ibid.*, p. 15.

30. Bulhakaw and Silitski, *Belaruskaia palitychnaia stsena i prezydentskiia vybary 2006 hodu*, pp. 222–3.

31. *Ibid.*, p. 218.

32. *Ibid.*, p. 223.

33. 'Exit Poll Gives Belarus' Lukashenko 84.2% of the vote', 20 March 2006, www.abc.net.au/news/newsitems/200603/s1595570.htm. The report mentioned that EcooM was 'considered to be close to the government', but expressed no scepticism about its results.

34. EcooM eventually set up a website www.ecoom.org/en.

35. See the report at www.pravda.com.ua/news/2006/3/20/39926.htm.

36. *RFE/RL Newsline*, 21 April 2006, www.rferl.org/newsline/2006/04/210406.asp#3-cee. See also www.iiseps.org/e3-06-1.html, accessed 2 May 2007.

37. See www.iiseps.org/e4-06-1.html, accessed 2 May 2007.

38. Waclaw Radziwinowicz, 'Lukashenka Won Less Than 50% of the Vote', *Gazeta Wyborcza*, 27 April 2006, http://serwisy.gazeta.pl/swiat/1,34192,3309580.html. Translated for the University of Ottawa's Ukraine List (UKL), by Jakub Krolczyk.

39. Lemez Lovas and Maya Medich, *Hidden Truths: Music, Politics and Censorship in Lukashenko's Belarus* (Copenhagen: Freemuse, 2006).

40. Karniajenka, 'Aspects of the 2006 Political Campaign', p. 89.

41. Vitali Silitski, 'Revolution of the Spirit', www.tol.org, 27 March 2006.

42. Korosteleva, 'Was There a Quiet Revolution?', p. 325; cf. Marples, *The Lukashenka Phenomenon*, pp. 70 and 72.

43. Vitali Silitski, 'Revolution of the Spirit', www.tol.org, 27 March 2006; Korosteleva, 'Was There a Quiet Revolution?', p. 325.

44. Evgeny Morozov, 'How Dictators Watch us on the Web', *Prospect*, 165 (18 November 2009).

45. Interview with leading EU official, 6 June 2008.

46. Information provided by sources in Belarus.

47. Alastair Rabagliati, 'Discrediting, Disconnect and Division in Belarus', p. 8.

48. Korosteleva, 'Was There a Quiet Revolution?', p. 326.

49. See the Pontis Foundation, 'Belarus after Election: The Naked Dictator', 13 April 2006, www.eurasianhome.org/doc_files/CP_%20Pontis_Belarus_after_Election_The_Naked_Dictator.pdf.

50. *Ibid.*

51. Dzmitriy Drihailo, quoted in Marples, *The Lukashenka Phenomenon*, p. 50.

52. Lionel Beehner, 'Belarus Opposition Undid Revolution', *Kyiv Post*, 19 April 2006.

53. Interview with EU official, 4 June 2007.

54. See 'What the European Union Could Bring to Belarus', at www.delblr.ec.europa.eu/page3242.html.

55. The increase in the gas price to $100 per 1,000 m³ in January 2007 cost Belarus an estimated $1.6 billion. The 'stabilisation loan' granted by Russia in December 2007 was $1.5 billion. See George Dura, 'The EU's Limited Response to Belarus' Pseudo "New Foreign Policy"', *CEPS Policy Brief*, 151 (February 2008), http://shop.ceps.eu/BookDetail.php?item_id=1598.

56. 'China Is Best Friend of Belarus', http://news.xinhuanet.com/english2010/indepth/2010-10/09/c_13549124.htm, dated 9 October 2010.

57. Author's interview with Andrei Dyn'ko, 7 October 2007.

58. Vital Silitski, 'Presidential Administration – An Uncertain New Line', in *Belarusian Yearbook 2009* (Institute of Belarusian Studies, 2010), at www.belinstitute.eu/images/doc-pdf/BY_2009_engl.pdf.

59. See www.charter97.org/index.php?c=ar&i=412&c2=&i2=0&p=1&lngu=en.

60. Feduta, *Lukashenko: Politicheskaia biografiia*, pp. 72 and 64–66.

61. Korosteleva, 'Was There a Quiet Revolution?', p. 328.

62. Vadzim Smok, 'Belarusianization: A New Wave?', *Bell*, 10 (2010); www.eesc.lt.

63. The Kwaśniewski report can be found at www.kwasniewskialeksander.eu/news.php?id=34&mode=view.

64. Ahto Lobjakas, 'Belarusian Opposition Backs EU U-Turn on Lukashenka', *RFE/RL Belarus, Ukraine and Moldova Report*, 8 October 2008.

65. David J. Kramer and Damon Wilson, 'When Sanctions Work', *The National Interest*, 12 August 2010.

66. See www.osce.org/odihr-elections/item_12_32542.html.

67. See the report at www.amnesty.org/en/library/info/EUR49/001/2009/en.

68. 'Smolensk Tragedy Is the Result of Kaczyński Decision, Lukashenko', http://telegraf.by/2010/04/smolensk-tragedy-is-the-result-of-kaczynski-decision-lukashenko.html.

69. See the IMF's *World Economic Outlook 2010*, www.imf.org/external/pubs/ft/weo/2010/02/pdf/text.pdf, especially the table at p. 215.

70. Lukianov, quoted in Luke Harding, 'Belarus Turns Off Flow of Russian Gas to Europe', *The Guardian*, 22 June 2010.

71. Interfax, 28 May 2009.

72. See www.youtube.com/watch?v=vD2TjnbPr8I and www.youtube.com/watch?v=b00wOpBGUMI&feature=player_embedded.

73. Tat'iana Vladimirovna, 'Sosedami glazami ekspertov', 20 June 2010, www.respublika.info/5046/povod/article40927/ and hwww.respublika.info/5048/povod/article41003/.

74. Balázs Jarábik, 'Shifting Positions: Who Is Promoting Democracy in Eastern Europe?', paper prepared for the GLOBSEC 2010 conference, September 2010, available at http://www.ata-sac.org/globsec2010/home/.

75. See www.consilium.europa.eu/uedocs/cms_Data/docs/pressdata/EN/foraff/117326.pdf.

76. See his comments at http://news.belta.by/en/news/elections/?id=599886.

77. The most likely source was via Viktar Rakhmanka, former boss of Belarusian Railways until his arrest in 2001, then the head of the Transport Division of the Investment and Building Department at Russia's Gazprom

78. Some, however, bought into his PR. See Owen Matthews and Anna Nemtsova, 'Russian Payback', *Newsweek*, 13 May 2010.

79. See the polling data at www.iiseps.org/epress15.html and www.swaboda.org/content/article/2095097.htm.

80. See http://www.belarus.by/en/press-center/news/lukashenko-winning-two-thirds-of-the-vote-would-be-a-good-result_i_0000001508.html.

81. See http://telegraf.by/2010/12/exit-polls-lukashenko-nabiraet-ot-742-do-791-golosov.html, 19 December 2010.

82. See 'Novye dannye nezavisimykh eksit-pollov: Lukashenko ne pobezhdaet v pervom ture', www.regnum.ru/news/polit/1358243.html, 19 December 2010.

83. The original report was at http://regnum.ru/news/polit/1358227.html, 19 December 2010. For the second figure, see n.82.

84. See www.iiseps.org/press1.html.

85. Author's interviews with bystanders, who wished to remain anonymous.

86. The NGO Viasna kept a commentary of events. See www.spring96.org/en.

Chapter 12 The Myth of the Belarusian Economic Miracle

1. Leonid Zlotnikov, 'The Belarusian "Economic Miracle" – Illusions and Reality', in Sabine Fischer (ed.), *Back from the Cold? The EU and Belarus in 2009* (Paris: EUISS Chaillot Paper, no. 119, 2009), pp. 65–78, at p. 66.
2. 'Vaennyia straty', in Latyshonak and Miranovich, *Historyia Belarusi*, p. 223.
3. The somewhat under-researched book *The Last Soviet Republic: Alexander Lukashenko's Belarus* (Bloomington, Ind.: Trafford Publishing, 2007) is allegedly by 'Stewart Parker', but the author in question has a very low international profile.
4. Jonathan Steele, 'Europe and the US Decide the Winner before the Vote', *The Guardian*, 10 March 2006. Cf. Roger Boyes, 'Next Stop Is the Belarus BlackBerry Revolution', *The Times*, 5 September 2005; Jo Durden-Smith, 'No More People Power', *The New Statesman*, 3 October 2005.
5. Feduta, *Lukashenko: Politicheskaia biografiia*, p. 339.
6. See http://www.imf.org/external/country/BLR/rr/glance.htm.
7. Kamil Kłysiński and Agata Wierzbowska-Miazga, *Changes in the Political Elite, Economy and Society of Belarus: Appearance and Reality* (Warsaw: OSW, CES Studies, no. 30, 2009), available at www.osw.waw.pl/sites/default/files/PRACE_30. pdf, at p. 56.
8. Interview with Yaroslaw Romanchuk, 26 June 2008, www.eurasianhome.org/xml/t/ expert.xml?lang=en&nic=expert&pid=1617&qmonth=0&qyear=0.
9. Alexei Pikulik, '. . . And Now, the End Is Near? Perspectives of Lukashenka's Political Survival and Beyond', *BISS Studies*, 30 November 2010, www.belinstitute.eu/images/ doc-pdf/sa201001en.pdf.
10. See www.belstat.gov.by, accessed 1 December 2010.
11. 'Russia's Trade with Belarus and Kazakhstan', *Russian Analytical Digest*, 87 (19 November 2010), www.res.ethz.ch., Figure 3, p. 14.
12. See http://belstat.gov.by/homep/en/indicators/ftrade1.php.
13. Dzianis Melyantsou and Andrej Kazakevich, 'Belarus's Relations with Ukraine and Lithuania before and after the 2006 Presidential Elections', *Lithuanian Foreign Policy Review*, 20 (2008), pp. 47–78.
14. Zlotnikov, 'The Belarusian "Economic Miracle"', p. 68.
15. *Ibid.*, p. 69.
16. *Ibid.*
17. Pikulik, '. . . And Now, the End Is Near?' – English adjusted. See also Pikulik, 'Comparative Pathways of Belarus, Russia and Ukraine' (EUI Ph.D Thesis, 2010).
18. Remarks by Valer Karbalevich, Strategia Centre, Minsk at the second annual BISS conference, Kiev, 11–12 November 2008; at http://belinstitute.eu/images/stories/documents/conference2009reporten.pdf.
19. See http://web.worldbank.org/WBSITE/EXTERNAL/COUNTRIES/ECAEXT/BELA RUSEXTN/0,,contentMDK:20629010~menuPK:328439~pagePK:141137~piPK:141 127~theSitePK:328431,00.html#econ.
20. See the figures at http://devdata.worldbank.org/AAG/blr_aag.pdf.
21. See http://belstat.gov.by/homep/en/indicators/population.php.
22. Zlotnikov, 'The Belarusian "Economic Miracle"', p. 70.
23. *Ibid.*, p. 71.
24. Vladimir Matikevich, 'Dollarovye millionery Belarusi', www.bat'ke.net, 15 July 2006.
25. Taras Mlenko, 'Tenevye millionery Belarusi', 6 August 2010, www.delo.ua/biznes/ kompanii/tenevye-millionery-belarusi-143727.
26. Mikalai Nekrashevich, 'Top 10 of Belarusian High-Ranking "Emigrants" to Russia', 24 May 2010, http://charter97.org/en/news/2010/5/24/29219/.
27. Jarabik and Rabagliati, *Buffer Rus*, p. 10.
28. Yaroslav Romanchuk, 'Who Benefits from Belarus–Russia Energy and Trade Wars?', *Bell*, 1:11 (February 2010), www.eesc.lt/public_files/file_1266564029.pdf.

29. Wojciech Kononćzuk, *Difficult Ally: Belarus in Russia's Foreign Policy* (Warsaw: OSW, 2008), p. 54, n. 62.
30. *Ibid.*, p. 42.
31. Pikulik, '. . . And Now, the End Is Near?' – English adjusted; www.belinstitute.eu/images/doc-pdf/sa201001en.pdf. See also one of Pikulik's key sources: Verena Fritz, *State-Building: A Comparative Study of Ukraine, Lithuania, Belarus and Russia* (Budapest: Central European University Press, 2007).
32. Jarabik and Rabagliati, *Buffer Rus*, p. 8.
33. Kruk, Tochitskaya and Shymanovich, 'Impact of the Global Economic Crisis on the Belarusian Economy', p. 8.
34. Mikhal Zaleski, 'World Financial Crisis as an Accelerator for Belarus' Reforms?', http://belinstitute.eu/images/stories/documents/sa62008en.pdf.
35. *Ibid.*
36. Peter Rutland and Oleg Reut, 'The Sorry State of the Customs Union', *The Moscow Times*, 23 March 2010.
37. See www.imf.org/external/country/blr/index.htm.
38. See the statistics at www.export.by/en/?act=news&mode=view&id=20457&page=19, dated 21 June 2010.
39. Kłysiński and Wierzbowska-Miazga, *Changes in the Political Elite, Economy and Society of Belarus: Appearance and Reality*, p. 57.
40. *Doing Business 2010: Belarus*, www.doingbusiness.org/Documents/CountryProfiles/BLR.pdf.
41. See www.doingbusiness.org/rankings, accessed 12 December 2010.
42. Dzmitry Kruk, Irina Tochitskaya and Hleb Shymanovich, 'Impact of the Global Economic Crisis on the Belarusian Economy', *BIIS Research Paper*, 4 February 2010, p. 11.
43. The following section is based on the interpretation of Vitali Silitski in a conversation with the author on 3 March 2009.
44. 'Belarus' Budget Deficit May Rise to 3% of GDP', 27 August 2010, http://news.belta.by/en/news/econom?id=574218.
45. Kruk, Tochitskaya and Shymanovich, 'Impact of the Global Economic Crisis on the Belarusian Economy', p. 3.
46. *Ibid.*, p. 2.
47. See the IMF's *World Economic Outlook 2010*, www.imf.org/external/pubs/ft/weo/2010/02/pdf/text.pdf, especially the table at p. 215.
48. Kamil Kłysiński and Wojciech Kononćzuk, 'Lukashenka Has to Choose: Reforms or Concessions to Russia', 27 October 2010, www.osw.waw.pl/en/publikacje/osw-commentary/2010-10-27/lukashenka-has-to-choose-reforms-or-concessions-to-russia.
49. See http://democraticbelarus.eu/node/9437.
50. See http://www.export.by/en/?act=news&mode=view&id=23332.
51. See www.telegraf.by, 15 October 2010.
52. Kłysiński and Kononćzuk, 'Lukashenka Has to Choose: Reforms or Concessions to Russia'.
53. See 'Belarus: Preparations for the Privatisation of Strategic Enterprises', 30 June 2010, www.osw.waw.pl/en/publikacje/eastweek/2010-06-30/belarus-preparations-privatisation-strategic-enterprises.

Chapter 13 The 2010s: Lukashenka's Juggling Act

1. Andrei Kortunov, 'Belorusskaia l'dina i rossiiskii iasberg', *Russian Council for International Affairs*, 17 August 2020, https://russiancouncil.ru/analytics-and-comments/analytics/belorusskaya-ldina-i-rossiyskiy-aysberg/.
2. Jason Motlagh, 'In Belarus, Clapping Can Be Subversive', *Atlantic*, 21 July 2011, www.theatlantic.com/international/archive/2011/07/in-belarus-clapping-can-be-subversive/242271/.
3. Uladzimir Akulich, Sierż Naūrodski and Aleś Alachnovič, 'The Belarusian Economy is Currently Experiencing Both Cyclical and Structural Recessions', *CASE Belarus*,

15 July 2016, https://medium.com/@CASEresearch/the-belarusian-economy-is-currently-experiencing-both-cyclical-and-structural-recessions-afd96703e6ea.

4. See the IMF data at www.imf.org/external/datamapper/GG_DEBT_GDP@GDD/SWE/BLR.

5. 'China's Global Development Footprint', *AIDDATA*, accessed 16 November 2020, www.aiddata.org/china-official-finance.

6. Tadeusz Giczan, 'The Rise of Belarusian Oligarchs', *CEPA*, 30 July 2020, www.cepa.org/the-rise-of-belarusian-oligarchs.

7. 'Natsional'naia platforma biznesa Belarusi-2018', *Telegraf.by*, 27 March 2018, https://telegraf.by/ehkonomika/389074-nacionalnaya-platforma-biznesa-belarusi-2018/.

8. See the data at https://webgate.ec.europa.eu/isdb_results/factsheets/country/details_belarus_en.pdf.

9. See the report 'IT Industry' by the National Agency of Investment and Privatization at https://investinbelarus.by/upload/pdf/ITper cent20industryper cent202018.pdf.

10. Vadim Sekhovich, '"Krasnye direktora", oligarkhi, druzh'ia iz Forbes. Chasnyi biznes i Lukashenko v proekte "Chetvert" veka", *Tut.by*, 27 June 2019, https://news.tut.by/economics/643329.html.

11. 'Glava gosudarstva posetil OAO 'Kommunarka", *President.gov.by*, 8 October 2004, http://president.gov.by/ru/news_ru/view/glava-gosudarstva-posetil-oao-kommunarka-2113/.

12. Giczan, 'The Rise of Belarusian Oligarchs'.

13. 'Belorusski sprut: "Khotinskii" biznes Aleksandra Lukashenko v RF', *Resursnaia Federatsiia*, 13 September 2016, http://resfed.com/article-2117.

14. Olga Karatch, 'Opinion: Four Russian Instruments of Control Over Belarus', *Belarus Digest*, 13 September 2016, http://belarusdigest.com/story/opinion-four-russian-instruments-control-over-belarus-27210.

15. Vadzim Smok, 'Belarus Cracks Down on Pro-Ukraine Donbass Fighters', *Belarus Digest*, 21 April 2016, https://belarusdigest.com/story/belarus-cracks-down-on-pro-ukraine-donbass-fighters/.

16. Katerina Andreeva and Igor' Il'iash, *Belorusskii Donbass* (Kiev: Folio, 2020).

17. Ryhor Astapenia, 'Migrants from Eastern Ukraine Put Pressure on Belarus', *Belarus Digest*, 3 August 2015, https://belarusdigest.com/story/migrants-from-eastern-ukraine-put-pressure-on-belarus/.

18. 'Vsesil'na li propaganda?', *IISEPS*, 5 July 2014, http://old.iiseps.org/06-14-08.html.

19. Margarita Balmaceda, *Living the High Life in Minsk: Russian Energy Rents, Domestic Populism and Belarus' Impending Crisis* (Budapest: Central European University Press, 2014), p. 120.

20. Interview with Dzianis Melyantsow, 31 March 2017.

21. Balmaceda, *Living the High Life in Minsk*, p. 120.

22. Interview at the Ukrainian National Security Council, 23 August 2017.

23. Bartosz Rutkowski, Marcin Rychły and Maciej Zaniewicz, 'The Complicated Story of Belarusian Opposition', *New Eastern Europe*, 1 (2016), pp. 131–7, http://competition2016.belarusinfocus.info/articles/complicated-story-belarusian-opposition/.

24. 'The Most Important Results of the Public Opinion Poll', *IISEPS*, 29 December 2015, www.iiseps.org/?p=3865&lang=en.

25. Interview with Katia Glod, 31 March 2017.

26. Andrei Yeliseyeu, 'Belarus at a Crossroads: Political Regime Transformation and Future Scenarios', *iSANS*, 22 July 2020, https://isans.org/analysis-en/policy-papers-en/belarus-at-a-crossroads-political-regime-transformation-and-future-scenarios.html.

27. 'Personnel for the Election', *Belarus Security Blog*, 28 February 2020, https://bsblog.info/personnel-for-the-election/.

28. Remarks by Makei at CER in London, 28 March 2018.

29. See https://minskdialogue.by/en/research/reports.

30. Interview with Yauheni Preiherman, 29 November 2017.

31. *Ibid.*

32. Remarks by Lukashenka at the Minsk Dialogue, 24 May 2018.

33. Remarks by Makei at the CER in London, 28 March 2018.

34. Interview with Dzianis Melyantsow, 21 August 2017.

35. 'Lukashenko's Family Strengthen Control Over the Belarusian Ruling Elite', *Belarus in Focus*, 22 April 2016, https://belarusinfocus.info/society-and-politics/lukashenkos-family-strengthen-control-over-belarusian-ruling-elite; interviews with Yuri Tsarik and Dzianis Melyantsow, 21 August 2017.

36. Interview with Yuri Tsarik, 30 January 2018.

37. *Ibid.*

38. Robert Coalson and Rikard Jozwiak, 'Worried About Moscow, Belarus's Lukashenka Drifts Toward Brussels', *RFE/RL*, 27 January 2015, www.rferl.org/a/belarus-lukashenka-drifts-toward-brussels/26816183.html.

39. Volha Charnysh, 'Police in Belarus: Guardian or Threat?', *Belarus Digest*, 4 February 2016, https://belarusdigest.com/story/police-in-belarus-guardian-or-threat.

40. 'Press-konferentsiia Prezidenta Respubliki Belarusi A.G. Lukashenko zhurnalistam rossiiskikh regional'nykh sredstv massovoi informatsii', *President.gov.by*, 17 October 2014, http://president.gov.by/ru/news_ru/view/press-konferentsija-prezidenta-respubliki-belarus-aglukashenko-zhurnalistam-rossijskix-regionalnyx-sredstv-10025/.

41. Vadim Mojeiko, 'Civil society: Between Repression and Collaboration with Business', *BISS*, 20 June 2019, https://belinstitute.com/en/article/3687.

42. S.A Tratstsiak, A.A. Kavalenia et al., *Belaruskaia Narodnaia Respublika w historyi belaruskai natsyianal'nai dziarzhawnastsi* (Minsk: Belaruskaia navuka, 2020).

43. See especially *Belorusskaia gosudarstvennost': ot istokov do kontsa XVIII v.* (Minsk: Belaruskaia navuka, 2018), volume one in the five-volume series edited by A.A. Kovalenia (Kavalenia) et al., *Istoriia belorusskoi gosudarstvennosti.*

44. Email from Piotr Rudkowski, 14 February 2018.

45. Piotr Rudkoŭski (Rudkowski), 'National Identity: State Policy and Public Opinion', *Belarusian Yearbook*, 2019, https://nmnby.eu/yearbook/2019/en/page12.html.

46. 'Public Opinion Poll: Support for Integration with Russia Plummeting in Belarus', *Belsat*, 10 February 2020, https://belsat.eu/en/news/public-opinion-poll-support-for-integration-with-russia-plummeting-in-belarus/; Anaïs Marin, 'The Union State of Belarus and Russia: Myths and Realities of Political-Military Integration', *Vilnius Institute for Policy Analysis*, 2020, https://vilniusinstitute.lt/wp-content/uploads/2020/06/Anais-Marin-Union-State-of-Belarus-and-Russia.pdf.

47. Grigory Ioffe, 'Belarus: Elections and Sovereignty', *Eurasia Daily Monitor*, 17:111 (29 July 2020), https://jamestown.org/program/belarus-elections-and-sovereignty/.

48. Piotr Rudkoŭski (Rudkowski), 'Soft Belarusianisation: The Ideology of Belarus in the Era of the Russian-Ukrainian Conflict', *OSW Commentary*, 253 (3 November 2017), www.osw.waw.pl/en/publikacje/osw-commentary/2017-11-03/soft-belarusianisation-ideology-belarus-era-russian-ukrainian. See also Vadim Mojeiko, 'Soft Belarusization: A New Shift in Lukashenka's Domestic Policy?', *Belarus Digest*, 21 April 2015, https://belarusdigest.com/story/soft-belarusization-a-new-shift-in-lukashenkas-domestic-policy/.

49. Aliaksei Dzermant, *Belarus'-Evraziia: pogranich'e Rosii i Evropy* (Imhoclub.by, 2020).

50. I.E. Savkina, *Chetyre kniagini – chetyre sud'by* (Minsk: Belorusskaia Pravoslavnaia Tserkov', 2020).

51. Dzmitry Mitskevich, 'Viejšnoryja: The Belarusian Defence Ministry Plays with Fire', *Belarus Digest*, 13 December 2017, https://belarusdigest.com/story/viejsnoryja-the-belarusian-defence-ministry-plays-with-fire/.

52. See https://vie.today/.

53. Andrew Wilson, 'Should the West be Wary of an Imminent "Union" of Russia and Belarus?', *Jamestown*, 20 December 2019, https://jamestown.org/program/should-the-west-be-wary-of-an-imminent-union-of-russia-and-belarus/.

54. 'Coercion to "Integration": Russia's Creeping Assault on the Sovereignty of Belarus', *iSANS*, 2019, https://isans.org/wp-content/docs/Belarus_report_eng_iSANS_10.03.2019_BRIEF_VERSION.pdf.

55. Kamil Kłysiński and Piotr Żochowski, 'The End of the Myth of Brotherly Belarus? Russian Soft Power in Belarus after 2014: The Background and its Manifestations', *OSW Studies*, 58 (November 2016), www.osw.waw.pl/sites/default/files/prace_58_ang_end_of_myth_net.pdf, at p. 17.

56. Vladimir Zotov, 'Bat'kiny natsisty', *Lenta.ru*, 3 April 2018, https://lenta.ru/articles/2018/04/03/belonazi/.

57. Yurii Baranchik, 'Belarus: elita uzhe vybrala preemnika Lukashenko', *Regnum.ru*, 6 August 2016, https://regnum.ru/news/polit/2164093.html.

58. Andrei Yeliseyeu, 'Fundamental Shifts in Anti-Belarusian Disinformation and Propaganda: Analysis of Quantitative and Qualitative Changes', *EAST Center*, 17 April 2019, http://east-center.org/fundamental-shifts-in-anti-belarus-disinformation-and-propaganda/; 'Re-Building of the Empire: Behind the Facade of Russia-Belarus Union State', *iSANS*, 19 December 2019, https://isans.org/analysis-en/reports-en/re-building-of-the-empire-behind-the-facade-of-russia-belarus-union-state.html.

59. Dmitrii Butrin, 'Druzhba nalogov. Rossiia i Belorussiia namereny v 2021 godu pereity na edinyi Nalogovyi kodeks i ne tol'ko', *Kommersant*, 16 September 2019, www.kommersant.ru/doc/4094365.

60. 'Media Find Out Contents of 31st "Road Map" on Belarus-Russia Integration', *Charter 97*, 18 March 2020, https://charter97.org/en/news/2020/3/18/369803/.

Chapter 14 The Revolution Without a Name

1. Aliaksandra Dynko, '"Ya nia vedaiu, khto b moh supratsiwliatstsa Maskve tak, iak Lukashenka". Vialikae interviiu z' S'viatlanai Aleksievich', *Radio Svaboda*, 10 February 2020, www.svaboda.org/a/30422633.html.

2. Andrei Yeliseyeu, 'Belarus at a Crossroads: Political Regime Transformation and Future Scenarios', *EAST Center*, 22 July 2020, https://east-center.org/wp-content/uploads/2020/07/Belarus-at-a-Crossroads-Political-Regime-Transformation-and-Future-Scenarios.pdf.

3. Stephen Hall, 'Tracing Authoritarian Learning in Belarus, Moldova, Russia and Ukraine' (UCL Ph.D Thesis, 2019), pp. 72–3.

4. Ray Furlong, 'Belarus Lives it Up as Neighbors Lock Down Over COVID-19', *RFE/RL*, 30 March 2020, www.rferl.org/a/belarus-lives-it-up-as-neighbors-lock-down-over-covid-19/30518084.html?ltflags=mailer.

5. Yeliseyeu, 'Belarus at a Crossroads'.

6. Andrew E. Kramer, '"There Are No Viruses Here": Leader of Belarus Scoffs at Lockdowns', *New York Times*, 25 April 2020; www.nytimes.com/2020/04/25/world/europe/belarus-lukashenko-coronavirus.html.

7. 'Millions Take Part in Belarus Civic Labor Day Amid Coronavirus', *Deutsche Welle News*, 25 April 2020, www.dw.com/en/millions-take-part-in-belarus-civic-labor-day-amid-coronavirus/a-53243951.

8. Ekaterina Pierson-Lyzhina and Oleksii Kovalenko, 'The Coronavirus Outbreak in Belarus, Russia, and Ukraine: Responses by the State, Business and Civil Society', *EAST Center*, 28 October 2020, https://east-center.org/wp-content/uploads/2020/10/The-coronavirus-outbreak-BLR-RU-UKR.pdf.

9. See the data at *Georank*, accessed 1 September 2020, https://georank.org/covid/belarus/sweden.

10. See the data at *Statista*, accessed 1 September 2020, www.statista.com/statistics/1110187/coronavirus-incidence-europe-by-country/.

11. Felix Light, 'How Poor Handling of Covid-19 has Caused Uproar in Belarus', *New Statesman*, 24 June 2020, www.newstatesman.com/world/europe/2020/06/how-poor-handling-covid-19-has-caused-uproar-belarus.

12. 'Strana dlia zhizhni', *YouTube*, accessed 11 November 2020, www.youtube.com/channel/UCFPC7r3tWWXWzUIROLx46mg.

13. Tadeusz Giczan, 'Belarusian Establishment Remains Monolithic. Or Does It?', *BNE IntelliNews*, 5 August 2020, https://www.intellinews.com/comment-belarusian-establishment-remains-monolithic-or-does-it-188987/.

14. 'Rossiiskie SMI v yune ne iskliuchali porazhenie Lukashenko. Otchet a prokremlevskikh narrativakh', *Media IQ*, 4 August 2020, https://mediaiq.by/article/rossiyskie-smi-v-iyune-ne-isklyuchali-porazhenie-lukashenko-otchet-o-prokremlevskih.

15. Henry Meyer, Irina Reznik and Aliaksandr Kudrytski, 'Putin's Unruly Ally Casts Eyes to West as Russian Ties Strain', *Bloomberg*, 13 June 2020, https://www.bloomberg.com/news/articles/2020-06-13/putin-s-unruly-ally-casts-eyes-to-west-as-russian-ties-strain.

16. 'Post-truth and Post-elections in the Post-Covid Belarus: Theory and Practice of Meddling', *iSANS*, 19 June 2020, https://isans.org/articles-en/post-truth-and-post-elections-in-the-post-covid-belarus-theory-and-practice-of-meddling.html.

17. 'Lukashenko: Zabyli, kak Karimov v Andizhane podavil putch? Nu tak my napomnim!', *Reform.by*, 4 June 2020, https://reform.by/lukashenko-zabyli-kak-karimov-v-andizhane-podavil-putch-nu-tak-my-napomnim.

18. 'Alexander Lukashenko Threatens to Execute the Peaceful Demonstrators by Firing Squad', *Our House*, 9 June 2020, https://news.house/40767.

19. 'Over 360 people Detained at "Solidarity Chains" Across Belarus', *Belsat.eu*, 25 June 2020, https://belsat.eu/en/news/over-360-people-detained-at-solidarity-chains-across-belarus/.

20. '260 Detained in Protests Across Belarus', *Viasna*, 15 July 2020, http://spring96.org/en/news/98243.

21. 'Analitychnaia tydnevaia spravazdacha pa vynikakh hazirannia: 6-12 lipenia 2020 hoda', *Viasna*, 13 July 2020, http://spring96.org/be/news/98194.

22. Galina Upasik, 'V spiske belorusskikh politzakliuchennykh 25 chelovek. Kto vse eti liudi', *Tut.by*, 16 June 2020, https://news.tut.by/society/691438.html.

23. '"Lukashenko otstal ot svoego naroda": belorusskie zhenshchiny o vyskazyvanii prezydenta o nikh', *BBC.com*, 15 July 2020, www.bbc.com/russian/institutional-53418368.

24. 'Esli bremia prezidentstva nagruzit' na zhenshchinu, "ona upadet, bedniaga", – Lukashenko', *Espreso*, 20 June 2020, https://ru.espreso.tv/news/2020/06/20/esly_bremya_prezydentstva_nagruzyt_na_zhenschynu_quotona_upadet_bednyagaquot_lukashenko.

25. @TadeuszGiczan, *Twitter*, 25 August 2020, https://twitter.com/TadeuszGiczan/status/1298330716942544896.

26. @TadeuszGiczan, *Twitter*, 19 September 2020, https://twitter.com/TadeuszGiczan/status/1307319829112803328.

27. @TadeuszGiczan, *Twitter*, 14 August 2020, https://twitter.com/TadeuszGiczan/status/1294287414383476737.

28. Sławomir Sierakowski, 'Belarus Uprising: The Making of a Revolution', *Journal of Democracy*, 31:4 (October 2020), https://www.journalofdemocracy.org/articles/belarus-uprising-the-making-of-a-revolution/.

29. Oleksiy Kupriyenko, 'The World's First Telegram Revolution: How Social Media Fuels Protest in Belarus', *Euromaidan Press*, 27 August 2020, http://euromaidanpress.com/2020/08/27/how-telegram-social-media-help-fuel-protests-in-belarus/.

30. 'Ermoshina pobedila v konkurse "Seksist goda-2010"', *Telegraf.by*, 14 January 2011, https://telegraf.by/in-belarus/ermoshina-pobedila-v-konkurse-seksist-goda-2010/.

31. '1,049,344 unikal'nykh podtverzhdennykh golosov na platforme "Golos"', *Golos*, https://partizan-results.com/?fbclid=IwAR3qJaiXPSBz8irb3AhlEhTh00ouB3bh6bcr1iIqwaGQlDkeZ7C5MnSFHh0.

32. @TadeuszGiczan, *Twitter*, 20 August 2020, https://twitter.com/TadeuszGiczan/status/1296411943465623552.

33. @TadeuszGiczan, *Twitter*, 9 August 2020, https://twitter.com/tadeuszgiczan/status/1292560483959156742?lang=en.

34. Polityczek.pl,*Facebook*,12 August 2020, www.facebook.com/watch/?v=2715374795384457. See also @RALee85, *Twitter*, 14 August 2020, https://twitter.com/RALee85/status/1294208593324113926.

35. @TadeuszGiczan, *Twitter*, 24 August 2020, https://twitter.com/TadeuszGiczan/status/1297842467795079168.

36. 'How Elections were Rigged in Vitebsk on August 9, 2020', *YouTube*, 10 August 2020, www.youtube.com/watch?v=DgkDrVj1qIo.

37. Andrei Eliseev, 'Matematika protiv Ermoshinoi: Kak v Belarusi fal'sifitsiruiut vybory', *Scribd*, uploaded 4 August 2020, https://www.scribd.com/document/471369567/Математика-против-Ермошиной-Как-в-Беларуси-фальсифицируют-выборы#download.

38. Katia Bonch-Osmolovskaia and Artem Shchennikov, 'Vbroshennyi prezident', *Novaya Gazeta*, 13 August 2020, https://novayagazeta.ru/articles/2020/08/13/86651-vbroshennyy-prezident.

39. Boris Ovchinnikov, 'Kak progolosovala Belarus' za predelami bol'shikh i srednikh gorodov. Popytka rekonstruktsii', 16 August 2020, https://medium.com/@barouh/как-проголосовала-беларусь-за-пределами-больших-и-средних-городов-попытка-реконструкции-1d1b026e5814.

40. Aleksei Zakharov, 'Metody podscheta: dobavliaia, otnimat', *Trv-science.ru*, 25 August 2020, https://trv-science.ru/2020/08/25/dobavlyaya-otnimat/.

41. Bonch-Osmolovskaia and Shchennikov, 'Vbroshennyi prezident'; Alya Shandra, 'How Alyaksandr Lukashenka Stole the Belarus Presidential Election', *Euromaidan Press*, 21 August 2020, http://euromaidanpress.com/2020/08/21/statistics-dont-lie-how-alyaksandr-lukashenka-rigged-the-belarus-presidential-election-exclusive/.

42. Ryhor Astapenia, 'What Belarusians Think About Their Country's Crisis', *Chatham House*, 21 October 2020, www.chathamhouse.org/2020/10/what-belarusians-think-about-their-countrys-crisis.

43. 'Sotsiolog: 50% plius 1 golos mogli ne nabrat' i Lukashenko, i Tikhanovskaya', *Deutsche Welle*, 4 October 2020, www.dw.com/ru/oleg-manaev-501-golos-mogli-ne-nabrat-ni-lukashenko-ni-tihanovskaja/a-55131952.

44. 'Final Report on 2020 Presidential Elections in Belarus', *Golos*, https://bit.ly/voice-belarus-report.

45. 'Faktor Sheimana', *Belorusskii partizan*, 6 October 2020, https://belaruspartisan.by/politic/514345/.

46. 'Human Rights Situation in Belarus: August 2020', *Viasna*, 2 September 2020, https://spring96.org/en/news/99352.

47. 'Belarus': Nasilie i militseiskii proizvol v otvet na poslevybornye protesty', *Human Rights Watch*, 12 August 2020, www.hrw.org/ru/news/2020/08/12/376082.

48. The video can be found on Google Drive at https://drive.google.com/file/d/1W3PM2xjlnF2xErd4u-coArHPqE7b2rRm/view.

49. Pavel Supanenka, 'The Rise of Belarusians: To Defeat the Dictator', *YouTube*, 11 October 2020, www.youtube.com/watch?v=CgF2n8_Zw4g&feature=youtu.be.

50. 'UN Human Rights Experts: Belarus Must Stop Torturing Protesters and Prevent Enforced Disappearances', *OHCHR*, 1 September 2020, www.ohchr.org/EN/NewsEvents/Pages/DisplayNews.aspx?NewsID=26199&LangID=E.

51. 'Vklyuchivshii "Peremen!" zvukorezhisser sayavil, chto v tiur'me ego bil zamglavy MVD Belarusi Barsukov', *Telegraf.by*, 17 August 2020, https://telegraf.by/obshhestvo/vkljuchivshij-peremen-zvukorezhisser-zayavil-chto-v-tjurme-ego-bil-zamglavy-mvd-belarusi-barsukov/.

52. 'Tortures in Minsk Prison', video tweeted by Franak Viačorka, @franakviacorka, *Twitter*, 13 August 2020, https://twitter.com/franakviacorka/status/1294008633903259648.

53. Sierakowski, 'Belarus Uprising'.

54. Ben Aris, 'The Belarusian Banshees', *BNE IntelliNews*, 13 September 2020, www.intel-linews.com/the-belarusian-banshees-191769/?source=belarus&inf_contact_key=89f 2e3e3b0a5c6a4087373726b6ee012cc0558ed5d4c28cbfab114022b1ec50d.

55. Michael Scollon, 'Belarusian Protesters Counter Authorities' Moves with Online Tactics', *RFE/RL*, 21 September 2020, www.rferl.org/a/belarusian-protesters-counter-authorities-moves-with-online-tactics/30850435.html?ltflags=mailer.

56. Alevtina Snihir, 'The Belarusian Diaspora Awakens', *GMF*, 17 August 2020, www.gm-fus.org/blog/2020/08/17/belarusian-diaspora-awakens.

57. See https://t.me/BlackBookBelarus.

58. @nexta_tv, *Twitter*, 24 September 2020, https://twitter.com/nexta_tv/status/1309092652676198400.

59. Viktor Belyaev, 'Belorusskie kiberpartizany vzlomali v subbotu okolo 30 saitov', *Thinktanks.by*, 11 October 2020, https://thinktanks.by/publication/2020/10/11/belorusskie-kiberpartizany-vzlomali-v-subbotu-okolo-30-saytov.html?mc_cid=b706ef53cc&mc_eid=8c76d3ed3f.

60. @nexta_tv, *Twitter*, 26 September 2020, https://twitter.com/nexta_tv/sta-tus/1309930574807797760.

61. 'Rabochie gruppi', *Koordinatsionnyi Sovet*, accessed 16 November 2020, https://rada.vision/rabochie-gruppy.

62. 'Belarus Workers Chant "Resign!" at Lukashenko on Factory Visit – Video', *Guardian*, 17 August 2020, www.theguardian.com/world/video/2020/aug/17/belarus-workers-chant-resign-at-lukashenko-on-factory-visit-video.

63. Conversation with Kamil Kłysiński, 29 October 2020.

64. Marharyta Fabrykant, 'Russian-speaking Belarusian Nationalism: An Ethnolinguistic Identity Without a Language?', *Europe-Asia Studies*, 71:1 (2019), pp. 117–36.

65. Interview with Oleg Manaev, 27 October 2020.

66. Interviews with Andrei Dynko, 1 April 2017, and Artyom Shraibman, 21 August 2017.

67. Aleksandra Boguslavskaia, 'Belorusy gotovy k dolgoi bor'be'. Sotsiolog o nastroeni-iakh protestuiushchikh', *Deutsche Welle*, 26 August 2020, www.dw.com/ru/belorusy-gotovy-k-dolgoj-borbe-sociolog-o-nastroenijah-protestujushhih/a-54704307.

68. Vladimir Socor, 'A Belarusian Revolution? What Kind? (Part One)', *Eurasia Daily Monitor*, 2 November 2020, https://jamestown.org/program/a-belarusian-revolution-what-kind-part-one/.

69. Katja Richters, 'The Belarusian Orthodox Church: From Reluctant Opponent to Re-gime Loyalist', *Berkley Center*, 11 September 2020, https://berkleycenter.georgetown.edu/responses/the-belarusian-orthodox-church-from-reluctant-opponent-to-re-gime-loyalist.

70. Cyril Hovorun, 'The Belarusian Protests and the Orthodox Church', *Berkley Center*, 28 August 2020, https://berkleycenter.georgetown.edu/responses/the-belarusian-protests-and-the-orthodox-church.

71. 'Metropolitan Epifaniy Called on the Belarusians to Establish Autonomous Orthodox Church (upd)', *Orthodox Times*, 13 August 2020, https://orthodoxtimes.com/metro-politan-epiphaniy-called-on-the-belarusians-to-establish-autonomous-orthodox-church/.

72. Andrei Makhovsky, '"I'm Not A Saint": Lukashenko Offers to Hand Over Power After Referendum', *Reuters*, 17 August 2020, www.reuters.com/article/us-belarus-election/im-not-a-saint-lukashenko-offers-to-hand-over-power-after-referendum-idUSKCN25D0IJ?il=0.

73. 'What's in Belarusian Riot Police's Arsenal?', *BNE IntelliNews*, 11 August 2020, www.intellinews.com/index.php/what-s-in-belarusian-riot-police-s-arsenal-189410/?source=belarus.

74. See the reports at http://en.kremlin.ru/events/security-council.

75. 'The Kremlin "Assistance" Operation in Belarus: The Other Kind of the Polite Green Man are Already on the Ground', *iSANS*, 21 August 2020, https://isans.org/columns-en/

the-kremlin-assistance-operation-in-belarus-the-other-kind-of-the-polite-green-man-are-already-on-the-ground.html.

76. 'Belarus: Lukashenko brandishes rifle in official clips released after Minsk protest', *YouTube*, 24 August 2020, www.youtube.com/watch?v=U-ltnESW6qY.

77. Christian F. Trippe and Ekaterina Sotnik, 'Belarus: How Death Squads Targeted Opposition Politicians', *Deutsche Welle*, 16 December 2019, https://www.dw.com/en/belarus-how-death-squads-targeted-opposition-politicians/a-51685204.

78. 'Human Rights Situation in Belarus: August 2020', *Viasna*, https://spring96.org/en/news/99352.

79. 'Human Rights Situation in Belarus: October 2020', *Viasna*, http://spring96.org/en/news/100211. See also 'Political Prisoners in Belarus, 2020', *iSANS*, https://isans.org/palitviazni/?lang=eng.

80. @TadeuszGiczan, *Twitter*, 14 August 2020, https://twitter.com/TadeuszGiczan/status/1294334174275481600.

81. Aleksey Kovalev and Yan Avseyushkin, 'Zachem Kreml' vyslal na pomoshch' Lukashenko zhurnalistskii desant?', *iSANS*, 11 September 2020, https://isans.org/articles/zachem-kreml-vyslal-na-pomoshh-lukashenko-zhurnalistskij-desant.html.

82. Andrei Eliseev, 'Peremeny v (bela)russkoi propagande: SShA i Soros podvinuli pol'sko-litovskii sgovor', *iSANS*, 24 September 2020, https://isans.org/columns/peremeny-v-belarusskoj-propagande-ssha-i-soros-podvinuli-polsko-litovskij-sgovor.html.

83. Amy Mackinnon, 'The Evolution of a Russian Troll', *Foreign Policy*, 10 July 2019, https://foreignpolicy.com/2019/07/10/the-evolution-of-a-russian-troll-russia-libya-detained-tripoli/.

84. Alexey Kovalev, 'But Help Came: How the Russian State Media Rescued Belarusian Broadcasters from Political Pluralism', *Meduza*, 15 September 2020, https://meduza.io/en/feature/2020/09/15/but-help-came.

85. Polina Titkevich, 'Ansambl' "Kosovskie piony": "Podumaite, pochemu inostrannye sily vmeshivaiuttsia v vashi vybory". Kakie eshche eksperty vystupaiut na belarusskom gosTV', *Media IQ*, 28 August 2020, https://mediaiq.by/article/ansambl-kosovskie-piony-podumayte-pochemu-inostrannye-sily-vmeshivayutsya-v-vashi-vybory.

86. Gigi Gigatashvili, 'Anonymous Pro-Russian Telegram Channels Target Protests in Belarus', *DFR Lab*, 25 February 2020, https://medium.com/dfrlab/anonymous-pro-russian-telegram-channels-target-protests-in-belarus-16ac3d0a1a12.

87. See ross-bel.ru.

88. Maksim Katz, 'Rossiiskaia propaganda v Belarusi', *YouTube*, 22 August 2020, https://www.youtube.com/watch?v=w7GNQ2ZUu7k. See also the commentary by Alexander Volvachev, 'Rossiisskie polittehnologi v Belarusi rabotaiut na Kreml', *Media IQ*, 25 August 2020, https://mediaiq.by/article/rossiyskie-polittehnologi-v-belarusi-rabotayut-na-kreml.

89. Dmitrii Kartsev, 'Lukashenko govorit, chto v programme oppositsii est' vykhod iz Soiuznogo gosudarstva s Rossiei. Eto Pravda? (Spoiler: neponiatno)', *Meduza*, 18 August 2020, https://meduza.io/feature/2020/08/18/lukashenko-govorit-chto-oppozitsiya-hochet-vyvesti-belarus-iz-soyuznogo-gosudarstva-s-rossiey-eto-pravda.

90. Andrei Yeliseyeu, 'Misogyny on TV: How Belarusian and Russian Propaganda Seeks to Discredit Svetlana Tikhanovskaya', *Visegrad Insight*, 13 October 2020, https://visegradinsight.eu/misogyny-on-tv/.

91. Maxim Solopov, 'Dictatorship is Our Brand', *Meduza*, 28 August 2020, https://meduza.io/en/feature/2020/08/28/dictatorship-is-our-brand.

92. Siarhei Bohdan, 'Belarusian State Apparatus – Strong from the Outside, Hollow from the Inside', *Belarus Digest*, 16 September 2020, https://belarusdigest.com/story/belarusian-state-apparatus-strong-from-the-outside-hollow-from-the-inside/.

93. 'Eismont: "Diktatura – eto nash brend, poriadok i normal'naia spokoinaia zhizn"', *Reform.by*, 8 March 2019, https://reform.by/jejsmont-diktatura-jeto-nash-brend-porjadok-i-normalnaja-spokojnaja-zhizn.

94. Solopov, 'Dictatorship is Our Brand'.
95. 'Lukashenko zadalsia voprosom o pol'ze diktatury iz-za problem s vodoi', *RBC.ru*, 28 June 2020, www.rbc.ru/politics/28/06/2020/5ef7f9789a79477be74d6435.
96. 'Popytka narusheniia vozdushnogo prostranstva Belarusi', *Tvr.by*, 24 August 2020, www.tvr.by/news/obshchestvo/popytka_narusheniya_vozdushnogo_prostranstva_belarusi/.
97. 'Lukashenko: High-Profile Diplomatic War on Belarus has Begun', *Belta.by*, 27 August 2020, https://eng.belta.by/president/view/lukashenko-high-profile-diplomatic-war-on-belarus-began-132936-2020/.
98. Andrei Eliseev, 'S informatsionnym suverenitetom Belarusi pokoncheno za tri nedeli', *iSANS*, 31 August 2020, https://isans.org/columns/s-informaczionnym-suverenitetom-belarusi-pokoncheno-za-tri-nedeli.html.
99. Andrei Yeliseyeu, '"Zmagars" as a Universal Expression of Evil: Belarusian Propaganda Has Put a Halter on a Long-Standing Pro-Kremlin Label', *iSANS*, 11 September 2020, https://isans.org/articles-en/zmagars-as-a-universal-expression-of-evil-belarusian-propaganda-has-put-a-halter-on-a-long-standing-pro-kremlin-label.html.
100. 'Belarus' ne drognet / liudi za mir v strane', *Youtube*, 24 August 2020, www.youtube.com/watch?v=QYsVik_Pr98&feature=youtu.be.
101. 'What Have Pro-Kremlin Media Strategists Achieved in Belarus?', *EUvsDiSiNFO*, 23 November 2020, https://euvsdisinfo.eu/what-have-pro-kremlin-media-strategists-achieved-in-belarus/.
102. Irina Khalil, 'Yabat'ki. Osnovnye priznaki rossiiskogo prisutstviia v Belarusi', *Novaya Gazeta*, 22 August 2020, https://novayagazeta.ru/articles/2020/08/22/86782-yabatki.
103. 'Why the Kremlin Needs Belarusian Political Parties', *iSANS*, 20 July 2020, https://isans.org/articles-en/why-the-kremlin-needs-belarusian-political-parties.html.
104. Gustav Gressel, Nicu Popescu and Andrew Wilson, 'Belarus and Armenia: How Russia Handles Uprisings', *ECFR*, 16 September 2020, https://ecfr.eu/article/commentary_belarus_and_armenia_how_russia_handles_uprisings/.
105. Kortunov, 'Belorusskaia l'dina i rossiiskii iasberg'.
106. 'Data Scientist Claims "Staggering" Fraud at Russia's Constitution Vote', *Moscow Times*, 3 July 2020, www.themoscowtimes.com/2020/07/03/data-scientist-claims-staggering-fraud-at-russias-constitution-vote-a70769. 'Here's Why Statisticians are Calling Putin's Constitutional Plebiscite the Most Fraudulent Vote in Russia's Recent History', *Meduza*, 6 July 2020, https://meduza.io/en/feature/2020/07/06/here-s-why-statisticians-are-calling-putin-s-constitutional-plebiscite-the-most-fraudulent-vote-in-russia-s-recent-history.
107. 'Gosti inauguratsii Lukashenko raskryli strannoe zakulis'e', *Moskovskii komsomolets*, 23 September 2020, www.mk.ru/politics/2020/09/23/gosti-inauguracii-lukashenko-raskryli-strannoe-zakulise-otnyali-telefony.html.
108. 'Esli belorusy voz'mut primer s kirgizov, mozhet priekhat' Putin na tanke', *Naviny.by*, 9 October 2020, https://naviny.media/article/20201009/1602216142-nuzhno-li-protestuyushchim-belorusam-brat-za-obrazec-kirgizskiy-scenariy?amp&fbclid=IwAR1rEpdMBpDCJWCZSZlOKzYDtVP9VoDalVCog4Ddam-EGemcL-ByTpMUSpus.
109. 'Opublikovano video pervogo za chetyre mesiatsa razgovora Tikhanovskoi s muzhem', *RIA Novosti*, 10 October 2020, https://ria.ru/20201010/tikhanovskaya-1579225173.html.
110. Tsikhanowskaya on *Telegram*, 13 October 2020, https://t.me/tsikhanouskaya/261.
111. Conversation with Belarusian analysts, 10 November 2020.
112. Figures posted by Pavel Latushka's People's Anti-Crisis Management group on Facebook, 14 November 2020, www.facebook.com/111554507424455/posts/125310752715497/?d=n.

Conclusions: Lukashenka's Rise and Fall

1. Marples, *The Lukashenka Phenomenon*.
2. Grigory Ioffe, *Reassessing Lukashenka: Belarus in Cultural and Geopolitical Context* (Basingstoke: Palgrave Macmillan, 2014).
3. V. Karbalevich, *Aleksandr Lukashenko: Politicheskii portret* (Moscow: Partizan, 2010).
4. Oleg Antonenko, '"Sasha, ty u finishnoi cherty". Bol'shoe interv'iu eks-prezidenta Pol'shi Aleksandra Kvas'nevskogo o Lukashenko, Putine i Belarusi', *BBC Russian Service*, 2 September 2020, www.bbc.com/russian/features-53991945.
5. Vitalii Silitski et al. (eds), *Sotsial'nye kontrakty v sovremennoi Belarusi* (St Petersburg: Nevskii prostor, 2009).
6. Jovita Pranevičiūtė-Neliupšienė et al., *Belarusian Regime Longevity: Happily Ever After. . .* (Vilnius: Vilnius University, 2014); Viachaslau Yarashkevich, 'Political Economy of Modern Belarus: Going Against Mainstream?', *Europe-Asia Studies*, 66:10 (2014), pp. 1703–34.
7. Matthew Frear, *Belarus under Lukashenka: Adaptive Authoritarianism* (London and New York: Routledge, 2019).
8. See Vitali Silitski, *Electorate of the Authority: Then and Now*, 5 October 2010, www.belinstitute.eu/index.php?option=com_content&view=article&id=745%3A2010-10-05-07-39-34&catid=5%3Areviews&Itemid=27&lang=en.
9. Andrei Yeliseyeu, *Facebook*, 6 October 2020, www.facebook.com/andrei.yeliseyeu/posts/10224814283291396.
10. Natalia Leshchenko, 'The National Ideology and the Basis of the Lukashenka Regime in Belarus', *Europe-Asia Studies*, 60:8 (October 2008), pp. 1419–33.
11. '$503 Average Salary by the Year's End, Government', *Telegraf*, 28 October 2010, http://telegraf.by/2010/10/503-average-salary-by-the-years-end-government.html.
12. From the *World Economic Outlook Database 2010*, accessed 19 November 2010, www.imf.org/external/pubs/ft/weo/2010/02/weodata/index.aspx.
13. Aleksei Pikulik, '. . . And Now, the End is Near?: Perspectives of Lukashenka's Political Survival and Beyond', *ODB Brussels*, 30 November 2010, https://odb-office.eu/policy-briefs/and-now-end-near-perspective-lukashenkas-political-survival-and-beyond.
14. See the data at www.iiseps.org/data10-391.html.
15. See www.president.gov.by/press10674.html and www.president.gov.by/press10676.html.
16. Interview with Natalia Leshchenko, 24 July 2007.
17. Vitali Silitski, *Contagion Deterred: Preemptive Authoritarianism in the Former Soviet Union (the Case of Belarus)*, https://cddrl.fsi.stanford.edu/publications/contagion_deterred_preemptive_authoritarianism_in_the_former_soviet_union_the_case_of_belarus. Andrew Wilson, 'Elections 2020 Through the Prism of Silitski's ideas', *BISS*, 11 June 2020, https://belinstitute.com/en/article/elections-2020-through-prism-silitskis-ideas.
18. Vitali Silitski, 'Preempting Democracy: The Case of Belarus', *Journal of Democracy*, 16 (2005), http://muse.jhu.edu/journals/jod/summary/v016/16.4silitski.html.
19. Bohdan, 'Belarusian State Apparatus'.
20. Interview with Oleg Manaev, 27 October 2020.
21. *Ibid.* See also Manaev's interview, '"Pakul' nia bachu sur'ieznykh prykmet, shto systema zatrashchala", satsyieliah Manaew', *Radio Svaboda*, 8 June 2020, https://www.svaboda.org/a/30658729.html?fbclid=IwAR3A4M-D27qKUzbAa7d736KK1-dujizt-pD4xDSLjR9g_KH0kb5BZ8rYNxKc.
22. Balazs Jarabik and Alastair Rabagliati, *Buffer Rus: New Challenges for EU Policy Towards Belarus* (Madrid: FRIDFE Working Paper no. 34, 2007), p. 1.
23. Pikulik, '. . . And Now, the End is Near?'.
24. See www.iiseps.org/data10-391.html. The poll was taken on 2–12 September 2010.

25. Quoted in Grigory Ioffe, 'Understanding Belarus: Economy and Political Landscape', *Europe-Asia Studies*, 56:1 (January 2004), pp. 85–118, Table 2, p. 105.
26. 'Vot i novyi povorot! Deputat Savinykh: Mnogovektornaia politika bol'she ne sootvet-stvuet zadachi razvitiia Belarusi', *Nasha Niva*, 21 September 2020, https://nashaniva.by/?c=ar&i=259423&lang=ru.
27. Siarhei Bohdan, 'Belarus Reluctantly Reverses Its Security Policies', *Belarus Digest*, 28 September 2020, https://belarusdigest.com/story/belarus-reluctantly-reverses-its-security-policies/. See also Yahor Lediadok, 'The Slavic Brotherhood's Future', *Meduza*, 16 October 2020, https://meduza.io/en/feature/2020/10/16/the-slavic-brotherhoods-future?utm_source=email&utm_medium=briefly&utm_campaign=2020-10-17.

Appendix The Belarusian Economy Since Independence

1. Zlotnikov, 'The Belarusian "Economic Miracle"', p. 68, n. 4.

INDEX